W9-CFZ-194

POPULATION AND ECONOMICS

Proceedings of Section V of the
Fourth Congress of the
International Economic History
Association, 1968

EDITED BY
PAUL DEPREZ

University of Manitoba Press
Winnipeg, Canada

Copyright © 1970
by
University of Manitoba Press

All rights reserved.   This book may not be
reproduced, in whole or in part in any form
without written permission from the publisher,
except that permission is hereby given for the
reproduction and use of parts or all of this work
for scholarly and teaching purposes provided that
credit is given to the author and publisher.

Library of Congress Catalog Card Number: 62-40077
ISBN 0-88755-109-2

LIBRARY
FLORIDA STATE UNIVERSITY
TALLAHASSEE, FLORIDA

PREFACE

The fourth Congress of the International Economic History Association was held from the 9th to the 14th of September 1968 at Indiana University, Bloomington, U.S.A.. When at that moment it was learned that the proceedings of this conference would not be published, the organizers of section V, dealing with Demographic History, tried to find other ways of having the reports and the communications published. It should be noted here that because of the willingness of the University of Manitoba Press, to whom we express our most sincere thanks, this difficulty was overcome.

The section of the Bloomington Conference this volume deals with was organized by David Eversley of the University of Sussex, and Woodrow Borah of the University of California (Berkeley). While the latter took on the Latin American part, the former was in charge of the remaining part of the section. Their help with the publication of the proceedings is greatly acknowledged by the editor.

Two of the communications however have not been published here. Dr. Saw Swee-Hok and his wife Dr. Cheng Siok-Hwa, formerly of the University of Malaya, Kuala Lumpur and presently of the University of Hong-Kong, and authors of a paper on "The Population of Singapore in the XIXth Century" did not wish to see their communication published. M.Allen C. Kelley's paper on "Demographic Cycles and Economic Growth: The Long Swing Reconsidered," has been published in the Journal of Economic History.

In order to increase the accessibility of the different studies it was decided that it was preferable to produce a bi-lingual volume instead of a multilingual one: consequently all non-English or non-French communications were translated into English. The communication by W. Koelmann was translated from German into English, while the studies by N. Sanchez-Albornoz (on the Province of Buenos Aires) and R. Mellafe were translated from Spanish.

I would like to extend my thanks to the staff of the Drafting Centre of the University of Manitoba who did an excellent job in re-working some of the graphs and maps.

Finally I wish to thank my research assistant Mr. G.A. Braun not only for his translation of the study by W. Koelmann but also for the considerable amount of time spent in proof reading some of the texts.

Paul Deprez.

LIST OF CONTRIBUTORS

Woodrow Borah,
> Department of History, University of California,
> (Berkeley), U.S.A.

Stanislaw Borowski,
> Poznan School of Economics, Poland.

Trent M. Brady,
> Department of History, University of Toronto,
> Canada.

Sherburne F. Cook,
> Department of Physiology, University of California,
> (Berkeley), U.S.A.

William M. Denevan,
> Department of Geography, University of Wisconsin,
> U.S.A.

Jean Ganiage,
> Sorbonne, University of Paris, France.

Akira Hayami,
> Faculty of Economics, Keio University, Tokyo, Japan.

Robert Horvath,
> Department of Statistics, University of Szeged,
> Hungary.

Wolfgang Koelmann,
> Historical Institute, Ruhr-University, Bochum,
> German Federal Republic.

Harvey Leibenstein,
> Center for Population Studies, Harvard University,
> U.S.A.

John V. Lombardi,
> University of Indiana, Bloomington, U.S.A.

Richard McNeish,
> Robert S. Peabody Foundation for Archaelogy,
> Andover, Mass. U.S.A.

Rolando Mellafe,
> Centro de Investigaciones de Historia Americana,
> University of Chile, Santiago de Chile, Chile.

Franklin Mendels,
> Department of History, University of California,
> (Los Angeles), U.S.A.

Goran Ohlin,
> Stockholm School of Business, Stockholm, Sweden.

Oliver Onody,
> National Bank for Economic Development, Rio de
> Janeiro, Brazil.

James Potter,
> The London School of Economics, England.

Nicolas Sanchez-Albornoz,
> Department of History, New York University, New York,
> U.S.A.

Carl O. Sauer,
> Department of Geography, University of California,
> (Berkeley), U.S.A.

Edward A. Wrigley,
> Cambridge Group for the History of Population and
> Social Structure, England.

TABLE OF CONTENTS

Part I

The Malthusian Problem
in Historical Perspective

HISTORICAL EVIDENCE OF MALTHUSIANISM

GORAN OHLIN

STOCKHOLM SCHOOL OF BUSINESS

In the last twenty years, very impressive progress has been made in the history of European population. The collection of demographic data has been more extensive, and the analysis more sophisticated than before. Appropriate demographic techniques have been developed and applied. The reconstitution of families from parish registers is the most striking of these methods, but the use of other sources has also become more judicious.

A great deal of information about relevant economic and social conditions has laso been systematized and explored. The history of epidemics has been considerably elaborated, and climatic variations have been charted and pondered.

It can hardly be said, however, that the great questions about the place of population growth in the process of social and economic change have received unambiguous answers. To some extent, the development of population history into a discipline of its own has also been accompanied by a growing scepticism about grand designs. The task of putting an accurate interpretation on the scraps of information available about past populations is arduous enough to provide full-time occupation to its practitioners, and like all producers of social statistics they are thoroughly distrustful of them. Moreover, the core of hard facts about demographic conditions in the past remains small, and statistical purists are inclined to stress the fragmentary character of these data and to take a stubbornly agnostic view of the mechanisms at work. As for the social historians who immerse themselves in a village, town, or region they are easily over-whelmed with the diversity of the results and shun generalisations which seem to mask rather than convey the complex truth.

Above all, however, a great number of the old controversies have been, as it were, transcended. It will no longer do to ask whether mortality or fertility determined the rhythm of growth in pre-industrial Europe, for it is apparent that both varied over a wide range. Even the classical issue whether population was on the whole determined by economic factors or whether, as an autonomous force, it wrought significant economic change shows signs of dissolving. One may now suggest that it depended on the time and the place, that the short run was very different from the long run, and that the demographic response to a change in the conditions of human life can take a great number of alternative forms, just as Schumpeter suggested that the economic response to population increase may range from stagnation to innovation.[1]

So far, the contours of a new conception of European population history can be only dimly perceived. But our ignorance has been raised to a higher level. At best, we may hope that the old reference to the complex interdependence between population and economy will cease to be a meaningless dodge and signify instead an interpretation which does justice to the mass of evidence and yet allows for some of those meaningful patterns which historical study must seek.

The short run: subsistence crises and epidemics

In population thought, most of the hypotheses are of ancient origin. "Malthusian" ideas had advocates before Malthus, just as they have had later ones. In this particular context, the term will not be used to refer to Malthus's moral philosophy but only to the view that population growth had a tendency to outrun the increase in the means of subsistence, and that the result was an increase in mortality, attributable to the increase in numbers. Needless to say, this is not doing justice to Malthus's own growing awareness of the role of the "preventive check" of restricted fertility, as contrasted with the "positive check" of rising mortality.[2]

One thing that burial records leave no doubt about is that mortality in pre-industrial Europe was indeed subject to very sharp fluctuations. Wherever the evidence is available -- in England, France, Sweden, and elsewhere -- harvest failure and high grain prices have been shown to be closely associated with very high death rates. Years of scarcity were marked by grain prices and death rates often 3-4 times as high as in surrounding years.

Subsistence crises of this kind were an integral part of the demographic regime of pre-industrial Europe. However, excessive mortality also occurred at times of good harvest and food supply, and it has been possible to piece together fairly good epidemiological explanations of many of these waves of mortality. Epidemic conflagrations seem, in fact, often to have over-shadowed the mortalities due to harvest fluctuation. However, it is also clear that years of food scarcity were also often years

of widespread epidemics. There has been much speculation on this,
and a strong tendency among earlier population historians to regard
epidemic mortality as a function, to a large extent, of undernutrition and the consequent weakening of resistance. In this
way, the primacy of food supply to demographic developments could
be upheld, as for instance Heckscher tried to uphold it in his
analysis of the short-term fluctuations in eighteenth-century
Sweden.[3]

    Modern medical opinion seems to take a dim view of
this notion. The case fatality of at least such virulent killers
as the plague does not seem to be lessened by adequate nutrition.
As Meuvret remarks, "current scientific theory may be driving us
too far in the other direction".[4]

    There is certainly no reason to dispute a general relation-
ship between undernutrition and health. And as for the
prevalence of epidemic disease in bad years, there is an
increasing tendency to stress the vagrancy which marked them, or
even the rat-infested grain shipments which were then sometimes
intensified.

    But a Malthusian interpretation of the steep and periodic
increases in mortality under the ancien regime requires more than
a demonstration of the obvious fact that food is vital to
survival. What has to be shown is that harvest failure, or the
incidence of epidemic disease was occasioned or aggravated by
population growth itself. Such a claim can hardly be substantiated, at least not in the simple version that would attribute
major significance to the modest increase arising from one decade
to another. In, e.g., the seventeenth century, subsistence crises
were simply too frequent to be put down to intervening demographic
growth.

    It is a very different matter to suggest that the frequency
of short-term fluctuations might have been a function of the
balance between population and resources. In some of the most
spectacular instances of sudden catastrophe, like the Black Death
or the great Irish famine of 1845 it is also impossible to deny
the relevance of the preceding rapid growth and population, and the
premonitory crises. Yet, these two disasters were evidently
unleashed by factors unrelated to the demographic situation. The
Black Death was part of a world-wide pandemic, and the potato
blight was not provoked by Irish fertility. The plague, one
suspects, would have dealth a heavy stroke to Western Europe no
matter what the prevailing economic situation had been. The blight,
on the other hand, found a one-crop society of extreme
vulnerability.[5] The two cases illustrate the extreme difficulty of
generalisation. What is clearly of central importance is precisely
the vulnerability of society to a great number of threats. Among
these threats are the ones that Malthus termed positive checks --
war, famine, and pestilence -- but above all, perhaps, climatic
fluctuation and harvest failure. All poor societies are naturally
vulnerable. In the case of harvest failure, their stocks and
transportation facilities are inadequate to protect them.

    The question then must be whether the vulnerability of
European society was in any systematic way influenced by population
growth, or whether there were basic changes in the threats to
which it was exposed. But this question leads away from short-

term fluctuations and into the intriguing matter of the long-run
swings of European demographic experience.

A brief comment is nevertheless necessary on the short-run
behaviour of fertility. Like mortality, but to a lesser extent,
fertility fluctuated with the harvest and, for that matter, with
mortality itself, though of course in the opposite direction. The
same was true of its components: the marriage rate and marital
fertility. The fluctuations in the marriage rate did not in the
short run affect the stock of fertile marriages enough to explain
the variation, and it is evident that the fertility of existing
marriages was also subject to considerable fluctuation in the
short run. This does not in itself pose the question of whether
birth control or family planning was practised. An entirely
satisfactory explanation is that periods of high mortality and
morbidity must have limited sexual activity. This in turn is
enough to account for the observed upsurge in fertility after
demographic crises, as the number of women who were then in a
position to conceive, being neither pregnant nor in a state of
postpuerperal sterility would then be markedly greater. Thus,
short-run variations in fertility do not seem to shed any light on
the Malthusian issues.

The long run: demography, economics or politics?

The long swings are far more complicated. Here, to be sure,
the Malthusian spectre does not arise in the guise of a single,
devastating blow, but rather in the form of an attrition which
then for some reason -- far less clearly indicated in the
Malthusian hypothesis -- gives way to new scope for expansion. If,
in the short run, mortality seems to be the most spectacular
variable, in the long run fertility comes into its own. Above
all, however, it is ovious that in the long run all aspects of
economic growth assume profound significance. Demographic history
can no longer be separated from the basic issues of economic
history. The question is rather whether, in the general scenario
of economic growth and development, the growth of population can
be attributed a certain primacy or whether it is basically a
dependent variable.

Allowing for a number of minor local variations it seems to
be generally accepted that populations in Western Europe have
known three major surges -- the first from approximately 1000 A.D.
to the 1300, the second covering the sixteenth century, and the
third beginning in the eighteenth century. Although this
observation serves to underline the fact that "the demographic
revolution of the eighteenth century was not unique",[6] there is
nevertheless reason to distinguish between the earlier swings and
the later. Our knowledge of the earlier ones is quite incomplete
and they are also of a different order, whereas the expansion of
European population from the eighteenth century on is relatively
well documented and marks a fundamental break with previous
conditions of mortality and, eventually, of fertility. In the
first wave of expansion, certain localities in Western Europe are
known to have been settled with a higher density than that of
modern times.[7] There is also evidence of distinct flagging even
before the Black Death which in any case cut down the population

by, say, one third. Recovery was not rapid, and the fifteenth
century seems generally to have been a time of stagnation. Low
rents and high wages convey the impression of populations moving
in an ample economic space. Roughly with the sixteenth century
relatively rapid growth sets in, accompanied by a clear
deterioration of the position of landless labour. The startling
figures for the wages of building craftsmen in England suggest
that around 1600 they were only about one third in real terms of
what they had been around 1500, and as Phelps-Brown and his
associates have shown European price history indicates something of
the same order on the continent.

A strictly Malthusian hypothesis of the long swings would of
course be that fertility in pre-industrial Europe was on a high
and "natural" level. Mortality on the other hand should have been
the main regulator. Long swings in mortality might have arisen as
a consequence of excessive growth, high densities, and low levels
of living succeeded by a breathing space, economic growth, etc.

Historians have often inclined to this view, and it is
vividly reflected in Le Roy Ladurie's work on Languedoc who paints
a magnificent picture of economic growth, stagnation and decline
in Languedoc between 1500 and 1700, in essentially Malthusian
terms.

However, close demographic inquiry has long tended to cast
doubts on the assumption of constant fertility. What Hajnal terms
the "European marriage pattern", with relatively late marriage and
extensive celibacy, involves a radical limitation of fertility.
Hajnal tentatively suggests that this pattern made its appearance
between the fourteenth and the eighteenth centuries.[8]
Reconstitution of families in the parish of Colyton has enabled
Wrigley to study the course of fertility for the whole period
1538-1837. This revealed that the mean age of marriage for women
varied considerably, while that of men remained more stable.
Moreover, what Malthus termed the "constancy of passion" did not
even produce a constant and "natural" level of age-specific
marital fertility. Instead, there is strong indication of family
limitation already in the seventeenth century, followed by a
renewed trend to larger families.

Genealogical studies, and certain French reconstitution
studies had rather tended to suggest that family limitation began
in the course of the eighteenth century and belonged to the
transition to a new demographic regime. But work in progress by
Ansley J. Coale and his associates confirms the impression that at
least in the nineteenth century, marital fertility in Europe
exhibited a very wide range of variation already before the onset
of systematic decline.

As for mortality, some direct and much indirect evidence
confirms the view that there was a significant rise in the
seventeenth century. The frequency of subsistence crises and
epidemics was higher than earlier. The eighteenth century, on the
contrary, brought a marked decline in the occurrence, followed by
their complete disappearance. In France, in Goubert's words, "un
monde demographique semble defunt." The actual evidence of a
decline in mortality is spotty before the end of the century, but
it is fairly consistent.

One question pertaining to the relevancy of a Malthusian or pseudo-Malthusian view of these changes is whether the higher mortalities of the seventeenth century did have their roots in increased density, rural overpopulation, etc., and whether the subsequent improvements had their origins in endogenous economic progress. Alternative explanations might be that secular climatic change or autonomous variations in epidemic incidence was an underlying factor.

Secular climatic change has been given increasing attention (especially by Utterstrom and Le Roy Ladurie). It was clearly sufficient to make for marked changes in agricultural conditions and may also have affected mortality directly. Its correlation with major demographic swings is not, however, compelling.

The history of epidemic disease also continues to be a major interest of demographers. The disappearance of the plague from Europe after the beginning of the eighteenth century has been especially subject to speculation. Biraben's thorough investigation of its history now suggests that the quarantine and other restrictive and protective measures should be given more credit for this than it has been customary to accord them.

However, there is too much evidence of genuinely demographic imbalance, in the seventeenth century and at other times of European history -- especially in the nineteenth century, when it is more clearly documented -- to dismiss the pertinence of a Malthusian or pseudo-Malthusian model in many situations. On the other hand, there is no ground for assuming that pre-industrial society contained no mechanisms for containing fertility and population growth. The issue now concerns the efficacy of such mechanisms, and the interplay between the demographic response and other forces affecting the conditions of economic growth.

It seems unlikely that the "engine of growth" of Western history could be identified with population pressure. Settlement and migration, urbanization and technological change are more likely candidates. This means that more emphasis must be placed on that enlargement of resources which vulgar Malthusianism dismissed as "arithmetic" progression, as against the expansive force of population. Thus, demographic history must shade into the general history of economic development.

REFERENCES

1. J.A. Schumpeter, "The creative response in economic history" Journal of Economic History, Nov. 1947. For similar, but more elaborated suggestions, see A. O. Hirschman, The Strategy of economic development (New Haven, 1958); Ester Boserup, The conditions for agricultural growth (London, 1965); Colin Clark, "Population Growth & Land Use", (New York, 1967).

2. The most useful guides to the whole Malthusian debate are probably J. A. Field, Essays on population and other papers (Chicago, 1931), and D. E. C. Eversley, Social theories of fertility and the Malthusian debate (Oxford, 1959)

3. E. G. in Eli F. Heckscher, An economic history of Sweden, p. 137.

4. J. Meuvret, "Demographic crisis in France from the sixteenth to the eighteenth century", in D. V. Glass and D. E. C. Eversley, (eds.), Population in history, p. 510. See also the extensive discussions in Paul Harsin and E. Helin (eds.), Problemes de mortalite. Actes du Colloque international de demographie historique (Paris, 1965).

5. Cecil Woodham-Smith's The Great hunger: Ireland 1845-9 also vividly brings out the issues of public policy.

6. K. F. Helleiner, "The vital revolution reconsidered", Canadian Journal of Economics and Political Science, XXIII (1957).

7. Emmanuel Le Roy Ladurie, Les paysans de Languedoc (Paris, 1966), p. 141.

8. J. Hajnal, "European marriage patterns in perspective", in Glass and Eversley (eds.) Population in History, p. 120.

2

POPULATION AND LABOUR FORCE POTENTIAL IN GERMANY 1815-1865

W. KOELMANN

RUHR UNIVERSITY, BOCHUM

(TRANSLATED BY G.A.BRAUN)

According to the Social and Economic History of Germany, the period 1815-1865 can be defined as the beginning of industrialization. Except for certain predecessors of only local importance, the German industrialization began only after the consolidation of the German States and the founding of the German Federation at the Vienna Congress. The Prussian Customs-union of 1818 and its expansion into the German Customs Union of 1843 were at the basis of a larger German domestic market. At the same time, in the 30's and 40's, railroad construction was started; this built up an internal German transportation system, making a domestic market possible. The years of the agrarian and general economic crises of 1846-1847 and the Revolution of 1848-1849 brought on a slump. After this, however, the influx of foreign capital and the political neutrality of Prussia during the Crimean War promoted a strengthening of industrial development. In the 1860's, even before Germany was politically united (1870-1871), she had become one of the industrial nations. Along with the economic developments there was also industrial development: the agrarian sector which had already been freed from old traditional ties by reforms at the beginning of the century had changed first into commercial agriculture and then into an industrial enterprise. We must emphasize the fact that important regional differences appeared in the particular stages of this process and also in the economic structures. This resulted in temporary differences which, even during the period of intense industrialization carrying on into the 20th century, were not completely leveled out.

It is within this framework that one must view the problems of population and labour force potential, the research of which even today is only beginning. Even though Karl Marx had already

attacked the problems of interdependence of population, labour
force potential and financial return of labour with the
establishment that the capitalist system was characterized by the
"progressive production of a relative overpopulation or an
industrial reserve army" (1); this problem has not received the
attention it deserves either in the economic or in the historic
scientific literature. Therefore, the German social historical
research placed priority on the connection between the evolution
from serfdom to a new labour base of an industrial society which
it related to the phenomenon of pauperism. They made it thus known
that "a slowly increasing primarily lower class population had
been freed but was still destined to economic immobility" (2);
the degree and the appearance, however, of such an emancipation
have not as yet been more thoroughly researched.

Any research of this subject is made particularly difficult
by the sources of data. The statistical observations for that
time period can hardly be satisfactory for a number of internal
and external reasons. Methods of keeping archives and concepts
differ from census to census and from state to state. The censi
taken by the Customs Union, however, can be regarded as fairly
dependable from 1843 onward whereas the standards for recording
the previous census had to be attained through research   This
had already been recognized by the statisticians of that time.
C.F.W. Dieterici who had served as director of the Prussian
Statistical Offices since 1834, had reservations on the
reliability of the population censi of Prussia, especially for
the years 1816 and 1819, since these censi "had not been carried
out with the required degree of precision" (3). This inaccuracy
of keeping records and archives cannot be overlooked. Moreover,
many of the problems of that time were not even observed by the
contemporaries nor were they able to see them. Thus, many loop-
holes remain in the statistical data and these can only be filled
by rough estimations. This holds especially true for business
statistics. Though there are large amounts of older statistical
data for different areas of the economy, the recording of overall
commercial statistics, (including the agricultural, business,
transportation and public sectors of the economy) began with the
occupational and commercial census of 1882. The data for the
agricultural sector became only available with the census of 1907.
This lack of material evidence permits us only to do a first
preliminary and incomplete analysis which will, in the future,
need many modifications before its results will be considered
acceptable.

Even though the phenomenon of the population need not be
defined, the concept of labour force potential must be given a
new definition for the researched period   This requires a
modification of the general formula,

whereby A = labour force potential

a_i = age.

This measure appears somewhat useful even though it refers to a definite period of economic and social development; these age groups and this measurement do not include the people who for physical (either mental or bodily sickness including former invalidities) or social reasons were not able to participate in the active work process. These last groups, however, are the important ones. They include the daughters of certain social classes, gentlemen and ladies of independent means as well as the greater portion of married women. Other groups including those of school age and students entering the work force at a later age are also excluded. Other than these, the definition of age groups need not be all inclusive for the 19th century. Indeed, one can accept the 15 year age delineation in spite of the phenomenon of child labour even though those who entered the active labour force earlier were still in a minority relative to the totals in the younger age groups. However, according to the understanding at that time there were no distinctly separate age groups. This originated from the discussion of the "laws dealing with disablement and old age pensions" of June 22, 1889 and from the conclusions according to which the old age pensions for people of 70 years and over were less than the foreseen disablement pensions. These only evened out the limitations of the productive capacity resulting from old age, but do not completely cover the costs of living.

Because of this, it is necessary to take into account all groups over 15 years without any upper age limit, but excluding all the so-called particular groups in order to obtain an accurate measure of the labour force potential. Thus

where J_i = Invalids, i.e., not fit for work for physical reasons;

S_i = Social cases, i.e., those who for social reasons (housewives and daughters of those (school children and students) who either do not enter or enter the work force at a later date, including those (middle class and pensioners) who left earlier.

A calculation standard may be obtained only on the basis of an occupational census, in which records of withdrawal of the special groups mentioned above are kept. The most detailed

statistics of this nature were compiled in the kingdom of Saxony
in 1849 and 1861. Using the above formula, one can calculate
from these statistics, that approximately 68% of those who are
15 years and older may be included in the potential labour force.
This factor has had a basic influence in our research.
        Because of the dissimilarity and incompleteness of the
material the analysis must be restricted to certain states and
provinces, between which, however, certain characteristic
differences must be expected. The following areas will be examined:

-- Northeast Germany, i.e., the Prussian provinces
   (East and West Prussia and Posen) which did not
   belong to the German Federation, as the area of
   agricultural restructuring and characterized by
   land expansion that followed the agrarian reform.

-- The Prussian provinces of Rhineland, Westphalia
   and Saxony and the Kingdom of Saxony as areas of
   commercial expansion and where the industry was
   in its initial stage.

-- The Dukedom of Baden and the Kingdom of Wurttemberg
   as the region of agrarian stagnation and retarded
   industrial development.

        In the change of the population noticeable differences
appeared between the chosen regions. Among these is a very
distinct group characterized by a peak growth comprising the
Kingdom of Saxony, Rhineland, Northeast Germany and the Province of
Saxony. Those regions of Germany which were the most rapid in
industrializing showed just as high a measure of population growth
as the Northeast Province which, after the reforms, entered into a
phase of agricultural expansion and commercial restructuring,
whereby a pattern of rationalizing and production expansion
appeared. In contrast to this, the two Northwest German States of
Baden and Wurttemberg remained far behind. Until 1849 the province
of Westphalia also belonged to this second group; after that it
began to move in the direction of the first group. From this one
can see that the development of the agricultural sector during this
time had the same effects as the development of the commerical and
industrial sectors. This was especially confirmed in the case of
Westphalia whose highly developed agricultural sector had already
expanded at the beginning of the century but whose industrial
expansion only really began after 1850.

        When observing the average yearly growth rates, the rate
for the years 1846-1849 becomes significant. Up until this time
period the growth rates dropped in almost all regions. A rise in
rates occurred only in Northeast Germany and Wurttemberg. This
result should, however, eertainly not be overemphasized; perhaps
only the strongest decline in the Kingdom of Saxony indicates any
significant change. Here the growth rates for 1837-1846 as
compared to 1816-1837 had decreased with approximately 3.7 per
thousand, while the growth in Northeast Germany and in Wurttemberg
and the small decreases in the other regions can perhaps be
interpreted as signs of paralleling growth when taken according to

TABLE 1

POPULATION AND POPULATION GROWTH IN SELECTED STATES
AND PROVINCES, 1816 - 1864

A. Population (in thousand)

	1816	1822	1837	1846	1849	1861	1864
Northeast Germany[a]	2.564	2.899	3.375	3.864	3.839	4.352	4.528
Kingdom Saxony	1.194	1.281	1.644	1.826	1.886	2.211	2.322
Province Saxony	1.197	1.313	1.564	1.742	1.781	1.976	2.044
Rhineland	1.871	2.032	2.474	2.763	2.811	3.216	3.346
Westphalia	1.066	1.140	1.326	1.446	1.465	1.618	1.667
Baden	1.000	1.082	1.250	1.361	1.364	1.364	1.418
Wurttemberg	1.394	1.455	1.605	1.721	1.740	1.719	1.743

B. Population Growth in Percentage Since 1816

	1816	1822	1837	1846	1849	1861	1864
Northeast Germany		11.3	31.6	50.7	49.7	69.7	77.0
Kingdom of Saxony		10.7	37.7	52.9	58.0	85.2	94.4
Province Saxony		11.0	30.7	45.6	48.8	65.1	70.8
Rhineland		10.9	32.2	47.7	50.3	71.9	78.9
Westphalia		10.7	24.4	35.6	37.4	51.8	56.3
Baden		8.2	25.0	36.1	36.4	36.4	41.9
Wurttemberg		10.4	15.2	23.5	24.8	23.3	25.1

C. Average Yearly Growth Rate (in per thousand)[b]

	1816/37	1837/46	1846/49	1849/61	1861/64
Northeast Germany	13.2	15.2	- 2.0	10.5	14.1
Kingdom of Saxony	15.4	11.7	11.0	13.3	12.2
Province Saxony	12.8	12.1	7.3	8.8	11.4
Rhineland	13.3	12.4	5.8	11.3	13.3
Westphalia	10.5	9.6	4.7	8.4	9.3
Baden	10.2	9.5	0.8	0.0	13.1
Wurttemberg	6.5	7.0	5.3	- 1.0	4.3

[a] 1816, 1822 and 1837 are estimated numbers.

[b] Because of the great inaccuracy of the original figures,
the growth rates for 1816-1822 and 1822-1837 are not
especially dependable.

. . . .

Table 1 (Continued)

Sources: Kingdom of Prussia and Prussian Provinces
(incl. Hanover)
PreuBische Statistik
Hrsg. vom Konigl. Statistischen Bureau in
Berlin
Bd. 48 A Berlin 1879

Kingdom of Saxony

1816 - 1836

Menatshefte zur Statistik des Deutschen Reichs
fur das Jahr 1879. Hrsg. v. Kaiserl. Statist-
itschen Amt. Juli-Dezemberheft. Bd. XXXVII,
Teil II der Statistik des Deutschen Reichs
(Heft 7 - 12) Berlin 1879

1837 ff

Zeitschrift des konigl. sachsischen
statistischen Landesamtes. 53. Jg. 1907,
Dresden (o.J.)

Dukedom Baden

Beitrage zur Statistik der inneren Verwaltung
des GroBherzogtums Baden. Hrsg. v. dem
Ministerium des Innern, Heft 1, Karlsruhe 1855,
Statistisches Jahrbuch fur das GroBherzogtum
Baden, Hrsg. v. GroBherzoglichen Statistischen
Landesamt, 41. Jg. 1914/15, Karlsruhe 1915,
S. 22 u. S. 78

Kingdom Wurttemberg

Hermann Losch: Die Bewegung der Vevolkerung
Wurttembergs in 19. Jahrhundert und im Jahre
1899.
in: Wurttembergische Jahrbucher fur Statistik
und Landeskunde.
Jg. 1900, Stuttgart 1901, H. II, S. 56 - 59

the inexact cardinal numbers. The years 1846-1849 showed a distinct decline in the rates in all areas with the exception of the Kingdom of Saxony. These years brought for Northeast Germany a decrease, for Baden a stagnation but they also brought a substantial slow down in the population growth of the West Prussian provinces and Wurttemberg. Here the population growth was hampered by the great agricultural crisis of 1846-1847, by the accompanying general economic crisis and by the revolution of 1848-1849.

The subsequent phases of 1849-1861 and 1861-1864 showed new increases in growth. According to this most regions only reached the level of growth rates of 1837-1846 in 1861-1864. However, another exception was portrayed by the Southwest German group who had shown population stagnation in the 50's or perhaps a slight decrease. Emigration influenced the population growth in a substantial way, for the first large wave of German emigration was essentially restricted to the area of Southwest Germany. After this and also as a result of the outbreak of the American Civil War, which brought to an end all immigration, the phase 1861-1864 showed renewed growth in which Baden, even during this short phase, reached the level of Rhineland while the growth rates for the population of Wurttemberg still remained approximately 1 per thousand lower than in the phase 1846-1849.

The population result from the outcome of two processes: the natural movement and the migration. Both are typified by large variations in the succeeding years, yet, one can identify certain phases in which at least the differences in levels of birth surpluses allow one to draw a certain synopsis, where N = births, P_0 = population at the beginning of the year, P_1 = population at the end of the year, I = immigrants, E = emigrants, D= deaths. If one follows the course of the figures in total, one can readily see that the phases do not emphasize any real differences in structure in relation to the population. The 1827-1834 exception was a result of the epidemic years 1831-1832. This was particularly evident for Northeast Germany which was struck in these two years with an excess mortality of 33,000, while in the other regions the increase in mortality and the decline in natality remained altogether relatively small. In contrast to this one can readily see the distinction for the periods 1847-1848 and 1849-1851 in all areas. During the agrarian crisis mortality remained relatively stable but the natality declined relatively more rapidly resulting in a noticeable decline of the birth surplus. Only in Northeast Germany did the death rate once again surpass the birth rate in the crisis year, caused by the rise of the epidemy. The following phase, 1849-1851, therefore, stood as a trend in the recuperation of births which had been severely hindered by the crisis. The birth surplus now reached a noticeable high. The differences between the last two phases 1852-1856 and 1857-1865 can be explained by the fact that the relatively strong years 1835-1846, had become fully reproductive in the latter: the appearance of, in relation to the total population, stronger age-groups within the reproductive period has been reflected in the number of births.

TABLE 2

NATURAL MOVEMENT IN CERTAIN DEVELOPMENT PHASES

	1816/26	1827/34	1825/46	1847/48	1849/51	1852/56	1857/65
Northeast Germany							
Birth rate	48.1[a]	39.9	42.1	38.6	48.2	43.0[b]	45.8
Death rate	27.8	36.5	30.5	42.6	32.7	38.0[b]	31.4
Natural growth	20.3	3.4	11.6	4.0	15.5	5.0[b]	14.4
Kingdom of Saxony							
Birth rate		41.0	40.8	39.3	43.0	39.4	42.5
Death rate		30.6	30.1	29.5	30.0	29.0	29.3
Natural growth		10.4	10.7	9.8	13.0	10.4	13.2
Prov. of Saxony							
Birth rate	39.1	37.8	37.5	36.2	39.4	37.1	39.1
Death rate	26.0	28.1	26.3	27.8	28.8	26.9	26.6
Natural growth	13.1	9.7	11.2	8.4	10.6	10.2	12.5
Rhineland							
Birth rate	36.8	36.2	37.6	34.3	37.0	34.2	36.9
Death rate	25.7	26.5	27.2	26.7	25.3	23.9	25.3
Natural growth	11.1	9.7	10.4	7.6	11.7	10.3	11.6
Westphalia							
Birth rate	36.7	35.2	36.6	32.7	36.2	33.2	36.5
Death rate	25.8	27.0	27.0	27.3	24.3	24.4	25.5
Natural growth	9.9	8.2	9.6	5.4	11.9	8.8	11.0

Table 2 (Continued)

	1816/26	1827/34	1835/46	1847/48	1849/51	1852/56	1857/65
Baden^c							
Birth rate	37.6	36.8	39.2	35.5	37.5	31.3	36.1
Death rate	27.0	27.6	28.9	28.0	27.5	26.5	25.8
Natural growth	10.6	9.2	10.3	7.5	10.0	4.8	10.3
Württemberg							
Birth rate	38.3	39.6	43.6	39.4	42.1	34.9	40.4
Death rate	30.1	31.7	33.9	32.0	31.1	31.3	31.9
Natural growth	8.2	7.9	9.7	7.4	11.0	3.6	8.5

[a] This death rate must be doubted since it contradicts the structural relationship of the population of Northeast Germany. There seem to be errors in the notification and registration of deaths, errors which cannot be eliminated.

[b] These rates were calculated for the epidemic year 1852 with an excess mortality of 10,187. If this year is excluded the rates become: Birth rate 42.3 per thousand; Death rate 35.4% and Natural growth 6.9%.

[c] For Baden 1817-1826: the original table shows only the live births, while the deaths also include the still born. Thus, the excess of births over deaths and the total number of births can be corrected with the help of migrational balances:

$$N = (P_1 - P_o) - (I - E) + D$$

Table 2 (Continued)

Sources: Prussian Provinces:

1816-54   Mittheilungen des statistischen Bureaus in Berlin.
          Hrsg. v. F.W.C. Dieterici
          9. Jg. Berlin 1856

1855   Statistik des Deutschen Reichs, N.F. Bd. 44
          Berlin 1892

Note: The kingdom of Lichtenberg (35,256 inhab.), absorbed in 1834
          is included in the totals for Rhineland.

Kingdom of Saxony:

          Zeitschrift des konigl. sachsischen statistischen
          Landesamtes. 53. Jg. 1907, Dresden o.J. S. 176

Baden:

          Beitrage zur Statistik der inneren Verwaltung des
          Grossherzogtums Baden. Hersg. v. dem Ministerium des
          Innern, Heft 1, Karlsruhe 1855.
          Statistisches Jahrbuch fur das Großherzogtum Baden
          Hrsg. v. großherzoglichen statistischen Landesamt
          41. Jg., 1914/15, Karlsruhe 1915, S. 22 u. S. 78

Wurttemberg:

          Hermann Losch: Die Bewegung der Bevolkerung Wurttembergs
          im 19. Jahrhundert und im Jahre 1899.
          in: Wurttembergische Jahrbucher fur Statistik und
          Landeskunde, Jg. 1900, Stuttgart 1901, H. II, S. 56-59.

By comparing the values for Northeast Germany and for Rhineland and Westphalia, one can readily see that the natural population movement in West Germany was of a different type than that of Northeast Germany. Even though a low in birth rates in 1847-1848 and a high in 1849-1851 were evidences in West Germany, the birth and death rates in that region were noticeably below the values of the rates for Northeast Germany. The reasons for the difference in values must be looked for in the differences in the age structure of the population which were subject to the differences in life expectancies. Here, once again, there are no basic differences in fertility: mortality remained the decisive factor.

This factor can be asserted by observing the average age at the time of death. For the period 1816-1860 it was 24.7 years for East and West Prussia, 23.9 years for Posen, 29.8 years for Rhineland and 31.3 years for Westphalia (4). This meant a difference of about 5.5 years between Northeast Germany and Rhineland and of about 7 years between Northeast Germany and the province of Westphalia. Accordingly, these values were probably in the first place interpreted as the difference in levels of child and infant mortality. Thus, the lower fertility brought with it a higher yield in live years for the population in the West German provinces, while the shorter lifespan of the North-east German population was experienced by higher birth rates.

Over and above this, social institutional factors and differences of community structure can serve as reasons. There were, for instance, noticeable differences in marriage rates which for Northeast Germany are significantly higher than for West Germany; but before all, there were important differences in the illegitimate birth rates. So was the illegitimate birth rate for the Province of East Prussia and for all phases since 1841, approximately one and a half times higher than for the Rhine Province. For example, for East Prussia it was 9.5 per thousand for 1851-1865 and 3.7% for the Rhine Province. The corresponding marriage rates for this phase were 9.5% and 7.9%. Thus, the differences between Northeast and West Germany can be attributed to a higher frequency of marriage and a higher illegitimate birth rate though in both provnces there were no exogenous elements or possible legal marriage prohibitions which would limit marriages. Therefore, reasons for such differences in marriage circumstances can only be found in the differences between marriage customs.

The birth and death rates for the Kingdom and the Province of Saxony lay approximately on the same level during the entire period. Even the low number of births for 1847-1848 and the high peak for 1849-1851 were not as clearly characterized as in Northeast Germany. The death rates were also subject to particularly insignificant variations. The same held for Baden and Wurttemberg. In these states the level of mortality was higher than in Saxony and West Germany and thus the surplus of births in total remained small. The particular fall in the rates during 1852-1856 was revealed in the Southwest German states to be due particularly high emigration of these years.

If the view that the natural population movement can be
confirmed by the differences between the regions postulated
earlier, one can see that the exogenous influences (epidemics,
crises and migration), as opposed to the endogenous factors, have
had a far reaching effect on the differences in life expectancies.
Thus, no real basic differences of population behaviour were
evident. This may also refer to the West German type since the
social institutional factors which stipulate its exceptional
position merely determine the level but not the placing of the
individual elements within the setting of the generation
structure. From this, the elements of nuptiality are the only
ones evidenced, not the elements of fertility with the
limitation of variances in illegitimate fertility and in mortality
as variables. Thus, the natural population movement of all
regions for the entire time period indicated a typical pre-
industrial generation structure just as Mackenroth had
described (5).

The growth of the entire population and the natural
population movement have already allowed us to see the influence
of migrations particularly for the Southwest German states.
Migrational balances show us to what degree the migrations have
influenced regional development. Only the Kingdom of Saxony
which was experiencing continual industrial expansion revealed
migrational gains for the entire period while Northeast Germany
registered gains in the periods 1826-1846 and 1849-1851. The
years of the agrarian crises brought with them the first
migrational losses. These losses, however, were almost entirely
eliminated by 1852. It was only after this that there was an
unbroken record of migrational losses. As the phase of the peak
agricultural growth reached an end they could support more
migrational losses. This marked the beginning of the internal
migrational movement of Northeast Germany, shifting the
population to the industrial population of the places located at
the edge of this area. Migrational balances in West Germany,
however, moved differently. Westphalia and even the Rhine
Province showed migrational gains until 1831 and 1846 respectively.
In the following phase however, Westphalia showed a continual
loss while the Rhine Province after 1856 registered renewed
migrational gains. Here, as well as in the small average yearly
losses in Westphalia in the previous phase, one can clearly see
the effects of the industrial development. In contrast to this,
the Southwest German states, with the exception of Baden, showed
continual population losses in the first phase. Their migrational
losses were relatively and, in some years absolutely higher than
those for Rhineland and Westphalia. The Northwest German area
was the exit point for the first large overseas migration from
Germany: the population figures for the 1850's clearly reflect
the first large wave of emigration. The described differences
of the natural population movement and migration are evidenced
in the size of the different age groups. These differences
resulted in the differences in the strength of the labour force
potential. It is here that the exceptional position of the

TABLE 3

Years	Northeast-Germany Absolute fig.	Annual average	Kingdom of Saxony Absolute fig.	Annual average	Province of Saxony Absolute fig.	Annual average	Rhine Province Absolute fig.	Annual average
1817/25	- 14.582	- 1.620	+129.074	+18.439[a]	+26.777	+ 2.975	+49.430	+ 5.492
1826/34	+ 34.600	+ 3.844	+ 18.392	+ 1.533	+ 2.048	+ 228	+38.302	+ 4.266
1835/46	+116.676	+ 9.723	+ 5.225	+ 2.613	+31.572	+ 2.631	+67.493	+ 5.624
1847/48	- 27.760	-13.880	+ 2.484	+ 828	+ 201	+ 100	-10.840	- 5.420
1849/51	+ 1.950	+ 650	+ 7.508	+ 1.502	-13.153	4.384	-13.521	- 4.507
1852/56	- 43.085	- 8.617	+38.212	+ 4.246	-29.409	- 5.882	- 9.264	- 1.853
1857/65	- 45.722	- 5.070			-40.576	- 4.508	+25.843	+ 2.871

Years	Westphalia Absolute fig.	Annual average	Baden Absolute fig.	Annual average	Wurttemberg Absolute fig.	Annual average
1817/25	+ 6.669	+ 741	+ 24.058	+ 2.673	- 10.459	- 1.162
1826/34	+17.695	+ 1.966	- 8.076	- 897	- 45.440	- 5.049
1835/46	- 9.842	- 820	- 23.088	- 1.924	- 36.783	- 3.065
1847/48	- 8.544	- 4.272	-115.710	- 7.855	- 18.258	- 9.129
1849/51	-14.453	- 4.818	- 46.147	-15.382	- 47.316	-15.772
1852/56	-21.658	- 4.332	- 74.248	-14.850	-101.903	-20.381
1857/65	-16.066	- 1.785	- 14.223	- 1.580	- 53.809	- 5.979

[a] 1828/34

Sources: See Table 2.

TABLE 4

LABOUR FORCE POTENTIAL

	1. In Thousand		
	1822	1849	1864
Northeast Germany[a]	1.196,4	1.667,7	1.893,4
Kingdom of Saxony[b]	588,0	882,9	1.022,5
Prov. of Saxony	588,7	800,5	883,6
Rhineland	887,9	1.251,5	1.458,6
Westphalia	495,6	644,8	724,9
Baden[c]	570,7	622,7	664,9
Wurttemberg[d]	671,3	801,4	844,5

	2. In Percent of the Total Population		
Northeast Germany	41,3	43,4	42,2
Kingdom of Saxony	45,9	46,6	46,0
Prov. of Saxony	44,8	44,9	43,9
Rhineland	43,7	44,3	44,1
Westphalia	43,5	44,0	43,9
Baden	46,4	45,7	46,6
Wurttemberg	46,5	45,9	48,3

	3. Growth			
	In Thousand		Yearly Growth Rate (per thousand)	
	1822/49	1849/64	1822/49	1849/64
Northeast Germany	471,3	225,7	12,4	8,5
Kingdom of Saxony	294,9	139,6	15,2	12,3
Prov. of Saxony	211,8	83,1	11,5	6,6
Rhineland	363,6	207,1	12,8	10,3
Westphalia	149,2	80,1	9,8	7,8
Baden	(52,0)	42,2	(5,8)	4,4
Wurttemberg	130,1	43,1	6,3	3,5

[a] Adjusted rates

[b] 1861, growth rate 1849-1861

[c] 1834: the growth rate for 1834-1849 would result for 1822 in a labour force potential of 532,200: the values for 1834 and 1849 are slightly over-estimated because the 14 years old have been included.

[d] 1821.

Sources:

Table 4 (Continued)

Prussian Provinces (incl. regions):

> 1822: Zeitschrift des konigl. preussischen statistischen Bureaus
> 1. Jg. 1. H. Berlin 1861
>
> 1849: Mittheilungen des statistischen Bureaus in Berlin.
> Hrsg. v. F.W.C. Dieterici, 3. Jg. (1850) Berlin 1850
>
> 1864: Preussische Statistik
> Hrsg. v. Kgl. statistischen Bureau in Berlin, H. 10
> Berlin 1867
> All numbers without the military population.

Kingdom of Saxony:

> 1822: Mittheilungen des statistischen Vereins fur das Konigreich Sachsen, 1. Lieferung, Leipzig 1831
>
> 1849: Statistische Mittheilungen aus dem Konigreich Sachsen. Hrsg. v. statistischen Bureau des Ministeriums des Innern. 3. Lieferung, Dresden 1854
>
> 1861: Zeitschrift des statistischen Bureaus des koniglich sachsischen Ministeriums des Innern. 9. Jg. Dresden 1863

Baden:
> 1834: Amtliche Beitrage zur Statistik der Staatsfinanzen des Grossherzogtums Baden, Karlsruhe 1851.
>
> 1849 u. 1864 Beitrage zur Statistik der inneren Verwaltung des Grossherzogtums Baden, Hrsg. v. Handelsministerium, H. 13, Carlsruhe 1862, H. 24, Carlsruhe 1867

Wurttemberg:

> 1821: Wurttembergische Jahrbucher fur vaterland-ische Geschichte, Geographie, Statistik und Topographie. Hrsg. v. J.D.G. Memminger.
>
> 1849: Wurttembergische Jahrbucher fur vaterland-ische Geschichte, Geographie, Statistik und Topographie. Hrsg. v. Kgl. statistisch-topographischen Bureau. Stuttgart 1852 (1854)
>
> 1864: Wurttembergische Jahrbucher fur Statistik und Landeskunde. Hrsg. v. Kgl. statistisch-topographischen Bureau, Stuttgart 1866.

agricultural northeast becomes clear. The lower average length
of life in this area meant at the same, a relatively stronger
distribution in the age groups under 15 years. For example,
in 1864 this age group represented 38% of the total population
whereas in Rhineland and Westphalia it represented only 35.3%.
In contrast to this, the Kingdom of Saxony which was an area
receiving continual industrial migration, had large age groups
to which belong the potentially active population, resulting in a
larger work force potential. The higher values for both the
Southwest states are revealed in an especially strong frequency of
the ag group over 65 years. Migration was particularly noticeable among the middle and younger age groups. When compared to
these, the West German provinces and also the Province of Saxony
took on an intermediate position.

By comparing the growth rates for the periods 1822-1849
and 1849-1864 one can see further differences. Here the influence
of the migrational movements was more clearly evident. The
Kingdom of Saxony, with continual migrational gains, showed the
highest yearly growth rates of the labour force potential followed
by the Rhine Province with migrational gains in the period up to
1846 and in 1857-1865. Northeast Germany at this time held the
third place after population increases caused by the 1826-1846
migration gains and by the rapid natural growth. The lowest
growth rates were recorded for the Southwest states which
experienced high migrational losses even though, when measured
against the total population, they had the largest work force
potential. The effect of the emigration was therefore not a
reduction of the labour force potential seen as part of the total
population, but rather a decrease in the growth of the total work
force.

The average yearly growth rates of the labour force
potential give a necessary measure for the expansion of employment
opportunities provided that employment conditions remain the same.
Only when the employment opportunities grew noticeably would a
full participation of the labour force be possible. It thus
becomes evident that the yearly requirements of employment
positions in the second period were lower than in the first one.
The Province of Saxony showed the largest absolute decline with a
difference of upwards of 4.9 per thousand, followed by Northeast
Germany with 3.9%. The changes in Wurttemberg however were
relatively more significant: from 1849 to 1864 the requirement
for employment positions was only half of what the requirements
had been for the period 1822 to 1849. In the western provinces of
Germany these requirements were only approximately one-fifth less.
From this it is evident that the labour market situation must have
been better in the second phase than in the first. An accurate
view of the labour market can thus be seen only when the growth
of the labour force can be compared to the real increase in
employment opportunities. However, since the necessary commercial
statistical material is not available (especially for agriculture)
one cannot make a very exact calculation. It is therefore
necessary to develop a method of approximation. One proceeds from
the assumption that the labour force potential of 1822 was fully

and effectively engaged as active population. 1822 is the most likely year since it is one of the few boom-years in Germany during the first half of the 19th century (6). Further, the level of employment structure is predicted to remain the same; thus the problem of increase in supply and demand of labour does not have to be taken into consideration. A long term measurement for average yearly growth rates can be calculated from the development of the mining, metal and textile industries in Rhineland between 1849 and 1861. This provides us with an estimated growth rate of 11.5 per thousand for this period, whereas for the period 1822-1849 one can attribute a growth rate of 4%. That we can use these growth rates as a measurement of the total labour market development is substantiated by Ipsens' calculations for the development of agricultural households in East Prussia between 1805 and 1867 (7). These calculations result in an average yearly growth rate of 6.3 per thousand in agriculture, whereas our estimated figures for all industries give an average yearly growth rate of 7%.

TABLE 5

ESTIMATED EMPLOYMENT OPPORTUNITIES

(in percentages of the Labour Force Potential)[a]

	1822	1849		1864	
	Employment Oppor- tunities (in 000)	Employment Oppor- tunities (in 000)	%	Employment Oppor- tunities (in 000)	%
Northeast Germany	1.196,4	1.332,6	79.9	1,582,0	83.6
Kingdom of Saxony	588,0	654,9	74.2	751,2	73.5
Prov. of Saxony	588,7	655,7	80.1	788,4	88.1
Rhineland	887,9	989,0	79.0	1.174,1	80.5
Westphalia	495,6	552,0	85.6	655,3	90.4
Baden[b]	532,5	593,1	95.2	704,1	105.9
Wurttemberg[c]	671,3	750,7	93.7	891,2	105.5

[a] Calculated at the hand of Table 4.

[b] See Table 4, note c.

[c] 1821.

The calculations make it readily apparent that until 1849 there was no overlapping between the available labour force and the employment opportunities. In the second period, the increase in the surplus labour market became noticeably smaller. In the provinces of Westphalia and Saxony the surplus was noticeably decreased while the southwest German states, according to these calculations, should have had a shortage of labour force.

However, this result would sooner seem to indicate that the data
which were at the basis of the growth rates in these areas have
been over-estimated rather than that the migrational wake had
prejudiced economic growth through a shortage of labour force.
The rates for the Kingdom of Saxony appear to be underestimated
although no consideration was given to the forced expansion.

Although these numbers taken by themselves, may be open to
criticism, they still tend to clarify the situation of overpopulation in the middle of the century. The population growth
of the first half of the century was by itself not to be surpassed
by economic growth whereas, in the Provinces of Westphalia and
Wurttemberg, migrational losses served to relieve the burden on
the labour market. The large surplus of labour force potential
over employment opportunities created increasing difficulties
for the masses. This reached a culmination point in the hunger
crisis of 1846-1848. The population grew at increasing rates and
soon surpassed the available living space. After 1849, however,
there were clear indications of relief which could remedy the
social catastrophe in Germany. There was a decrease or even a
retrenchment of the surplus growth.

This result was reached on the grounds of two premises:
an overall growth that started in the period prior to the middle
of the century and over and above this, the acceptance of a stable
level of employment opportunities. Both assumptions are too
optimistic for partial presentation even though contemporary
sources illustrate that at least in regional terms the increase of
labour demand was not as high as reflected in the estimated
statistics, and that consequently there was a gradual decrease in
income. This incongruity does not reveal itself in structural
unemployment as it does in most fully industrialized societies.
Rather, it is indicated in a diminution of the value of individual
employment positions and in the phenomenon of underemployment.
Although the computed "surplus labour" also worked, their inclusion
in the work process meant at the same time a decrease in income of
everyone and an increase in the tendency towards pauperization.
The consequence of such a development was a greater geographical
mobility. A lessening of the basis for subsistance drew along
with it a weakening if not a loss of the social ties. This was
the reason for the increasing migrational pressures and was
revealed in the migrational balances. Overseas migrations which
accounted for an approximate loss of 1.4 million persons from
Germany during the 15 year period between 1845 and 1859 (8)
merely depicted the peak of total mobility. At present, little
is known about the strength of internal migrational movements.
In Berlin alone, by taking a random count, there were approximately
17,500 persons who left and approximately 30,500 persons who moved
into Berlin in 1851; thus, a total migrational turnover of 47,500
persons in one year meant an approximate 13,500 person increase
for Berlin (9). Such high rates of internal mobility - migrations
to regions of apparently higher living standards - clearly
characterized the mobility of trade structures in the beginning
of the period of industrialization. This internal mobility was
not only of a regional nature but also affected the inter-

occupational mobility - a continuous change in employment opportunities - which became one of the basic problems of industrial progress in the first stages of industrialization.

The social political writers of that period have continually made it known that the problem of overpopulation could be remedied by the expansion of employment opportunities. The Westphalian social politician, Friedrich Harkort, already in the 1840's claimed that "the people should have the opportunity to provide for their own needs; the opposite would be scandalous for the business enterprise" (10). Yet, against this interpretation which was aimed at a positive alleviation of the problem of poverty through economic expansion stood the larger spread views of the Mathusians. Insofar as one accepts Malthus, that population growth inevitably will outgrow the subsistence possibilities and then, through preventive or repressive corrective factors, must be brought back to its initial level, one must consequently draw the conclusion that population growth could be prevented by insufficient work opportunities. An extreme form of this observation can be found in the writings of Karl August Weinhold, a M.D. of Halle who proposed to eliminate from reproduction entire sectors of the population (11), as a drastic solution to the problem. There were, however, many more moderate suggestions. They were especially aimed at a diminishing right-to-marriage and right-to-settlement. Such repressive measures were found in the legislation of certain German states. Even the liberal state of Prussia which, influenced by the classical Liberalism of the ministerial bureaucracy, made careful efforts to avoid all legal interference in commercial and business affairs, saw itself forced to introduce in 1842 restrictions on the right-of-settlement and on citizenship rights for incoming foreigners (this referred basically to immigrants coming from other states of the German Federation). Although the right-of-settlement remained free for all citizens of Prussia, the poor and the foreigners not fit for labour (such as the dependents of prisoners), could be refused by the local authorities and would only be allowed to reap the benefits of citizenship when they could produce evidence of a good reputation and of the possibility of self-support (12). The Southwest German states placed more severe restrictions on marriage and on the right of choice of residence. Women who wanted to marry a citizen of the community had to indicate possession of one hundred and fifty guilders, while for the men, it was merely a matter of proving citizenship before being permitted to marry. This also held true for the citizens of Baden. Here community citizenship was tied to the presentation of evidence indicating freedom from debt, the capacity to practise a profession and proof of purchasing power of 500 guilders initially, amount that was later raised to 1,000 guilders (13). Thus, the communities were given the power to return all those who could be expected to become a burden and require public relief. Whether and to what extent these regulations were carried out is not as yet known. It would, however, seem unlikely in view of the periods of growth, that these regulations would have had much of an effect on the total population even though they might have noticeably aggravated the destinies of certain lives.

Neither migration or any other such measures were able to relieve the problem of overpopulation. Our data would seem to indicate an improvement of the situation for the 1850's and 1860's which marked the beginning of the process of industrialization. Despite periodic crises, the disparity between labour force potential and employment opportunities grew smaller until the entire labour force was utilized. A proximity of this situation was only attained in the 1890's. It was only at that time that industrialization brought relief from the catastrophe which had threatened during the development in the 1850's. Bruno Hildebrand, a member of the old historical school of National Economics, had already given such an interpretation to the process of industrialization at the time when the crises of overpopulation was reaching an all time high. He characterized "the momentary unemployment on food shortage" as "the necessary sacrifice with which one must purchase progress for mankind" (14). Without underestimating the seriousness of the situation, he anticipated the significance of the industrialization process in the ensuing decades. At the same time, it was recognized and made known, that the crises of the mid-century did not depict the closing phase of process leading to a final catastrophe, but rather, it marked the beginning of a new era.

REFERENCES

1. Marx, Karl: Das Kapital; Kritik der politischen Okonomie,
    in Karl Marx und Fr. Engels, Werke. re-edited by the
    Institute for Marxismus-Leninismus, Berlin, vol. 23, Berlin,
    1962, p. 657.

2. Jantke, Carl: Zur Deutung des Pauperismus; in Die Eigentum-
    slosen, Munich, 1965, p. 15.

3. Die Statistischen Tabellen des preussischen Staats nach der
    amtlichen Aufnahme des Jahres 1843, edited by W. Dieterici,
    Berlin, 1845, p. 22.

4. Keller Fr. Eduard: Der Preussische Staat, vol. 1, Minden,
    1864, p. 396.

5. Mackenroth, Gerhard: Bevolkerungslehre, Theorie, Soziologie
    und Statistik der Bevolkerung, Berlin-Gottingen-Heidelberg,
    1953, pp. 120 and foll.

6. With the economic "recovery of the years 1821, 1822 and of
    the first half of 1823" (Schumpeter, Joseph A.:
    Konjunkturzyklen. Eine theoretische, historische and
    statistische Analyse des kapitalistischen Prozesses, volume
    1 (=Grundriss der Sozialwissenschaft, volume 1) Gottingen,
    1961, p. 310), "whereby the wages held better than the
    retailprices" (Abel, Wilhelm: Agrarkrisen und
      Agrarkonjuktur, 2nd edition, Hamburg-Berlin, 1966, p. 215)
    could the available labour force potential probably for
    the first time be fully employed.

7. Ipsen, Gunther: Die Preussische Bauernbefreiung als
    Landesausbau, in Zeitschrfit f. Agrargeschichte und Agrar-
    soziologie, vol. 2, 1954, p. 51.

8. Burgdorfer, Friedrich: Die Wanderungen uber die deutschen
      Reichsgrenzen, in: Allgemeines Statistisches Archiv,
    volume 20, 1930, pp. 189 and foll.

9. Baar, Lothar: Die Berliner Industrie in der industriellen
    Revolution, Berlin, 1966, pp. 172 and foll.

10. Harkort, Friedrich: Die Vereine zur Hebung der unteren
    Volksklassen nebst Bermerkungen uber den Central-Verein in
    Berlin, Elberfeld, 1845, p. 14.

11. Weinhold, Carl August: Von der Uberbevolkerung in Mittel-
    europaz und deren Folgen auf die Staaten und ihre
    Civilization, Halle, 1827, pp. 45 and foll.

12. Gesetz uber die Augnahme neu anziehender Personen vom 31.
    Dez. 1842; Gesetz uber die Verpflichtung zur Armenpflege,
    vom. 31 Dez. 1842; Gesetze uber die Erwerbung und der Verlust

References (Continued)

der Eigenschaft als preussischer Underthan, sowie uber den
Eintritt in fremde Staatsdienste, vom. 31 Dez. 1842 in
Gesetz-Sammlung fur die Koniglich Preussischen Staaten,
1843, Berlin (no date given).

13.   Gesetz uber die Rechte der Gemeinde-Burger und die
Erwerbung des Burgerrechts, vom. 31 Dez. 1831, partially
reproduced in Merker, Uber den Erwerb der Heimat und die
solidarische Verpflichtung zur Armenpflege, Berlin, 1833,
pp. 216-227.

14.   Hildebrand, Bruno: Die Nationalokonomie der Gegenwart und
Zukunft und andere gesammelte Schriften, volume 1,
Editor, Hans Gehrig (=Sammlung sozialwissenschaftlicher
Meister, volume 22), Jena, 1822, p. 187.

3

DEMOGRAPHIC DEVELOPMENT AND THE MALTHUSIAN PROBLEM

IN THE POLISH TERRITORIES UNDER GERMAN RULE,

1807-1914

STANISLAW BOROWSKI

POZNAN SCHOOL OF ECONOMICS,

POLAND

I.   THE AIM, SCOPE AND SOURCE MATERIALS OF THE PAPER.

In this paper the author endeavours: (1) to analyse population development in the area between the Nysa, Odra, Wisla and Lower Niemen in the years of 1807-1914; (2) to confront the Malthusian population theory in the first century after its publication with the long run demographic development in the area under research.

The subject of the analysis comprises: marriages, births and deaths; the total, natural and migrational increase of population; changes in population density, in its age and sex distribution as well as in its division according to residence and means of living.

The Malthusian theory has become a basis of a debate lasting until present days. Participants in that debate have included theoreticians in demography, experts in national and international population policy and historical demographers. From the long list of problems discussed we have chosen only three questions.

The first one concerns the mutual relation between the development of resource (especially of food) and the development of population. The Malthusian model: (food production increases according to arithmetic order and population in geometrical order) -- has seldom been verified in Europe in post-Malthusian times. The point of our discussion will be: when and to what extent has the Malthusian model and the demographic development diverged in the investigated area.

The second question refers to the relationship between the socio-economic and demographic factors. We will examine which factors have checked and which have stimulated the demographic development.

The third question refers to demographic influence on economic and social conditions in the discussed area.

For comparison purposes we have divided that area into three regions corresponding to former administrative units, namely Silesia equivalent to the Prussian province of Siberia, Great Poland with boundaries fixed by Vienna Congress of 1815 as those of the Grand Dukedom of Poznan and finally, Pomerania comprising three Prussian provinces: Pommern, Westpreussen and Ostpreussen. Today, except for four districts belonging to the German Democratic Republic, Silesia is a part of Poland. Similarly, all of Great Poland and the major part of Pomerania belong to Poland. Some western districts of Pomerania (Regierungsbezirk Stralsund) are situated in the German Democratic Republic and an eastern part of Pomerania (approximately Regierungsbezirk Konigsberg) belongs to the USSR. Thus, about 90% of the investigated area constitutes the western and northern territories of Poland. Today, the total area is a point of scholarly scientific and political interest in Europe.

In the years 1807-1914 we can distinguish three periods of demographic development: 1807-1840, 1840-1871, 1871-1914.

During the first period the state authorities managed to centralize the results of parish registration of natural movement but they had no interest in migratory movements of population. During the censuses population had been counted but not registered. Until the beginning of 1830's the census work was done by great landowners or their officials who in those times also performed state administrative duties.

Population development was approximately of stationary character. Years of birth surplus and years of death surplus alternated. As a rule there was also migrational surplus.

In these times several economic and social reforms took place which indirectly had a positive impact upon population growth. We shall therefore regard the years 1807-1840 as a period preceding the demographic revolution in the investigated area.

In the second period of 1840-1871 the registration and statistics of natural movement of population had been improved and observation of migrations for statistical purposes began. During censuses, population was registered by name and the results aggregated by administrative units. The census work was done by state officials of the regional administration.

The population previously stationary was now slowly growing. The surplus of deaths over births had occurred from time to time but it was not significant. The number of emigrants, especially after 1860 had grown from year to year.

In that time the agricultural production increased, the development of modern industry began, the home market became larger and larger, and the capitalistic system prevailed. It was a transitional period from a demographic situation with nearly equal levels of mortality and natality to a demographic growth situation with considerable surplus of births over deaths; from a traditional socio-economic system including feudal elements to a modern system based on growing industry.

In the third period, the recording of vital statistics was initiated with the creation in 1874 of offices for registration of births, marriages and deaths. Current reports from these offices were sent to the Prussian Royal Office of Statistics. The population census was perfected. Persons and their characteristics were registered in individual forms which were elaborated in the central office. Because of non-reliability of current registration of migrants, the Prussian authorities ceased to collect data of this kind in the 1880's, except for figures on overseas emigration.

In that period the death rates began to fall. The birth rates on the contrary were growing at first and later on followed the trend of the death rates. In the progressive development of population the emigration caused increasingly greater losses.

Simultaneously, further development of agriculture, industry, transport, trade and commerce and of other services was observed.

The beginning of a permanent fall of death rates marks the demographic revolution and the fall of birth rates -- the beginning of demographic counter-revolution. Therefore, the years of 1871-1914 will be subsequently referred to as the period of demographic revolution and counter-revolution.

The sources of our investigation mentioned above consist of hand-written and printed materials comprising the result of registration of births, deaths and migration of population, occupational and agricultural censuses, the estimates of agricultural production and of the agrarian reforms.

These source materials were collected and elaborated by Statistical Offices of the Warsaw Dukedom, of the Prussian state and of the German Reich. The reader will find detailed information about these sources in our statistical tables.

II. THE PERIOD PRECEDING THE DEMOGRAPHIC REVOLUTION, 1807-1840.

During the entire period the natural movement of population showed great and rapid changes. The amplitude of those changes was small in Silesia that was rather well economically developed. and very large in more under-developed Great Poland. Yearly changes have been presented in Figures 1 to 3. When considering five year changes we may find that the death rates fluctuated between 27.3 and 42.1 deaths per thousand population and the birth rates between 41.2 and 53.3 live and dead births per thousand population (Table 1).

TABLE I. BIRTH RATES, DEATH RATES AND RATE OF NATURAL INCREASE (IN °/o/o)

Years	Silesia			Great Poland			Pomarania		
	Birth rate	Death[a] rate	Rate of increase	Birth[a] rate	Death[a] rate	Rate of increase	Birth[a] rate	Death[a] rate	Rate of increase
1806-1810				45.3	42.1	3.2			
1816-1820	47.4	32.3	15.1	53.3	29.1	24.2	50.7	28.8	21.9
1821-1825	45.9	30.7	15.2	48.5	28.6	19.9	47.8	27.3	20.5
1826-1830	42.9	33.0	9.9	40.2	38.0	2.2	42.1	30.6	11.5
1831-1835	41.9	33.8	8.1	40.3	37.9	2.3	40.9	35.1	5.8
1836-1840	41.2	31.8	9.4	43.4	29.2	14.2	40.8	29.1	11.7
1841-1845	41.2	30.0	11.2	46.6	30.1	16.5	42.0	28.1	13.9
1846-1850	39.1	33.2	5.9	43.7	37.6	6.1	42.3	33.8	8.5
1851-1855	38.7	33.0	5.7	43.3	39.3	4.0	43.3	35.1	8.2
1856-1860	40.2	30.0	10.2	43.6	32.8	10.8	43.7	30.3	13.4
1861-1865	40.7	29.2	11.5	44.7	29.4	15.3	43.8	28.2	15.6
1866-1870	43.2	30.7	12.5	45.6	33.0	12.6	41.2	31.9	9.3
1871-1875	41.7	31.1	10.6	46.0	31.6	14.4	41.5	28.5	13.0
1876-1880	41.4	30.1	11.3	46.4	28.6	17.8	42.7	28.6	14.1
1881-1885	40.0	30.7	9.3	43.3	28.6	14.7	41.2	28.8	12.4
1886-1890	40.8	29.3	11.5	44.3	26.3	18.0	41.9	27.1	14.8
1891-1895	41.2	28.8	12.4	42.8	24.0	18.8	40.3	25.4	14.9
1896-1900	41.2	26.8	14.4	43.6	23.6	20.2	39.7	24.5	15.2
1901-1905	39.2	25.4	13.8	42.3	22.4	19.9	37.5	23.1	14.4
1906-1910	36.5	22.5	14.0	39.5	19.9	19.6	34.5	20.2	14.3
1911-1941	33.2	21.0	12.2	35.2	18.5	16.7	32.0	19.8	12.2

[a] Dead births included

Source: A.G.A.D., A.Z.96., Z.K.P.S.B. 1961. P.S., H.5-245.

The death rates in towns were approximately 12% higher than in
the rural areas.
   There is speculation that the high birth and death rates
have been caused by incomplete results of population censi.
Some demographers estimated the number of persons omitted during
the highly incomplete census of 1816 to be between 5% to 13% of
the total population. We will not undertake any discussion on
details and only say that the mentioned percentages were over-
estimated.
   In the years of 1816-1819 the population censuses were
taken each year. The next census was in 1821 and the following
ones took place every third year. The birth and death rates
have been based on the average population calculated from these
three censuses. Therefore, the greatest difference between the
calculated rates and the true ones should be less than 5%.
Assuming that all births as well as all deaths were recorded and
that the censi give us the real total population, we have
calculated the net migration. (Table 2)

TABLE 2. YEARLY AVERAGE OF NET MIGRATION BY REGIONS, 1816-1910

Years	Silesia	Great Poland	Pomerania	Total
	Number of Persons			
1816-1822	+ 3 957	- 1 157	+15 145	+17 945
1823-1831	+ 4 448	+ 5 418	+ 3 014	+12 880
1832-1840	+20 016	+ 7 068	+15 993	+43 067
1841-1849	- 1 376	- 878	- 1 795	- 4 049
1850-1861	- 1 146	- 1 083	+ 1 055	- 1 174
1862-1871	- 9 551	-11 111	-21 672	-42 335
1872-1880	-11 456	-13 883	-31 747	-57 086
1881-1890	-21 068	-23 294	-63 163	-107 525
1891-1900	-15 102	-21 813	-48 011	-89 925
1901-1910	-12 994	-18 028	-46 908	-77 930
	Per 1000 Population			
1816-1822	+ 1.9	- 1.3	+ 6.4	+ 3.4
1823-1831	+ 1.9	+ 0.5	+ 1.1	+ 2.0
1832-1840	+ 7.4	+ 6.0	+ 5.1	+ 6.1
1841-1849	- 0.5	- 0.7	- 0.5	- 0.5
1850-1861	- 0.4	- 0.8	+ 0.3	- 0.2
1862-1871	- 2.7	- 7.2	- 4.8	- 4.4
1872-1880	- 2.9	- 8.4	- 6.7	- 5.5
1881-1890	- 5.1	-13.4	-12.9	-10.0
1891-1900	- 3.3	-11.7	- 9.4	- 7.4
1901-1910	- 2.6	- 8.8	- 8.7	- 6.2

Continued ......

Table 2. (Continued)

Years	Silesia	Great Poland	Pomerania	Total
	Percentages of Natural Increase			
1816-1822	+10.4	- 4.8	+24.9	+14.6
1823-1831	+17.4	+100.01	+ 8.6	+19.5
1832-1840	+84.0	+55.8	+50.6	+66.3
1841-1849	- 5.8	- 6.3	- 4.8	- 5.4
1850-1861	- 4.0	- 8.9	- 2.3	- 1.3
1862-1871	-23.2	-53.1	-40.9	-36.8
1872-1880	-25.5	-51.1	- 4.8	-41.4
1881-1890	-49.3	-82.8	-95.0	-78.3
1891-1900	-25.4	-61.7	-63.0	-49.6
1901-1910	-18.9	-45.9	-61.8	-42.4

Sources: Calculated from Mittheilungen 1848-1859.
Z.K.P.S.B. P.S., H.5-234.

The positive net migration, especially in Silesia, recently has become a subject of controversy. In questioning the likelihood of a positive net migration a number of arguments were used: incompleteness of the population censi; the economic under-development of Silesia; a considerable out-migration and the lack of information about in-migration.

According to our appraisal, the calculated net migration is highly probable. The incompleteness of the census results has not been sufficiently proved. It concerns chiefly the first censi between which the positive net migration was rather low. But the highest net migration occurred between the later censi which were rather complete and reliable.

It is true that the area under research was economically under-developed in those times and that there was a considerable emigration of population, especially of population living from textile trade. But, we have to keep in mind that the area represented a higher level of development in comparison with the territories east and south of the investigated regions. The historical regularity in migrational movements is that the population flowed from low income areas to regions with high per capita incomes. In the investigated area the pull factors for immigrants from the eastern and southern territories were the demand for a labour force caused by agrarian reforms, construction works and the beginning of modern industry. As a rule these immigrants entered illegally and therefore were not registered by public authorities even though they were tolerated. With reference to the most under-developed region of Great Poland we have found plentiful information on: (1) migrational inflow mainly from the east, and (2) on construction of new houses in rural and urban areas. In regard to the regions of Silesia and Pomerania the problem of immigration and housing development has not been yet thoroughly examined.

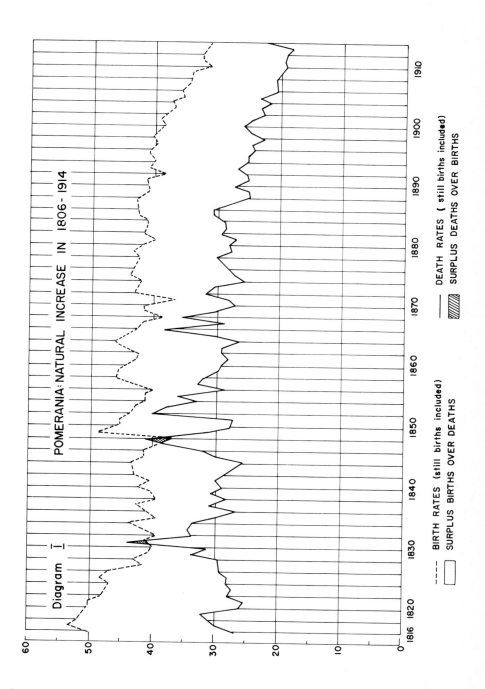

Diagram I

POMERANIA: NATURAL INCREASE IN 1806-1914

---- BIRTH RATES (still births included)
□ SURPLUS BIRTHS OVER DEATHS

—— DEATH RATES (still births included)
▨ SURPLUS DEATHS OVER BIRTHS

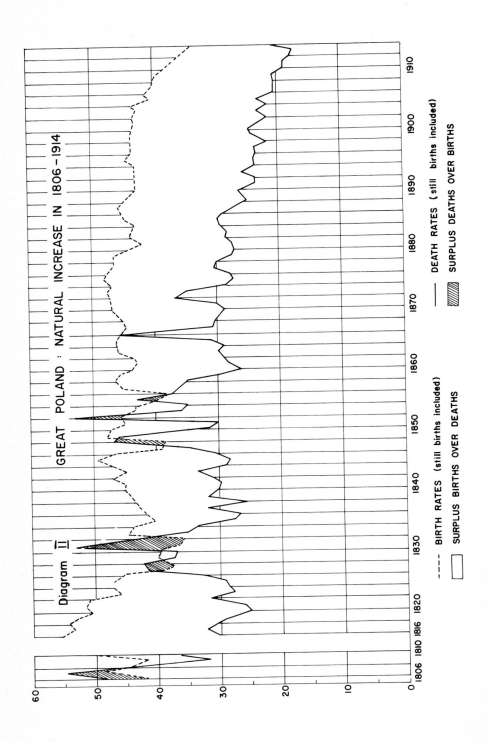

GREAT POLAND : NATURAL INCREASE IN 1806-1914

Diagram 11

---- BIRTH RATES (still births included)
—— DEATH RATES (still births included)

SURPLUS BIRTHS OVER DEATHS
SURPLUS DEATHS OVER BIRTHS

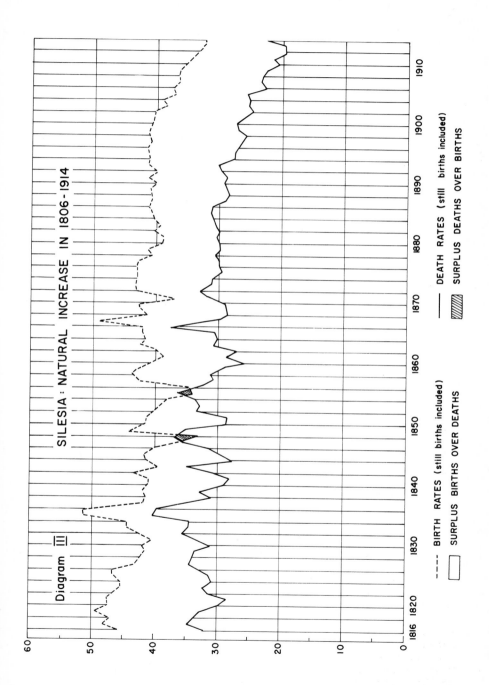

SILESIA : NATURAL INCREASE IN 1806-1914

Diagram III

---- BIRTH RATES (still births included)

SURPLUS BIRTHS OVER DEATHS

——— DEATH RATES (still births included)

SURPLUS DEATHS OVER BIRTHS

Population density decreased from the south to the north. In 1816 it amounted in Silesia to 48, in Great Poland to 29, in Pomerania to 22 persons per square kilometer and in 1840 to 70; 43 and 35 respectively. (Table 3, page 8)

The percentage of persons in the age group of 14 years and younger used to oscillate between 37% and 41% of the total population. These percentages were slightly lower in the towns than in the countryside. Population in the productive age of 15-60 amounted to 54%-57% but these percentages were higher in towns than in the countryside. Elderly persons of 61 years and over represented about 5% of the total population.

In Silesia, the percentages of urban population oscillated about 20%, in Great Poland 28% and in Pomerania 24%. During the entire time period preceding the demographic revolution these percentages did not change significantly. As the natural increase of the urban population was significantly lower than the increase of the rural population, the stable distribution of population between towns and countryside was possible thanks to little migrational surplus in towns. (Table 4, page 9)

For that period detailed information on distribution of population according to means of living is available for Great Poland only. About 78% of population made their living from agriculture and 12% from industry and handicraft. (Table 5, page 10) Those percentages likely did not change in Pomerania; in Silesia, however, the part of population living from non-agricultural sources was probably slightly higher.

Many social and economic factors limited the population capacity of the investigated regions. The feudal agrarian order and the three field system were the main causes of the low food production. The primitive land and water carriage made difficult the transportation of agricultural products. Therefore, in each decade of the first half of the XIXth century (1806-1807, 1825-1828, 1831-1832, 1847-1848), famines occurred, usually together with wars (1806-1807, 1831, 1848) or epidemics (1831-1832). The diagrams reveal the rapid increase of death rates and even a surplus of deaths over births. In the sense of Malthusian theory the population growth was limited by the positive checks. This situation improved from the end of the 1830's onward.

A characteristic trait of the agricultural feudal society at the beginning of the XIXth century was the considerable percentage of non-marriageable population. In the country only the farm owners and tenants, functionaries and handicraftsmen attached to landlords and a part of free workers and cottagers could marry and maintain a family. An important part of the rural population consisted of adult but non-married peasant children and agricultural servants staying with the peasants or with the landlords. The peasants with their children and their servants cultivated their farm areas and those of the landlords. In the towns, on the other hand, only the craftsmen and traders and a part of free workers and cottagers were married. The servants staying with craftsmen and traders and the other part of free workers and cottagers were not able to maintain a family. Thus, we see some other checks of population development similar to the Malthusian preventive checks. About 1840 their impact on

TABLE 3. POPULATION GROWTH AND DENSITY PER SQ. KM.

Year	Population in Thousands			Index Numbers			Density per sq. km.		
	Silesia	Great Poland	Pomerania	Silesia	Great Poland	Pomerania	Silesia	Great Poland	Pomerania
1810		781.2			95.3			29	
1816	1942.1	820.2	2139.9	100.0	100.0	100.0	48	29	22
1822	2194.7	958.8	2596.2	113.0	116.9	121.3	54	33	27
1831	2464.4	1056.3	2938.1	126.9	128.8	137.3	60	36	30
1840	2858.8	1233.9	3366.7	147.2	150.4	157.3	70	43	35
1849	3061.6	1352.0	3685.0	157.6	164.8	172.2	75	46	38
1861	3390.7	1503.5	4256.6	174.6	183.3	198.9	83	51	44
1871	3707.2	1583.8	4569.2	190.9	193.1	213.5	92	55	49
1880	4007.9	1703.4	4879.9	206.4	207.7	228.0	99	59	53
1890	4224.5	1751.6	4913.2	217.5	213.6	229.6	105	61	52
1900	4668.9	1887.3	5195.1	240.4	230.1	242.8	116	65	55
1910	5226.0	2099.8	5484.6	269.1	256.0	256.3	130	72	58

Source: A.G.A.D., A.Z. 96. Mittheilungen des Statistischen Bureau's in Berlin 1849-1859 (Mittheilungen) Z.K.P.S.B. 1861. P.S., H. 5-234.

TABLE 4. THE URBAN AND RURAL POPULATION

| Year | Percentages of Urban and Rural Population[a] | | | | | | Index Numbers for Urban Population | | |
| | Silesia | | Great Poland | | Pomerania | | Silesia | Poland | Pomerania |
	Urban Population	Rural Population	Urban Population	Rural Population	Urban Population	Rural Population			
1810	.	.	25.3	74.7	.	.	.	82.2	.
1816	20.4	79.6	29.3	70.7	26.7	73.3	100.0	100.0	100.0
1822	20.0	80.0	27.4	72.6	24.7	75.3	110.8	109.5	112.1
1831	20.2	79.8	27.5	72.5	24.2	75.8	125.9	121.1	124.0
1840	19.5	80.5	28.6	71.4	23.1	76.9	141.4	135.6	136.1
1849	20.1	79.9	26.6	73.4	23.3	76.7	156.1	149.9	150.6
1861	21.5	78.5	28.0	72.0	24.6	75.4	184.8	175.3	183.7
1871	24.6	75.4	26.9	73.1	25.4	74.6	230.5	177.3	203.6
1880	27.0	73.0	28.0	72.0	27.4	72.6	273.8	198.5	235.9
1890	29.9	70.1	28.9	71.1	29.6	70.4	319.6	211.1	254.5
1900	33.3	66.7	32.6	67.4	32.9	67.1	393.9	256.0	299.2
1910	34.8	65.2	34.4	65.6	36.4	63.6	460.1	300.7	349.2

[a]The Total population = 100

Source: See Table 3.

TABLE 5. THE OCCUPATIONAL STRUCTURE[a] OF POPULATION IN SILESIA, GREAT POLAND AND POMERANIA IN 1810-1907[1]

Year	Total	OF WHOM IN THE FOLLOWING OCCUPATIONS					
		Agriculture	Industry and Handicraft	Commerce and Transport	Professions Public Administration, Army and Clergy	Indoor Domestic Service[b]	Without or Unspecified Occupation
				SILESIA			
1861	100.0	43.9	37.5	3.7	3.5	2.7	8.7
1882	100.0	45.8	33.8	6.6	4.5	2.4	6.9
1907	100.0	35.6	36.5	8.9	4.6	1.5	12.8
				GREAT POLAND			
1810	100.0	78.5	12.2	3.4	1.7	2.0	2.2
1861	100.0	54.2	27.8	3.6	5.2	3.8	5.4
1882	100.0	64.0	16.9	5.4	5.0	3.1	5.6
1907	100.0	56.6	18.5	7.1	5.8	1.4	10.6
				POMERANIA			
1861	100.0	57.8	28.0	3.3	3.2	2.7	4.9
1882	100.0	58.0	19.6	6.7	5.0	3.5	7.2
1907	100.0	50.5	20.0	8.5	6.4	1.8	12.8

[a] In 1810 and 1861 the economically activer persons refer to those without permanent assistance from family members; in 1882 and 1907 all economically active persons.

[b] In 1882 and 1907 also labourers at changeable jobs.

[1] Main occupations only. Indoor domestic service treated in the source as economically inactive persons.

Source: A.G.A.D., A.Z. 96. P.S.H. 10. S.D.R., Bd. 4. 210.

population growth began however to decrease.

In the period preceding the demographic revolution there were also some factors stimulating demographic growth. The high death rates caused naturally high birth rates. The years of famines, wars and epidemics were followed by compensatory time periods with a high natality. These time periods were the longer and the natality the igher when the famine, wars and epidemics had lasted longer and caused more deaths. The percentages of elderly people, of 61 years and over, were very low (ca 5%). Thus, the population was rather young and this contributed to a high fertility.

In the years 1807-1840 the economy and social life were always under the pressure of demographic factors. In the investigated regions there was a surplus of population which in the conditions of those times could not find jobs, sufficient food and housing.

Under the impact of the French revolution and of some interests of the state and especially because of the demographic pressure, the rural population gained personal freedom in 1807-1809, and economic freedom in 1811-1823. Thereafter some other agrarian reforms were introduced. The freedom of moving from place to place, the new division of rural population into the landowners and the landless, the abolishment of corvee and of other peasant obligations as well as of the commons, gave a start to technical progress, growth of employment and production in the agriculture.

All this, along with the urban overpopulation caused similar reforms in industry, commerce and trade at the beginning of the 1830's. I.a. the towns had been liberated from the feudal authority and the craftsmen from the last dependencies of the guilds.

Consequently, the labour force resources and reserves had been used for capital accumulation which was the basis of the capitalistic system; both progress and exploitation.

Confronting all these changes with the Malthusian population theory one may say that Malthus tried to examine the nature of poverty. He saw its basis in overpopulation. But he did not foresee that a new economic system with technical progress and production growth could arise from the poverty and victims of the human mass. All these could enlarge the population capacity of regions and improve the standard of man's living.

III. THE TRANSITIONAL PERIOD, 1840-1871

The natural movement of population became more stable than in the previous time period. The birth and death rates diminished in the more developed Silesia and Pomerania but remained almost unchanged in Great Poland. In the entire area, the five year average death rate (per thousand) fluctuated between 28.1 and 39.3%, the rate of live and still births aggregated between 38.7 and 46.6 (Table 1). As a rule the death rates in towns were higher than in the country, the birth rates, however, were higher in the rural areas than in the urban ones.

In contrast to the former period the completeness of

census results is beyond discussion and there is no doubt about the natural and migrational increase resp. decrease in population.

The investigated area was becoming a scene of lively migrational movement. More and more emigrants were leaving for different regions, especially for the western and overseas countries. They were replaced by immigrants flowing in from regions east and south of the area under research. The net migration was negative and became continuously larger (Table 2).

Between 1840 and 1871, the population density increased considerably: in industrialized Silesia the population density increased from 70 to 92 persons per square kilometer; in Great Poland from 43 to 55 and in Pomerania from 35 to 49 (Table 3).

Except for some local areas the number of females was equal or higher than that of males.

The percentages of children 14 years and less increased slightly in comparison with the previous time period. These percentages were about 4% lower in towns than in the country-side. The share of population in the age group 15-60 was about 4% higher in towns than in the country-side. The portion of older people, 61 years and over, remained at a level of 5%. These percentages of age structure show the influences of country-town migration.

The share of urban population in Silesia rose from 20% to 25% of the total population, in Pomerania from 23% to 25%, but in Great Poland there were no significant changes (Table 4). In 1861, 44% of the total population in Silesia found their source of living in agriculture, in Great Poland 54% and in Pomerania 58%. In the same year industry and handicraft were the source of living for 38% of the total population in Silesia, for 28% in Great Poland and for 20% in Pomerania (Table 5).

In the transitional period famines (1847-1848), epidemics (1852, 1856, 1866) and war appeared suddenly causing higher levels of mortality, (even a surplus of mortality over natality). The calamities, however, lasted only a very short time and between them the increase of population was considerable. Thus the calamities did not check the population growth to the same extent as in the previous period.

The number of unmarried people, rather large in the pre-revolutionary time period, was diminishing. More extensive and intensive agriculture, lively developments in construction industry and transportation enabled the employers to offer more jobs with the possibility of maintaining a family. The demand for a labour force, growing production of food, houses and of other consumer goods, developing land and railway transport resulted in the exchange of people, products and culture between rural and urban areas: all those were the basic stimuli of population growth in the transition period.

The population growth animated mutually the socio-economic life. Great labour force resources and reserves favoured the basic capital formation. Human masses not fully employed and receiving relatively low wages in comparison with growing properties were getting radical. Those who became landless during previous agrarian reforms were demanding that the lost or still cultivated farm areas should be their own. Those who kept the farm areas as their own after reforms were organizing peasant circles for self-help purposes. The urban proletariat was demanding a solution of social problems. The first steps in organizing cooperatives and trade unions was made. The demographic and socio-economic growth was correlated with development in education health service, literature and the arts.

Thus in the transition period the Malthusian positive and preventive checks were exerting even lower pressure on population growth. But new factors also appeared stimulating that growth.

IV. THE PERIOD OF DEMOGRAPHIC REVOLUTION AND COUNTER-REVOLUTION 1870-1871.

The rapid changes in the natural movement of population were stopped and a falling tendency appeared. At first the death rates began to fall. Later on the birth rates started to follow but at a slower rate. The curve formed by those rates took the shape of a falling area of a convex parabola (See Figure 1-3). When comparing the years 1871-1875 and 1911-1914 we may see that the death rates in Silesia fell from 31.1% to 21.0%, in Great Poland from 31.6 to 18.5% and in Pomerania from 28.5 to 19.8%. At the same time the birth rates diminished: in Silesia from 41.7 to 33.2%, in Great Poland from 46.0 to 35.2% and in Pomerania from 41.5 to 32.0% (Table 1).

The natural increase, sometimes amounting to 2% of the average population was absorbed in a great part by emigration to the western and overseas countries.

In the total investigated area the yearly migrational loss rose from 37,000 in 1872-1880 107,000 in the 1880's with a subsequent decrease to 78,000 in the first decade of the twentieth century. In other words, the losses absorbed from 41% to 78% of the total natural increase (Table 2).

Between 1871 and 1910 the population density in industrialized Silesia rose from 92 to 130 persons per square kilometer, in Great Poland from 55 to 72 and in agricultural Pomerania from 49 to 58 (Table 3).

In the whole area the number of females was higher than the number of males. The surplus of females was caused by natural factors, by urbanization and by a great number of male emigrants. Important changes may be observed in the age distribution. In 1900 the percentages of children 14 years or less oscillated around 40%. In the towns these percentages were falling to 34 and in the country they rose to 43. In the same time the percentages of population of the working age in the total area amounted to 53% in the entire area, to 59% in towns, and in the country-side to 50%. The population was evidently ageing: the share of elderly people 61 and over increased to 8%.

In 1910 the percentages of urban population in all regions under research oscillated around 35% (Table 4). In 1907 the population living from agriculture in Silesia amounted to 36% of the total population, in Great Poland to 57% and in Pomerania to 51%. The industry and handicraft in Silesia constituted a source of living for 37% of population, in Great Poland for 19% and in Pomerania for 20%.

Between 1871 and 1914, the socio-economic factors influencing the demographic processes had, in comparison with the previous time periods, greatly changed. One of the most significant results of agrarian reforms was the increase in food production. In Great Poland, for instance, the production of the four basic grains (wheat, rye, barley and oats) increased more than fourfold between 1810 and 1910; the production of potatoes more than 60 times, while the production of cattle, sheep and pigs combined almost doubled. Besides the numerical growth the increasingly higher quality of the products, especially of the animal products, was of great importance. In the same period the population of Great Poland increased 2.5 times. Similar changes were noticed in other regions (Tables 3, 6 and 7).

TABLE 6.   PRINCIPAL CROPS PER CAPITA
(in 100 kilogram)

Year	Silesia		Great Poland		Pomerania	
	The Four Basic Grain Production	Potatoes	The Four Basic Grain Production	Potatoes	The Four Basic Grain Production	Potatoes
	Per Capita of the Total Population					
1810	.	.	2.0	0.4	.	.
1878	4.4	8.9	5.5	12.9	5.6	7.3
1910	4.7	16.7	8.4	23.5	8.7	14.6
	Per Capita of the Agricultural Population					
1810	.	.	2.6	0.5	.	.
1882	6.5	10.8	6.4	12.1	6.4	9.2
1907	15.1	36.4	16.7	45.3	15.4	25.4

Source: Archiwum Głowne Akt Dawnych, Archiwum
Zamojskich/A.G.A.D., A.Z./96. Wojewodzkie
Panstwowe, Poznan/W.A.P.P./, Maj Biała 243b.
Preussische Statistik /P.S./, H. 4;5;66;81;211;
225;234. Statistik des Deutsche Reichs/S.D.R./
Bd. 4;204;210;240.

TABLE 7.   CATTLE, SHEEP AND PIGS PER 100 PERSONS[a]

| Year | Per 100 Persons of the Total Population | | | Year | Per 100 Persons of the Agricultural Population | | |
	Great Silesia	Poland	Pomerania		Great Silesia	Poland	Pomerania
1816	45.2	34.6	64.4	1849	.	81.0	.
1861	40.6	53.5	53.6	1882	92.6	86.5	98.0
1910	36.6	60.8	68.1	1907	131.1	121.6	140.3

[a]One unit of cattle = 10 sheep - 4 pigs (based on
practice of the Prussian Statistical Office "Zeitschrift
des Koniglich Preussischen Statistischen Bureau's
/Z.K.P.S.B./1891, p. 215.

Source: Z.K.P.S.B. 1961. PS., H 218, 219, 234,
S.D.R. Bd. 4, 212. Tabellen und amtliche
Nachrichten, Berlin, 1849-1858.

From the beginning of the transition period one may
observe a very quick development of railway communication.
Simultaneously with the increase in food production the railway
transport facilitated the creation and development of great
human agglomerations making their living from non-agricultural
production. This resulted in the specialization of regions,
subregions, centres and towns such as the typical industrial
centres in Silesia, agricultural Great Poland with food
processing industries, agricultural and commercial centres in
Pomerania. The agglomeration of population, improving transport
and economic specialization had a beneficial effect on the
development of the regional markets, on the increase in
agricultural and non-agricultural production and on the increase
of employment and incomes.

As mentioned above, the agrarian reforms gave a start to
an intensive process of housing development in the country. The
landlords were building more and more houses for the land-
labourers families. The peasants, freed from the old dependences
began to build their own houses adapted to the needs of their
families. From the 1830's an increasing degree of housing
development had been observed in towns. At last the lively
housing development was beneficial for the frequency of marriages
and for the family size.

Contrary to the pre-revolutionary time period in rural
and urban areas more jobs were created. The landlords and owners
of great peasant farms tried to secure the manpower for the
entire year in offering family houses or dwellings to married
workers. Chiefly the seasonal labourers and foreign workers were
single. In the towns, on the other hand, under the conditions of
a developing market, the skilled servants were able to found
their own workshops and maintain families. A competing industry

developed simultaneously with the handicraft industry, assuring
stable and slowly rising wages which allowed a large part of
employed workers to marry while still young and to maintain a
family.

The economic growth favoured the development of the
material and of the non-material culture and offered an improved
health protection. The number of the sanitary personnel and
particularly of physicians, accoucheurs and midwives grew as well
as the level of the medical education and the efficiency of health
service. In Great Poland, for instance, in the years 1810-1898,
the number of physicians per 10,000 inhabitants grew from 1 to 2.5
of the accoucheurs and midwives from 0.7 to 3.6, whereas in the
years of 1825-1905 the number of health establishments increased
from 1 to 5 per 100,000 inhabitants.

Thus the high production of food and of other goods,
development of transport, construction of houses, school education
and ever more efficient health service, the increasing number of
jobs and rising incomes -- all favoured a decrease in mortality
and the maintaining of a high fertility.

From 1871 to 1914 we may observe not only the fall of
mortality but also, although with some lag, a permanent decrease
of fertility. In those times a positive correlation of incomes
with family size had consolidated and lasted until World War II.

At the same time the aspiration to an ever higher
standard of living seemed to weaken that correlation. In the
area under research the world wide regularity with which the
birth rates follow the permanently falling mortality, appeared
very evident. The emigration of rather young people, the ageing
of population, the surplus of females in urban and industrialized
areas -- all caused the decrease of fertility.

On the other hand, the demographic development created an
increasingly greater demand for goods and favoured savings and
investments.

The animated migrational movement between country-side
and towns, the outflow of emigrants to the western and overseas
countries and the inflow of immigrants from the eastern and
western regions meant the transfer of population from low income
regions to high income ones. In the investigated area a
scarcity of labour force was noticed. There were attempts to
replace the lacking manpower by mechanization in agriculture and
by technical progress in the total economy.

V. CONCLUSIONS

Let us elaborate on certain conclusions drawn from our
confrontation of the examined demographic development with the
Malthusian theory.

In the area between the Nyssa, Odra, Wista and Lower
Niemen the thesis on the mutual relation between the development
of resources, especially of food, and the development of
population has been verified for the pre-industrial period and
preceding the demographic revolution. In the transition period
this thesis corresponded only to some extent to the historical
reality. But in the period of demographic revolution and

counter-revolution, the thesis discussed and the demographic development fully diverged. In the latter period the resources grew much faster than the population in the investigated area: thus the growth of resources became the real basis for demographic growth.

It is possible to observe the Malthusian positive (famines, epidemics and poverty) and the preventive checks (impossibility of marriage) in the pre-revolutionary period and to a minor degree during the transition period. These checks ceased to exert any influence on population development during the demographic revolution and counter-revolution. In the last period a new type of checks appeared corresponding to the changed socio-economic conditions, namely: personal income affecting the number of children in a family, aspiration to an ever higher standard of living, women surplus in the industrialized and urbanized area, emigration of young people and the beginning of a ageing of the population.

Malthus treated one-sidedly the relation between the socio-economic and demographic factors. He saw the negative influence of (the relative) overpopulation but overlooked its consequences in building a new economic system. In the period preceding the demographic revolution, and in the case of investigated regions, the relative overpopulation exerted heavy pressure on the agrarian order, contributed to reforms in agriculture, in industry, in commerce and trade, in transportation and in other services. The great labour force resources made possible the basic capital accumulation, technical progress and the prevalence of capitalism. In the capitalistic system the push role of demographic factors resulted in the creation of ever growing demand for consumer goods, and a tendency toward saving and investment.

The Malthusian theory arose in concrete conditions of space and time. During his long life the author has revised many times its theses according to the historical experience. For socio-economic conditions of his own time and for similar conditions of later periods, the theory may play a diagnostic role. That theory could not and cannot be a basis for diagnosis and forecasting purposes in periods with more developed conditions.

REFERENCES

1)   S. Borowski, Emigration from the Polish Territories
     under German rule, 1815-1914, "Studia Historiae
     Oeconomicae", Vol. 2, Poznan 1968, p. 151-184.

2)   S. Borowski, Ksztartowanie sie rolniczego rynku pracy
     w Wielkopolsce w okresie wielkich reform agrarnych,
     1807-1860 (The development of the Market for
     Agricultural Labour in Great Poland at the time of the
     Major Agrarian Reforms of 1807-1860) Poznan 1963,
     PWN, pp. 664.

3)   A.M. Carr-Saunders, World Population, Past Growth and
     Present Trends, London 1964, Frank-Cass, pp. 336.

4)   C. Clark, Population Growth and Land Use, London 1967,
     MacMillan, pp. 406.

5)   B. Drewniak, Emigracja z Pomorza Zachodniego 1816-1914
     (Emigration from the Western Pomerania, 1816-1914),
     Poznan 1966, Wydawnictwo Poznanskie, pp. 120.

6)   D.H.C. Eversley, Social Theories of Fertility and the
     Malthusian Debate, Oxford 1959, Clarendon Press,
     pp. 314.

7)   A. Fircke, Rückblick auf die Bewegung der Bevölkerung im
     Preussischen Staate wahrend des Zeitraumes vom Jahre
     1816-1874, "Preussische Statistik", Bd. XLVIII A.,
     Berlin 1879.

8)   D. V. Glass, Population Policies and Movements in
     Europe, II edition, London 1967, Frank Cass, pp. 490.

9)   B. Kaczmarski, Ocena spisow ludnosci na Slasku z
     pierwszej porowy XIX w. (Evaluation of the Population
     Censuses in Silesia in the First Half of the XIXth
     Century), "Przeszrosc Demograficzna Polski", Vol. I,
     p. 17-66.

10) T. Ladogorski, Zrudzenia pruskiej statystyki ludnosci
     pierwszej porowy XIX w. i proby jej korekty na Slasku
     (Illusions of the Prussian Population Statistics of the
     First Half of the 19th Century and the First Trials to
     Correct the Figures for Silesia) "Przeszrosc Demograficzna
     Polski", Vol. III.

11) Z. Pavlik, Nastin populacniho vyvoje sweta (Evolution of
     the World Population) Praha 1964, Ceskoslovenska
     Akademia Ved, pp. 308.

12) V. F. Wilcox, International Migrations, Vol. I, II,
     New York 1929-1931.

4

AMERICAN POPULATION IN THE EARLY NATIONAL PERIOD

J. POTTER

(LONDON SCHOOL OF ECONOMICS)

1. Background: Malthus and Colonial America

It is scarcely necessary to remind members of such a
Conference that the Rev. T.R. Malthus based his demographic law
directly upon American experience. He wrote in the Essay on the
Principle of Population of 1798:

> "In the United States of America, where the means of
> subsistence have been more ample, the manners of the
> people more pure, and consequently the checks to early
> marriage fewer than in any of the modern states of
> Europe, the population has been found to double itself
> in twenty-five years.
>
> This ratio of increase, thought short of the
> utmost power of population, yet as the result of
> actual experience we will take as our rule; and say,
>
> That population, when unchecked, goes on doubling
> itself every twenty-five years, or increases in a
> geometrical ratio."

Malthus refers in several passages to the great speed of
American population growth, "a rapidity of increase, probably
without parallel in history". The newest settlements in America
had the most rapid growth, being greatest at the frontier where
the settlers devoted themselves solely to agriculture. To this

observation, Malthus added the footnote formulating the second part of his law:

> "In instances of this kind, the powers of the earth appear to be fully equal to answer all the demands for food that can be made upon it by man. But we should be led into an error if we were thence to suppose that population and food ever really increase in the same ratio. The one is still a geometrical and the other an arithmetical ratio, that is, one increases by multiplication, and the other by addition."

Various eighteenth century writers before Malthus had given different estimates of the period of time within which population doubled itself, and several of these writings are found to have been in Malthus's own library (now the Malthus Collection, at Jesus College, Cambridge). The earliest of these is Benjamin Franklin's Observations concerning the Increase of Mankind of 1751. In clause 7, Franklin wrote:

> "Hence marriages in America are more general, and more generally early, than in Europe, and if it is recknoned there that there is but one marriage per annum among 100 persons, perhaps we may here reckon two; and if in Europe they have but four births to a marriage (many of their marriages being late) we may here reckon eight; of which, if one half grow up, and our marriages are made, reckoning one with another, at twenty years of age, our people must at least be doubled every twenty years."

Later, in the same work, Franklin returned to the same theme, now stating the period of doubling as a supposition:

> "Thus there are supposed to be now upwards of one million of English souls in North America (though it is thought scarce 80,000 have been brought over-sea) and yet perhaps there is not one the fewer in Britain, but rather many more, on account of the employment the colonies offered to manufactures at home. This million doubling, suppose but once in 25 years, will, in another century, be more than the people of England, and the greatest number of Englishmen will be on this side of the water."

There can be little doubt that many contemporary and present-day ideas of population growth in colonial America originate with Benjamin Franklin. Somewhat later, Michael Sadler, in The Law of Population (London, 1830) attempted to trace the origins of Malthus's ideas. Because of similarities of views and wording, he claimed that the immediate influence was the Rev. Townsend's Journey Through Spain. (1) Sadler continues the trail from Townsend to the Rev. Robert Wallace; (2) Elsewhere both Malthus and Townsend are said to have derived ideas from Dr. Price; (3) Dr. Styles; (4) and Dr. Franklin.

Price's Observations have the greatest amount of detail about the American colonies, more even than is found in Franklin's

work. The author speaks of a doubling of population in New Jersey
in 22 years and a doubling in New England in 25 years. In Volume
II of the Malthus copy, part of the following passage has been
marked with a line in the margin for emphasis:

> "One of the most obvious divisions of the state of
> mankind is, into the wild and the civilised state.....
>   Our American colonies are at present, for the
> most part, in the first and happiest of the states
> I have described; and they afford a very striking
> proof of the effects of the different stages of
> civilization on population. In the inland parts
> of NORTH-AMERICA, or the back settlements, (5) where
> the modes of living are most simple, and almost
> everyone occupies land for himself, there is an
> increase so rapid as to have hardly any parallel."
> (Price Observations, ii, 258-9)

These are certainly not the only pre-Malthusian writings
discussing the period of doubling. The French philosophes
Count Buffon and Abbe Raynal both cite Franklin in speaking of a
25-year period of doubling in America. The second Hollis
Professor of Divinity at Harvard University, Edward Wigglesworth
the Younger, published a pamphlet in Boston in 1775, Calculations
on American Population, predicting the size of the American
population as far as the year 2000 A.D. Wigglesworth firmly
asserts that the American colonies had doubled their population
every 25 years from the time of the first plantations,
"principally from the natural increase of the inhabitants." (6).

It is not the purpose of this paper to estimate the
accuracy of Malthus's assumptions about the natural rate of
growth of population in colonial America. These assertions
were attacked by contemporaries, particularly of course by his
opponent William Godwin. Michael Sadler also refused to accept
Malthus's "pretended proofs", entitling one of his chapters
"Of the erroneousness of the supposed facts and deductions
relative to particular states of America, on which the geometric
theory is founded." (7).

If one assumes the aggregate figures shown in the First
Census, that of 1790, to be reasonably accurate, then it is
indisputable that, in total, the population of colonial America
increased at a rate closely approximating to that of the
Malthusian postulate - indeed slightly faster. Separate estimates
for particular colonies are made difficult by boundary changes
and still more by the internal mobility of the population. It is
clear, however, that growth was uneven, both in place and time.
New England grew at the slowest rate, partly because of net
emigration from the region. The Middle Colonies grew at the
fastest rate, helped by the arrival of other Americans (e.g.,
those from New England) and by the waves of new settlers from
Europe. The trends in the South are complicated by slavery and
by internal re-distribution within the region, Virginia for
example losing ground to the Carolinas and Georgia.

The general picture of fast growth in the newest
settlements, whether through migration or natural increase, and
slower growth in the older areas, whether through emigration or

slower natural increase, seems to be confirmed by the available
statistical evidence. What must remain uncertain, however, is
the contribution to aggregate growth made by the fresh arrivals
from Europe. The suggestions - one can hardly call them
serious estimates - of some historians, uninterested in the
demographic significance of their figures, would place
immigration at such a high level that the resultant natural
growth rate falls far below the Malthusian level, in extreme
cases to half. If some of these high figures are discarded,
above all on the ground that available shipping in the eighteenth
century simply could not have handled such a traffic, and
calculations are made based for example on possible passenger
space, then one reaches a total figure for immigration not
exceeding half a million throughout the colonial period (and
probably nearer one quarter of a million). Such an estimate
then lowers the natural rate of growth below that shown by the
aggregate figures. Although the natural growth rate is
consequently reduced to a level slightly below the Malthusian
rate, the difference is not significant and one is left with the
conclusion that the natural growth rate of population in colonial
America probably was somewhat under, but very close to, the
Malthusian rate of doubling every 25 years.

2.   <u>Decline in Rate of Natural Increase, 1790-1860</u>
          The total American population continued to grow at a
rate of about 34/35 per cent per decade from 1790 to the Civil
War, varying only between 36.4 per cent in the 1800s and 32.7
per cent in the 1830s. This near-constancy in the aggregate
rate of growth, however, conceals a number of important and
obvious changes during the period:

  a) The Negro population was proportionally at its
    greatest - just over 20 per cent of total
    population - at the end of the eighteenth century.
    Negroes constituted 19 per cent of total
    population in the First Census of 1790. This
    proportion declined steadily in the next decades
    and by 1860 had fallen to 14 per cent (continuing
    to fall, in fact, until the lowest point of 10
    per cent was reached in 1920).

  b) Towards mid-century, immigration came to contribute
    increasingly to total growth. As this growth rate
    was constant, the natural rate of increase must have
    begun to decline earlier in the century.

  c) A vast redistribution of population occurred both
    within, and more particularly beyond, the area of
    settlement of 1790. By 1860, 45 per cent of the
    American population lived outside the original
    states of 1790.

  d) Urban growth through this period was slow but uneven.
    The aggregate figure of 20 per cent urban in 1860
    conceals great regional variations; even within
    New England, only 2 per cent of Vermont's population
    lived in towns in 1860, whereas both Rhode Island
    and Massachusetts were over 60 per cent urbanised.

These developments make it hazardous to generalise about American demographic history in this period. Aggregate growth rates, influenced by the factors indicated, varied greatly from region to region and from state to state. In 1790 Virginia had the largest population both of whites only, of Negroes and, therefore, of total numbers. By 1860 she still had the largest Negro population, but ranked seventh in white population and fifth in aggregate. Pennsylvania, second in white population and in aggregate in 1790, was still second in both respects in 1860. Massachusetts, third in white population (fourth in aggregate) in 1790 had fallen to sixth in white population (and sixth also in aggregate) in 1860. New York, the most populous state in 1860, had risen from fifth place in 1790.

These changes of ranking, of which only the most obvious examples have been given, are the clearest indication of the regional differences in growth rates. The usual assumption has been that the explanation lies entirely in migration, internal and external, and that the natural growth rate behaved in much the same way - i.e., was slowly declining - in all regions. Accordingly, various writers have made calculations of the American birth rate, showing a steady decline from 1800 to 1860 and beyond.

It is not until 1850 that the Census data, by showing state of birth, make possible any calculations of internal mobility and of contribution of immigration. Once such calculations become feasible, then considerable regional differences emerge in the rates of natural growth. With allowance made for gains from immigration from outside and for gains or losses from internal migration, then the resultant growth rates vary greatly; while a roughly calculated national figure for the decade 1850-60 is of a 26 per cent natural growth rate, that for New England alone is 12 per cent and for Rhode Island and Connecticut 6 and 8 per cent respectively.

3. White Fertility Ratios

The early Censuses provide sufficient details of the age and sex structure of the population to allow white fertility ratios to be calculated for the separate states. The following table shows the ranking by states in ascending order.

TABLE I

WHITE FERTILITY RATIOS BY STATES AND TERRITORIES, 1800-1869
NUMBER OF CHILDREN 0-9 YEARS PER WOMEN 16-44 YEARS (1800-1820)
AND 16-49 YEARS (1830-1860)

1800

Rhode Island	145
Massachusetts	148
Connecticut	151
Delaware	151
Maryland	160
Washington D.C.	160
NEW ENGLAND	164
New Hampshire	170
New York	178
TOTAL U.S.A.	182
Virginia	182
MID ATLANTIC	183
SOUTH ATLANTIC	185
New Jersey	185
Pennsylvania	188
North Carolina	192
Maine	198
South Carolina	204
Vermont	207
Georgia	212
Indiana	213
Kentucky	238
EAST SOUTH CENTRAL	239
Tennessee	241
EAST NORTH CENTRAL	244
Mississippi	250
Ohio	250

1810

Rhode Island	141
Massachusetts	142
Connecticut	143
Washington D.C.	147
New Hampshire	155
NEW ENGLAND	156
Maryland	160
Delaware	169
New Jersey	174
Virginia	178
Vermont	178
SOUTH ATLANTIC	181
TOTAL U.S.A.	182
Pennsylvania	184
MID ATLANTIC	185
North Carolina	186
Maine	188
New York	190
Louisiana	190
South Carolina	195
Michigan	200
Mississippi	205
Georgia	210
Illinois	215
Kentucky	227
EAST SOUTH CENTRAL	228
EAST NORTH CENTRAL	229
Tennessee	230
Ohio	231
Indiana	232
Missouri	236

1820

Massachusetts	127
Connecticut	128
Washington D.C.	129
Rhode Island	131
NEW ENGLAND	138
New Hampshire	139
Vermont	147
Maryland	151
Delaware	160
Maine	163
New Jersey	163
New York	167
MID ATLANTIC	170
Virginia	171
TOTAL U.S.A.	173
SOUTH ATLANTIC	174
Pennsylvania	175
Michigan	177
North Carolina	182
Louisiana	185
South Carolina	185
WEST SOUTH CENTRAL	189
Georgia	202
Kentucky	208
Ohio	213
Arkansas	214
EAST SOUTH CENTRAL	215
EAST NORTH CENTRAL	216
Missouri	218
Tennessee	220
Mississippi	222
Indiana	224
Alabama	225
Illinois	230

1830

Massachusetts	94
Connecticut	98
Rhode Island	100
D.C.	104
New Hampshire	106
NEW ENGLAND	107
Maryland	116
Vermont	119
Delaware	123
New Jersey	129

1840

Rhode Island	88
Massachusetts	88
Connecticut	91
New Hampshire	97
D.C.	99
NEW ENGLAND	100
Vermont	113
New York	114
Maryland	114
Delaware	120

1850

Massachusetts	76
Rhode Island	80
Connecticut	81
New Hampshire	84
NEW ENGLAND	87
D.C.	91
New York	95
Vermont	99
MID ATLANTIC	105
New Jersey	106

Table I (contd.)

Maine	130	MID ATLANTIC	120	Maine	106
New York	131	New Jersey	121	Maryland	111
MID ATLANTIC	133	Maine	125	New Mexico	113
Pennsylvania	137	Pennsylvania	130	Delaware	118
TOTAL U.S.A.	141	TOTAL U.S.A.	135	Pennsylvania	118
Virginia	141	Virginia	137	Louisiana	118
SOUTH ATLANTIC	143	SOUTH ATLANTIC	141	TOTAL U.S.A.	119
North Carolina	146	North Carolina	142	Virginia	123
South Carolina	150	South Carolina	145	North Carolina	123
Louisiana	157	Louisiana	145	South Carolina	124
Ohio	168	Michigan	146	SOUTH ATLANTIC	125
Michigan	168	Wisconsin	149	Ohio	130
Florida	175	Ohio	151	Michigan	131
Georgia	175	Florida	154	EAST NORTH CENTRAL	138
EAST NORTH CENTRAL	175	EAST NORTH CENTRAL	158	Utah	139
EAST SOUTH CENTRAL	178	Kentucky	160	WEST SOUTH CENTRAL	140
Tennessee	181	WEST SOUTH CENTRAL	161	Kentucky	141
WEST SOUTH CENTRAL	182	Iowa	166	Tennessee	141
Mississippi	190	Illinois	168	Illinois	143
Indiana	192	Tennessee	170	EAST SOUTH CENTRAL	144
Illinois	195	EAST SOUTH CENTRAL	171	Alabama	145
Alabama	197	Indiana	171	Missouri	146
Missouri	200	WEST NORTH CENTRAL	175	WEST NORTH CENTRAL	148
Arkansas	202	Georgia	175	Wisconsin	148
		Missouri	176	Georgia	148
		Mississippi	184	Indiana	148
		Alabama	185	Minnesota	150
		Arkansas	195	Iowa	155
				Texas	155
				Mississippi	159
				Arkansas	165
				Florida	167
				Oregon	181
		New Hampshire	77	EAST NORTH CENTRAL	128
		Rhode Island	79	Tennessee	132
		Massachusetts	80	Pacific	132
		Connecticut	83	Illinois	132
		NEW ENGLAND	85	Georgia	134
		D.C.	94	Kentucky	134
		New York	95	EAST SOUTH CENTRAL	135
		Vermont	95	Indiana	136
		Maine	97	Kansas	136
		New Jersey	102	Missouri	137
		MID ATLANTIC	103	Alabama	137
		Maryland	106	Nebraska	138
		Pennsylvania	115	Mississippi	140
		Michigan	115		
		TOTAL U.S.A.	116		

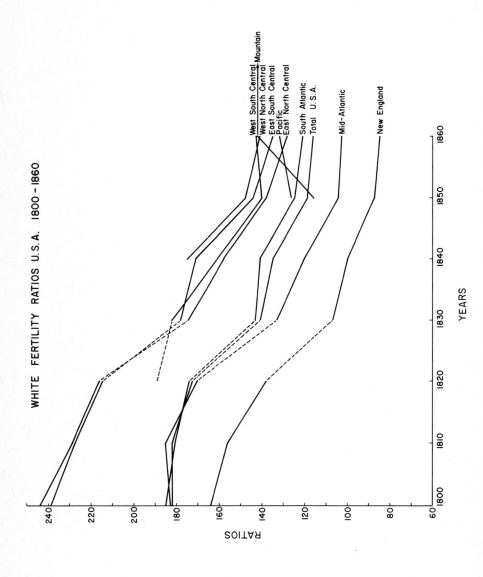

WHITE FERTILITY RATIOS U.S.A. 1800 - 1860

Table I (contd.)

South Carolina	117	WEST NORTH	
Delaware	118	CENTRAL	141
Colorado	118	Wisconsin	142
Louisiana	119	Iowa	146
North Carolina	120	Florida	147
Ohio	121	Minnesota	148
SOUTH ATLANTIC	121	Arkansas	155
California	121	Texas	158
Virginia	124	Washington	160
Nevada	125	Utah	178
New Mexico	128	Oregon	192

The foregoing Table and graph I (8) reveal a number of interesting features. The graph in particular clearly shows that fertility ratios were generally declining in all areas, but at very different levels. The decade 1850-60, probably reflecting among other things the consequences of immigration, shows a slight halt to the declining trend.

New England states group themselves together with the lowest fertility ratios in every Census year. The Middle States are generally next highest after New England. The close grouping of the South Atlantic States, coming next highest, is quite remarkable (1830: Va. 141; S.A. tot. 143; N.C. 146; S.C. 150; 1850: Va. 123; N.C. 123; S.C. 124; S.A. tot. 125). The areas of newest settlement, after the very first initial period, soon begin to show high fertility ratios, West North Central leading in 1840, 1850 and 1860.

The state data presented above are themselves only part of the story. From 1830 it is possible to break the state figures down by countries and cities. Out of the mass of subsequent detail it is possible only to cite a few examples here:

TABLE II

FERTILITY RATIOS IN CERTAIN CITIES, 1840 and 1850

1840 City		1850 City		1850 State	
Boston	77	Boston	69	Massachusetts	76
Providence	83	Providence	76	Rhode Island	80
New York City	85	New York City	77	New York	95
Philadelphia	90	Philadelphia	84	Pennsylvania	118
Chicago	92	Chicago	100	Illinois	143
Baltimore	92	Baltimore	91	Maryland	111
Cincinatti	93	Cincinatti	94	Ohio	130
Louisville	102	Louisville	97	Louisiana	118
New Orleans	110	New Orleans	76	Kentucky	141

The general pattern emerging from both the state figures and sub-divisions is that the lowest fertility ratios are usually found in the most urbanised states (Rhode Island, Connecticut, Massachusetts). Within those states, fertility ratios are highest in the rural divisions and counties, lowest in the more urbanised counties. All cities, wherever situated and whether at high or at low fertility ratios, have a lower ratio than the total ratio for the state in which they are situated. As with the state figures, the divisional and city figures generally show a declining trend over time.

One other factor to be mentioned may explain the appearance of New Hampshire in 1860 as the state with the lowest fertility ratio (Table I). Mobility affected the age and sex structure of the population. With the exception of the movement of females into some New England factory towns, a migrating group generally contained proportionately more males than the society they were leaving. Consequently, migrant receiving areas had large male surpluses; emigration areas tended to be left with female surpluses. The presence of surplus women in a population lowered the fertility ratio, as in the case of New Hampshire in 1860 which had a considerable female surplus.

The evidence thus confirms the assumption of a declining natural rate of population growth in the U.S.A. from the beginning of the nineteenth century, but points to very marked regional differences. Above all, the differences in fertility ratios appear to associate the declining growth rate directly with the process of urbanisation.

4. Possible Explanations

It is not proposed to examine in detail all possible interpretations of the data presented above. Since the declining trends are found in all regions and at all levels of fertility ratios, a simple universal interpretation, with urbanisation as the only explanation, cannot be expected. Yet the general proposition that the decline is predominantly associated with urban growth, though not to the exclusion of other factors, does appear to be justified by the evidence.

   a)   Health in Towns, and particularly child mortality, has to be considered as a relevant factor. It is not until much later in the century that evidence becomes available to allow a statistical study in this area. (9)

   b)   Age and Sex Structure are of obvious relevance. Immigration and the high internal mobility of the population greatly disturbed the pattern, injecting young male settlers into new areas, tending to leave behind an aging population and/or a female surplus. Urban growth also disturbed the pattern but sometimes in a different direction, attracting female migrants either into factory and workshop employment, or domestic work. As mentioned earlier, an excess of women over men in the fertile age-groups tended to lower the fertility ratio because of reduced opportunities for marriage.

Again only a few examples can be given to demonstrate the
irregularities in the age and sex structure; these are shown in
Table III. By comparing these with the fertility ratios given
earlier (Table I and II), some correspondence does appear between
the existence of a female surplus and the evidence of a lowe
fertility ratio.

TABLE III

PERCENTAGE OF TOTAL POPULATION IN FERTILE AGE-GROUP
female surpluses underlined

	1820 (16-44 years)		1840 (16-49 years)	
	M.	F.	M.	F.
U.S.A.	19.6	19.4	24.5	23.4
Connecticut	19.2	21.1	24.9	26.0
New England (tot.)	19.5	20.9	25.1	25.6
New York	20.4	19.6	25.9	25.1
Middle Atlantic States	20.0	19.5	25.1	24.7
Virginia	19.4	19.6	23.0	23.6
East South Central (tot.)	18.5	17.6	22.9	21.1
Ohio	19.3	17.8	24.1	22.5
Lowell, Mass.			21.7	49.2
Portland, Maine			26.4	27.5
Chicago, Ill.			23.9	33.1
Philadelphia, Pa.			25.8	29.8
Louisville, Ky.			34.0	25.8
Wisconsin			39.5	19.4
Milwaukee, Wisc.			36.7	24.1

c) Family Limitation. The final section of this paper is
   devoted to the possibility of deliberate family
   limitation in early nineteenth century America. (10)
   From the 1820s, evidence begins to appear of a very
   considerable literature, overt and clandestine, on
   sexual matters, with peak periods of output
   apparently in the 1830s, the 1850s, and from the
   Civil War (which had a direct influence) until the
   passing of the restrictive 'Comstock Law' of 1873.

Apart from a few early works (such as the curious,
anonymous Aristotle's Master Piece Completed, New York 1788,
reprinted 1817, giving inaccurate information about the safe
period), the best known writings of this period were Robert
Dale Owen's Moral Physiology (published in New York in 1830, and
advocating coitus interruptus) and Charles Knowlton's Fruits of
Philosophy (sub-titled The Private Companion of Young Married
People) first published anonymously in New York in 1832
(advocating douching); the second edition, this time under
Knowlton's name, was published in Boston in 1833 by Abner
Kneeland, editor of the Boston Investigator; by 1839 the book was
in its ninth edition). In The Young Man's Guide (Boston, 1835),
William A. Alcott wrote:

"The world abounds in impure publications....If these books contained truth, and nothing but truth, their clandestine circulation would do less mischief. But... on the contrary, they contain much falsehood, especially when they profess to instruct on certain important subjects. Let me repeat it then, they cannot be relied upon."

Similarly, Sylvester Graham in A Lecture to a Young Man on Chastity (Boston, 1837) complained that

"Unprincipled book publishers have found out that works on this subject will sell rapidly and they have not neglected such opportunity to get gain....Works denouncing marriage and the Bible and encouraging promiscuous commerce between sexes; works pretending to teach how pregnancy might be avoided and thus encouraging illicit commerce....are already flooding our country and spreading corruption in their course...."

In the outburst of writing in the 1850's, several writers spoke of the wide circulation of the type of literature that, as strict moralists, they deplored. "An Old Physician" (possibly Alcott again) in The Physiology of Marriage (Boston, 1856) attacked "the manufacture and sale, all over the land (clandestinely of course) of such books, prints, etc." and deplored the "wide circulation" of a book by "a physician of New England" (presumably Knowlton), "whose avowed object was to teach people, both in married life and elsewhere, the act of gratifying the appetite without the necessity of progeny."

Other works were themselves vehicles for advertising. The Married Woman's Private Medical Companion (New York, 1853) by Dr. sic A. M. Mauriceau, "Professor of Diseases of Women" (11) consisted almost entirely of a verbatim, but unacknowledged, reprint of Owen's Moral Physiology, with footnote announcements of a mail order service for such commodities as "Portugese Female Pills, at $5. a box", "M. Desomeaux' Preventives at $10. a package"; and "French Secrets at $5 a dozen". In 1856 Henry's Private Adviser (Vol. 1, no. 1, October 15, 1856, announcing a book by J. Henry, The Chart of Life, which apparently never appeared) listed the known methods of birth prevention; onanism, injections, "introduction of a sponge for instance", the condom, "of course efficacious", preventive powders, and several others.

It is difficult, of course, to assess the significance of these publications. The moralists no doubt exaggerated the extent of their circulation. One interesting group of writings paid particular attention to the alleged demoralising effects of city life; postponement of marriage; neglect by wives of the home in favour of "the party, the concert, the call, the steamboat excursion, the lecture, the theatre, or the exhibition"; the imitation in cities of "foreign manners and customs"; and general licentiousness.

It cannot be assumed of course that the methods of birth control advocated in the writings, or the practical means available, were effective. Quack remedies abounded. A.K. Gardner, A.M., M.D. in The Causes and Curative Treatment of Sterility (New York 1856),

cited with apparent approval the "popular" opinion that conception
was not possible if the female remained in a standing position, as
also the view that "violent dancing" after intercourse would
prevent pregnancy. Indeed James C. Jackson in The Sexual Organism
and its Healthful Management (Boston, 1864) recommended as the best
method "jumping and dancing, followed by a douche". Other writers
advocated post-coital coughing and sneezing, while Henry's
Private Adviser referred to a "galvanic machine" priced at $10,
apparently designed to kill the male sperm after intercourse by
administering an electric shock to the female.
　　　More importantly, a group of writers, some of whom were
seeking to remedy sterility, others to provide prevention, made
various suggestions concerning the female safe period. The view
that all the writers reiterated, however, was that conception could
and did only result from intercourse within seven days (12) after
the woman's monthly period. This recommendation remained
unchanged from Aristotle's Master Piece (of the late eighteenth
century) mentioned earlier, through all the nineteenth century
writings. In other words, the advice widely advocated was
erroneous and more likely to lead to an increase than to a decrease
in births.
　　　Finally, the writings contained very frequent reference to
the alleged increasing incidence of abortion in early nineteenth
century America. The advocates of birth control in fact regarded
the need to reduce abortion as one of the main reasons for their
advocacy. (13) The moralists disapproved both of the advocacy of
birth control and the existence of abortion. This attack reached
a quite frenzied climax in the atmosphere at the time of the
passing of the 1873 Comstock Law. Dr. Lewis (14) in Chastity, or
our Secret Sins (New York, 1874) quoted a paper by Dr. Nathan Allan,
of Lowell, Mass., read to the American Social Science Association,
which declared that in America "the crime of abortion has become
more common than it ever has been at any previous time or in any
other country in the history of the world." But as early as the
1850's various publications had made highly emotional attacks
upon "those in our cities that make the procuring of abortion their
profession", (Henry) the perpetrators of "crimes without name"
(Alcott).
　　　The nature of the evidence precludes any firm conclusions.
But it can be claimed that there was a considerable interest in
some parts of America in the early nineteenth century in reducing
the number of births, by one method or another of family
limitation.

(REFERENCES)

1) The Rev. Joseph Townsend, Rector of Pewsey, Wiltshire. The work is in three volumes and is dated London 1791. It is not to be found in the Malthus Collection, which neverthe less includes numerous books of travel and geography.

2) Various Prospects of Mankind, Nature and Providence (1761). Wallace was Minister at Moffat. The Malthus Collection includes an Anonymous work, A Dissertation on the Numbers of Mankind in Ancient and Modern Times (Edinburgh, 1753), attributed elsewhere to Wallace. This work makes no mention of America, but says (p. 5) "And thus we shall find mankind to double themselves in each period of 33 1/3 years", and attributes populousness to the cultivation of simple virtues: "....Twas simplicity of taste, frugality, patience of labour and contentment with a little, which made the world so populous in ancient times. The decay of these virtues, and the introduction of a corrupted and luxurious taste, have contributed in great measure to diminish the numbers of mankind in modern days."

3) Richard Price, Concerning Observations on the Expectation of Lives, the Increase of Mankind .... (a collection of writings published in London in 1769, the first item of which, "In a Letter to Benjamin Franklin Esq......." was read to the Royal Society on 27 April 1769). This work by Price is in the Malthus Collection. When examining Malthus's books I found in this volume a hand-written double sheet of notes, probably in Malthus's hand. The writer of these notes twice asked: "in what number of years would such population double itself" and "how soon will the population be doubled?". If the writing is indeed in Malthus's hand, it would be evidence that it was Price (and beyond him, Franklin) who stimulated Malthus's interest in this subject.

4) Ezra Styles (or Stiles), President of Yale College, 1778-1795, "The Interest of Great Britain considered with regard to her Colonies, together with Observations concerning the Increase of Mankind...." (Boston and London, 1760). The second part is a reprint of Franklin's Observations, referred to on the title page as "the very ingenious, useful and worthy author of this Pamphlet B.....n F.....n, Ll.D. ". Another work by Styles, A Discourse on the Christian Union (Boston 1761), has some calculations of population increase and mentions a doubling in 20 or 25 years, dependent on "the nature of the climate".

5) Cf. T. R. Malthus, Essay, "In the back settlements, where the inhabitants applied themselves solely to agriculture, and luxury was not known, they were found to double their own number in 15 years, a most extraordinary instance of increase." (the passage to which Malthus added the footnote containing his second 'Law'). Cf. also the passage from Malthus cited above, on page 1 - "a

rapidity of increase probably without parallel in history."

6) There are very close similarities of wording between Wigglesworth's and Malthus's writings about population, but Wigglesworth's short pamphlet is not in the Malthus Collection, and I have found no correspondence between the two.

7) Michael Thomas Sadler, The Law of Population (London, 1830), Book II, Chapter II, pp. 401ff.

8) Similar calculations may be made from 1830 for different age groupings: e.g., no. of children 0-4 years per woman of 20-29 years, or 0-4 years per women 15-50. While different features emerge from different calculations, the broad trends are the same in all calculations.

9) On the medical evidence, see in particular R. H. Shryock, Medicine and Society in America, 1660-1860 (New York, 1960).

10) It is altogether fitting that this paper should be presented at a Conference held at Indiana University, since it is based on research carried out in 1965 in the Library of the Institute of Sex Research (the Kinsey Institute) of Indiana University. The section which follows is a very short summary of a large mass of material on the subject.

11) The name of this author was later given by Edward Crapsey in The Nether Side of New York (New York, 1872) as a foremost abortionist.

12) The number varied between writers, but most accepted ten days as the extreme limit.

13) e.g. Knowlton (1832), "of artificial abortions, which are doubtless produced daily within the United States, I scarcely need speak." Henry (1856), "the horrible practice of procuring abortions, now so prevalent among married people, is caused by the want of simple and reliable means of prevention."

14) Whose other writings continued such interesting titles as Our Girls, Chats with Young Women, Weak Lungs and How to make them Strong, Our Digestion, or My Jolly Friend's Secret, New Gymnastics for Men, Women and Children, and Gypsies, or Why we went gypsying in the Sierras.

5

POPULATION THEORIES, NON-TRADITIONAL INPUTS AND

THE INTERPRETATION OF ECONOMIC HISTORY

HARVEY LEIBENSTEIN

HARVARD UNIVERSITY

I. Neo-Malthusian Models

This paper emphasizes non-traditional elements in the
theories of production and population growth, and considers their
consequences and interactions.

The system of ideas that relates population growth to
economic welfare developed by Malthus and others lend themselves
readily to formulation into rigorous and simple models. This has
been done by Peacock, Baumol, Nelson, Leibenstein, and others.
Theories of this type are classical in their nature; the major inputs fall into the traditional categories of land, labor and
capital. Technical progress or changes in the state of the arts
are usually handled exogenously.

For the interpretation of the economic history of some
periods theories of this type, whether formal or informal, have
frequently been presumed to be useful. One reason is that the
units involved are readily measurable. Labor can be measured in
terms of numbers of workers. Land can be measured in terms of
acres or other normal units. While capital must be aggregated
and measured in value terms, they are values which are determined
by market prices. (Land, of course, can also be measured in terms
of price.) This is not to suggest that historians in fact
always use rigorous models of this type, but that in a rough way
the general mould into which such theories fall are likely to be
part of the mental furniture of historians, economists, and others

who consider the "population-resources" problem. The relation between different proportions of traditional inputs can be examined and deductions made from the changes in proportions. Conclusions from such models need not be of a Malthusian character.

These "Neo-Malthusian" (and "Post-Malthusian") theories have two sides to them. One side involves a theory of production: in general, the proportions of the traditional inputs determines output per worker. (Some specific models may also contain a theory of distribution which determines how total output is divided between owners of land, labor and capital.) Thus, a one-to-one correspondence is seen to exist between inputs and outputs. The other side usually involves a simple and rudimentary theory of population growth. For the most part the attack on Malthusian type theories has been on the presumed fertility assumptions of the theory, whereas I will want to argue that the production side of the theory is probably the more vulnerable.

The importance of these theories for the contemporary scholar is not the Malthusian conclusions but the classical mould that we have inherited. The mould has been found much more acceptable than the conclusions. In this paper we question the "mould," - that is, the "population-material resources balance" framework into which the population problem has usually been cast.

II. "The Residual" or "Measure of Our Ignorance"

The Neo-Malthusian debate frequently turned on whether one happened to be an invention-innovation optimist or an invention-innovation pessimist, i.e., whether one believed that the current rate of material inventions would continue or one believed that this too was subject to considerable diminishing returns. The experience of the last century or so supports the optimists. Extrapolating from the rates of growth within the last half-century in countries that have had positive economic growth, it would appear that at least the potential economic growth is greater than the rate of population growth. The argument of the technological pessimists must depend for the most part on theory rather than experience, i.e., on the belief that some resources such as land are in fact fixed, and that, in fact, the substitutes for such resources are likely to be considerably inferior to the fixed resources so that significant diminishing returns result.

However, recent research suggests a possible conclusion that was not expected -- that we have been looking at the unimportant aspects of the problem. The rate of growth cannot be explained primarily by changes in the traditional inputs of capital, land, and labor. Rather, traditional inputs seem to explain only somewhere between 10% to less than 50% of the growth that takes place in most countries (1). What has been called the "residual" (2) seems to "account" for most of the economic growth. While there has been considerable speculation about the nature of the "residual" inputs, and while we know with some degree of definiteness what some of them must be, we cannot say what all of them happen to be. Nevertheless, this finding is of great importance, and I want to argue in this paper that it is a critical element in any reinterpretation of the Neo-Malthusian viewpoint, or of any set of relations between population and resources.

In what follows I want to discuss some of the potential non-traditional inputs, how they may contribute to economic growth and how they may possibly interact with population growth to determine output per capita.

III.   Incentives and Effort Aspects

The conventional theory of production assumes that the incentive aspects are more or less at a maximum or constant. This is most readily seen in the modern theory of the firm in which it is usually assumed that it is in the interest of every firm to minimize the costs of production given input prices and the nature of the technique. My own belief, which I have emphasized in a recent paper, is that incentives vary considerably between firms (including farms), that firms do not minimize costs, that the degree to which firms approach cost minimization differs considerably between firms, industries, countries, and so on, and that these variations are statistically significant.

We have to separate the assumptions in our theories made for purposes of convenience and those which appear to be reasonable simplified sketches of reality. The cost minimization assumption is a highly convenient one, since it permits a one-to-one relation between quantities of inputs and quantity of output. Yet, it s seems to me that an alternative set of assumptions is a better sketch of reality, and yields different results about the nature of production.

These are as follows: (1) Not all inputs are purchasable in terms of the units in which they are used in production. (2) Some aspects of the production function are not fully known by the firm. (3) There is no fixed trade-off between the units under which inputs are purchased (e.g., time) and those in which they are used (e.g., effort). (4) Beyond some point there is diminishing utility to effort. (5) The objective of the firm is not completely determined and specified external to the firm. In other words, it depends on the preferences for a variety of things of those who make up the interrelated groups that are the constituents of the organization that we call the firm. (6) Finally, and of great importance, is the fact that not all inputs are traded.

The basic idea to be developed is that human inputs, essentially varieties of labor inclusive of management and entre-preneurship, can put forth different degrees of effort in response to different incentives both within firms and in the economy at large. Effort should not be interpreted here in a narrow physical sense, although physical effort is one dimension. Other possible dimensions of effort are: (1) the act of choosing between different activities; (2) the degree of care in carrying out such activities; (3) scanning the "information field" inside and out-side the firm; (4) various "search activities," i.e., looking for a new means of performance in terms of techniques of production or characteristics of the product; (5) the degree of perserverence in carrying out activities; (6) the degree of cooperation with co-workers; etc.

For our purposes the most important efforts are those that introduce change. There are likely to be considerable differences in different contexts in the degree of effort put forth which result in the use of more efficient as against less efficient techniques even without changes in the physical capital employed - for example, the employment of more efficient flow of materials. Most important are the differences in the degree of effort directed towards the introduction of innovations - i.e., the search and development of information and the marshalling of other inputs in order to introduce innovations. This last includes entrepreneurial activities.

The incentives structure and their induced efforts include not only those involved in the production of consumer goods, and the production of physical capital goods, but also those involved in the accumulation of human capital through education, on-the-job training, etc. We must also include the "negative efforts" to production - the efforts put forth by various people to resist the adoption of profitable innovations. Of course, these facts or their possibilities are not especially new. What is of interest in recent research is that it has been shown that elements such as these are likely to be of great importance (3).

IV. The Nurture-Nature Borderline - Intelligence and Family Size

A large literature has accumulated which shows that, on the average, children that come from families with relatively few siblings or with no siblings do disproportionately better at intellectual and related pursuits than those with many siblings (4). It has not been determined whether it contains a genetic component.

At present we know little about the relation between population quality, entrepreneurial capacities and contact with siblings. But there is a relation between intelligence and entrepreneurship, although intelligence is only one of the qualities requisite to entrepreneurship. There is some data that suggests that an unusual proportion of those who have considerable intellectual achievements to their credit were either only children, first born, or came from families in which there was a relatively large age gap between siblings (5). It seems plausible that the ability to think abstractly would be developed earlier or would on the whole be greater if children learned the concomitant verbal skills either from adults or from siblings considerably older than themselves (6). While it is difficult to separate the level of intelligence from acquired skills, there is evidence to suggest that a young child's intelligence level can actually be raised by a culturally nurturant upbringing or by training (7), or by the kinds of environmental stimuli available in an urban setting (8); and that there is a close connection between family size and intellectual capacity. Intellectual capacity, and the attendant ability to manipulate abstractions that typifies educated intelligence is unquestionably important to economic development. It is evident in the contribution of professionalized skills to the economy, i.e., in the work of engineers, lawyers, doctors, architects, and teachers at various levels. It seems likely that acquired intellectual capacities are also related to managerial skills. It would appear then, that the smaller the rate of population growth and the smaller the family size, the greater the extent to which these skills could be developed per person, on the average.

V. The Quality Replacement Rate

In considering the influence of population growth two basic aspects must be assessed simultaneously: (1) the effect of the growth rate, and (2) the effect of the changing age structure (9).

A crucial effect of population growth is to supplant old workers by young ones. Various members of the existing labor force leave because of death, retirement, or change in social status, while young people enter as they reach working age and/or acquire training. The newcomers to the work force will in many cases be different in quality from those that leave. Thus, as a consequence of population growth and education, the qualitative nature of the work force changes. Among the important factors affecting economic growth are (1) the work skills of the population and (2) the attitudes of the population. The attitudes of the work force are shaped by religious, social, cultural, and political traditions. Some basic attitudes that affect growth are those that determine degree of adherence to traditional occupations and procedures (10). Such attitudinal changes will usually influence the degree of labor mobility (11), the extent of participation of women in the work force (12), and the age at which people normally enter the work force (13). In addition, they will affect the willingness of people within a given occupation to accept new techniques, equipment, or new organizational forms.

Consider the effect of the rate of population growth on the assumption that the age structure remains stable. To achieve a quality shift those entering the work force must be different in terms of education and training, than those leaving. One circumstance under which this can happen is if the proportion of children receiving a given degree of education is greater than it was when the members of the current adult population were themselves children. Assume that this proportion is invariant with respect to the rate of population growth. The greater the rate of population growth, the larger the extent to which people with a given degree of education replace uneducated people who leave the work force.

To illustrate the implications involved, let us consider a numerical example. Suppose for purposes of illustration that the length of working life is fifty years. In a stationary population with a stable age structure two per cent would retire (14) every year and two per cent would enter. If those entering are of a new quality compared to those in the population initially, then after twenty-five years fifty per cent of the population will represent the new quality and fifty per cent the old. For example, fifty per cent will be literate and fifty per cent illiterate. But if the population grows at two per cent per year and the entry rate rises to four per cent, then at the end of twenty-five years approximately seventy per cent will be literate.

Now, consider a five year period and compare a stationary population in which entry rates and retirements are at two per cent per year with one in which the entry rate is six per cent. In the stationary population at the end of five years, only ten per cent are literate, whereas in the rapidly growing population over twenty-five per cent will become literate in the same period.

Of course any other acquired skill -- such as a high school education -- can be substituted for simple literacy in this calculation. A similar line of reasoning can be followed in the case of physical improvement in the labor force as a result of superior nutrition (15).

Now consider the age structure. The greater the degree to which the age structure is skewed towards children, the greater is the replacment of more educated people for less educated. In addition, high rates of population growth which have recently gone up, or increasing rates of population growth, will normally be associated with a fall in the average age of the population (16). Such changes will also work to replace educated people by more educated ones. The rate of replacement rises as the average age of the population falls.

A similar analysis can be made for the attitudes of the population. For example, we can visualize the replacement of tradition-bounded people by less tradition-bounded individuals as a result of population and education.

VI. Some Indirect Costs of Population Growth

We have considered the possibility that population growth may change the work quality and tradition boundedness of the population by assuming that the rate and pattern of population growth has no influence on the predetermined proportion exposed to education, etc. Obviously, expenditures on education will not increase in direct proportion to the young in the population (17). The capacity to levy taxes will depend somewhat on real income per capita. There are alternative claims on public revenues, such as the need for investment funds for industrialization (18). These claims will vary with the rate and pattern of population growth. In a largely agricultural population, the greater the rate of population growth, the less land per man; the greater the degree of fragmentation, and hence, the smaller the output per man (19). High growth rates will normally increase the burden of dependency (20) and decrease potential taxable revenues. Population growth may raise population replacements to a higher quality from an economic viewpoint, but it will simultaneously make it more difficult to provide a given amount of education for the same proportion of children entering the population (21) or to provide other influences that may cause attitudes to change.

It is to be emphasized that education is unlike traditional inputs in many respects. We know that in a general way education pays off from a productivity viewpoint, we do not know much about the marginal productivity of education. Most research on returns to education has really been on the average returns to marginal years of education. What we do not know very much about is the marginal returns to marginal years of education. The present writer's view is that it is not at all impossible that the marginal returns for some marginal years of education may be zero when a given type of education expands very rapidly. (A recent study by the author on returns to education in Greece leads him to believe that this may have occurred with respect to secondary education for the period 1960 to 1964.) Education is also complicated by the fact that its inputs are diverse, its quality is rarely constant, and many of its influences on productivity are

very indirect. Hence, unlike traditional inputs, we cannot
simply add educational inputs and harvest productivity outputs at
the other end of the pipeline.

Even more elusive than education are those inputs
responsible for technological change - especially entrepreneurial
capacities. The innovation rate will depend on perception and on
the ability to take advantage of economic opportunities, and hence
on entrepreneurial capacities. Returning to a previous section,
we might recall that not all inputs necessary for production are
marketed, and that some are unavailable or not equally available
to all individuals. Only some people are entrepreneurs. These
are likely to be the ones who are able to fill the gaps in
necessary inputs or capable of creating substitutes for unavailable inputs, and, in general, are able to perform as "input
completers" (22). Once again entrepreneurship is an elusive input
and not easily augmented in the sense in which traditional inputs
are augmentable.

The main point of the previous remarks is that while with
the traditional inputs we were able to rely on a production
function which operated as a one-to-one correspondence in the
sense that we were able to visualize that we could add something
tangible to our stock of inputs and obtain at the other end a
tangible output. Once we deal with the non-traditional inputs
this simple input-output relationship no longer holds.

VII.   Conclusions

The "population-resources" problem must be looked at in a
new light. We no longer ask the question what effect do different
rates of population growth have on income by examining their
effect on land resources and capital per man. To illustrate how
we might re-orient our thinking on the "population-resources"
problem we might consider sub-questions of the following kind:
(1) What are the effects of population growth on the supply of
educational services, on the demand for education, and on the
dynamics of population replacement? (2) What are the effects of
population growth on entrepreneurial capacities, on the level of
education, and on the distribution of population between countryside and urban areas that may indirectly affect entrepreneurial
capacities? (3) What effect does population growth have on the
quality of the work force? We have seen that family size will to
some degree affect individual capacities through its effects on
the nurture, health and energy of the population. However, the
degree to which these elements are important as a determinant of
productivity is at the present time unknown. (4) Finally, what
effect, if any, does population growth have on the motivating
forces produced in the society and its relation to the degree and
direction of effort put forth by the population on productive
activities and especially on the rate of adoption of productive
innovations? For the most part this paper suggests that we
should reorient our thinking on the "population-resources" question
away from the traditional categories of land, natural resources
and capital towards the analysis of the impact of population
growth on "non-traditional" inputs.

REFERENCES

1. For example, Simon Kuznets concludes "that the direct
    contribution of man-hours and capital accumulation would
    hardly account for more than a tenth of the rate of growth
    in per capita product - and probably less. The large
    remainder must be assigned to an increase in efficiency in
    the productive resources - a rise in output per unit of
    input, due either to the improved quality of the resources,
    or to the effects of changing arrangements, or to the impact
    of technological change, or to all three." Modern Economic
    Growth, pp. 80-81.

2. The "residual" has been aptly named by Moses Abramowitz as
    "the measure of our ignorance." This appellation errs on
    the side of humility.

3. See H. Leibenstein, "Allocative Efficiency vs. X-Efficiency,"
    A.E.R., June 1966.

4. Cf. William D. Altus, "Birth Order and Its Sequelae,"
    Science, January 7, 1966. This section of the paper is in
    part based on a short paper presented to the World
    Population Congress, 1965.

5. A. Anastasi, "Intelligence and Family Size," Psychological
    Bulletin, Vol. 53, No. 3, pp. 187-209.

6. D. McCarthy, "Language Development in Children," in
    L. Carmichael, Manual of Child Psychology, New York, John
    Wiley & Sons, 1946, pp. 558-559.

7. E. A. Haggard, "Social Status and Intelligence," Genetic
    Psychology Monographs, Vol. 49, 1954, pp. 141-186.

8. H. Jones, "The Environment and Mental Development," in
    L. Carmichael, A Manual of Child Psychology, op.cit., p.655.
    See also S. Smith, "Language and Non Verbal Test
    Performance of Racial Groups in Honolulu Before and After a
    Fourteen Year Interval," Journal of Genetic Psychology, Vol.
    26, pp. 51-93.

9. N. Keyfitz, "Age Distribution as a Challenge to Development,"
    unpublished ms. (mimeo), p. 10. I am indebted to
    Professor Keyfitz. This section is, in part, inspired by
    his work.

10. A. Coale and E. M. Hoover, Population Growth and Economic
    Development in Low Income Countries, A Case Study of India's
    Prospects, Princeton University Press, Princeton, 1958,
    pp. 108-109.

11. N. Keyfitz, op. cit., p. 12.

References (Continued)

12. Internal Labor Organization, "The World's Working Population, Some Demographic Aspects," *International Labor Review*, Vol. 73, No. 2, p. 173.

13. Coale and Hoover, *op. cit.*, pp. 231-233, 314.

14. "Retirement" is used as a general term for all those that leave the work force for any reason whatsoever including death or illness.

15. J. M. Tanner, *Growth at Adolescence*, Charles C. Thomas, Springfield, 1955, pp. 83-97. See also Rose Frisch and Roger Revelle, "Variations in Body Weights Among Different Populations," in The World Food Problem, President's Science Advisory Committee, Washington, 1957, pp. 1-41.

16. Keyfitz, *op. cit.*, pp. 3-6.

17. F. Harbison and C. A. Myers, *Education, Manpower, and Economic Growth, Strategies of Human Resource-Development*, McGraw-Hill, New York, 1964, p. 19.

18. Coale and Hoover, *op. cit.*, pp. 188-189.

19. C. B. Mamoria, *Agricultural Problems of India*, Kitab Mahal, Allahabad, 1960, pp. 230-234.

20. Coale and Hoover, *op. cit.*, pp. 332-333.

21. *Ibid.*, pp. 247-249.

22. For a fuller treatment on these matters see the author's "Entrepreneurship and Development," *A.E.R.*, May 1968.

6

INDUSTRY AND MARRIAGES IN FLANDERS

BEFORE THE INDUSTRIAL REVOLUTION

FRANKLIN F. MENDELS

UNIVERSITY OF CALIFORNIA, LOS ANGELES

The study of historical demography has been marked in recent years by important innovations. In particular, the use of information contained in parish registers in reconstituting family histories over long periods has greatly enhanced our knowledge of pre-industrial demographic mechanisms. There is still, however, much to learn concerning the interrelations between demographic and economic changes and differences.

This paper focuses on one of the ways in which population and economy interacted in "pre-industrial" society. It examines the effects of "industrial" export demand on marriages in eighteenth-century Flanders. It follows in its method the work of several demographers and economists, for statistical regression analysis is used to observe stabilities in the relationships between one demographic variable, marriage, and its economic determinants[1]. It is observed that annual oscillations in the number of marriages can be correlated with changes in the grain market. The same changes in the grain market, however, had opposite effects on marriages in areas with subsistence agriculture and areas with a commercial agricultural organization. Moreover, where an important part of the labor force was engaged in the domestic linen industry, oscillations in the number of marriages were generated by fluctuations in the international linen market as well as fluctuations in the domestic grain market. Finally, it is observed that market fluctuations generated demographic fluctuations in an asymmetric manner: the response of marriages to favorable market changes was clearly observed but unfavorable changes in market conditions did not possess a stable relationship with marriage fluctuations.

A large part of the population of so-called pre-industrial Europe was in fact engaged in the production of industrial commodities. Long before the Industrial Revolution, millions of peasants

were transforming in their cottages the mineral and vegetable products
of the land into such commodities as iron, cloth, or beer. Much of
this activity remained part-time and seasonal and it is therefore
somewhat arbitrary to categorize the peasants involved in it as
agriculturalists or industrialists. In spite of this difficulty
of classification, the importance of domestic industry for our
understanding of the functioning of peasant society before modern
industrialization cannot be overestimated. In particular, if the
peasants of "pre-industrial" Europe derived a sizeable share of their
income from the manufacture and sale of industrial goods on the
market, one should expect fluctuations in the conditions of the
markets for such goods to affect their income and hence their
demographic behavior. Yet, surprisingly, recent research into the
economic determinants of demographic fluctuations in various regions
of Europe has focused on the price of grains, an indication of the
abundance of food. The mechanism of subsistence crises has thus been
carefully defined by historical demographers and considered as the
primary economic determinant of short-term demographic fluctuations
even for the case of areas known for their dense network of cottage
industries with remote commercial outlets (2).

Eighteenth-century Flanders possessed a large textile industry.
Most of its products consisted in relatively cheap linen cloth
produced in the countryside even though the region was more renowned
for its laces, **serviettes,** and other luxury goods manufactured in
Bruges, Ghent, Courtrai, Lille, and their suburbs. In 1738, in the
midst of great difficulties plaguing the urban industry, 20 percent
of the adult male population of Bruges was still employed in the
textile industries (3). At the end of the century, 122,000 adult
persons were engaged in spinning or weaving in the Département de
l'Escaut (or Province of East-Flanders) for a total adult (age
15 and above) population of approximately 370,000 persons (4).
Within the countryside, sharp patterns of industrial location
existed and were further strengthened during the course of the
eighteenth century. The domestic industry took its greatest
extension where the soils were least appropriate for cereal farming
and, moroever, these areas also had the highest rural population
densities, the highest rates of population growth, and the highest
degree of farm fragmentation. Thus, some areas of Flanders were
not engaged at all in any cottage manufacture; this was the polder
zone --or maritime Flanders-- where demographic growth was less
rapid and more steady in the eighteenth century, where farms were
much larger and population sparser (5).
Most rural weavers were independent craftsmen. They purchased
most of their flax and sold their finished cloth at the market.
They employed wife and children as well as a servant or two. At the
market, the linen was purchased by merchants and hence shipped to
France, Holland, and mostly to Spain and her American colonies (6).
In these markets, the Flemish linens were in competition with the
products of the rural industries of Brittany, Silesia, Ulster,
Scotland, and other European regions. Thus, the Flemish linen
industry only produced a small share of a major international
trade flow and was submitted to the impact of its fluctuations.
In other words, the price faced by the Flemish peasants and merchants
was determined on the international market by the interaction of

international forces of demand and supply which were exogenous to the
Flemish economy. Domestic producers could vary their output and
merchants their sales but such actions could not by themselves have
any noticeable effect. On the contrary, however, Louis de Wulf,
a merchant from Ghent, noted in 1770 that

> whoever knows of the exports of our fabrics knows
> that it is the trade with Andalousia, whence all
> merchandise is carried to Spanish America, that
> rules the progress of our fabrics and sustains
> them. The least sterility in trade would raise
> or lower prices by 15 or 20 percent, as daily
> experience shows (7).

Together with cloth, the Flemish peasants also produced some of the
food needed for their sustenance but the small size of their holdings
and the poor quality of the sandy soils of the interior prevented
most families from relying exclusively on agricultural sources of
support. Industry was carried out as a complement from which
additional food could be purchased after exchange at the market.
If this is so, the higher the price of linens and the lower the
price of food, the better off were the peasants.
  Flemish agriculture was remarkably advanced technologically, as
we are told by the travellers who came especially from foreign
countries to observe it (8). However, while product per hectare
must have been relatively high and still progressing in the course
of the century thanks to the spread of potato cultivation, farms in
the interior of Flanders were progressively becoming smaller through
a fragmentation that went hand in hand with population growth (9).
This situation was different in maritime Flanders, where a food
surplus was produced and exported to foreign countries as well as to
the rest of Flanders. The cash which was obtained by the peasants
of the interior in the production of linens could thus be used
principally in the purchase of food produced by the commercial
agriculture which had developed in the polders. Agricultural
techniques on their heavy soils were less labor-intensive but more
capital-intensive than in the interior. Most of the agricultural
labor force consisted of agricultural laborers. Thus, contrary
to the peasant-farming system of the interior, hiring in the
commercial farms must have been a function of past or expected
future food sales, given labor's marginal productivity. If this
is so, the higher the price of food, the better off were the farmers
and agricultural laborers.
  Available evidence indicates that there was no increase in real
wages during the eighteenth century in any area of Flanders (10).
A dense population living on scarce land in the interior could
barely subsist in spite of the complement of income that was obtained
in part-time industry and despite improvements in agriculture.
Unemployment was always a possibility for the rural and urban
proletariat. Yet, in the weeks when a large labor force was needed
to pull the weeds from the flax fields and to harvest, most of the
laboring population was employed and some areas were even able to
foster temporary immigration. However, agricultural activities were
highly seasonal and the agricultural innovations that were introduced in the course of the century even tended to increase the
seasonal character of employment (11). Thus, there was during every

winter a long period of slackened demand for labor during which many
had to depend on charity. It was among this pool of potentially
unemployed workers that the Flemish linen industry found its labor
reserve. The observed stagnation of real wages during a period of
industrial and demographic expansion must be seen as the result of
the persistence of seasonal unemployment for a large share of the
labor force.

It appears from observations summarized here that the Flemish
economy conformed in several essential ways with the Ricardian
framework of economic structure and growth with "unlimited" supply
of labor (12). In subsistence agriculture, the marginal productivity of labor during a part of the year must have been lower than
the real wage, whose minimum was set by custom. Thus, the agrarian
labor force was larger than the competitive optimum. The existence
in a large sector of the economy of a labor reserve willing to
accept employment at a customary wage rate kept wages from rising
in commercial agriculture and urban industry through the competition
of migrants. Wages obtained in commercial agriculture and urban
industry were higher than in subsistence agriculture, but the
differences remained approximately constant during the eighteenth
century (13). The process of economic expansion, which involved
a doubling of the output of the linen industry, was facilitated
by the availability of seasonally unemployed labor. Agricultural
production was permitted to progress together with industry and
population.

The population of the Flemish cities went through a period of
decline from 1700 to approximately 1750. Growth resumed in the
second half of the century but it was not until 1800 that the
initial urban population level was attained again. In the meantime,
the industrialized areas of the countryside experienced a short
crisis in the early part of the century, but a remarkable growth
in its second half. Finally, maritime Flanders had a regular but
slow population growth in this period (14). These findings and in
particular the contrasts which have been observed within Flanders
among several geographic areas point to the need of research into
the economic and demographic mechanisms that underlie them.

In the present paper we present a test of the hypothesis that
nuptiality was during the period under consideration a mechanism
by which the population adapted itself to economic opportunities
and their fluctuations. It has been shown that Spanish linen
prices could act on the Flemish economy as exogenous determinants
of economic changes. It is thus possible to use the Spanish
linen price series published by Professor Hamilton as an indicator
of the changes in demand for linens in Flanders. Several cereal
price series could be used as indicators of change in agriculture,
but since rye was the main staple and Ghent the principal market,
the indicator of market changes for the Flemish rural industry
was taken to be the ratio of linen prices obtaining in Spain and
rye prices in Ghent, both measured in terms of silver to allow for
changes in the relative value of Spanish and Flemish currencies (15).
For the villages of maritime Flanders where no industry had
established itself but where the principal economic activity was
commercial agriculture, linen prices cannot have entered into the
economic plan of their inhabitants but rye prices alone.

Annual percentage changes in the chosen price variable were regressed against annual percentage changes in the number of marriages in selected villages and towns. The use of a non-conventional measure of nuptiality was necessitated by the absence of estimates of the annual population at risk of marriage or, rather, of estimates calculated independently from the measured numbers of celebrated marriages. Indeed, since population enumerations were rare and incomplete, estimates of the population of various villages have been made by several researchers, but the method of calculation which they used involved the application of multipliers to marriages --and other variables-- and the average of several possible estimates thus obtained for a given date. Thus, in order to avoid any circularity, it seemed preferable to utilize numbers of celebrated marriages as they were obtained from parish registers, rather than dividing them by such estimates to obtain rates. The annual percentage changes used to measure the intensity of fluctuations minimize the difference between rates and absolute numbers. It can be shown that the percentage changes in the number of marriages are the closer to percentage changes in the marriage rates as the amplitude of marriage fluctuations relative to fluctuations in total population is larger (16).

Rather than calculating regression coefficients only for runs where each year's observations were included, the data were separated into two categories of observations and the coefficients were separately calculated for runs including only cases when price changes were favorable for the linen producers and then for observations when price changes were unfavorable. This was done with the expectation that, by analogy with the reaction of consumption and investment to changes in actual or projected income, marriages may not respond symmetrically to upward and downward changes in economic opportunities and income.

In order to allow for the effect of expectations and habit persistence on marriages, the independent price variables were lagged; an unweighted sum of prices (or price ratios) with lags of up to three years was actually used. Time was also included as an independent variable both in a linear and quadratic form to allow for the possibility of historical change in the "elasticity" of reaction of marriages to economic fluctuations. Finally, a dummy variable was added into the equation to measure the effect of the invasions of the 1700's and 1740's with the disruptions that accompanied them.

The regressions were run on two cities, Bruges and Ghent, and on groups of villages in the sandy (industrialized) area, in the transitional (industrialized) area between the sandy zone and the polders, and finally in the polder zone (commercial agriculture). In each of the areas the data run from 1689 to 1778.

The regression equation had the following form:

$$\left(\frac{\dot{M}}{M}\right)_t = a + \sum_{\lambda=0}^{3} b_\lambda \left(\frac{\dot{P}}{P}\right)_{t-\lambda} + c_1 t + c_2 t^2 + d_0 D_t + d_1 D_{t-1} + e_t$$

where a is the intercept; b is the coefficient of response of marriages to economic changes; c_1 measures the effect of time; c_2 measures the non-linear effect of passing time; d_0 measures the effect of the "war" dummy variable; d_1 measures the effect of the same, lagged one year; e is the regression residual; t is time; M is the number of marriages; $M = M_t - M_{t-1}$; P is the price variable: in the case of regressions run on villages of the polder zone, it is the price of rye, and elsewhere the ratio of rye price to linen price; $\dot{P} = P_t - P_{t-1}$; λ is the lag; D is a dummy variable for invasion years: $D = 0,1$.

The results of the regression analysis are shown in Table I. The coefficients c_1, c_2, d_0, d_1 are not shown in this table, for their standard errors were consistently large in comparison with their estimated value. The upper value of each cell is the regression coefficient. The lower figure is the t-ratio. Starred ratios are those corresponding to a coefficient significantly positive or negative at a five-percent level of significance.

Table I a.

Regression coefficients. Case of favorable (negative) rye-linen ratio change in previous year $N = 45$

	Ghent	Bruges	Sandy	Trans.	Polders
a	-1.1759	-.5643	-.9088	.3517	-1.1626
	-2.5089*	-.8088	-1.2524	.4226	-.7497
b_0	-.0236	-.0384	-.0450	-.0450	.1045
	-1.8875	-1.7033	-1.9224	-1.6739	2.0860*
b_1	-.5518	-.3003	-.4038	-.4941	-.4918
	-5.7863*	-2.1157*	-2.7351*	-2.9178*	-1.5585
b_2	-.0007	-.0020	-.0043	-.0049	.0060
	-.3739	-.7267	-1.4784	-1.4766	.9657
b_3	-.3242	-.0118	-.6192	-.3905	-1.3900
	-.9489	-.0233	-1.1704	-.6437	-1.2294

Table I b.

Unfavorable (positive) rye-linen ratio

$N = 42$

	Ghent	Bruges	Sandy	Trans.	Polders
a	.0318	.2581	-.1971	-.9366	.3932
	.0553	.4132	-.2230	-1.3546	.2488
b_0	.0336	-.0060	-.0570	-.1000	-.1556
	.6863	-.1124	-.7591	-1.7019	-1.1588

Table I b. (continued)

b_1	.0017	.0223	.0055	.0199	-.0724
	.0959	1.1237	.1956	.9064	-1.4449
b_2	.0047	-.0000	-.0128	.0155	.0183
	.6072	-.0025	-1.0785	1.6743	.8637
b_3	.0250	-.0012	-.0875	.2132	-.4599
	.2374	-.0106	-.5425	1.6889	-1.5935

Table I c.

Rye prices. All cases   N = 86

Fertile

a	5.3165
	.1468
b_0	.0871
	2.1303*
b_1	-.0552
	-1.3833
b_2	.0301
	.7424
b_3	-.0380
	-.9457

Sources: See note 15.

Table I a. and I b. shows that for the observations where the previous year had been characterized by a favorable change in the price ratio where there was industrialization, a significant increase in the number of marriages followed with a one-year lag. There was, however, no similar response to unfavorable changes in the price ratio. When all observations were merged (these results are not shown here) the selected price ratios had no significant effect on the annual changes in the number of marriages. Table I c. shows that the marriages in the areas with commercial agriculture and large farms responded symetrically and positively to changes in food prices.   It is clear here that the demographic mechanism of the industrialized countryside resembled more that of the towns than that of the area of commercial agriculture. The positive response of marriages to changes in cereal prices in some areas of the countryside --the polders-- is contrary to generally accepted conclusions concerning the mechanism of subsistence crises in pre-industrial rural society.

The "time" and "war" variables which had been included in the regression equations had no significant effect on marriages (their coefficients are not displayed in Table I).

At this stage the differences in demographic structure and evolution among the various economic-geographic areas of Flanders are not completely accounted for. It has been shown here, however, that the demand (price) for an industrial commodity added a powerful stimulus of demographic fluctuations where manufacturing served as a complement to agricultural means of subsistence for a significant section of the population.

Moreover, the asymmetry of reaction of marriages to economic shocks deserves some attention. It may have been caused by the existence during the entire period of restraints on marriages caused by the pressure of population on scarce means of subsistence and revealed by a high age of marriage (17). If a social mechanism is permanently operating under tension, that is, in this case, if the age of marriage is already close to an upper --psychological or physiological-- boundary, it is perhaps to be expected that movements away from such a boundary are easier to induce than movements toward it (18). Insofar as regional changes in nuptiality could affect the regional rate of population growth, such an asymmetry in the reaction of nuptiality could contribute to the difference in the demographic trends between the industrial and purely agricultural areas of Flanders, for this asymmetry could, ceteris paribus, tend to promote irreversible population growth as long as the relevant prices continued their stimulating fluctuations, and irrespective of their long-run trend. Naturally, however, the course of population change depended on other variables as well as on the one to which consideration has been given here.

According to the well-known mechanism of subsistence crises, positive changes in food prices are generally held to have had a negative influence on population in the short run and on the demographic variables that determined its fluctuations. It should not be too surprising, however, when a careful analysis is made of economic systems in sub-regions of an area, that one should distinguish within so-called pre-industrial society the regions that operated as providers of a food surplus from those which had to import food and paid for it with the proceeds of a domestic industrial occupation. Large farms benefited, and did not suffer, from high food prices; agricultural employment in commercial farming regions increased in periods of high prices.

It must be noted that in a closed economy the periods of agricultural and industrial prosperity might have coincided and fluctuations in the prices of industrial and agricultural commodities might have been closely correlated if industrial commodities found their principal outlet among the landlords and wage laborers. This, however, was not necessarily true but it has been argued by some (19). At any rate, it cannot be disputed that, in the words of Professor Labrousse, "the further away the locus of consumption is from the locus of production, and the more attenuated the probability of concordance of agricultural and industrial crises, of the rise of staple prices and of industrial unemployment (20)." Thus, for small and industrially specialized regions, the concomitance of industrial and agricultural causes of income or demographic changes did not necessarily hold, and, just as the prosperity of the rural weavers of eighteenth-century Brittany depended more on the fluctuations of the Spanish and Portuguese crops than on the vagaries of the French climate (21), one adds a significant and truly exogenous cause of demographic fluctuations --both rural and urban-- in eighteenth-century Flanders by introducing a measure of the oscillations of industrial demand.

The areas of the countryside which were engaged in a part-time textile industry with market destination responded to particular types of economic stimuli, in particular to changes in the demand for and price of the products of the cottage manufactures. These sections of society were still dominated by the primary need to find food, but they solved the subsistence problem by roundabout ways which already resembled some of those used by "industrial" society.

REFERENCES

An earlier version of this paper was written while the author was supported by a Demographic Fellowship from the Population Council. Computations were carried out with the financial support of the Population Council and the Research Committee, Graduate School, University of Wisconsin. The author has benefited from comments by the participants to the Colloquium on Historical Demography, University of Sussex, April 1968 and to the Bloomington conference. Professor T.H. Hollingsworth's valuable suggestions are gratefully aknowledged. The responsibility for remaining errors is solely the author's.

1) G. U. Yule, "Changes in Marriage and Birth Rates in England and Wales during the past Half Century," Journal of the Royal Statistical Society, Vol. 69 (1906), 100-132; V. L. Galbraith and D. S. Thomas, "Birth Rates and the Interwar Business Cycle," Journal of the American Statistical Association, Vol. 36 (1941), 465-476; D. Kirk, "The Influence of Business Cycles on Marriage and Birth Rates," Demographic and Economic Change in Developed Countries (Princeton, 1960), 241-260; M. Silver, "Births, Marriages, and Economic Fluctuations in the United Kingdom and Japan," Economic Development and Cultural Change, Vol. 14 (1966), 302-315.

2) See for instance Pierre Goubert, Beauvais et le Beauvaisis de 1600 à 1730 (Paris, 1960).

3) J. Craeybeckx, "Les industries d'exportation dans les villes flamandes au xviiè s.," Studi in Onore di Amintore Fanfani (Milan, 1962), IV, 413-468.

4) Faipoult, Mémoire statistique du Département de l'Escaut (Paris, 1805), P. Deprez (ed.) (Ghent, 1960)

5) P. Deprez, "The Demographic Development of Flanders during the Eighteenth Century," D. V. Glass and D. E. C. Eversley (eds.), Population in History (London, 1965), 608-631; P. Olyslager, De localisering der Belgische nijverheid (Antwerp, 1947). The pattern of industrial location and its relationship with demographic, social, pedological, and other variables has been studied by Paul Deprez in his unpublished dissertation (University of Ghent, 1960), which, generously, he allowed me to use.

6) J. Bastin, "De Gentse lijnwaadmarkt en linnenhandel in de xviie eeuw," Handelingen der Maatschappij voor Geschiedenis en Oudheidkunde te Gent, new series, Vol. 21 (1967), 131-162. H. Coppejans-Desmedt, Bijdrage tot de studie van de gegoede burgerij te Gent in de xviiie eeuw (Brussels, 1952).

7) Quoted by J. Lefèvre, Etude sur le commerce de la Belgique avec l'Espagne au xviiiè s. (Brussels, 1922), p. 179.

8) E. H. Slicher van Bath, "The Rise of Intensive Industry in the Low Countries," J. S. Bromley and E. H. Kossman (eds.), Britain and the Netherlands (London, 1960), 130-143.

9) P. Deprez, "De boeren," J. L. Broeckx et al. (eds.), Flandria Nostra (Antwerp, 1957), I, 123-165; "De Kasselrij van Oudburg in de 18e eeuw. Bijdrage tot de studie van de sociale en economische struktuur van het platteland," Unpublished Dissertation, University of Ghent, 1960. There is an abundance of monographic studies of Flemish rural history. Much is owed to the work of D. Dalle, C. de Rammelaere, J. de Brouwer, P. Lindemans , A. de Vos, and G. Willemsen.

10) C. Verlinden, "Introduction," Dokumenten voor de geschiedenis van prijzen en lonen in Vlaanderen en Brabant (Bruges, 1965), II, xxv; Deprez, "De Kasselrij. . .," op. cit.; J. Craeybeckx, "De handarbeiders," Flandria Nostra, op. cit., I.

11) F. Mendels, "industrialization and Population Pressure in Eighteenth-Century Flanders," Unpublished Dissertation, University of Wisconsin, 1969, Chapter III.

12) F. Mendels, op. cit.

13) This is consistent with a neo-Ricardian framework. See W. A. Lewis, "Development with Unlimited Supply of Labor," The Manchester School, Vol. 22 (1954), 132-191.

14) D. Dalle, De bevolking van Veurne-Ambacht in de 17de en 18de eeuw (Brussels, 1963); Deprez, "The Demographic Development. . .," op. cit.

15) Data sources:

Prices: E. J. Hamilton, War and Prices in Spain 1651-1800 (Cambridge, 1947); P. Deprez, "Graanprijzen te Gent en te Deinze in groten Vlaams, 1555-1795," Dokumenten, op. cit., I, p. 64; "Maten, gewichten, en munten," ibid., II, pp xxix-xxxix.

Marriages:

Bruges: A. Wyffels, "De omvang en de evolutie van het Brugse bevolkingscijfer in de 17e en 18e eeuw," Revue Belge de Philologie et d'Histoire, Vol. 36 (1958), 1243-1274.

Ghent: H. van Werveke, De curve van het Gentse bevolkings-cijfer in de 17e en de 18e eeuw (Brussels, 1948)

Sandy zone:
           Ertvelde, Oosteeklo, Lovendegem, Sleidinge, Waarschoot, and Zomergem.
           G. Vanlaere, "De demografische ontwikkeling van Assenede, Bassevelde, Boekhoute. . .," Handelingen

der Maatschappij voor Geschiedenis en Oudheidkunde te Gent (HMGOG), new series, Vol. 15 (1961), 49-105; A. de Vos, "De bevolkingsevolutie van Evergem. . .," Appeltjes van het Meetjesland, Vol. 8 (1957), 1-72.

Fertile zone:
Boekhoute and Watervliet.
G. Vanlaere, op. cit.

Transition zone:
Assenede, Bassevelde, Erembodegem, Iddergem, Terafelne, Welle, Oordegem-Smetlede, Schorisse, St-Blasius-Boekel, St-Maria-Horebeke, St-Kornelis-Horebeke, Zegelsem. G. Vanlere, op. cit.; J. de Brouwer, "De demografische evolutie. . .," Cinq études de démographie locale xviiè-xixè s. (Brussels, 1963), 71-120; C. de Rammelaere, "De bevolkingsevolutie in het Land van Schorisse (1569-1796)," HMGOG, Vol. 10 (1959), 53-97.

16) F. Mendels, "Economic Fluctuations and Population Change in 18th Century Flanders," Paper read at the Annual Meeting of the Population Association of America, Cincinnati, 1967.

17)

Age of first marriage for cohorts born in 1700-1779

		1700-19	1720-39	1740-59	1760-79
Vieuxbourg	M	27.3	27.9	26.3	24.2
	F	25.2	26.3	24.2	22.0
Adegem	M	25.8	26.0	26.5	23.5
	F	24.4	25.3	26.4	23.4
Sainghin	M	31.2	31.9	30.8	29.7
	F	28.4	29.1	28.0	26.6
Elversele	M	29.4		29.5	
	F	28.0		28.5	
		(1700-49)		(1750-96)	

Sources: P. Deprez, "The Demographic Development of Flanders. . .," op. cit.; F. Verhoeyen, "De bevolking van Elversele in de 17de en 18de eeuw," Unpublished Thesis, University of Ghent, 1961; R. Deniel and L. Henry, "La population d'un village du Nord de la France: Sainghin-en-Mélantois, de 1665 à 1851," Population, Vol. 20 (1965), 564-602.

18) N. Georgescu-Roegen, "Evolution versus Mechanics," Analytical Economics, (Cambridge, Mass., 1966), 83-91

19) C. E. Labrousse, Esquisse du mouvement des prix et des revenus en France au xviiiè s. (Paris, 1933), II, p. 532

20) Ibid.

21)   Ibid., p. 541.

Part II

The Pre-industrial Society in Europe, Asia and Africa

7

DEMOGRAPHIC HISTORY OF PRE-INDUSTRIAL SOCIETIES

J. POTTER

LONDON SCHOOL OF ECONOMICS

I have been asked at rather short notice to undertake the task of Rapporteur for this session on pre-industrial societies, despite the obvious disqualification that most of my own work has been concerned with periods and places that can hardly rank as pre-industrial. My task is not made any easier by the comprehensive nature of this morning's Rapport by Goran Ohlin, most of whose remarks were equally applicable to both industrial and pre-industrial societies. I shall therefore be content to interpret the role of Rapporteur as one of seeking to pose questions which seem relevant to the subject under discussion rather than trying to make a substantive contribution to the discussion.

I should like to begin however by placing the discussions of this Demography section of the Conference in the context of our meetings here in Bloomington at the Fourth International Economic History Congress. The stock-in-trade of most economic historians is national history. For innumerable reasons, not least the mental incapacity of most of us to comprehend more than a tiny portion of human experience, we busy ourselves for the most part with the detailed study of one country, usually but not always our own native country.

We acknowledge to ourselves, and sometimes proclaim in public, that such studies are of limited value since our lack of knowledge of other countries and other periods deprives us of any yardstick for measurement or comparison. Occasionally we piously plead for international rather than national economic history. Occasionally the bolder ones among us, like Dudley Dillard, try to write international economic history.

We were reminded in the Addresses of Welcome with which we were greeted at the opening plenary session of this Congress that in meeting together as we are doing this week we have a special

task, nay duty, to try to transcend our normal nationally intro-
verted viewpoints and to achieve a broader vision of our subject.
Without discourtesy to our hosts, we may change the words of the
English poet to read: 'What should they know of America who only
America know.' We would no doubt all agree that if a Conference
of this nature is to serve any useful purpose, that should be,
apart from the personal satisfaction derived from meeting
colleagues from all parts of the world, to make us think in terms
of international economic history. Yet in the few sessions
already held at the Conference, one point has already emerged
with unmistakable clarity: even the simplest of cross-national
comparisons are fraught with difficulty. As an economist friend
of mine puts it, to compare satisfactorily the price of a loaf of
bread in London with the price of a loaf of bread in Moscow would
require a Ph.D. thesis. The moment one proceeds to larger
questions, the measurement of living standards, the analysis of
economic growth, the problems multiply to infinity. All too
frequently the choice seems to rest between highly particularised
detail, unique to time and place, or platitudinous generalisation
to which economic history has little to contribute.

The thought nevertheless occurs that in this demographic
section of the Conference we may be somewhat better off than are
our colleagues in other branches of economic history. Because we
are dealing with the basic elements of human existence, conception and birth, courtship and marriage, disease and death, it
is possible that those of us who work in demographic history may
be able to identify significant comparisons or meaningful truths
of universal application such as elude the students of other
branches of our subject. In a word, I am asking whether demographic history can claim to be international with greater
justification than the rest of economic history.

In a session devoted to pre-industrial societies this seems
to offer a challenge of crucial importance, not only to us as
historians but also as social scientists interested in the world
today. Can we indeed identify common demographic patterns in all,
or even in most, pre-industrial societies? Or if not, can we at
least identify significant contrasts that might in turn lead to
helpful generalisations? Have pre-industrial societies common
demographic features? There are a number of possibilities:

1. We may discover similar trends with the evidence
suggesting that these are caused by similar circumstances.
2. We may discover similar trends brought about by patently
dissimilar causal factors. For example the observed datum
that the age of marriage has risen (or fallen) may be the
consequence of quite different, and possibly diametrically
opposite, social or economic changes. (And similar the datum,
a change in the age of marriage, will not necessarily in all
circumstances have the same effect on fertility).
3. We may discover similar trends which are nevertheless
occurring at different levels or at different rates; the
direction may be the same but everything else different.
That the impact will be different in these conditions is
obvious if we consider, for example, death rates falling but
at very different levels. All too often however the

significance of differing rates of change has been ignored:
one example, all too rarely noticed, is the differing speed
of natural population growth in North America and Western
Europe, especially in the first half of the nineteenth
century.
4. We may discover, not surprisingly, dissimilar trends in
dissimilar conditions.
5. More disturbingly, we may discover dissimilar trends in
conditions which at least prima facie appear to be somewhat
similar (as for example the differing growth rates of the
French and the German populations in the nineteenth century).
6. We may discover contradictory traits within the same
society. Rising living standards appear to affect population change sometimes in one direction, sometimes in
another. The difficulty of predicting demographic behaviour
obviously springs from contradictions of this kind.

A European observer studying the American scene at once
becomes aware of some of these problems of generalisation;
certainly he is not inclined to make an assumption of similarity.
Brought up as we are on Malthusian and Ricardian precepts, we
gradually come to recognise that American demographic history is
both anti-Malthusian and anti-Ricardian. So far from population
outrunning food supplies, the American experience has increasingly tended in quite the opposite direction: the expansion of food
output has, especially and progressively over the past century,
proceeded faster than the expansion of population. Instead of
population surplus and food famine, the twentieth century
American dilemma (at any rate one of them) has been the constant
tendency of agriculture to over-produce; and the result has been
for American agriculture a kind of Malthusian crisis in reverse.
    Secondly the European assumption that Ricardo was speaking
a truism when he wrote that new land is likely to be marginal,
i.e. less productive, land has been negated in the American experience. For most of the colonial period and all through the
nineteenth century and even beyond, the expansion of the
American frontier meant that new land was not necessarily poorer
land and often was indeed more fertile land. The Ricardian
generalisation at once appears inapplicable to the American
scene.
    This is in fact saying no more than that land supply is a
crucial factor in the relationship between population and food-
supply, as Malthus himself recognised. Can we therefore proceed
to look for similarities, on the one hand in all territorially
expanding societies, the U.S.A., Canada, Australia, Russia, to
name the most obvious examples, and on the other for similarities
in all economies of fixed territorial size?
    The process of population movement, however, may or may not
be a frontier phenomenon. Obviously people have moved into
already settled as well as into unsettled areas. In either case,
just as the existence of a frontier, in the sense of unsettled
territory, creates divergent experience, so also does the act of

migration, whether it is to a frontier or not.

Above all, migration is a selective process. A cohort of migrants will not be identical with a cohort of the people who remain behind in a number of significant particulars. Most of these are obvious and well-known. A migratory group is very likely to have a different age and sex structure from the society left behind and (where applicable) also from the society which it enters. This different age and sex structure must affect the birth rate of both, even if the fertility rate remains constant. And the fertility rate may not remain constant. Further the ratio of dependants to producers is changed by this difference in age composition, a factor which may have great social significance.

These important factors (frontier conditions and migration) create differences between certain societies, but in these cases they are associated with some form of change. Is it any easier to generalise about conditions preceeding economic and social change? Do pre-industrial societies offer a fixed set of circumstances which make it possible to derive universal truths about demographic behaviour?

It is not altogether clear from the papers before us in this session what is meant to their authors by the description 'pre-industrial'. All the papers refer to relatively recent times; the earliest date mentioned is the seventeenth century. Moreover no clear distinction is made between 'pre-industrial' and 'pre-economic development'. One suspects for instance that the term 'pre-commercial' would have sufficed just as well. If this is so, then we are at once begging the largest of all the questions we have to deal with, the connection between demographic behaviour and economic change. From this point of view industrialisation may only be one special form, and perhaps a relatively unimportant one, of economic development. Should not this session be posing questions about traditional societies, stagnant over the centuries, not yet experiencing the erosions of economic change springing from whatever quickening agency.

The questions raised by such pre-growth societies certainly have universal importance. The very notion of 'subsistence level' - so often regarded as some kind of absolute - sets its own problems; indeed it has already been asserted (by Professor Postan) that there is no such thing. Is there a minimum diet (measurable in terms of calories, or by any other device) which human beings require in order to live? The evidence is not convincing. Nor is it clear that the same minimum would apply in equatorial regions as in arctic regions, or that all branches of the human species have the same requirements. One may certainly agree with the suggestion that human life has at times continued on quite incredibly small food supplies - even no food at all by normal definitions of the word.

Nevertheless we merely proceed from here to further questions. Given conditions of poor diet, or famine, the effects such conditions have in inducing low fertility, or poor infant survival rates, or high susceptibility to disease, or generally short life-expectation, have to be investigated (an obvious example from more recent times is the association of deaths from influenza during the first World War with the deterioration of diet below that level to which people were accustomed).

But, as Ohlin points out, doubt has recently been cast even on these assumptions and the connection between adequacy of diet and resistance to disease may be a tenuous one.

This raises a further problem, whether there is in stagnant societies a long-run situation of equilibrium between population and food maintained mainly by epidemics - a question which is largely, but not entirely, the basic Malthusian problem. Historically, however, further questions suggest themselves. How long do we find it has taken societies, at different times and in different places, to make up for the experience of a demographic catastrophe? And what have been the effects of this sudden cataclysmic experience? If, at year 1 population has equalled, say, 10,000; and in year 2 famine or plague reduces that population to say, 5,000, how many years are required to reach year X when the population has been restored to 10,000? But perhaps even more importantly, it cannot be assumed that the population of 10,000 at year X is identical with the original population of 10,000 at year 1. What differences are found in its age and sex structure? Has it changed in physiological (or mental, or any other) quality in respects which are significant for economic life?

The last sentence has introduced a word which is almost anathema in respectable academic circles. Men are not only born free but also equal, so how can one speak of quality in this context? Increasingly however, economic historians are recognising the significance of education in economic processes. We are merely pushing the question one stage further back by asking about the fitness of the human body. An individual's life expectation for example must influence his economic behaviour (e.g. his leisure preference, or his propensity to save - indeed his conduct in every respect), just as much as do his religious beliefs, his taboos, his know-how. Similarly a village of weak, disease-ridden people is likely to have a different economic performance from one of healthy, strong individuals. Health is at least one factor determining both the will and the ability to work. The association therefore between diet and disease and human capabilities is one to be investigated.

Many interesting questions are raised by the papers presented to this session. All too little is known about the size of the household and the function of the family in early societies, and we have before us a number of interesting suggestions. One contribution discusses the existence of an annual cycle in the individual's pattern of life; births, marriages and deaths are not spread evenly over the calendar year. The significance of the incidence of marriage and of the age of marriage is brought to our attention and it is pointed out that postponement of marriage after the age of 20 years may be more significant than postponement at an earlier age. In all these respects we should no doubt like to have not a handful of case-studies but large numbers of studies carrying as much authority as those before us today.

Returning to my opening remarks, I cannot fail to be impressed by significant similarities in the papers even though they come as they do from different continents. Above all there is a similarity of resources and a similarity in methods. It is striking that we all are confronted by the limitations imposed by the raw materials at our disposal. There is often a surprising likeness in the source of those data, emanating sometimes from religious institutions, occasionally from some civic authority. In using these materials in whichever country we are working, we are at least discussing, and perhaps practising, similar techniques: we are thinking of the possibilities of family reconstruction; we are thinking of the potentialities of the computer. In our problems and methods of research at least we appear to speak an international language. It is surely therefore appropriate to conclude with a plea for an enormous expansion of the use of our common language to build up a far greater stock of information to which we can all turn in future years in our attempts to answer the broader questions I have been raising.

8

EUROPEAN HISTORICAL DEMOGRAPHY

E. A. WRIGLEY

UNIVERSITY OF CAMBRIDGE, ENGLAND

European historical demography has made great progress in
recent years. The quantity of results published has increased
sharply and their technical quality is often higher than in the
past. Since there is sometimes a 'bandwagon' aspect to any sudden
spurt in research work which may produce results more notable for
their volume than their value, it may be well to try to assess what
has been achieved already and what should be attempted in the near
future.

Most of the documentary sources known and used at present by
historical demographers have been exploited sporadically by historians and others over many decades. Thousands of English parish
registers, for example, were consulted by incumbents at Rickman's
request in the 1830s to enable him to make estimates of the size of
the population of the country from Elizabethan times onwards. No
subsequent research operation has involved the use of more than a
small fraction of the registers then examined. In the eighteenth
century men like Short, Price, Howlett, Wales and Eden understood
the importance of these records and made extensive use of them.
And even earlier, in the later decades of the seventeenth century,
there was a keen interest in population questions. Petty, Graunt,
King and others variously consulted parish registers, Hearth Tax
returns, and lists made under the Marriage Duty Act of 1694. What
has distinguished recent work, therefore, has not been the citing
of new evidence but rather the use of new methods and the asking of
questions which reflect a new appreciation of the interconnections
between economic, social and demographic history.

The most striking achievements in the analysis of the raw
material of historical demography have sprung from the realisation
that it can be a prime source of information about the characteristics of 'natural'fertility and other fundamental demographic

103

characteristics. Louis Henry, who has done more than any other man
to bring this about, wrote recently:

> "Contrary to what a superficial view might suggest, historical
> demography is not simply a marginal part of demography. It
> is demography itself, just as demography, being a study of
> human populations in time, is history itself." (1)

Where suitable data sources exist historical demography is sometimes
more favourably placed than contemporary demographic studies because
the demographic experience of each generation in the past is complete, and there is no uncertainty about the future like that which
causes so much difficulty in the study of cohorts which are still
living. Moreover historical demography is not so severely cramped
by the restrictions imposed by government statistical services
seeking to preserve the confidentiality of personal information.

There are several sources which may permit the life histories
of individuals to be studied in sufficient detail to yield precise
estimates of fertility, mortality and nuptiality. Parish registers
form perhaps the most important of these sources, but peerage
records, genealogies and the records of religious communities like
the Quakers, can all be used for the same purpose.

The most exhaustive method of analysing data of this type is
that known as family reconstitution. Where it can be undertaken
with success very full analysis of fertility and some aspects of
mortality and nuptiality is feasible, but though the nominal
ordering of records for demographic analysis through family
reconstitution is a very promising method, it also involves many
problems. For instance, it is usually difficult to argue from the
sample of reconstituted families to the population as a whole,
either because the group involved is distinguished from the bulk
of the population by its religion or status (the Quakers, or the
peerage), or because, although the original source covers the whole
population (the parish registers), those who stay at home all their
lives are over-represented in the sample. Or again, care must be
taken to make allowance for under-registration and to attempt to
discover its extent. Family reconstitution is also a rather time
consuming and expensive operation and is therefore often seen to
best advantage when part of a larger research project in which
aggregative methods and techniques which lie half-way between
simple aggregation and full reconstitution are also used. The
study of French demographic history from the late seventeenth to
the early nineteenth century undertaken by the Institut National
d'Études Démographiques and now approaching completion is an
excellent example of this type of project.

It is important to recognise the value of choosing a suitable
sampling design before embarking on any research which entails the
processing of a large quantity of information in a standard form.
Much time may be wasted unnecessarily in working through a large
body of such data when an appropriate sampling method could cut the
labour involved substantially without seriously affecting the
accuracy of the result. Where the bulk of the data is so great
that sampling of some sort is inevitable, a good sampling design
is even more important. The failure to appreciate this point has
gravely prejudiced the value of many aggregative studies in the
past. A wider understanding of it more recently has helped
historical demography considerably.

The improvement of techniques in historical population studies since the Second World War is visible not only in the more effective use of running records of birth, marriage and death, but also in the analysis of census material whether collected by the state or by the ecclesiastical authorities. For example, the estimation of fertility and mortality using assumptions derived from the study of stable population characteristics may permit a much more effective analysis of census data than was once normal in the absence of vital statistics.

To recite only the achievements of historical demographers in extending the knowledge of fertility and mortality in the past, however, is to neglect the most important aspect of the development of historical demography. The conjunction of adjective and noun does not connote simply the extension, so to speak, of the activities of the Registrar-General or a census bureau into the past. The reason why historical demography is an exciting subject lies in the discovery and demonstration that it can provide a calculus of behaviour central to much of the activity of man in the past. To be able to follow the impact of famine and disease upon a community in the wake of bad harvests, identifying those within the population who were susceptible because of their age, occupation or position within the family, is much more than an exercise in demography sensu stricto. Similarly, to be able to tabulate the number of families with resident grandparents or containing a second married couple from a pre-census listing, provides an insight into the organisation and functioning of society with far wider implications than could be drawn from an analysis, say, of the age distribution of the population. The prevalence of the extended family and the circumstances under which it may be formed are topics of profound importance to the understanding of the economic, social and legal dispositions of a community. Or again, statistics of age at marriage, or illegitimacy, or pre-marital conception, or family limitation are far more than naive demographic facts. They are a first step towards the unravelling of social relationships or economic arrangements which can tell us much about the structure of a society.

Behind these general remarks there lies an issue which deserves fuller consideration. Whereas traditional demography worked with large aggregates and dealt with the characteristics of populations en masse, the recent achievements of historical demography, both in the minutiae of technical demography and in a general historical setting, have been closely connected with the concentration on individual families as the unit of study. The scale of investigation in recent historical demography has much to do both with its nature and its success.

History is, amongst other things, the study of the interconnectedness of events. There are nodes within the whole network of events whose characteristics reflect its functioning sensitively and are for this reason especially well worth study. Historical demography has staked a claim to attention in recent years because it appears to be strategically placed in this respect. And here the scale of investigation is very important. A national figure expressing fertility or mortality is an average of conditions which may vary immensely by region, social class, occupational group, and so on, and by combinations of these characteristics. Such a figure is far too clumsy to be a sensitive index to any but the most general changes or conditions. When the family is the unit of study, on the other hand, there is, in principle at least, vastly greater flexibility and sensitivity. By combining families which have certain characteristics or groups of characteristics in common, the full range of demographic conditions can be examined and correlated with these characteristics. Those Genevan bourgeois families, for example, which began to practise family limitation in the late seventeenth century would probably have been lost in the mass if information about fertility had been obtainable only for Geneva as a whole – and there would therefore have been no possibility of investigating further the social pressures which pushed the group into new patterns of behaviour (2).

Where there is a large mass of nominally ordered information about individuals – from wills, inventories, Poor Law accounts, rate books, settlement papers, enclosure awards and the like, all that concerns a particular family can be articulated round the reconstituted record of that family, or round the details of a family recorded in a census document. This makes it possible to test hypotheses about the interrelations between conditions or events which it would otherwise be difficult to test satisfactorily. For example, it may be asserted that the older daughters in a family stand a better chance of early marriage than the younger; or that areas of partible inheritance are areas of early marriage; or that the demographic characteristics of 'closed' parishes are different from those of 'open' parishes; or that the religious attitudes of a particular period both enjoined and enforced a strict code of sexual behaviour; or that assortative mating was a strongly marked feature of a certain community and that this had significant effects on the concentration of wealth in a few families; or that wage paid labour during the industrial revolution tended to lose patterns of behaviour which had previously served to moderate fertility; and so on. These and many similar questions can be examined with a new precision where interlinkage of nominally ordered information is feasible, whether or not the sources used are primarily demographic or cover a much wider spectrum. Moreover, bodies of data of this sort help to provoke new questions as well as enabling old questions to be more fully answered.

The recent improvements in technique in historical demography, in short, because they have shown the value of rigorous methods of establishing and testing linkages between nominally ordered records, even though undertaken initially for purely demographic purposes, probably presage the extension of this logic to a wider area of social and economic behaviour in the past, with the individual family as the basic building block. When data are held in such a convenient form they lend themselves to the testing of hypotheses about a wide range of social and economic activity in the past, and, especially when a suitable sampling technique is used, results of great interest may be attainable with relatively little effort. This is especially true when the data are processed by computer.

The last few paragraphs are perhaps somewhat euphoric. The types of analysis described or suggested are possible only where the source material is full and rich. In western Europe, for example, the absence of suitable records precludes family reconstitution until the sixteenth or seventeenth centuries even in the

most favoured areas. The developments of recent years in
historical demography are relevant only to the early modern period
and even then only to some parts of western Europe or places of
European settlement (though China and Japan may prove to be massive
exceptions to the rule that other areas are less promising).
Moreover, the number of detailed analyses of registers, census
documents and listings is still very limited even for purely demographic purposes, and studies which embrace a wider field are still
rarer. The dialectical interchange between hypothesis and
empirical studies is in a very early stage. For example, neither
the provenance nor the prevalence of the 'European' family has
been determined, nor have the theoretical implications of Hajnal's
definition of it been fully examined (3). But enough has been
adumbrated in general discussions and sufficient garnered in
empirical studies to create confidence that historical demography
in the next decade will both provide a great deal of hard fact
about fertility and mortality in the past and bring into being a
body of material so ordered that history will benefit not only
from the rigour of the statistical testing of hypotheses and the
economy of good sampling design, but also from the opportunity to
make effective use of some sociological and anthropological concepts. Indeed the matrix of linked information which can be made
available in favourable circumstances should prove of interest to
demographers, economists, sociologists, social anthropologists and
human geographers, as well as to historians; but most of all to
those who honour the divisions between these subjects largely in
the breach.

(REFERENCES)

1) L. Henry, 'Historical demography', Daedalus (spring 1968),
   p.395, issued as vol. 97, no. 2 of the Proceedings of the
   American Academy of Arts and Sciences.
2) L. Henry, Anciennes familles genevoises (Paris, 1956)
3) J. Hajnal, 'European marriage patterns in perspective', in
   D. V. Glass and D. E. C. Eversley (eds.), Population in History
   (London, 1965)

9

DEMOGRAPHIC ASPECTS OF A VILLAGE IN TOKUGAWA JAPAN

AKIRA HAYAMI

KEIO UNIVERSITY, TOKYO, JAPAN.

1. Introduction

Tokugawa Japan[1] bequeathed to us an abundant supply of materials for population study. Although these materials cannot be compared to modern scientific demographic data, they are excellent for their day. Japan in the Tokugawa period was a rare example of a well documented pre-modern state.

There are two reasons for this fortunate situation. First, when Japan was finally unified in the late sixteenth century, the shogun and the provincial feudal lords became very much interested in the quantitative aspects of the regions they governed and hence conducted surveys on the size and population of their domains. These early surveys were the first attempt of its sort since the eighth and ninth centuries when a type of census had been carried out.

Second, as a result of the strict ban put on Christianity by the Tokugawa government, a registration of the religious faith of every individual was carried out every year. The people were ordered to report what religious body they belonged to and to avow themselves Buddhists. In general, all the people, both urban and rural, were ordered to enter the name of their family temple in the register of their town or village, the basic unit for this national survey.

This religious registration system was put into effect on a nationwide level about 1670. At first, the system had nothing to do with census-taking, but later it also came to be utilized for that purpose. Besides the names and the family temples of individuals, their sex, age, and relationship to their household head, and such matters as the reason and the date for any change in residence were entered. The form of these registrations differed in various parts of the country. The fact, however, that census-like registrations existed in many provinces, and especially the fact that they were conducted annually, should be considered a significant event facilitating the demographic study of the Tokugawa period. As a result of the existence of the two types of data described above, Japan is fairly well endowed with demographic materials.

This report is the result of a demographic study I made using the example of Yokouchi village in Suwa county in the province of Shinano. The materials for this village are, from the point of view of a continuous study over a period of years, the best which I have discovered to date. I have made a study of various aspects of the demographic history of this village by combining the traditional method of population study with a tracing of the demographic behavior of families through the method of family reconstitution.

In Suwa han, the domain to which this village belonged, shumon aratame cho or religious registrations were drawn up for every village for 201 years from 1671 to 1871. The form of the survey continued to being almost the same throughout the period. There are shumon aratame cho extant for the village of Yokouchi for 144 years out of this 201 year period.

In general, there is no one method for determining to what extent these materials can be trusted, but for Yokouchi village the materials for the first half of the period can be relied upon to a greater extent than those of the latter half. This generalization is based on the extent to which the materials are continuous, on the extent to which births are reported, and on the extent to which the reasons for any changes are recorded. Thus, if this span of 201 years is divided into 25 year periods, the reliability of Period II (1701-1725) is the highest in every respect. There is the least amount of continuity in the materials from Period V (1776-1800) on. Also, the recording of births is incomplete in Periods VII and VIII (1826-1871).

The method used for studying these materials was first, at the most basic level, to record on cards--one card for every family for every year--the name, sex, age, and relationship to the head of the household of every person in the family and to note the reasons for any changes in the household. Using these cards it was possible to make horizontal studies on the village for any year for which there were materials. And because there is no break in the continuity of the materials of over four years, it was possible to make vertical times studies on each family. The next step was to record on one card the demographic behavior of each couple in order to obtain from the basic cards more detailed material concerning marriage and births. For this it was possible to adopt the method developed in the 1950s by Henry Fleury.

This method of dealing with the basic materials, that is of using the family reconstitution method carried out in the studies on the historical demography of Western Europe, was extremely valuable in tracing long-term demographic changes. And because the shumon aratame cho for this village record all family members in one place, family reconstitution was extremely easy to carry out, in comparison with the work European demographers have in reconstructing families from birth, marriage, and death records.

The village under study, Yokouchi, is situated on the edge of the Suwa basin in Nagano prefecture in central Japan. (Fig. I) At

the beginning of the Tokugawa period, this village was estimated at
350 koku on the lord's cadastre, which meant that the cultivated
land produced about 1,800 bushels of grain. The altitude, about
2,600 feet above sea level, is so high that agriculture cannot be
carried out in the winter. In the second half of the nineteenth
century, sericulture and the manufacture of spinning silk were developed in the Suwa basin, but it is not clear how these developments
were related to population growth.

Fig. I. Map

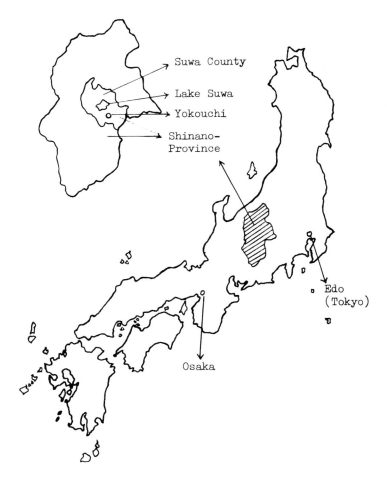

Suwa County

Lake Suwa

Yokouchi

Shinano-
Province

Edo
(Tokyo)

Osaka

2.   Demographic observations of the village
General trend The demographic history of this village as it appears
in the records started with 189 persons and 27 households in 1671.
The population grew steadily in the first hundred years, and had
grown to 524 persons by 1771. These figures are the registered population which is based on the number registered in the shumon aratame

cho. If we obtain the actual population by subtracting from the registered population those who went out to work and by adding those who entered the village to work, the increase is from 184 persons to 493. In any event, the increase in population was rapid, and moreover, it continued over a 100 year period. The average growth rate per year was as high as 0.9%. (Fig. II)

Fig. II. Population Trends, Number and Mean Size of Households

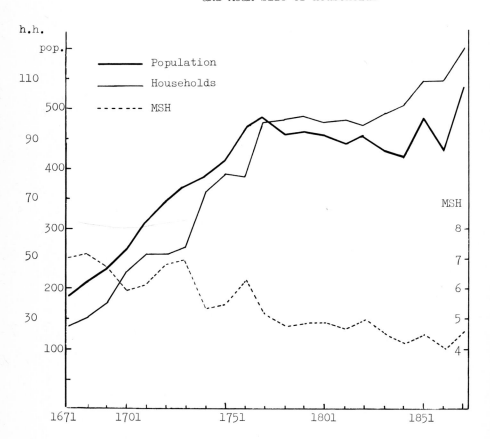

Compared to the growth in population, the growth in the number of households was even greater. During the same period the number of households increased 3.6 times, from 27 to 98. Naturally this meant a decrease in the average number of family members, namely, a change toward smaller families. In general it can be said that in the sixteenth and seventeenth centuries there was a movement away from the large households of the pre-Tokugawa period which contained subordinate labor toward the creation of the nuclear family in the farming villages. In this village also, according to the materials of the beginning of the period, more than 15% of the households had more than ten members. Compared to this, by the middle of the eighteenth century, the figure had become less than 9% and the average number of persons per household had fallen from 7.0 persons to 5.9. (Table I)

Table I. Distribution of Households by the Number of Married Couples and by the Household Size

Year	1671	1722	1771	1823	1871
Married Couples per Household					
0	2	3	14	15	32
1	13	28	57	65	69
2	9	15	21	20	17
3	3	5	4	1	1
4	-	-	1	-	-
Average	1.48	1.43	1.17	1.07	0.88
Household Size					
1	-	-	1	5	9
2	1	2	6	9	9
3	1	6	14	14	20
4	3	6	18	22	20
5	4	4	23	17	32
6	2	10	10	15	15
7	4	5	9	8	8
8	2	5	4	5	4
9	5	4	3	1	-
10	4	4	5	1	-
11	1	3	3	-	1
12	-	-	-	3	-
13	-	-	1	1	-
14	-	-	-	-	1
15	-	2	-	-	-
Average	7.00	6.67	5.36	4.87	4.45

This phenomenon was not based on a fall in the birth rate. In the early period there remained to some extent households which included unmarried blood relatives and unrelated members such as genin and gejo, subordinate male and female workers. These gradually disappeared and small families composed of only one couple and their children became the general trend. Consequently, the percentages of the married went from 47.2% for males and 55.9% for females aged 16-50 in the fourth quarter of the seventeenth century to 54.2% for males and 76.1% for females in the third quarter of the eighteenth century. (Table II) It is thought that this trend toward small families was already relatively well developed in the period for which we have materials but it is necessary to take note of this because it is one of the most important factors in the rapid population growth in the first half of the Tokugawa period.

The above population trends underwent a complete change in the fourth quarter of the eighteenth century. First, the total population of the village was stabilized and up until the new population increases in the latter half of the nineteenth century, there were some short-term changes but the population as a whole remained almost completely stationary. The growth rate for the second 100 year period averaged 0.05% per year. Families became nearly as small as was possible, but even so, the number of households increased out of proportion with the increases in population, and the average number

Table II. Proportions Married

(1) Male

(per cent)

Age \ Periods	1671-1700	1701-1725	1726-1750	1751-1775	1776-1800	1801-1825	1826-1850	1851-1871
16-20	-	2.2	-	-	-	2.7	1.2	0.4
21-25	39.8	33.6	18.0	13.5	9.0	22.9	10.5	8.6
26-30	54.4	74.1	58.7	51.8	35.4	53.4	64.2	36.2
31-35	65.6	92.7	88.9	73.0	58.8	74.8	80.0	68.6
36-40	80.6	91.0	82.2	90.7	90.2	84.0	83.3	76.6
41-45	78.7	89.0	88.4	95.9	86.6	93.6	97.7	89.1
46-50	89.7	94.6	97.6	98.2	89.4	90.0	85.7	79.6
16-50 Total	47.2	64.5	50.1	54.2	48.7	62.6	50.0	46.4

(2) Female

(per cent)

Age \ Periods	1671-1700	1701-1725	1726-1750	1751-1775	1776-1800	1801-1825	1826-1850	1851-1871
16-20	42.5	54.2	45.8	45.5	30.3	32.8	19.7	18.8
21-25	53.3	72.5	74.6	81.5	57.4	82.9	67.9	56.4
26-30	82.1	85.6	78.3	81.8	66.3	89.1	97.6	84.6
31-35	75.4	92.8	100.0	83.5	93.0	83.6	82.6	82.5
36-40	61.2	78.4	100.0	77.3	94.3	92.3	98.7	84.4
41-45	47.8	74.4	82.2	89.7	87.0	89.6	72.4	86.3
46-50	44.6	70.8	73.9	88.0	73.9	81.0	66.7	71.9
16-50 Total	55.9	73.9	74.7	76.1	68.9	78.9	64.6	68.3

of persons per household became still smaller, decreasing to between
4.7 and 5 persons. The percentage of the married, after reaching a
peak in the first half of the period, leveled off, and in the long
run perhaps tended to decrease.

Age structure Next let's look at the age structure by period.[2]
In the first half of the 200 year period, the half in which there
was a high population growth rate, and particularly up until the
seventeenth century, the typical form of the recorded population was
pyramid shaped. However, in the second half of the period, from the
second half of the eighteenth century, the typical form was closer to
the bell-shaped pattern. This may have been due in part to a decline
in the percentage of infant and child mortality, but it can better be
understood as a contrast between the first 100 year period in which
there was a high birth rate and the latter 100 year period in which
the high birth rate had ended. (Fig. III)

From the above it is clear that there was a rapid increase in
population from 1671 to 1775, and that after that, up until the
1850's, the population remained stationary. The reasons for this
population increase were a rise in the percentage of married persons,
and resulting from this, a change toward smaller families and a continued high birth rate.

Birth and death rates During the period in which shumon aratame cho
were carried out, only the babies who survived were registered, and
thus it is not known what the true birth rate was. However, we can
consider the percentage of persons recorded at the age of one or two
compared to the current population an index of the birth rate. For
the fifty year period from 1671-1725 this rate was 3,5%-4,0%, and
during the next fifty years it was 2,5%-3,0%. During the final 100

Fig. III. Age Composition

(1) 1676-85 Average

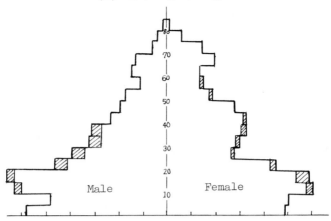

The shaded area indicates the population
working outside the village.

years it was 2,0%-2,5%. The figures for this last period are too
low, however looked at, but this is thought to be due to the unreliability of the historical materials. However, it is certain that
during the first 100 years there was a continuously high birth rate.
(Table III)

Table III. Birth and Death
Numbers and Rates

(per thousand)

Periods	Births		Deaths	
	Number	Rate	Number	Rate
1671-1700	235	36.2	170	26.2
1701-1725	316	40.9	202	26.2
1726-1750	287	29.7	209	21.6
1751-1775	318	27.5	198	17.1
1776-1800	243	21.0	233	20.2
1801-1825	283	24.9	236	20.8
1826-1850	253	22.8	216	19.5
1851-1871	224	22.5	174	17.5
Total	2159	28.2	1639	19.6

On the other hand, if we look at changes in the death rate calculated from the number of deaths of persons clearly shown in the
records to have died, we see a rate for the first fifty year period
of 2,5%, and after this period a rate of around 2,0%. These figures
also are too low to be trusted. This is due to the fact that the
recorded deaths are more imperfect than the recorded births.

The above figures are low due to the fact that infants who died
before being recorded in the shumon aratame cho are not included, and
some adjustment should be made to includes these figures. However,
because the life expectancy was extended and infant mortality decreased to a certain extent, the death rate in the second hundred
year period was probably lower than in the first hundred year period.

It is not known whether or not the material concerning infant

(2) 1751-60 Average

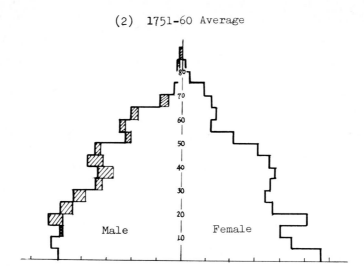

(3) 1826-35 Average

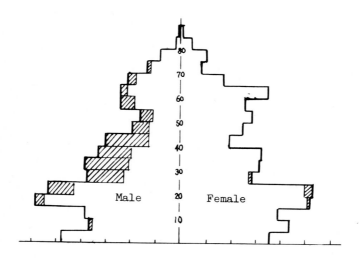

mortality became more unreliable over time, but in the first hundred
year period, on the average, out of 1,116 persons whose births were
recorded, 26% died by age five, and 31% by age 10. If we added to
this the infant and child deaths which were not recorded, it would
probably be seen that nearly 40% of the babies born died before
reaching age 10. However, the infant death rate was improved in the
first hundred year period, and while the death rate was 39% up to age
10 from 1671-1725, during the next fifty year period it fell to 26%.
(Table IV)

Table IV. Child Deaths

Periods of birth	Sex	No. of births	Number of deaths by age						Survival rate at 10
			1	2	3	4	5	6-10	
1671-1700	m.	119	-	18	6	15	4	6	0.59
	f.	108	-	14	4	9	5	5	0.66
	t.	227	-	32	10	24	9	11	0.62
1701-1725	m.	157	-	19	12	14	6	4	0.67
	f.	145	2	18	19	12	8	7	0.55
	t.	302	2	37	31	26	14	11	0.60
1726-1750	m.	155	-	9	8	7	7	13	0.72
	f.	123	-	10	8	5	5	10	0.69
	t.	278	-	19	16	12	12	23	0.70
1751-1775	m.	160	1	9	9	4	5	9	0.77
	f.	149	-	5	10	5	3	6	0.81
	t.	309	1	14	19	9	8	15	0.79
Total	m.	591	1	55	35	40	22	32	0.69
	f.	525	2	47	41	31	21	28	0.68
	t.	1116	3	102	76	71	43	60	0.69

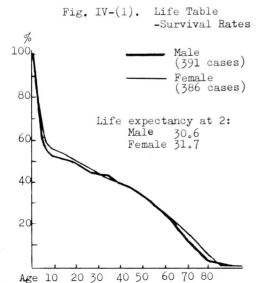

Fig. IV-(1). Life Table -Survival Rates

Male (391 cases)
Female (386 cases)

Life expectancy at 2:
Male 30.6
Female 31.7

% 100 80 60 40 20

Age 10 20 30 40 50 60 70 80

Life table If we study the
probability of deaths based
on the age of death, the
curve gradually shifts upward, and along with this,
the life expectancy at age
two is extended. In the
period 1671-1700, the life
expectancy for males was
24.8 years and that for females 29.8, but in the period
1726-1750, it rose to 34.8
years for males and 35.2 for
females. If we look at
changes in the average life
expectancy for each age
group, we see that there was
a remarkable lengthening of
life expectancy for males
under age 20 and for females
under age 40. These changes
correspond to changes in the

Fig. IV-(2). Probability of Death for Age Specific Groups

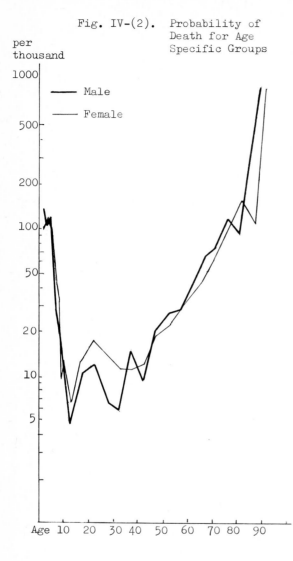

per thousand

composition of age groups and an increase in the proportion of the productive population in the total population. (Fig. IV)

Marriage Next, if we look at the age of marriage, we can see a distinct trend for females. The average age of marriage for females in the seventeenth century was 18.8 years, but in the first quarter of the eighteenth century, it dropped to 16.9 years. Gradually rising, it reached 21.7 years in the latter half of the nineteenth century. For males there was a stable trend of between 25.6 and 28.5 years. (Fig. V)

Flowing out of labor Another interesting aspect is the population exodus, especially that of the male labor force. In the beginning, the numbers were not very large, and those who left were generally employed in agriculture in neighboring areas. Naturally, a certain number of persons from other villages came into Yokouchi, but very soon the destination of persons leaving their villages changed from neighboring villages to Edo (now Tokyo) where they became employed in the commercial or service sectors. The numbers of those who left Yokouchi village began to increase from the second quarter of the eighteenth century, and at the peak, about 30% of the male labor force worked in Edo or other places. (Fig. VI)

What we know about the demographic history of this village from the basic figures is as follows: At the beginning of the 200 year period, the type of large farms which depended on subordinate labor was still in existence. Consequently, there were many unmarried persons. The marriage rate and consequently the birth rate were limited to a low level. But at the next stage, small farming became predominant, and the family became the unit for farming. Unmarried persons rapidly disappeared and the marriage and birth rates soared to their

Fig. V.   Mean Age at Marriage

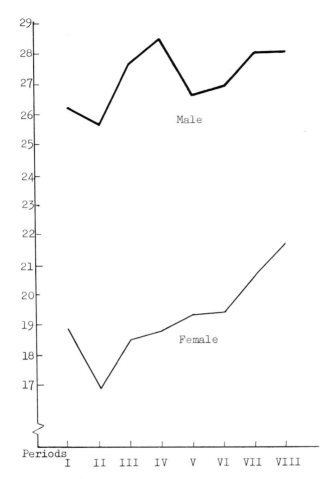

maximums. But when the exodus of labor began, the rates went down
and the population was stabilized.

This population stagnation in the latter half of the Tokugawa
period has been frequently spoken of as a Malthusian equilibrium.
Perhaps the economic conditions became so unfavorable that the inhabitants of the village had to choose between bringing down their
standard of living or controlling the number of births. There was
very little room for bringing down the living standard, and this led
them to choose the second method. In the first place, they began to
delay the age of marriage, and then to control the number of births,
usually through abortion or infanticide. From 1671-1725, married
women who survived until age 45 with their husbands had 6.5 births
if the women married between ages 15-20, 5.9 births if married at
21-25, and 1.5 if at over 26. In contrast to this, a hundred years
later, from 1776 on, women averaged 3.6-3.8 births whenever they

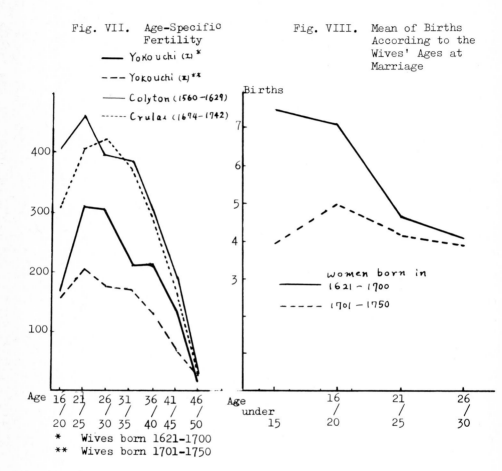

Fig. VII.   Age-Specific
            Fertility
      ——— Yokouchi (Ⅰ) *
      ― ― ― Yokouchi (Ⅱ) **
      ——— Colyton (1560-1629)
      ----- Crulai (1674-1742)

Fig. VIII.   Mean of Births
             According to the
             Wives' Ages at
             Marriage

women born in
——— 1621 - 1700
― ― ― 1701 - 1750

 * Wives born 1621-1700
** Wives born 1701-1750

Fig. IX. Fertility According to the Age
at Marriage

(1) Wives born 1621-1700   (2) Wives born 1701-1750

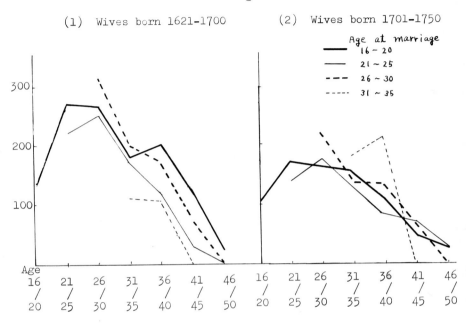

Fig. VI. The Proportion of the
Population Working
Outsides of the Village

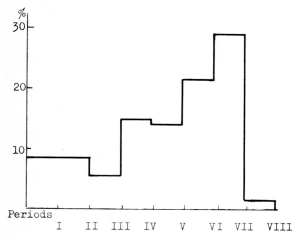

Periods
    I   II   III   IV   V   VI VII VIII

married. I think this
change was due to the
practice of birth con-
trol. (Table V)

3. FRF Analysis
    Next I want to
report the results of
tracing the demographic
behavior of married
couples in the first 100
year period, the period
for which the materials
are most reliable. In
this village, there was
a total of 168 married
couples in which the
wife was born before
1700. Among these, 39
were already registered
as married in the first
year for which we have
materials, 1671, and
consequently it is not
known at what age they
began their married
life. There were 56
women for whom the
period of married life
is known, and who con-
tinued to be married
until the end of the
possible childbearing
age at 50. And there
were 73 women whose
married life ended be-
fore the end of the
childbearing age. For
those whose married life
ended before the child-
bearing age was over,
in 33 cases the husband
died, in 28 cases the
woman herself died, 11
marriages ended in di-
vorce, and the reasons

Table V. Average Number of Births
by Age at Marriage

	Age at marriage	Average number of births	Cases
Females married 1671-1725	under 20	6.5	39
	21-25	5.9	7
	26-30	1.5	2
	over 31	2.3	3
Females married 1726-1775	under 20	4.2	67
	21-25	3.4	19
	26-30	3.0	6
	over 31	1.0	1
Females married 1776-1821	under 20	3.7	50
	21-25	3.6	39
	26-30	3.8	6
	over 31	1.5	2

for the remaining 23 are unclear. After a wife died or was divorced,
80% of the husbands remarried. In contrast to this, the remarriage
rate for women after their husband died or divorced them was a very
low 20%.
    If we look at the number of births by age groups of married
women, we see that the annual number of births for women aged 16-20
was 0.166, for women aged 21-30 it was just over 0.3 births, for
women aged 31-40 just over 0.2 births, and practically none for women
over 40. The peak in births is between ages 21-30, and the number

falls in a staircase pattern for each succeeding age. The number of births in the under 20 age group is surprising small. The age of marriage and the number of births are naturally correlated, as are the number of years the marriage continued and the number of births, but there is a higher correlation between age and the number of births. Consequently, there is a greater effect from postponing the age of marriage past 20 than by reducing the age of marriage to less than 20. Under the age of 20, as the age of marriage is raised one year the number of births varies by only 0.2. In contrast to this, the number of births varies by 0.3 per year for every year that the age of marriage is raised in the 21-30 age group. There is evidence for this in the fact that as a whole the birth rate fell from the second half of the eighteenth century due to the fact that the average age of marriage was raised to over 20. (Fig. VII, VIII and IX)

Next, if we look at the interval between births of mothers born before 1700, we see that the average interval from marriage to the birth of the first child is 3.2 years, and the interval between the first and the second child is 3.1 years. The interval between the second and third child was 3.3 years. The average interval between the fifth and sixth child rose to 3.9 years, but after this the gap narrowed to around 3 years. The fact that the order seems to have almost nothing to do with the average interval between births means that women who bore many children continued to bear them at about the same intervals to a firly advanced age. The fact that the number of births falls as a whole with an increase in age is due to an increase in the number of women who completely stopped having children.

Because there are few examples, it cannot be definitely said that there is a difference in the sex ratio according to the order of birth. Even so, the following extremely interesting trend can be observed. Namely, of first born children, 77 were males and 88 females, a sex ratio of 87.5, while of last born children 74 were males against 55 females, or a sex ratio of 134.5. Gradually the percentage of males increased. It was not possible to prove whether this was due to natural or artificial influences.

4. A Conclusion

The example of this village is only one out of tens of thousands in the Tokugawa period, but the population changes for Japan as a whole are almost the same as for this village. It has been considered up to now that the total population of Japan in the beginning of the seventeenth century was 18 million, but this is a completely unscientific estimate. I have shown that this figure, viewed in the light of local historical materials of the first half of the seventeenth century, is an overestimate, and that the population was probably less than 10 million. In 1721, the first national population survey was carried out by the Tokugawa government, and this survey reported a population of 26 million. In any case, from the seventeenth century to the beginning of the eighteenth century, the population of Japan increased rapidly. This increase, to some extent, was due to the increase in the urban population due to the rapid establishment of castle towns. However, the increase in the farm village population was even greater. As can be seen in the case of Yokouchi village, it was possible for the population to triple in a hundred year period. However, after 1721, there was almost no change in the national population according to the Tokugawa government surveys. The survey became increasingly inaccurate, but up until the final survey in 1846 the recorded population fluctuated at around 26-28 million. In 1872, the new household registration system came into existence. Reliable national population figures based on this registration showed a population of 35 million, and thus the population in the latter part of the Tokugawa period was not at all stationary. In certain areas there was continuous growth. However, the growth rate in the latter half of the Tokugawa period was in any case lower than that of the first half. The changes in the national trends and in the trends of Yokouchi village resemble each other.

Hasty conclusions should be avoided, but it is my opinion that the various figures drawn from this village can be taken as a national model. We don't know when the rapid population growth in Yokouchi village began to take place, but it is probably that it began at the same time that the change to small families began to take place, following changes in agriculture. At the same time there was probably an improvement in housing and food, and a rise in the standard of living. Thus the infant and child mortality rate fell and the average life expectancy was lengthened. As a result, the increase in population was greater than the birth rate.

No problems arose as long as this increased population was combined with an increase in other production requisites, in the case of this village, with an increase in cultivated land. However, in the second half of the eighteenth century, the area which could be reclaimed into cultivated land reached its limit. Further increases in the population resulted in an exodus of the population to go to work in the cities. Furthermore, the excess in population caused great changes in the demographic history of this village from this time on. The people in Yokouchi were forced to somehow cope with more people than the village could support. Leaving the village to work elsewhere formed one solution. In addition, the age of marriage for females was raised, and to some extent there was a decrease in the percentage of the married.

However, we cannot say that the population stagnation in the latter half of this 200 year period resulted from the above factors. In explaining the sharp contrast between the first and second hundred years, it is surmised that population control was being carried out. Conversely, the demographic history of this village in the first hundred year period is an example of a transitional period in which population control was not necessary. An average yearly growth rate of slightly under 1% is not at all exceptional; rather if other factors remain in balance, this is a normal growth rate. This situation can be seen in other villages which I have analyzed. In these villages also, it was possible to reclaim land for cultivation. In short, the above example shows that when it was not necessary to control the size of the population, and when there were no famines or epidemics, it was possible for an increase of this extent to take place in the pre-industrial society of Japan.

I began this type of research into the demographic history of the Tokugawa period using series of shumon aratame cho or religious registrations only a few years ago organizing an informal study group. Collecting and organizing the materials and then translating them into statistics takes a tremendous amount of time, and thus up to now we have only be able to report on the results of a very few analyses. However, if work progresses as expected, it will be possible

to obtain a number of studies similar to this one. Because
there are numerous good materials, it should be possible for
me and the group to report on a number of similar studies in
the very near future. (3)

R E F E R E N C E S

(1) Japan from 1600 to 1870

(2) It should be noted that both the calendar year and the
calculation of age in the Tokugawa period differed from that
of the West.   The differences in the calendar have been largely
ignored in this paper, but all ages mentioned have been calculated according to the Japanese method. This method is to count
a person as being one year of age at birth, and to add one year
at the beginning of every new calendar year. Thus it is
necessary to subtract approximately one year from every age
mentioned in order to obtain the age according to the Western
method of calculation.

(3) These are our selected list of articles written in English.
A. HAYAMI, "The Population at the Beginning of the Tokugawa
Period." Keio Economic Studies. Vol. 4, 1966-67.
A. HAYAMI, "The Demographic Analysis of a village in Tokugawa
Japan: Kando-Shinden of Owari Province, 1778-1871."   Keio
Economic Studies. Vol. 5, 1968.
A. HAYAMI, "Population History of a village in Pre-industrial
Japan." (to be published in the "DAEDALUS Historical Demography
Special Issue.")

10

THE INTERDEPENDENCE OF ECONOMIC AND DEMOGRAPHIC

DEVELOPMENT IN HUNGARY (FROM THE MIDDLE OF THE

XVIIITH TO THE MIDDLE OF THE XIXTH CENTURY)

ROBERT HORVATH

(SZEGED UNIVERSITY, HUNGARY)

Many scholars have dealt with the problem of the interdependence of economic development and population growth in
Europe, - the most recent being Prof. John HABAKKUK of Oxford
University in England in his scholarly paper, published in
1962. (1) However, due to the wide varieties of the different
growth patterns and population trends, it is interesting to
enter more thoroughly into the details of these problems, by
studying the whole complex in the different areas, roughly
corresponding to the national economic and political boundaries. (2)

Despite the fact, that the problem of an overall Hungarian
historic demography has not yet been solved (3) and that a
synthesis of Hungarian economic history, based on available
demographic, economic and social statistics is also making its
first steps in these days (4), it is an alluring task to widen
the research work in this direction. Therefore the scope of
this paper is to describe in a rather sketchy way the interdependence of the population problem and the economic development in Hungary by summarising my own studies in this field.
However, the period covered does not start from the liberation
from Turkish domination of the main parts of this country (1718),
but from the fifties of the XVIIIth century, i.e. the decade
from which the first reliable population data are available. (5)
It ends with the beginning of the War of Independence (1848-49),
that is to say, with the period which may be considered the

pre-statistical era in Hungary. The activity of official statistics in the modern sense of the word was started in this com
country only after these historical events. (6) This section
of Hungarian economic and demographic history corresponds
roughly to the pattern of the agrarian type of social development in the pre-capitalistic era, such as the War of Independence marks the rise of capitalist development in Hungary.

By entering first into the problem of population change,
the most outstanding point in the period under survey, - covering a century -, is the poor quality of our limited information,
which prevails for the period before 1850 for Hungary as in
most European countries taken into consideration by Prof.
HABAKKUK's paper. Even its institutional origins seem to be
more stationary in Hungary than in most European countries west
of Hungary, since the emancipation from serfdom was somewhat
slower and occurred in 1848 and the process of industrialisation
was upheld by the somewhat colonial position reserved for this
country in the bigger economic framework of the Hapsburg-
Empire. The very beginning of the industrialisation on a large
scale corresponding to capitalist development - as the most
recent studies have once again stressed (7) -, is not more
remote than the forties of the XIXth century, when KOSSUTH and
his followers initiated their campaign for the protection of
the national manufacturing industry (1844). (8).
The overwhelming agrarian character of the Hungarian
feudal society and the rigid framework of the feudal land-
tenure system has not permitted an expansion of population
growth of more than 1.0 percent per annum, - i.e. less than
the average rate in Europe. As another slight difference to
the West-European trend, the distribution of this secular
yearly average of 1.0 percent was also more uneven: its
maximum rate was reached at the beginning of the period in
question. At the end - as the author of the present paper
supposes - it ought to be even lower, considerably under 1.0
percent for the whole country.
This supposition may be deducted and generalised from
the pilot-studies of the author resulting from his rediscoveries
of Professor HATVANI's data concerning the vital statistics of
the town of Debrecen for 1750-54 (9) and those of János FEJES
for the entire Kis-Hont county in Northern Hungary for the year
1803 (10). Debrecen had, in the four - year period mentioned,
some 27,000 inhabitants and the population of Kis-Hont county
was approximately 16,000 in the above mentioned year./- The
most frequently quoted data from the Hungarian statistical
literature, covering the last decade of the XVIIIth and the
first half of the XIXth centuries, are pointing in the same
direction.
The lag behind the European population growth may be
attributed to the fact that the economic resources of the
country were not wholly mobilised, despite other special factors
at work, among them the resettling of the regained territories

from Turkish domination and the fertility of the famous Hungarian soil. This latter played a very considerable part in this
process, and was clearly demonstrated in the works of the best
Hungarian classical economist, Gregor BERZEVICZY. He was
of the opinion, that the yearly subsistence of the whole
Hungarian population might have been produced at the end of
the XVIIIth century in the county Bihar (East Hungary on
the Transylvanian border). (11) Such a view was commonly
held by a number of economic and statistical writers of this
time.

      The traditional mechanism of population change, described
by Prof.HABAKKUK in his above mentioned paper, was based on
the establishment through marriage of a separate household for
serf-population, with a fixed age at marriage. This was
done in order to maintain the accustomed standard of living.
However, I want to stress the point, that this pattern of
population development involved the exclusion of a fragment
of the population from marriage-possibilities by the autonomous population movement, as the size of serf-tenure was
pressed downwards to the lowest possible economic limit, -
i.e. to a quarter-tenure.

      This is also confirmed by the statistical observations
of LE PLAY in his famous series of monographs concerning
the living conditions of worker's families from the two
worlds. LE PLAY was describing the life of a Hungarian serf-
family in the forties of the XIXth century near the borough
Hatvan in the Northern part of the Great Hungarian Plain (12).
The facts presented by him were checked by the most eminent
Hungarian historian of his day, Michael HORVÁTH, making LE
PLAY's data of strong documentary character. He has found,
that in an average serf-family there are always one or two
elder brothers or sisters, working as helping hands, and
thus deprived of marriage possibilities. This confirms the
views of our eminent contemporary scholar, Prof. SAUVY, concerning the well-functioning of traditional population groups
on a firm institutional basis (13). LE PLAY, in conclusion,
was of the opinion that the average Hungarian serf-family
was better fed, than all others enumerated in his collection
of monographs for Europe, but their dwelling and other living
conditions were extremely simple although sanitary enough,
i.e. appropriate to peasant living conditions of those days.

      This kind of population development, however, was
narrowed down through the expropriation of the collective
pastures of villages by the big-landowners, when the beginnings
of capitalist farming were gaining ground in the country, -
especially during the end of XVIIIth and the beginning of the
XIXth century. This roughly corresponds to the time, when
the inner colonisation of the liberated areas from Turkish rule
came to an end. The best Hungarian statistician of this period,
Martin SCHWARTNER, Professor of the only university of the
country, the University of Pest, expressed the idea some twenty
years before RICARDO, that the interests of the big landowners and the landed gentry were opposed to the country's
population interests, including the best economic use of land.

The interests of the latter favoured especially the extension of extensive animal farming, capital accumulation and credit possibilities (being almost nil) resulting in the diminution of the number of land-tenures. (14).

Originally the territories regained from Turkish domination were redistributed by the so-called"Neoacquistica" - Commissions set up by the Hapsburg-administration, with the aim of an inner colonization of the country. The migrants were coming mainly from the northern and to some minor extent from the western part of the country, which had been liberated from Turkish rule. Also, foreign immigrants were called in from Mid-European and Western countries by the Hapsburg-rulers and by the new big-landowner class, established through the activity of the said Commissions. This kind of development came to an end with the exhaustion of inner colonization possibilities by the end of the XVIIIth century. (15)

This traditional mechanism of population growth, identified by Prof. HABAKKUK as the functioning of the Malthusian preventive check, was supplemented by other factors corresponding in his line of thought to the positive checks in the form of wars, diseases, famines and misery. The presence of these factors may be observed also in Hungary in the period under survey, but there is more than scanty statistical evidence available concerning their effects on population development.

As a matter of fact, no major war devastated this area in the period under review. The 7 Years War of MARIA THERESIA and the Turkish War of JOSEPH II were fought abroad. The Napoleonic Wars involved again the armies of the Hapsburg-Empire, but only the campaign of 1809 has transformed a part of Transdanubia (i.e. the western part of the country) to a battlefield (near to the town Győr). Here the Hapsburg armies with a strength of 50.000,- of whom only the half were counted as Hungarian nationals -, lost some 3000 soldiers in action. (16) From this time on up to the War of Independence in 1848-49, no major disturbances occurred. In the statistical and demographic literature of the period the population losses due to war were treated only in general terms and not in figures. More emphasis was laid on the unfavourable effects of the recruiting system. According to the said sources, it was damaging the population stock not only numerically by rending marriage impossible owing to the 12 years service-time, but also qualitatively by enrolling the most healthy individuals (17).

Diseases were connected closely to wars, especially pest-epidemics brought in from Turkish territories through the intermediary of Hungarian troups and communicated to the armies of other European powers. This was also referred to by SÜSSMILCH in his "Divine Order". (18) However, with the introduction of inoculation and vaccination at the turn of the XVIIIth and XIXth centuries, pest cases were no longer recorded. Those recorded were sporadic and restricted to the Turkish border. Later on, of the massive epidemics recorded only the cholera epidemics of the years 1830-31 and 1866-67

may be further quoted, and the famines connected with them in
some regions of the country, owing to the rigid "cordon sanit-
aire" introduced, (19). Paul MAGDA when giving a statistical
and geographical description of the country at the end of the
second decade of the XIXth century, was of the opinion, that
the subsistence level of the country-people was very uneven,
owing more to the existing differences of cultivated soil, than
to the fluctuation of harvest results, - especially in the highlands. (20) Many economic thinkers from TESSEDIK to BERZEVICZY
denounced the deficiencies of the inner communication system;
both the lack of inner markets and the ensuing impossibility to
eliminate local insufficiencies in the alimentation of the
population. (21)

As signs of misery, mention must be made of the
problem of the village poor, - whose number seemed to be
increasing during the period under survey acording to a small-
sample of TESSEDIK taken from the borough Szarvas and covering
the years 1776-85 and 1806-1818. (22) Another feature of the
same problem was represented by the increase of the number of
popular bandits "betyars" fighting the rich and the oppressors
let them be Austrians or Turks, the memory of which is preserved
in the folklore of the time.

The above synthesis points to the direction that the
traditional pattern of population change in the first half of
the period in question, i.e. from 1750 to 1800, were influenced
more actively by the extraordinary phenomena in Hungary than in
the second one, i.e. from 1800 to 1850. During this whole period
the vital statistical evidence reveals a great uniformity
according to my former research (23) - and as a consequence,
the pressure of population despite a greater fragmentation of
holdings must have been considerably greater in the second half
of the said period, than in the first half. This population
trend may be considered as the demographic basis of the first
modern tendencies for industrialisation in the forties, as outlined above.

In spite of his observations, concerning the beginnings of capitalist development in agricultural production,
SCHWARTNER has made an optimistic forecast of future population
trends. When weighing the future possibilities of industrialisation he estimated (1809-11) that the population of the whole
country would be doubled in fifty years time. However, the
first real Hungarian demographer, John FEJES, in his first
Hungarian treatise on demography of the same time (1812), fixed
this period with a more realistic and accurate approximation of
120 years. The basis of his interpretation was provided by
his statistical data for his home county Kis-Hont (Northern
Hungary), with poorer soil than average and with the first
recorded appearance of families with one child. (24)

In the preceding section of our paper many aspects of the
economic development of Hungary in those days had already been
mentioned or referred to, - especially the main phenomenon

consisting of the abundancy of unused land, devastated by the
Turks and subsequently by the liberating armies. The rise in
agricultural output was fostered especially by the new methods
brought up as a consequence of the Agrarian Revolution, i.e.
by the introduction of root crops, artificial grasses, potatoe-
planting, crop-rotation and also by the use of agricultural
machines.

As I pointed out some years ago, this evolution was first
focused upon by Prof. HATVANI, who discussed problems of
agricultural technology, - as early as the fifties of the
XVIIIth century, in his lectures at the Old Helvetian College
in Debrecen. This evolution has gained ground by the activity
of his followers, especially by TESSEDIK and PETHE from the
eighties on in the same century. (25) These new methods were
adopted mainly on the big estates, but the technical progress
has had rapid access also in the settlers-region and gradually
also on the serf-tenures.

The rise in prices was to be observed during this
Hungarian evolution as well as the rise in Europe. This was
clearly shown by the statistics of prices accumulated by
TESSEDIK from the years 1767-1804. (26) It revealed however, -
according to my interpretation -, not only the "inflexibilities
in the supply of agricultural products in face of a growing
population" as Prof. HABAKKUK formulated it, but also the
incompatibility of the communication system in the country with
the exigencies of a more market-oriented economy. Similarly,
the surplus demand created by wars and the first experiences
of the Hapsburg-administration with paper-money up to the
twenties of the XIXth century had played also an important role
in this process.

The problem of transport facilities appropriate to a
capitalistic minded agricultural production was in Hungary a
more difficult one than in England during the Industrial
Revolution, - despite the fact that big rivers were abundant
in the country and the horse-stock was also suited to local
traffic conditions. In general, horses were used not only for
passenger transport, but also as traction power in the grain
trade for pulling the ships upstream. Indications of decreasing
quality and quantity of the horse-stock are available from
the eighties of the XVIIIth century on, when the technical
progress in agriculture increased the number of the first
primitive machines in use. The deterioration of the situation
was shown by the first printed work at the end of the 20's of
the XIXth century written by Stephen SZÉCHENYI, the greatest
political reformer of the early capitalist development of
Hungary. This work entitled "On horses" documented with
with statistics the fact that the density of horses per square-
mile in the country was already lower than in selected
European countries. (27) The spreading of windmills (according
to the Dutch model) on the Great Hungarian Plain considerably
alleviated this pressure later on, (28) but the subsequent war
periods had exercised a slow-down effect. The cattle-trade
solved its transportation problems for domestic demand and
also for export without difficulties by driving a yearly

export stock of 80,000 cattle on foot, (though with a considerable loss, - according to statistical sources.) (29)
    During the whole period the need for development of the
internal river communication-system was strongly felt in the
country. Many blueprints were elaborated for the building of
canals between the Danube and Tisza and the Francis-canal in
South-Hungary became a reality at the beginning of the XIXth
century linking together the rivers Temes and Bega. Later on,
the regulation of water level of the Tisza and the lower section
of the Danube was begun through canalisation and the first chain-
bridge between Buda and Pest was built under the influence of
SZECHENYI. (30) The latter event rendered it possible to unite
the two cities in following years (1876), thus laying the
economic foundations of the development of a real industrial
center in the country. Nevertheless, the absence of railway-
communication is striking in the whole period under survey.
The beginning was dated from the year 1847, when the first
trunk-line between the towns Pest and Vac was built (34 kms)
in the Northern direction from the natural economic center of
the country.
    This underdeveloped state of the communication-system, was
due to the retarded establishment of the first centers for an
iron manufacturing industry, even if steam-power was occasionally
introduced. However, their geographic distribution was a very
uneven one similar to the few cloth and porcelain manufactures
founded in this time. A more solid impetus was given to this
trend of industrialisation by the economic policy advanced by
KOSSUTH in the forties and by the break-out of the War of
Independence with the need of massive production of military
equipment within the country. During the Napoleonic Wars,
according to my sources, the solution of this problem was reached on the guild-basis. (31) As main industrial area, the mining
region of Northern Hungary was mentioned by LE PLAY in his
description of a typical Hungarian industrial worker-family
just before the War of Independence . (32)
    From my whole line of thought - I think - any idea of an
overvaluation of industrial progress in the period under survey
must be avoided. This is proved also by the fact that the
main trend of population development was concentrated on the
agricultural area and not in towns. Another characteristic
might be the fact, that the economic literature even in the
last decades of the period, as represented by the works of
MAGDA, ERDELYI and FENYES, (33) treated almost exclusively
the problems of land economics. The only scientific material
dealing with questions of modern industrial society was contributed by the most outstanding personality of the Hungarian
economic policy of the epoch, KOSSUTH. Nevertheless, his
approximation was dated from his second London-emigration
during the years 1858-59, while he was under the influence of
the Industrial Revolution in England and its theoretical
literature. (34)
    Economic development was in the whole period slowed down
in a special way by the almost total absence of accumulation of
capital and the institutional framework of credit. SZECHENYI
stressed in his 1830 work, "On credit", the absurdity of

feudal legal conditions prohibiting the selling and hypothecation
of the estates of the nobility. This represented a major draw-
back (35) toward the transformation into capitalist modes of
production.

The scarcity of capital came to light even earlier in
a). the report of the few Hungarian merchants who were prepared
for the use of the Commercial Commission of the feudal Diet of
1790 and b). in the economic writings of BERZEVICZY between
1797-1819. Here the necessity of the creation of a banking and
credit system and the foundation of big commercial and transport
companies with the participation of the wealthiest magnates was
already dealt with. (36) However, the realisation of these
claims was connected to the industrial policy of KOSSUTH inaugur-
ated in the 1840's, furthering the founding of a commercial
bank ready to fulfil the functions of a Hungarian National Bank,
too. (37) The importance of this new development could be
understood only with regard to the fact that the central financial institutions of the Hapsburg-Monarchy never extended
their field of activity - (or if the did, then only sporadically)
- in this period to the Hungarian economy.

IV.

Summarising the results of the second and third sections
of my paper, one may say, that the interdependence of economic
and population development in Hungary during the period dealt
with seems to correspond narrowly with the RICARDO-type
mechanism as elaborated by W.A.LEWIS and referred to by
HABAKKUK. According to it, population growth was the leading
factor in economic development encouraging the spreading and
widening of more intensive production methods and this factor
created the opportunities for further investments from the
demand side. This explanation is also in close conformity with
the solution elaborated by MARX himself in his "Capital",
following not only the line of true Ricardian traditions but
on a larger scale that of economic, historical and statistical
evidence. (38)

This picture of Hungarian development during the transition period of an agrarian feudal society on the threshold of
capitalism is in its essence, very similar to that of the
Prussian society, analysed in the main works of SÜSSMILCH
between 1741-1762. (39) However, comparing Hungarian and
Prussian intiial conditions to capitalist development,. the
Prussian society was in a more favourable position owing to
different factors. Ths most important among them seems to be
the small-holder policy of FREDERIC the Great, representing
an early attempt to supplant a capitalist agricultural
development on to the shoulders of an economically impoverished
and weakened nobility. The possibilities of such an experiment
were given by the more remote and less devastating demographic
and economic effects of the 30-Years War, and by the subsequent
and more advanced industrialisation and urbanisation of the
Prussian held territories.

Despite this agrarian policy of the soldier-king, motivated also strongly by imperialistic tendencies, the first set-backs of a capitalistic social transformation were already felt in the 1750's. SUSSMILCH was especially impressed by their similarity to that of the social effects of Industrial Revolution in England. In a recent reassessment of SÜSSMILCH's "Divine Order" I already stressed the point that to be able to avoid these harmful effects he arrived at an alternative conception of social evolution similar to the Prussian way of capitalist development based on the small-holder system. (40). The importance of this idea was recognised again in the XXth century as a hypothetic "third-way" alternative between capitalist and socialist economic development and was fostered by the agrarian reformers from HENRY GEORGE to DAMASCHKE and renewed at a higher level as a solution of an overall social reform by W. ROPKE. - This may be stated without any p practical effects.

A last remark of methodological importance is furnished by the similarity of the possible theoretical criterions as formulated by C. LÉVY. (in accordance to the suggestion of Professor SAUVY, (41) concerning the interdependence of demographic and economic - and in a larger sense social - development) between contemporary under-developed countries and our historical example of Hungary, - the problems of morality conditions and that of international aid set apart. The criterions enumerated by LÉVY - such as physiologic fecundity, rudimentary hygenic conditions, feeble alimentation, poor energy consumption, analphabetism, overwhelmingly agrarian occupational pattern, low status of women, employment of children, absence or feeble representation of middle-classes, hierarchic society -, may also be employed - mutatis mutandis - in our case. (42)

Thus, the views concerning the necessity of a complex analysis of the interdependence of demographic and economic development and its demonstration on England and France and in some selected European countries - in the volume edited and contributed by Prof. P.V.GLASS and theoretically synthetised in general by D.E.C. EVERSLEY - are again amply confirmed and justify the renewed efforts in this direction (by the International Economic History Association. (43)

From my rudimentary synthesis-given in the two main parts (II and III) of the present paper - it may be contemplated as established, that the role played by industrialisation in the proper sense cannot fully be analysed in this, but only in the subsequent period of real capitalist development in Hungary, up to World War II.

However, this part of our study based on sources and documents of a real statistical character must be reserved for a separate paper, not only for its different problems but also owing to its different method. Most probably its material cannot even be elaborated and dealt with in one homogeneous study, but must be cut in two, as a consequence of the territorial changes stipulated by the peace-treaties after World War I, and because of the ensuing artificial formation of a new economic unit with its different population in size and in demographic, economic and social properties.

R E F E R E N C E S

1). J. HABAKKUK: Population Problems and European Economic
Development in the Late Eighteenth and Nineteenth
Centuries, Papers and Proceedings of the Seventy-fifth
Annual Meeting of the American Economic Association,
1962, American Economic Review, 1963, Number 2, pp.
607 et seq.

2). Ibidem, where Prof. HABAKKUK stresses the importance of
the study by areas. Such an effort was undertaken first
by the author of the present paper with the title: The
number of the population of Hungary and the Hungarian
Demography, Történeti Statisztikai Kozleményeks,1959 ,
N. 1-2, pp. 118. and seq. (In Hungarian)

3). The volume Historical Demography of Hungary, Edited by
J. KOVACSICS, Budapest, 1963, has not solved this
problem, as it is written by its contributors-with
only one exception - by using exclusively historical
and not historical demographical methods. (In Hungarian)

4). There are many outstanding monographs available, but as
from a synthesis, mention must be made from the
university sripta of Prof. Zs.P. PACH's Hungarian
Economic History and the economic historical parts of
the more recent General Hungarian Historical Text-
books for university purposes. (In Hungarian)

5). R. HORVÁTH : Prof. Stephen Hatvani and the Beginnings of
Statistics in Hungary, Budapest, 1963, - a monography.
(In Hungarian with French and Russian Summaries).

6). R. HORVÁTH : The Significance of the Formation of the
First Official Statistical Service in Hungary, Statisztikai Szemle, 1958, N.2, pp.171 et seq. (In Hungarian)

7). T.I. BEREND - GY. RÁNKI : Historical Interpretation and
the Past of our Economic Development, Nepszabadság,
1965. 10th April, pp. 4-5. (In Hungarian).

8). R. HORVÁTH : The Progressive Ideas of Kossuth in his
Lectures on Political Economy at London University,
Acta Universitatis Szegediensis, Juridica et Politica,
Tomus X, Fasciculus 3, Szeged, 1963. (In Hungarian
with French and Russian Summaries).

9). HORVÁTH, as under 5.

10). R. HORVÁTH: Les Débuts de la Démographie en Hongrie:
János Fejes, Population, 1965, N.1, pp.109 et seq.

11). R. HORVÁTH: The Ideas of Gregor Berzeviczy on Economics and Population, Ibid., Tom. XI, Fasc. 7, Szeged, 1964. (In Hungarian with French summary)

12). P.G.F. LE PLAY : Les Ouvriers Européens, Paris, 1895.

13). A. SAUVY : Théorie Générale de la Population, Vol I. Economie et Population, Paris, 1952.

14). HORVÁTH, as under 5). - with reference to M. SCHWARTNER: Statistik des Königreichs Ungern, 2d Edition, (Ofen). Buda, 1809, Vol.I. pp.94 et seq.

15). HORVÁTH, as under 2). - where this problem was treated also in the context of the nationalities. This latter problem is therefore excluded from the line of thought of the present paper.

16). P. BAY : Napoleon in Hungary, The Emperor and his Soldiers in the Town of Győr, Budapest, 1941. pp.41 et seq. (In Hungarian)

17) HORVÁTH, as under 9). - and from the same author: Les Débuts de la Démographie en Hongrie : Janos Fejes, Population, 1965, N.1. pp.109 et seq.

18). R. HORVATH : Quelques Données inconnues sur la Mortalité de la Peste de Debrecen (1739-40) et celle de Choléra en Hongrie (1831, 1866, 1872-73). Bulletin de l'Institut International de Statistique, 33e Session, Paris, - and from the same author: "L'Ordre Divin" de Süssmilch, Population, 1962. N.2. pp.267 et seq.

19). HORVÁTH, as under 18), and from the same author: La Statistique de la Peste de Debrecen (1739-40) et du Choléra de Pest (1831) en Hongrie et leurs Conséquences Sociales, Acta Univ. Szegediensis, Jur et Pol. Tom XI, Fasc. 4, Szeged, 1962.

20). The Author of the present paper has treated these problems in detail in a paper in manuscript entitled: Paul Magda's Contributions to Hungarian Statistics and Economics . ibid., Szeged, 1968, (In Hungarian).

21). HORVÁTH, as under 11), - and from the same author: Tessedik as a social scientist, Körös Népe, Vol.IV, 1963, pp.27 et seq. (In Hungarian)

22). HORVÁTH, as under 21).

23). R. HORVÁTH : The Scientific Study of Mortality in Hungary before the Modern Statistical Era, Population Studies, 1963, N.2, pp.187 et seq.

24). HORVÁTH; as under 17).

25). HORVÁTH : Stephen Hatvani and the Origins of Economics in Hungary, Közgazdasági Szemle, 1960, N.1. pp.74 et seq. (In Hungarian)

26). HORVÁTH, as under 21).

27). R. HORVÁTH: Stephen Széchenyi and the Statistics, Statisztikai Szemle, 1967, Nr. 5 pp. 461 et seq. (In Hungarian with Russian and English summaries).

28). HORVÁTH, as under 21).

29). P. Magda: The Statistical and Geographical Description of Hungary and the Military Confines, Pest, 1819, pp. 54 et seq. (In Hungarian)

30). HORVÁTH, as under 27).

31). BAY, as under 16), - pp. 95 et seq.

32). LE PLAY, as under 12).

33). MAGDA, as under 29). and R. HORVÁTH: Alexis Fényes, the progressive Hungarian Statistician and man of reform (1808-76), Act. Univ. Szegediensis, Jur. et Pol., Tom. III, Fasc. 6. Szeged, 1957, - with reference to the works of Fényes and Erdélyi. (In Hungarian with French and Russian summaries).

34). HORVÁTH, as under 8).

35). HORVÁTH, as under 27).

36). R. HORVÁTH: Problems of the Development of Hungarian Financial and Price Statistics, Statisztikai Szemle, 1967, Nr. 8-9, pp.884 et seq.

37). HORVÁTH, as under 8).

38). HORVÁTH, as under 11).

39). HORVÁTH, as under 18).

40). Ibidem.

41). Institut National d'Etudes Démographiques: Le "Tiers-Monde" , Sous-développement et Développement, Réédition par A. SAUVY, Travaux et Documents, Cahier No. 39, Paris, 1961. Analyse du Problème by G. BALANDIER, p. 135.

42). Ibidem, Les Critères du Soud-développement by C. LÉVY,
     pp. 137 et seq.

43). Population in History, Essays in Historical Demography,
     Edited by D.V. GLASS, London 1965, - and : Population,
     Economy and Society by D.E.C. EVERSLEY, in the same
     volume, pp. 23 et seq. - Another kind of synthesis is
     represented by the work of J. STASSART : Les Avantages
     et les Inconvénients Economiques d'une Population
     Stationnaire, Collection Scientifique de la Faculté
     de Droit de l'Université de Liège, No. 20, Liège, 1965.

11

LA POPULATION EUROPEENNE DE SOUSSE AU XIXEME SIECLE

JEAN GANIAGE

SORBONNE, PARIS

I. - Sousse et ses habitants

L'installation de familles européennes sur les côtes orientales de Tunisie était un phénomène récent, puisqu'elle ne remontait pas au delà de 1820. A Sousse, à Sfax comme à Djerba, les Maltais avaient frayé la voie de l'immigration italienne. Servis sans doute par la lointaine parenté entre l'arabe tunisien et le dialecte parlé dans leurs îles, quelques uns d'entre eux étaient venus se fixer sur le continent. D'autres les avaient rejoints, bientôt imités par une poignée de Siciliens et de Napolitains. Plusieurs négociants marseillais ou génois de Tunis, intéressés dans le commerce des huiles, installaient comme correspondants à Sousse certains de leurs parents, à mesure que les navires venus

d'Europe commençaient à fréquenter les ports du Sahel.
Les tournées périodiques des missionnaires capucins de
Tunis ne pouvaient bientôt suffire aux besoins d'une colonie
catholique en plein essor. En novembre 1836, Sousse était
érigée en paroisse, une paroisse démesurément étendue
d'ailleurs, puisque son ressort englobait toutes les côtes
orientales de la Régence, depuis le cap Bon jusqu'à l'île
de Djerba (I). En 1860, la population européenne de Sousse
était évaluée à plus de 600 personnes (2), ce qui commençait à
poser des problèmes de cohabitation avec les Musulmans, même
dans une cité commerçante où se cotoyaient les éléments les
plus divers.
Sousse était en effet une ville des plus actives. Malgré
la médiocrité de son port, elle s'affirmait comme une capitale
régionale dont l'influence se faisait sentir dans le Sahel
aussi bien que dans les steppes de l'intérieur. La ville
était le principal marché des huiles de Tunisie; les nomades
y apportaient la laine et les peaux de leurs moutons.
D'Europe venaient sucre et café, les cotonnades anglaises et
les scieries de France, de la quincaillerie, des armes et de
la poudre, introduites en contrebande. Le trafic du port
variait en fonction de la récolte. Certaines années, Sousse
l'emportait sur La Goulette pour la valeur des exportations,
mais le volume des importations se maintenait à un niveau
très bas, la plupart des navires arrivant sur lest pour
charger des huiles où des grignons. De 1861 à 1865,en cinq
ans, la moyenne des échanges ne dépassait guère 4 millions
de francs, 2 à 3% des importations du pays, mais plus du
quart de ses exportations.
L'artisanat traditionnel commençait à souffrir de la
concurrence européenne. Le tissage des toiles était en pleine
décadence; la fabrication des sandales ne se maintenait que
grace à une clientèle rurale peu exigeante. Aussi le développement urbain demeurait-il limité. En 1860 encore, la
ville restait enfermée dans son enceinte du XIIIe siècle,
un quadrilatère bastionné dont la superficie ne dépassait
pas 35 hectares. Avec 8,000 habitants environ, dont 1,700
Juifs et quelque 600 Européens, Sousse était cependant la
quatrième ville de la Régence (3).
Comme les Juifs, les Européens avaient été relégués
dans le bas de la vieille ville. Ils s'entassaient au nord-
est de l'enceinte fortifiée, dans un étroit quartier voisin
de la porte de la Mer, à peu de distance du ribat et de la
grande mosquée. Faute de place, certains avaient du
s'installer au delà des remparts. Sur les terrains vagues
en bordure de la mer, ils avaient édifié de misérables
cabanes où ils campaient dans la promiscuité de leurs
volailles et de leurs chèvres qui vagabondaient sur "la mer
des ordures" (bahar ez zebla). Après chaque averse, le
quartier franc était anvahi par les eaux qui dévalaient de
la ville haute; des égouts à ciel ouvert y répandaient une
boue noirâtre et nauséabonde. Dans ce quartier malsain et
dépourvu d'eau potable, typhoide et dysenterie étaient à
l'état endémique. Les épidémies les plus graves, typhus et
surtout choléra, se manifestaient généralement à la fin du

printemps. Venant d'Egypte où de Tripolitaine, elles se pro-
pageaient du sud au nord, par Sfax ou Djerba, suivant une
progression régulière que n'arrivaient pas à entraver des
mesures de quarantaine insuffisantes.

Vers 1860, les Maltais, sujets britanniques, formaient
près des trois quarts de la colonie européenne. Les Italiens
venaient ensuite; mais ils étaient encore loin de former un
groupe homogène, partagés qu'il étaient en Siciliens,
Napolitains, Génois et Toscans, de dialectes et de genre de
vie différents. Les Français n'étaient pas plus d'une cin-
quantaine, quelques Corses, des négociants marseillais, des
Italiens naturalisés où protégés. L'Autriche n'était repré -
sentée que par une famille de commerçants, les Bogo, des
Italiens passés depuis longtemps sous la protection impériale(4).

En 1881, les Maltais étaient encore les plus nombreux
au sein d'une colonie que ne s'était pas sensiblement accrue.
Mais après l'établissement du protectorat, l'immigration de
Siciliens se developpa sur un rythme rapide, tandis que
s'installaient des familles de fonctionnaires et d'employés
français. Dès avant 1890, les Italiens étaient devenus les
plus nombreux. La recensement de 1906, le premier en date, en
dénombrait, 2,823 dans la ville, en regard de 1,469 Français et
de 874 Maltais seulement (5). Sousse avait vu sa population
doubler en un quart de siècle; mais elle le devait essentielle -
ment à l'immigration étrangère. Sur quelque 18,000 habitants
en effet, les Musulmans étaient moins de 10,000, les Européens,
5,241 et les Juifs indigènes environ 3,000 (6).

Une ville nouvelle s'était crée à l'extérieur de la
médina, toujours enfermée dans ses remparts. Dès le début du
protectorat l'armée avait installé un camp près de la
Kasbah. Un nouveau quartier s'édifiait à l'est, sur le front
de mer. Mais c'est du côté du nord que la ville nouvelle
prenait tout son essor. Le bastion qui prolongeait l'enceinte
au nord-est ayant été rasé, on put bâtir sur l'ancienne
"mer des ordures" et tracer des rues et des avenues régulières.
Au delà, deux quartiers siciliens, Capace grande au nord et
Capace piccolo au sud, se développaient en désordre dans
des régions sablonneuses où le terrain était très bon marché(7).

Visiblement, le niveau de vie de la colonie européenne
était très bas; mais, faute d'indications suffisantes, il est
difficile de se faire une idée des moyens d'existence de la
plupart des familles. A la veille du protectorat, la classe
dirigeante était représentée par une demi douzaine de
négociants, un officier et un médecin français au service
du bey, un pharmacien maltais, les employés de la ligne
télégraphique française. Napolitains et Siciliens étaient
le plus souvent pêcheurs ou maçons. Quelques Maltais étaient
désignés comme commerçants, mais la plupart d'entre eux
n'avaient pas de profession définie. Vivaient-ils tous de
contrebande, ainsi que l'assuraient les rapports des consuls
de France et d'Angleterre, qui leur attribuaient un trafic
clandestin de cotonnades, d'armes et de poudre en provenance
de Malte, d'huile et de laine en direction de l'étranger (8) ?
Les accidents mentionnés périodiquement dans les registres,

naufrage de barques maltaises, équipages massacrés par des bédouins, explosions de poudre, tendraient à le confirmer.

Presque tous étaient illettrés : 7 à 8% des Maltais seulement étaient capables de signer leur nom au moment de leur mariage, proportion qui tombait à moins de 5% chez les femmes. En revanche, presque tous les Français et près de la moitié des Italiens savaient lire et écrire. En 1892 encore, malgré l'ouverture d'écoles françaises et italiennes, près de la moitié des Européens de Sousse étaient illettrés et, en 1901, sur les registres paroissiaux, on pouvait recenser plus du tiers d'analphabètes, presque tous Siciliens où Maltais.

2 - Etude démographique (9)

Les jeunes gens et jeunes filles du quartier franc de Sousse se mariaient essentiellement entre eux. En raison de l'éloignement et de la précarité des moyens de transport, les relations avec les centres de peuplement européen les plus proches, Sfax où Tunis, étaient réduites à peu de chose. Entre 1850 et 1880, le taux d'endogamie dépassait 95%; il était encore de plus de 75% au début du XXe siècle. Les mariages avec des jeunes gens du dehors se limitaient pratiquement au milieu assez étroit des familles de négociants et de notables. Maltais où Siciliens, le petit people du quartier franc se mariait presque toujours sur place. Mais l'installation de nouveaux venus, immigrants fraîchement arrivés d'Europe où familles originaires de Tunis, élargissait périodiquement le cercle de leurs relations. Certains retournaient chercher femme au pays natal, mais il est difficile de préciser l'importance de phénomène.

Cet isolement n'était pas compensé par des relations avec les autres communautés de la ville. Nous n'avons trouvé aucune mention de mariages avec des Musulmans, convertis où non. Avec les Juifs, les unions étaient si rares (deux en cinquante ans)

Tableau I

Naissances, mariages et décès par année civile

Années	M	N	D	Années	M	N	D
1850	6	. 19	. 38	1880	9	. 36	. 17
51	2	. 17	. 3	81	7	. 35	.
52	4	. 28	. 9	82	12	. 55	. 25
53	4	. 23	. 11	83	16	. 64	. 44
54	3	. 18	. 12	84	11	. 55	. 33
55	7	. 28	. 10	85	22	. 81	. 36
56	3	. 25	. 22	86	28	. 95	. 42
57	8	. 21	. 11	87	23	. 96	. 45
58	5	. 29	. 7	88	26	.126	. 44
59	3	. 27	. 11	89	25	.111	.

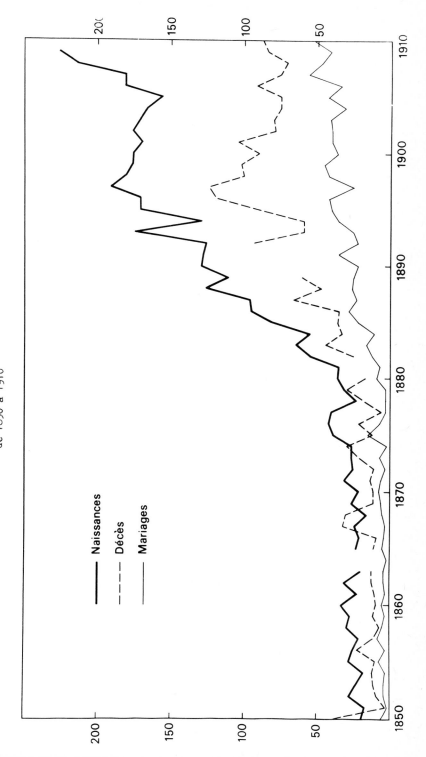

Graphique n° 1
Naissances, mariages et décès
de 1850 à 1910

Années	M	N	.D	Années	M	N	D
1860	5 .	33 .	9	1890	22 .	129 .	
61	3 .	22 .	10	91	35 .	128 .	
62	4 .	31 .	12	92	22 .	126 .	93
63	4 .	20 .	12	93	25 .	175 .	59
64	2 .	17* .	9*	94	35 .	129 .	59
65	5 .	23 .	11	95	40 .	171 .	90
66	4 .	21 .	9	96	42 .	171 .	119
67	3 .	24 .	32	97	25 .	191 .	124
68	5 .	16 .	30	98	42 .	182 .	100
69	6 .	26 .	11	99	45 .	177 .	102
1870	7 .	21 .	11	1900	36 .	176 .	90
71	6 .	31 .	12	01	40 .	170 .	104
72	3 .	24 .	10	02	40 .	177 .	79
73	7 .	26 .	20	03	41 .	172 .	80
74	2 .	26 .	28	04	31 .	166 .	75
75	15 .	39 .	10	05	43 .	156 .	75
76	7 .	42 .	22	06	34 .	181 .	91
77	3 .	40 .	6	07	56 .	181 .	75
78	3 .	23 .	18	08	47 .	213 .	71
79	3 .	31 .	29	09	41 .	226 .	84

* Aucun acte de juin à septembre 1864, la presque totalité de la population européenne ayant été évacuée pendant l'insurrection.

qu'on pouvait les tenir pour quantité négligeable (10). Comme dans la plupart des Echelles du Levant, les diverses communautés ethniques continuaient de vivre en marge les unes des autres, séparées par le strict cloisonnement des barrières confessionnelles.

Entre les catholiques, d'ailleurs les différences d'origine s'effacaient assez lentement. Les Maltais épousaient surtout des compatriotes, tandis que les Italiens, moins nombreux au début, manifestaient plus d'éclectisme. En revanche, toutes les familles de négociants étaient alliées entre elles, sans distinction de nationalité. Les Serra, les Mainetto, les Carleton, agents consulaires de Naples, de Sardaigne et de Grande-Bretagne, mariaient entre eux leurs enfants, de même que les Moro et les Vignale, Génois d'origine, les Monge et les Saccoman, sujets et protégés français.

Tableau II   Répartition des mariages selon
l'origine des conjoints
(1850-1880)

	Maltais	Italiens	Français	Divers	Total
Maltaises	85	17	1		103
Italiennes	10	20	1	2	33

	Maltais	Italiens	Français	Divers	Total
Francaises	1	2	5	1	9
Autres		2	4		6
Ensemble	96	41	11	3	151

(1890-1910)

	Maltais	Italiens	Français	Divers	Total
Maltaises	62	48	14		124
Italiennes	26	440	35	2	503
Françaises	15	16	132		163
Autres	1	3*			4
Ensemble	104	507	181	2	794

*Dont une Juive tunisienne

Avec le temps, la disproportion numérique entre les
sexes tendait à s'atténuer, malgré la persistance de
l'immigration. L'âge au mariage traduisait une évolution
sensible depuis les premières années. Sans doute les filles
se mariaient-elles encore très jeunes, certaines à 14 ans,
la plupart entre 15 et 20 (52% des cas). Du moins ne
voyait-on plus de mariées de 12 et 13 ans, comme cela se
produisait quelques années plus tôt dans le quartier franc
de Tunis. Entre 1850 et 1880, l'âge moyen au premier mariage
était de 27 ans pour les hommes et de 21 pour les femmes,
Maltais et Maltaises se mariant un peu plus tôt que les
Italiens. Les jeunes gens épousant des veufs où des veuves
étaient légèrement plus agés ceux qui épousaient d'autres
célibataires (11). Quant aux veufs et aux veuves, autant
qu'on en puisse juger d'après une vingtaine de cas, ils
avaient 41 ans et près de 31 ans en moyenne, au moment de
leur remariage.

Tableau III   Distribution des âges au mariage

| Age au | H O M M E S | | F E M M E S | | Age au |
mariage	Célib.	Veufs	Célib.	Veuves	mariage
14 ans			5		14 ans
15-19	4		50		15-19
20-24	37		40	1	20-24
25-29	57	1	22	3	25-29
30-34	18	2	7	2	30-34

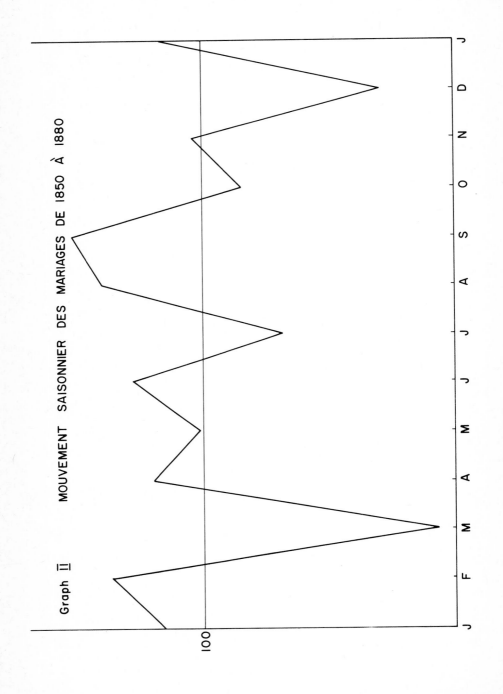

Graph II

MOUVEMENT SAISONNIER DES MARIAGES DE 1850 À 1880

Age au mariage	HOMMES Célib.	HOMMES Veufs	FEMMES Célib.	FEMMES Veuves	Age au Mariage
35-39	11	2	2	2	35-39
40-44		2		1	40-44
45-49	1	3			45-49
50 ans	1	1			50-56
Indét.	11	4	13	3	Indét.
Total	136	15	139	12	Total

La répartition des mariages au cours de l'année, comparable à celle de la paroisse de Tunis à la même époque,
offre bien des analogies avec celle de la France et de l'Italie
sous l'Ancien Régime. Elle accuse en effet des variations
mensuelles imposées par le calendrier de l'Eglise. En mars
et décembre, on retrouve ainsi les interdits du careme et
de l'avent. Mais juillet et octobre apparaissent également
comme des mois de faible nuptialité, sans qu'il soit possible
de l'expliquer (12).

Tableau IV   Mouvement saisonnier des mariages
                    (1850-1880)

Mois	Nombre absolus	Nombre Journaliers	Indice Mensuel
J	15	0,48	115,2
F	16	0,56	135,8
M	1	0,03	7,68
A	15	0,50	120
M	14	0,46	111,8
J	16	0,53	127,9
J	9	0,29	69,6
A	18	0,58	139,2
S	19	0,63	151,9
O	11	0,35	84,9
N	13	0,43	103,9
D	4	0,13	30,9
Total	151	4,99	1200

L'accroissement du nombre des naissances enregistrées
à Sousse pendant un demi siècle traduit assurément l'essor
de la population. Il souligne également le maintien d'une
fécondité des plus élevées. Si l'on retient le chiffre
de 620 habitants vers 1860, le taux de natalité apparait

supérieur à 40%. Nous retrouvons des moyennes presque aussi
fortes cinquante ans plus tard: 34,2% pour l'ensemble de la
colonie, en 1906, 38% dans le groupe italo-maltais, seulement
25% chez les Français (13).

Tableau V

Répartition des familles selon leurs dimensions

Nombre de naissances par famille	Familles complètes Nombre de		Familles incomplètes Nombre de		Ensemble des familles nombre de	
	familles	naissances	familles	naissances	familles	naissances
0	1	0	4	0	5	0
1	1	1	4	4	5	5
2	0	0	6	12	6	12
3	0	0	9	27	9	27
4	2	8	5	20	7	28
5	1	5	4	20	5	25
6	1	6	9	54	10	60
7	3	21	9	63	12	84
8	5	40	9	72	14	112
9	6	54	5	45	11	99
10	9	90	1	10	10	100
11	6	66	1	11	7	77
12	2	24	2	24	4	48
Total	37	315	68	362	105	677

Chez les familles que nous avons reconstituées (14), la
moyenne des naissances est de 6,4 par couple, 8.5 pour les
familles complètes, 5.3 pour les autres. Les premières naissances
survenaient généralement moins d'une année après le mariage, la
durée moyenne de l'intervalle étant de 14.8 mois. Comme on
pouvait s'y attendre, les cas les plus fréquents correspondent
à des intervalles de 9 et 10 mois. (15). S'il est impossible
de départager naissances prématurées et conceptions antenup-
tiales, du moins pouvons nous constater que celles-ci n'étaient
pas fréquentes, guère plus de 5% des femmes se trouvant enceintes
au moment de leur mariage. Le nombre des naissances illégitimes
était encore plus faible : 13 sur 808 en trente ans, ce que
correspond à un taux de 1.6%.

Nous avons retrouvé des résultats classiques en ce qui

Graph. no. 3

Fécondité légitime

Comparaison avec quelques populations anciennes

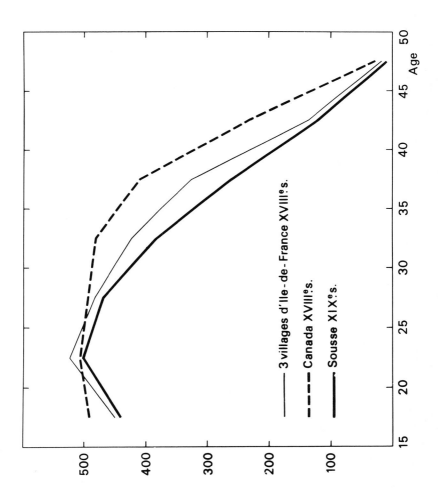

concerne l'espacement des naissances. La durée de l'intervalle intergénésique passe en effet de 25 à 14 mois,selon que le premier enfant a survécu où non, ce qui souligne le rôle de l' allaitement maternel.
Le tableau VI illustré par le graphique no.3, permet de suivre les variations du taux de fécondité légitime, selon l'âge des femmes. La courbe, que dessine une crosse très régulière, atteint son point le plus élevé entre 20 et 24 ans,elle s'abaisse ensuite progressivement pour atteindre sa valeur la plus faible entre 45 et 50 ans. Le taux de fécondité légitime est égal à 11, un résultat très proche de celui que nous avions trouvé pour la paroisse de Tunis à la meme époque (10,87). Ainsi se confirme le très haut niveau de fécondité de cette population maltaise et sicilienne qui continuait de vivre en régime prémalthusien jusque dans les dernières années du XIXe siècle.

Tableau VI   Fécondité légitime

| Nombre de | A G E   D E   L A   F E M M E | | | | | | |
	15-19	20-24	25-29	30-34	35-39	40-44	45-49
Naissances	80	179	176	130	78	31	2
Femmes-années	171	356.5	375.5	335	287	233	199.5
Naissances pour 1,000	467,7	502,1	468,7	388	271,7	133	9,8

A une forte natalité correspondait un taux de mortalité relativement peu élevé en année moyenne (16 à 17 pour mille aux alentours de 1860). Les vieillards étant peu nombreux, il s'agissait essentiellement de décès d'enfants en bas âge ou d'accidents (16). Mais le retour périodique des épidémies de choléra et de typhus contribuait à relever singulièrement ces moyennes. Sur 462 décès recensés de 1850 à 1880, 62 au moins devaient en effet leur être attribués: 22 entre mai et juillet 1850, 6 en juillet-août 1856, 19 en juin-juillet 1867 (choléra), 13, l'année suivante, et 2 en 1872 (typhus) sans compter les cas de variole, mentionnés de façon épisodique.
Il n'est guère de famille qui eût été épargnée. Parfois le sort s'acharnait sur un foyer, témoin cette famille maltaise où le choléra enlevait en moins de trois semaines le mari, la femme et cinq de leurs sept enfants (17). Si les nourrissons étaient épargnés, les enfants de I à 10 ans, les adultes de 35 ans et plus, les vieillards surtout apparaissaient comme les victimes habituelles du fléau. Compte tenu de ces épidémies, le taux général de mortalité ne devait pas être éloigné de 25% entre 1850 et 1880. Vers 1906, en revanche, il n'était plus que de 15,3%.
Dans les familles que nous avons reconstituées, près

de 20% des enfants mouraient avant leur premier anniversaire, la
plupart dans les trois premiers mois de leur existence. Il ne
semble pas que les conditions sanitaires se soient rapidement
améliorées après l'etablissement du protectorat, car, à en juger
d'après le nombre de décès d'enfants de moins d'un an entre 1900
et 1909, le taux de mortalité infantile restait encore supérieur
à 14% (18).

La répartition des décès au cours de l'année souligne le
caractère meurtrier des épidémies. Sur la courbe des variations
mensuelles, le maximum de juin se dessine avec netteté (19).
Après 1890, en revanche, les écarts se réduisent, tandis que
l'allure de la courbe se transforme : si l'on voit se maintenir
une surmortalité estivale, sensible surtout chez les jeunes
enfants, désormais les mois d'hiver l'emportent sur tous les
autres pour la fréquence des décès.

Malgré le manque de recensements réguliers, les moyennes
et les courbes, comme tous les renseignements tirés de registres
paroissiaux, permettent d'étudier de façon assez précise le
comportement démographique de cette colonie européenne.

Tableau VII

Mouvement saisonnier des décès
(marine étrangers exclus)

Mois	I - De 1850 à 1880		2 - De 1892 à 1910	
	Nombres absolus	Indice mensuel	Nombres absolus	Indice mensuel
J	24	60,5	172	122,4
F	32	88,3	135	105,4
M	30	75,6	132	93,9
A	51	132,9	113	83
M	39	98,3	112	79,7
J	71	185	148	108,9
J	48	120,4	154	109,6
A	31	78,2	151	107,6
S	33	86	118	86,8
O	41	103,2	128	91
N	36	93,8	137	100,7
D	31	78,2	157	111,8
Total	467	1200	1657	1200

Pendant cette période, le phénomène le plus marquant est
l'accroissement rapide d'une population qui double par trois
fois en moins d'un demi siècle. Sans doute un tel gonflement
des effectifs ne peut-il s'expliquer que par l'importance de

graph. no.4.   Mouvement saisonnier des décès

——— de 1850 à 1880   - - - de 1892 à 1910

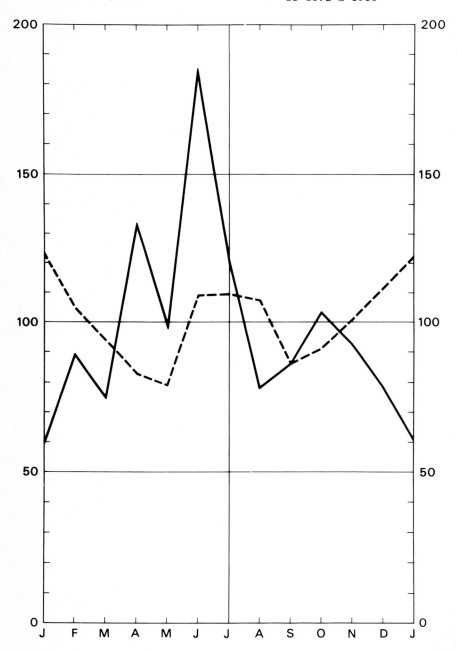

de l'immigration. Mais l'accroissement naturel joue son rôle, lui aussi, les taux de natalité et demortalité en témoignent. A Sousse, comme à Tunis, les familles du quartier franc vivaient encore pour la plupart en régime prémalthusien. Jusqu'à la fin du XIXe siècle, dans les foyers siciliens ou maltais, les naissances se succèdaient à raison d'une tous les deux ans en moyenne, l'allaitement des enfants rythmant de façon régulière l'espacement des conceptions.

Mais cette fécondité élevée était compensée par la forte mortalité qui sévissait chez les enfants en bas âge, le retour périodique des épidémies, choléra ou typhus, qui enlevaient leurs victimes par dizaines. A un siècle de distance, nous retrouvons ainsi chez ces Maltais et ces Italiens du midi émigrés sur les rivages tunisiens un comportement démographique qui n'est pas sans rappeler celui des paysans français à la fin de l'Ancien Régime. Reste à établir des comparaisons plus suggestives avec les régions d'origine, Malte, les archipels et l'ouest de la Sicile, lorsque celles-ci auront été étudiées à leur tour sur le plan démographie.

Orientation bibliographique

Etudes historiques ou régionales

R.P. ANSELME DES ARCS - Mémoires pour servir à l'histoire de la mission des Capucins dans la Régence de Tunis, 1624-1865 - Rome, 1889, in-8°, 142 p.

CUBISOL (Charles) - Notices abrégées sur la Régence de Tunis - Bone, 1867, in-8°, 88 p., 16 pl.

DESPOIS (Jean) - La Tunisie orientale, Sahel et basse steppe, 2ème éd. - Paris, 1955, in-4°, 554 p., ills.

DUNANT (Jean) - Notice sur la Régence de Tunis - Genève, 1858, in-8°, 261 p.

GANIAGE (Jean) - Les origines du protectorat français en Tunisie (1861- 1881) - Paris, 1959, in-8°, 776 p., 41 pl.

LOTH (Gaston) - Le peuplement italien en Tunisie et en Algérie - Paris, 1905, in-8°, VII-503 p. 26 fig., 10 pl.

MALTZAN (Heinrich, freiherr von) - Reise in den Regenschaften Tunis und Tripolis - Leipzig, 1870, 3 vol. in-8°, ills.

PELLISSIER de REYNAUD (E.) - Description de la Régence de Tunis - Paris, 1853, in-4°, 455 p., carte.

PERPETUA (G) - Geografia della Tunisia, descrizione particolareggiata della Reggenza ... Torino, 1882, in-8°, 215 p.

Etudes démographiques

COHEN-BALLOUM (Claire) - Etude démographique de la population
   européenne de Sousse au début du XXe siècle. Tunis, 1962,
   mss.

GANIAGE (Jean) - La population européenne de Tunis au milieu
   du XIXe siècle. Etude démographique - Paris, 1960, 102 p.
   4 pl., 9 gr.

GANIAGE (Jean) - Trois villages d'Ile-de-France au XVIIIe siècle
   Etude démographique - Paris, 1963, 148 p., 5 pl., 15 graph.

GAUTIER (Etienne) et HENRY (Louis) - La population de Crulai,
   paroisse normande. Etude historique - Paris, 1958,
   in-8°, 272 p., ills.

HENRIPIN (Jacques) - La population canadienne au début du
   XVIIIe siècle. Nuptialité, fécondité, mortalité
   infantile - Paris, 1954, in-8°, XXXII-118 p., ills.

HENRY (Louis) - Anciennes familles genevoises. Etude démographique : XVIe-XXe siècle - Paris, 1956, in-8°, 234 p.,
   ills.

HENRY (Louis) - Fécondité et natalité en régime naturel -
   Communication présentée à la 28° session de l'Institut
   International de Statistiques, 1953.

VALMARY (Pierre) - Familles paysannes au XVIIIe siècle en
   bas Quercy. Etude démographqiue - Paris, 1965, in-8°,
   192 p., ills.

NOTES

(I)   Sfax puis Monastir ayant été tour à tour érigées en
      paroisse en 1842 et 1863, les dépendances de Sousse se
      réduisirent aux colonies de Hammamet et Nabeul, distantes
      de 75 et 92 kilomètres, où vivaient une quinzaine de
      familles européennes.
(2)   600 Européens en 1856 (Arch. Résid. Dossier de 1 agence
      consulaire de Sousse), chiffre repris par Guérin pour
      1862, 640 en 1870. Les estimations de la mission
      catholique étaient de même ordre : 600 "chrétiens" en
      1856, 620 trois ans plus tard. Il ne semble pas y avoir
      eu de Grecs à Sousse à cette époque. Le seul protes-
      tant de la ville, John Stevens, vice-consul de Grande-
      Bretagne, avait épousé une Française et leurs enfants
      furent baptisés à l'église catholique.
(3)   Fait à signaler, l'évaluation de la population de Sousse
      ne pose guère de problèmes à cette époque. Les
      estimations des contemporains concordent généralement
      entre elles. Pellissier de Reynaud accorde 7,000 hab-
      itants à la ville en 1842, dont 400 Européens. Vingt ans
      plus tard, Guérin avance le chiffre de 7,600, y compris

600 Chrétiens. On peut tirer des évaluations de même ordre à partir des registres fiscaux et des rapports consulaires : 8,000 habitants environ, dont quelque 1,700 Israélites. En juin 1863, 426 Juifs de Sousse étaient inscrits sur les registres de la mejba, indigents compris (171). Vingt autres continuaient de figurer sur les rôles, bien qu'ils eussent émigré à Tunis.

(4) Les patronymes étaient très variés, plus d'une centaine. Les plus répandus étaient évidemment des noms d'origine maltaise, mais aucun d'entre eux ne s'imposait de façon particulière. Les plus courants, Borg, Micallef, Bonello, Xiberras, Rizzo, Azzopardi, Muniglia, Vella, Fenech, Darmanin, ne représentaient, à eux dix, guere plus de 30% des naissances.

(5) Le nombre des Maltais avait été réduit par des mesures de naturalisation individuelles. Parmi les Italiens, on comptait quelques familles de Livournais, des Juifs de lointaine origine andalouse. Mais le gros de la colonie était composé désormais de Siciliens, originaires pour la plupart de Trapani, de Palerme et surtout de petites iles comme celle des Femmes, Pantellaria, Favignana.

(6) Le recensement de 1906 n'avait pas été étendu à la population tunisienne.

(7) J. Despois : La Tunisie orientale, p. 699

(8) Rapport du vice-consul Stevens, chargé d'enquêter sur la contrebande maltaise. Sousse, 7 juillet 1858 (Arch. Tun. doss. 117, c.94).

A partir de 1865, les professions, plus fréquemment indiquées dans les actes de mariage, permettent de recenser chez les Maltais 18 commerçants, 6 ouvriers, 4 charretiers ou cochers, 4 marins ou pêcheurs, 2 boulangers, 1 meunier, 1 tailleur, 1 ébéniste et 1 tailleur de pierres. Mais on peut s'interroger sur l'activité réelle de ces commercants dont la plupart étaient incapables de signer leur nom.

(9) Cette étude démographique repose sur le dépouillement systématique des registres paroissiaux de la ville de Sousse entre 1836 et 1906 et la reconstitution des familles selon la méthode Henry. Comme ceux de Tunis, de 1843 à 1881, les registres de la côte ont été tenus ou recopiés par le chancelier de la mission des Capucins, le Frère Anselme des Arcs. Pendant toute cette période, ils présentent les mêmes qualités que ceux de l'église Sainte-Croix dont nous avons tiré parti dans notre étude sur la population européenne de Tunis. Après le départ de la mission catholique, en avril 1881, pendant plusieurs années les registres furent assez mal tenus, notamment en ce qui concerne les décès. Certains actes, manifestement recopiés, font double emploi; des feuilles ont disparu; la fréquence des additifs et des actes de notoriété souligne des omissions. Trois registres enfin ont été égarés, ceux des décès pour 1889, 1890 et 1891. C'est la raison pour laquelle nous n'avons pu donner à la reconstitution des familles l'ampleur que nous aurions souhaitée. Nous avons du nous limiter à 128 couples

mariés à Sousse ou à Tunis entre 1839 et 1869, auxquels
nous avons adjoint 8 familles de Monastir, Nabeul et
Hammamet, qui relevaient alors de la même paroisse. Après
élimination des familles "inconnues", c'est-à-dire celles
dont la durée d'union était impossible à déterminer, res-
taient 105 couples, 101 de Sousse, 2 de Hammamet, 2 de
Monastir et Nabeul, sur lesquels nous avons fondé
notre étude. Pour la période postérieure à 1900, nous
avons surtout utilisé le diplome d'études supérieures
de Claire Cohen-Balaloum : Etude démographique de la
population européenne de Sousse au début du XXe siècle,
soutenu en 1962 devant la Faculté des Lettres de Tunis.

(10) Faute d'état civil tunisien, il n'est évidemment pas
possible de faire la part des mariages mixtes et des
conversions de chrétiens à l'Islam. Mais le temps des
renégats était révolu depuis longtemps et, d'autre part,
la claustration des femmes musulmanes, la sévérité
des châtiments ne pouvaient guère favoriser les relations entre Européens et indigènes. L'effort de
prosélytisme des missionnaires se limitait aux Juifs,
mais la rareté des conversions souligne le peu de
succès de l'enterprise : 3 baptêmes d'enfants trouvés
en cinquante ans, 2 conversions d'adultes, dont une
suivie d'apostasie,

(11) 27,1 et 27,8 ans pour les hommes, la moyenne d'ensemble
étant de 27,2 ans; 21 et 23 ans pour les femmes, la
moyenne générale étant de 21,1 ans (âge modal : 17).

(12) On pourrait évoquer la fréquence des épidémies en
juillet (choléra de 1850, 1856 et 1867), mais cette remar-
que vaut également pour le mois de juin, qui apparaît
comme une période de forte nuptialité.

(13) 897 naissances de 1904 à 1908, 5,241 habitants recensés
en 1906.

(14) Nous n'avons retenu que les couples dont les dates de
mariage et de fin d'union étaient connues, ainsi que
l'âge au moins approximatif de la femme, 105 au total, que
nous avons répartis en familles "complètes" et
"incomplètes", selon que la femme avait atteint ou non
l'âge de 50 ans dans l'état de mariage.

(15) 23 et 20 cas, sur un total de 121 intervalles.

(16) Mis à part les marins étrangers, de 1850 à 1870, on peut
faire état de 9 victimes de naufrages ou d'assassinat
par des bédouins, de 3 victimes d'explosion de poudre.
A cela s'ajoutaient les enfants écrasés par une charrette
ou piqués par un scorpion.

(17) Famille Grech-German: décès de mai-juin 1850.

(18) Comparaison avec le nombre des naissances survenues pendant
la même période, compte tenu d'un décalage de 6 mois
(D'après les relevés de C. Cohen-Babaloum).

(19) Plus de 15% des décès annuels entre 1850 et 1880.

12

LA MODERNISATION DEMOGRAPHIQUE DE L'ESPAGNE:

LE CYCLE VITAL ANNUEL 1863-1960

NICOLAS SANCHEZ-ALBORNOZ

NEW YORK UNIVERSITY

L'Espagne occupe, dans l'évolution générale d'une population du "type ancien" au "type moderne", une position intermédiaire entre les pays les plus avancés et ceux du Tiers Monde
où, pour la plupart des nations, cette évolution vient à peine
de commencer. Avec les autres pays de la périphérie de l'Europe
elle partage cette place qui est ni d'avant-ni d'arrière-garde.
Ceci correspond par ailleurs étroitement à l'évolution du pays
sur les autres plans. En feuilletant n'importe quel annuaire
international, on se rend très vite compte que l'Espagne occupe
une même position intermédiaire sur le plan économique et social.
D'autre part l'excellent petit livre de M. Jorge Nadal sur
l'histoire de la population espagnole vient de définir d'une
façon très nette la position de l'Espagne dans le contexte
international (1). Ajoutons encore que nous entendons par
"modernisation" non seulement la phase initiale de la
"révolution démographique", caractérisée une brusque chute de
la mortalité et par un accroissement naturel élevé, mais aussi
la phase "mûre" caractérisée par une mortalité basse, un
vieillissement de la population et par un accroissement naturel
moyen voire lent. D'une façon générale, la "révolution
démographique" peut être modérée, comme dans le cas de l'Europe,
ou explosive telle qu'elle se manifeste actuellement dans les

pays sous-dévéloppés. L'urbanisation elle aussi est reliée à
cette modernisation.

Ceci dit il nous soit permis d'énoncer l'objet de cet
essai, car il s'agit bien d'un essai et non d'une étude appro-
fondie. Voici réuni, à partir d'une brève recherche empirique,
un faisceau d'hypothèses. A certains égards nous serions même
tentés de considérer cet exposé comme un projet d'enquête.

D'après M. Nadal, le schéma de l'évolution démographique
de l'Espagne est différent de celui des pays les plus
dévéloppés, non pas parce que le pays ait suivi des voies
différentes, mais parce qu'il y ait eu décalage dans toutes les
phases de son évolution démographique. La réduction de la
mortalité catastrophique, et notamment des épidémies, a commencé
au 18e siècle, suivant de près le reste de l'Europe. La
réduction de la mortalité non-catastrophique par contre n'est
évidente qu'après la Première Guerre Mondiale. La baisse de la
fécondité, toute lente au début, doit attendre le déclenchement
de la Guerre Civile, soit 1936, pour baisser brusquement. Le
viellissement est déjà perceptible dans le recensement de 1950
et il y a des signes avertisseurs d'une stagnation future de la
population.

Que l'Espagne a su vaincre au 19e siècle les épidémies,
notamment le choléra et la fièvre jaune, ainsi que les catastro-
phes   alimentaires dues aux crises de subsistance dont nous
avons souligné la persistance (2), est un fait incontestable,
mais le fait que la mortalité dite normale ait pu resister
aussi longtemps à la baisse nous laisse cependant rêveur. Les
faits sont pourtant là. Observons les courbes de la natalité et
de la mortalité pour la seconde moitié du 19e siècle ou les taux
correspondants (3) et nous ne constaterons que des lignes trop
parallèles. Ce n'est que vers 1890, et encore à peine, que la
mortalité commence à s'infléchir. Comparons les dates de 1863
et 1900, dates sur lesquelles nous reviendrons plus tard. En
1863, le taux brut de natalité est de 37,8 pour mille et le taux
brut de mortalité 28,8 pour mille ce qui donne un taux d'accroissement naturel de 9 pour mille; en 1900 les taux respectifs
sont 33,8, 28,8 et 5 pour mille. Tous ces taux indiquent clairement qu'il n'y ait pas eu de progrès.

La question qui se pose est s'il y a un autre moyen pour
déceler les changements intervenus dans la mortalité? Lors de
l'étude des effets démographiques des crises de subsistance
nous avons observé un cycle vital annuel considéré comme carac-
téristique d'une population du type "ancien", c'est-à-dire une
accumulation relative des naissances en hiver, résultant de
conceptions printanières, et une forte poussée de mortalité
estivale causée par des maladies de l'appareil digestif (4).
En passant par contre au cycle annuel contemporain (5) les
conceptions s'étalent régulièrement sur toute l'année, tandis
que le pic de la mortalité a changé de place: il ne se situe
plus en été, mais en plein hiver. Les fortes mortalités estiva-
les ont disparu et ce sont maintenant les maladies causées par
la dégénérescence ainsi que les maladies pulmonaires qui fauchent
les vies. Notons que la combinaison particulière des courbes
des naissances et des décès dans le cycle ancien, impose un
rythme très particulier au mouvement annuel de la population:

Graph. 2.   NATALITE.

Taux d'accroissement ou de diminution par rapport à la
moyenne mensuelle des naissances.

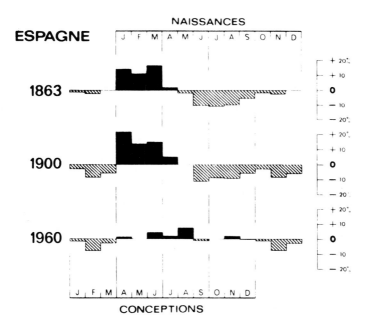

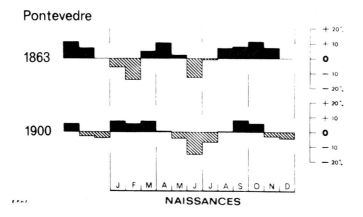

forte croissance en hiver (faible mortalité et natalité élevée)
et absence de croissance en été (natalité faible et mortalité
élevée).

Le cycle du type ancien se retrouve-t-il ailleurs qu'en
Espagne? Nous n'en savons rien. Il est cependant fort probable
qu'il joue dans les pays méditerranéens et, sous une autre forme,
dans les pays scandinaves par example. Quand est-ce que ce cycle
a commencé à se modifier en Espagne? Cherchons une date vers
le milieu du siècle qui en gros sépare 1863 et 1960 (6). Celle
du tournant du siècle n'est que par trop tentante: faisons donc
le point en 1900.

Les conceptions printanières

Le tableau I et le graphique 1 qui s'y rattache font ressortir
une ligne presque parallèle entre les naissances de 1863 et
1960. Les mois pendant lesquels la natalité est caractérisée
par une déviation positive par rapport à la moyenne sont janvier,
février, mars et en moindre mesure avril. Décomptés les neuf mois
de gestation de l'enfant cela équivaut à des conceptions survenues
aux mois d'avril, mai, juin et juillet.

Tableau 1

Naissances: déviations (en pourcentages et par rapport à
la moyenne) des moyennes mensuelles.

	Espagne				Pontevèdre	
	1863	1900	-	1960	1863	1900
Moyenne mensuelle	50.566	52.320		54.544	991	1239
Janvier	14.4	21.4		0.9	- 6.1	7.4
Février	10.8	13.5		0.2	-14.7	5.4
Mars	16.6	15.1		3.9	4.4	7.5
Avril	2.0	5.2		1.3	10.6	0.7
Mai	- 2.2	- 0.7		7.2	1.8	-4.6
Juin	-10.3	-11.6		- 1.4	-13.1	-15.4
Juillet	-11.2	- 9.1		- 0.6	- 0.9	- 7.2
Août	-10.2	- 9.6		1.5	6.5	0.3
Septembre	- 5.6	- 5.8		- 0.7	7.7	7.7
Octobre	- 1.6	- 3.0		- 1.6	11.1	5.5
Novembre	- 2.6	- 8.9		- 8.0	6.7	-2.9
Décembre	0	- 6.1		- 2.8	- 0.3	-4.2

Graph. 1.   MORTALITE.

Taux d'accroissement ou de diminution par rapport à la
    moyenne mensuelle des décès

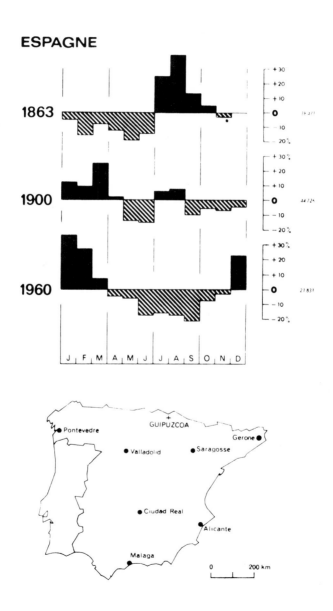

En cet égard les espagnols paraissaient s'être comporté, en 1863 aussi bien qu'en 1900, d'une manière tout à fait instinctif, tandis que leurs descendants d'aujourd'hui, moins spontanés, étalent les conceptions à leur gré sur toute l'année.
A présent seule une certaine préférence pour concevoir en août (les vacances?) semble se dessiner ce qui accentue les naissances du mois de mai. Tout comme dans le passé la Carême reste une période de conceptions réduites.
Vue la forte susceptibilité des enfants aux maladies infectieuses de la saison chaude, plus forte encore en pays méditerranéens, les conceptions printanières constituent autant une réaction instinctive qu'une réponse intelligente à la crainte, basée sur une expérience très ancienne, de la forte mortalité des enfants en bas âge pendant l'été. Les risques semblaient peut-être moindres si les enfants voyaient le jour en hiver.
L'autre observation concerne l'existence d'une pointe, d'un faible accroissement des naissances en septembre - octobre. Ceci correspond à un double cycle annuel dans les provinces du Nord-Ouest de l'Espagne: toute la Galicie, les Asturies et la Montagne de Santander, face à l'Atlantique, les provinces de l'ancien royaume de Léon (Léon, Zamora et Sala- manque) plus Avila ainsi que l'Estrémadure (Caceres et Badajoz) (Voir le cas de la province de Pontevedra, tableau 1). A quoi correspond ce cycle secondaire des conceptions de la fin de l'automne et du début de l'année? Nous n'avons pas d'explication pour cette singularité.
La question qui reste est de savoir quand le comportement des espagnols en matière de conceptions a changé? Voilà un problème que le démographe aura peut-être intérêt à préciser, mais qui a surtout sa place dans l'historiographie des menta- lités, la conception étant dans une certaine mesure un acte volontaire de l'individu. Que le couple se laisse aller à ses instincts ou adopte un comportement dicté par les croyances ou coutumes constitue déjà en soi un choix.

Mortalité estivale et mortalité hivernale.

Quittons le terrain, somme toute assez gai, de la natalité pour passer à un autre aux couleurs plus sombres, à savoir celui de la mortalité. Que s'est-il passé sur ce point entre 1863 et 1900? Le graphique 2 et le Tableau 2 fournissent l'évidence d'un changement profond.

Tableau II Décès: déviations (en pourcentages et par rapport à la moyenne) des moyennes mensuelles.

Espagne

	1863	1900	1960
Moyenne mensuelle	38.471	44.726	21.831
Janvier	-5,2	11,9	36,3

	1863	1900	1960
Février	-16,0	9,2	26.7
Mars	-8,1	24,4	7,7
Avril	-12,4	2,1	-4,7
Mai	-19,4	-14,1	
Juin	-14,4	-14,8	-17,5
Juillet	24,5	5,9	-16,2
Août	38,8	7,6	-17,4
Septembre	12,9	-10,2	-21,2
Octobre	4,6	-5,5	-7,6
Novembre	-3,1	-6,7	-2,9
Décembre	0	-4,6	22,7

	Alicante		Guipuzcoa		Pontevèdre		Gèrone	
	1863	1900	1863	1900	1863	1900	1863	1900
Moyenne Mensuelle	893	965	394	394	696	926	755	735
Janvier	-3,2	6,8	2,5	-2,5	28,5	33,4	-9,0	37,8
Février	-8,5	24,6	-8,1	9,3	5,4	21,3	-20,0	44,6
Mars	-22,7	34,0	-6,5	52,0	-4,8	59,3	-10,7	23,2
Avril	-9,0	-2,0	0,5	22,5	-11,3	9,2	-21,0	0
Mai	-27,8	-16,5	0,5	-7,3	-12,7	-12,5	-26,8	-14,8
Juin	-17,9	-15,8	-17,2	-23,8	-20,1	-33,5	-26,9	-26,6
Juillet	23,2	-0,4	-5,3	-21,3	-3,2	-32,8	30,6	-34,5
Août	36,6	-7,0	30,9	-11,1	12,7	-23,7	64,1	5,0
Septembre	8,0	-12,0	28,9	-19,5	4,0	-16,3	16,6	-14,8
Octobre	-5,3	-6,7	4,6	-13,4	-2,7	-5,8	5,2	-19,5
Novembre	-6,9	-10,1	-11,6	6,0	0	-7,4	-1,5	-6,2
Décembre	-3,0	-0,8	-18,5	10,1	7,1	0,5	0,4	-5,3

	Valladolid		Saragosse		Ciudad Real		Malaga	
	1863	1900	1863	1900	1863	1900	1863	1900
Moyenne Mensuelle	789	771	1130	1098	707	804	1150	1236
Janvier	-10,4	12,4	-1,6	-7,2	-17,3	2,1	-2,6	11,6
Février	-11,2	7,5	-19,8	-11,2	-22,7	-6,3	-16,0	-4,7

	1863	1900	1863	1900	1863	1900	1863	1900
Mars	-6,2	14,9	-20,6	28,7	-18,1	41,1	-12,3	-4,0
Avril	-10,6	-5,0	-14,6	7,1	-25,0	-7,0	-22,7	-12,9
Mai	-23,9	-19,3	-16,9	-13,7	-28,8	-28,7	-13,4	-10,6
Juin	-32,1	-26,0	-12,0	-24,4	-12,5	-19,1	26,8	17,6
Juillet	-2,8	-1,0	40,3	10,4	61,9	41,0	68,2	33,8
Août	41,5	13,2	49,5	16,8	58,1	13,4	29,3	16,8
Septembre	33,0	-5,1	13,3	-7,8	17,4	-1,2	2,4	-5,9
Octobre	21,2	9,2	0,9	-7,6	5,2	1,3	-8,4	-15,1
Novembre	-3,7	-0,9	-4,6	-5,4	-8,4	-15,0	-28,7	-14,1
Décembre	2,0	0,9	-4,0	16,1	-19,1	-20,8	-21,3	-13,8

En 1863, juillet-août et septembre, et dans un degré moindre octobre, étaient des mois pendant lesquels se produisait une sur-mortalité par rapport à la moyenne mensuelle, tandis que l'hiver paraissait une saison relativement saine. En 1960, la situation est complètement renversée: le printemps et l'été semblent être très favorables à la santé tandis que l'automne et le plein hiver sont des périodes vraiment néfastes. Entre les deux dates extrêmes, le tournant du siècle apparaît dans une perspective de transition: la mortalité estivale décroit, sans pour autant disparaître complétement; seul les mois de juillet et août dépassent légèrement la moyenne annuelle. Un second cycle, plus prononcé que le cycle antérieur se dessine et le mouvement saisonnier en 1900 est la réflection de cette dualité.

Dans un pays aussi composite et mal intégré en somme qu'était l'Espagne en 1900, ce qui est vrai pour le pays tout entier, ne l'est forcément pas pour chacune des différentes régions. L'analyse régionale que nous avions élagué en ce qui concerne les naissances, s'impose ici.

Nous avons évité le procédé un peu long du calcul des écarts par rapport à la moyenne annuelle des décès de chacune des 49 provinces espagnoles   pour lesquelles nous possédons des données, ainsi la répartition du pays en zones de comportement homogène. Nous avons préféré choisir et présenter ici huit cas bien espacés entre eux et suffisamment représentatifs de la région à laquelle ils appartiennent. Nous nous excusons du fait que nous n'avons pas justifié les raisons pour lesquelles chaque exemple fut choisi.

Dans le cas de la Catalogne par exemple nous avons omis Barcelone, à cause de son caractère trop urbain, ainsi que la province de Lérida, trop rurale par rapport aux conditions générales de la région (voir également tableau 2).
D'après ces cas nous pouvons distinguer quatre types d'évolution de la mortalité:
a. du double cycle au cycle d'hiver.

Ceci est le cas pour Pontevedra. Le double cycle, signe précurseur, apparaissait déjà en 1863 dans toute la province ainsi qu'en Galicie, Leon et Oviedo. Des deux pics, celui de l'hiver était le plus important; le cas extrême étant Santander où le plein été était la saison la plus saine. Etait-ce pour cette raison que la reine Isabelle et la Cour d'Espagne avaient pris l'habitude d'aller bourgeoisement en villégiature sur le côte de Santander?.. En 1900 le pic estival a complètement disparu.
b. Inversion complète du cycle.

Un tel phénomène peut être observé à Alicante et Guipozcoa. Alicante représente en quelque sorte la position la plus évoluée de la côte du Levant, de Barcelone jusqu'au sud. Au-delà de la frontière septentrionale d'Alicante commençaient des structures bien différentes. Quant à Guipozcoa, au nord, elle résume bien l'évolution du Pays Basque auquel elle appartient.
c. du double cycle à la prépondérance hivernale.

Ceci est le cas pour Valladolid, Saragosse et Gérone; en d'autres termes le centre-nord de l'Espagne composée de la Vieille-Castille, l'Aragon et la partie septentrionale de la Catalogne.
d. du double cycle à la prépondérance estivale.

Sont dans ce cas: Ciudad Real, la Nouvelle-Castille, Malaga et l'Andalousie, en d'autres mots les régions les plus méridionales et les plus retardées.

De cette analyse on peut tirer les conclusions suivantes. Primo qu'un changement qualitatif de la mortalité, dans le sens de la "modernisation" s'est manifesté pendant les 37 ans écoulés entre 1863 et 1900. Ce changement ne s'est pourtant pas déclaré par un fléchissement dans le volume des décès, ni par une baisse dans le taux national brut de mortalité. Il est pourtant bien évident et suffisamment significatif pour justifier d'avancer la date initiale de la révolution démographique en Espagne. Secundo, et il fallait s'y attendre, tout le pays ne prit pas le même chemin en même temps: une distinction se fait entre des régions qui sont plus avancées et d'autres qui sont nettement en rétard sur le mouvement général. Comme dans la plupart des pays méditerranéens, l'évolution suit une ligne qui va du Nord au Sud.
Que les maladies d'origine gastrique aient diminué n'a rien de surprenant. Ce fut en effet à cette époque qu'un marché national de produits agricoles fut constitué et que les crises de subsistance disparaissaient lentement; nous sommes enclin à admettre que les habitants du pays étaient ravitaillés plus facilement et plus régulièrement, donc mieux nourris du point

de vue strictement quantitatif. Ceci a pu avoir une influence
très considérable sur la mortalité ordinaire. La question qui
se pose est de savoir s'il faut attribuer la diminution de la
mortalité estivale entre 1863 et 1900 à la diminution de la
mortalité infantile ou à une réduction de la mortalité des
adultes? La réponse n'est guère facile puisque la mortalité
infantile était toujours très forte en 1901 et de l'ordre de 186
pour mille (7) et puisque Biraben et Henry ont observé le fait
que le double cycle annuel existait encore en 1950/51 pour les
enfants espagnols décédés dans la première année de leur existence, ce qui prouverait la persistance de certains traits.

Reste également à savoir pourquoi un tel changement ne
s'est pas manifesté dans une modification du volume des décédés
ou dans une baisse du taux brut de mortalité. Comment se fait-il
qu'une diminution des maladies de l'appareil digestif a pu être
remplacée et neutralisée par un accroissement des maladies
pulmonaires et des maladies de dégénérescence? Un accroissement
des maladies de dégénérescence ne pouvait intervenir que dans le
cas d'un vieillissement généralisé de la population. Est-ce
que la baisse de la mortalité est due à l'amélioration des conditions alimentaires seule ou à l'influence conjugée de celle-ci
et de la diffusion des connaissances et des pratiques sanitaires?
Dans un tel contexte des études sur la consommation, les salaires
et le niveau de vie de l'époque seraient les bien venues.

Disons finalement qu'un comparaison de l'évolution de la
population urbaine et rurale est tout aussi indispensable. En
1900 en effet, le port de Cadix, chef-lieu de la province du
même nom, fut caractérisé par une hausse des décès en période
d'hiver, tandis que la campagne environnante enregistrait une
fluctuation à double pointe, celle de l'été étant plus forte que
celle en hiver (8). Cette observation cependant ne se trouve
pas confirmée pour les autres capitales andalouses, Malaga et
Grenade.

REFERENCES

* Les graphiques accompagnant le texte ont été tracés de main
de maitre par Mme. Françoise Vergneault-Belmont au Laboratoire
de Cartographie de l'Ecole Pratique des Hautes Etudes, à Paris.
Je tiens à lui exprimer mes remerciements les plus vifs.

1. La población española (siglos XVI a XX), Barcelone, 1966.

2. Voir España hace un siglo: una economía dual, Barcelone,
   1968, notamment chapitres II et III.

3. Nadal, op. cit. pags. 130-132. Voir aussi, plus brièvement
   Jean Daric "Evolution démographique en Espagne", Population
   II (1) 1956, pags. 93-94.

4. Nous nous sommes inspirés sur ce point chez J.-N.Biraben et
   L. Henry, "La mortalité des jeunes enfants dans les pays
   mediterranéens", Population, 12 (4), 1957, pags.615-44.

5. <u>Anuario Estadístico de España.</u> 1961, pag. 116. Les données
   sur 1863 se trouvent a Instituto Geográfico y Estadístico,
   <u>Movimiento de la población de España en el decenio de</u>
   <u>1861 a 1870</u> Madrid, 1877, et celles de 1900 à Id.,
   <u>Movimiento annual de la población de España</u>, 1900, Ière
   Partie, Madrid, 1901.

6. Nous avons préferé l'année 1863 à toute autre de cette
   période car elle semble relativement "normale", c'est-à-
   dire qu'elle ne souffre pas l'influence d'une épidémie
   (choléra de 1865), ni d'une crise alimentaire (1963)
   ni des suites de celles-ci.

7. Antonio Arbelo, <u>La mortalidad de la infancia en España</u>,
   <u>1901 - 1950</u>, Madrid, 1962. La moyenne de la mortalité
   infantile de 1861 à 1870 était de 235 pour mille. En
   une trentaine d'années, elle était donc déjà descendue
   de 21 pour cent.

8. Cadix-province: nombre de décès survenus par mois de janvier
   à décembre pendant l'année 1900, 1277, 1195, 1428, 1138
   1003, 1231, 1301, 1237, 1058, 1050, 1128, 1172.
   Cadix-ville: ide.: 233, 227, 248, 206, 200,186, 183, 173,
   163, 161, 180, 198.

Part III

The Historical Demography
of Latin America

13

THE HISTORICAL DEMOGRAPHY OF LATIN AMERICA:

SOURCES, TECHNIQUES, CONTROVERSIES, YIELDS

WOODROW BORAH

DEPARTMENT OF HISTORY

UNIVERSITY OF CALIFORNIA, BERKELEY

To say that historical-demographic studies of Latin America, whether of the whole or any part, are in their infancy hardly distinguishes them from such studies of other areas, for all historical demography is as yet sparsely developed. What is distinctive is a difference which Latin America shares with areas like sub-Saharan Africa, namely, that history can be held to begin only with European recording. In Latin America prehistory thus comes at least to 1492 and in many regions into the eighteenth or even nineteenth centuries. Periods are considerably different from those of Europe, and techniques and conceptions that for Europe and the Middle East would be applied only to human occupations millennia old must be applied in Latin America to fairly recent ones. Although techniques and materials are not themselves so dissimilar, the differences in recency of the periods to which they can be applied amount in the end to a very considerable variation. Any extended study of historical demography for Latin America means a far greater familiarity with techniques normally reserved in the Old World for archaeologists and historical geographers. Since it is the advent of the Europeans that makes the first and perhaps most conspicuous difference, we are brought to a division into periods that is different from that used for Europe: prehistoric, protohistoric, and first European contact. To these follow two periods that parallel European experience: the eras of protostatistical recording and of systematic gathering of statistics. Nevertheless, these last two also have local flavor. I.shall organize discussion in terms of these five periods, and define each in the discussion.

There is little work that covers all or most of these periods in a single study. Attempts to estimate world population at various points in time do include all of America, and give global estimates for America, sometimes with some kind of regional breakdown. For the end of the eighteenth century and later, they are based upon reporting that gives a reasonable basis for global figures; for earlier periods, they are more apt to be based upon simple speculation or some theory of symmetry (1). The one study which does cover Latin America from 1492 to roughly the present is Angel Rosenblat's attempt to estimate the Indian population and other racial components for all of America in 1492, 1570, 1650, 1800, and 1939-1950. Initially prepared as a seminar paper in Spain in the 1930's, it has been republished a number of times, with no change in the estimates but with enormous additions to the footnotes. In general, Rosenblat belongs to that group of scholars who discard most contemporary testimony as wild exaggeration and arrive at very low aboriginal populations for 1492. Except for the West Indies, he postulates relatively small demographic damage because of the European conquest, a slow replacement of Indians by mixed bloods, and from the seventeenth century on, a steady growth of population (2). His estimates are much challenged at both ends of the time span: for the earliest point because of discarding so much testimony and pushing figures sharply downward; for the latest point because of the inherent difficulty, after centuries of steady interbreeding, in assigning any validity to racial groupings in census counts. At the time of its first publication, Rosenblat's study was perhaps most useful because it brought together in one volume the material and discussion then available. It has continued to be a widely consulted and useful compendium, though now no longer able to encompass a burgeoning publication of new material and discussion.

Most demographic studies of Latin America have tended to cluster at the two ends of Rosenblat's time span. Anthropological, geographical, and historical studies have tended to concentrate upon the question of numbers at the time of European entrance into the New World. This has been hotly debated since at least the middle of the eighteenth century, and perhaps even since the sixteenth. It remains a burning question today (3). The discussion has seldom gotten beyond estimates of numbers. Straight demographic study of Latin America, as of Europe and the United States, has tended to analyze the most recent censuses and compendia of vital statistics. Its aim has been to know the present and predict the future; historical inquiry is seldom part of the plan.

Regional studies have tended to follow the same pattern, and are in addition extraordinarily fragmentary and scattered. Most historical-demographic discussion of regions, i.e., countries, districts, and cities, has tended to be a chapter or a few paragraphs in a more general historical essay. There are, however, two notable regional works that are both histories of population from the sixteenth to the twentieth century and illuminating guides to sources. They are Rodolfo Barón Castro on the population of El Salvador (4) and Nicolás Besio Moreno on the population of Buenos Aires (5), the latter attempting to arrive at estimates for crude birth, marriage, and death rates as well as mere numbers. Most recently, there has appeared a survey of materials and historico-demographic work for Argentina (6), which is a model of the kind of guides we need but badly lack for other countries.

1.   The Prehistoric Eras
Prehistory may be defined as the long corridors of time that

stretch from the earliest entrance of man into America until just
before European-brought disturbances, direct and indirect, began to
alter Indian culture and population. The span of time is at the
very least fifteen to twenty thousand years, is often stated as
thirty to fifty thousand, and may well be more, for the tendency of
study in past decades has been to give greater antiquity to man's
presence in America (7). The range of cultures is from hunting and
gathering, through the development of agriculture, to the elabor-
ately stratified and intricately organized societies that the
Europeans found. Professor MacNeish's studies (8) and his paper in
this symposium give an excellent idea of the long stretch of time
and the range of cultures. As in the Old World, prehistory means
absence of writing, but the criterion will not fit exactly because
Meso-America did develop systems of writing, hieroglyphs in the
Maya zone, and pictographs in the Mixtec-Zapotec-Nahuatl zone north
of the Isthmus of Tehuantepec. Of Maya hieroglyphs, we can read
dates and a few names (9); of the pictographs, a good deal more, so
that for the Mixteca, genealogies and histories of ruling houses
can be read back to 692 A.D. (10). However, such records have been
little used. For the last centuries before the coming of the
Europeans, we also have legends that were recorded either in
pictographs or in European writing (11). Their value for demographic history is largely corroboratory. Understandably, most
studies of prehistoric populations tend to concentrate upon the
eras of sedentary and denser settlement, that is, since the
beginning of the first millennium B.C.
 Inevitably, since the materials available for prehistory and
the methods of treatment do not yet permit attention to the refined
and detailed questions of current demography, discussions of
prehistoric populations tend to center upon determination of gross
numbers and direction of change. Scholars ask what kind of human
culture, what numbers must be postulated to maintain the kind of
political and social structures that archaeological examination
indicates, what densities are appropriate to the kinds of technology
found, what numbers of workers were needed to build the pyramids,
temples, and other structures. As the discussion moves from
technology and social structure to numbers and back, it has in it a
very real possibility of circular argument, but a very beneficial
one in which steady examination back and forth does reveal new
insights. One interesting characteristic of all estimates for
America is that the numbers and territorial densities postulated are
often much lower than those for comparable societies and technologies
in Eurasia and Africa (12). The difficulty is somewhat masked by
calculating the American densities in terms of number of persons
per hundred square miles or hundred square kilometers (13).
Another series of questions, which does not estop estimates of
number, concentrates upon change and direction of change in numbers,
especially by dating occupation and abandonment of houses and land.
Findings here are more easily proved, but there remains much debate
between scholars who find relatively unchanging straight-line
patterns of increase in the regions they study and those who find
cyclical movement, i.e., that numbers tend to build up, reach a
maximum, undergo very considerable attrition, and move through the
same cycle again. Perhaps the most notable instance of cyclical
finding is S. F. Cook's study of the Teotlalpan, with its

postulation of five-hundred year cycles, the latest of which may be reaching its climax at the present time (14). A different question just becoming prominent is the extent to which the absence of rapid long-distance communication in America and isolation from the Old World may have meant freedom from massive epidemics. Since discussion is usually focused upon this question in terms of the impact of diseases brought by the Europeans from Eurasia and Africa, I shall discuss it in the section on first European contact. However, all such questions apply to the periods of protohistory, of early European contact, and even to later ones.

Estimates of prehistoric population in America are based essentially upon examinations of the nature and extent of human occupation and land use. The techniques and conceptions brought to the study are drawn from a wide range of fields: anthropology and especially archaeology in its widest sense; geology with its study of underlying forms and its inspiration for stratigraphic analysis; geography with its attention to climate, soils, land forms, land use, and erosion; botany and zoology, with their attention to complexes of biota and changes in them; and even chemistry. Conceptions drawn from the biological sciences, most of all ecological succession and balance, become especially important even though their application, if the ideas are drawn too directly from studies of animal populations, sometimes creates scandal among scholars still intent upon maintaining a firm separation between God's finest creation and the rest of His handiwork. The application of ideas of ecology and ecological balance has been especially prominent in the work of Carl Sauer and S. F. Cook. On the basis of techniques used, scholars working on prehistoric human population in America may be divided very roughly into two groups. On the one hand, are the biogeographers and palaeobiologists, who arrive at estimates through determination of complexes of biota and changes in those complexes, as well as direct evidence of land use; on the other hand are the anthropologists and archaeologists, who apply more commonly known methods of determination of human occupation and activity, especially study of artifacts, but are developing very rapidly a whole new range of techniques and skills. We may indicate briefly the techniques of both groups in a listing of kinds of problems and conceptions used to arrive at estimates of human population:

a). Studies of complexes of biota and changes in them. Central to what one might call succession studies is the conception that complexes of plants and animals will tend to reach certain compositions of species in given conditions of soil and climate, and that certain kinds of failure to do so, or changes in the complexes, indicate disturbance by man. At best, the scholar can judge the technology and even the relative density of the human use of the soil and biota that sets up the kind of disturbance found. Thus the presence of clearings in otherwise well-wooded regions or what should be well-wooded regions raises the presumption of human activity and occupation, usually destruction of forest for cultivation. Presence in the biota of an overlarge percentage of species of a kind normally associated with a brush cover in what should be forest raises the presumption of disturbance by man, and again the scholar can attempt to gauge the extent of the disturbance (15). A brilliant study that illustrates the techniques well is Carl L.

Johannessen, Savannas of Interior Honduras (16). Another brilliant study, based on historical evidence, is Lesley Byrd Simpson's Exploitation of Land in Central Mexico in the Sixteenth Century (17), which examines the replacement of Indians by European-introduced livestock in sixteenth century central Mexico, in effect, of one large mammal by others. I should emphasize that the application of biogeography and palaeobiology to the study of past human populations is only now being worked out, for the application involves the formulation and testing of sophisticated conceptions of succession and climax in complexes of biota and the effect of various forms of human disturbance. The existence of very extensive grasslands in temperate South and North America in regions where trees grow readily raises a series of as yet unresolved problems (18). In general, the discussion has proceeded with relatively little heat and much attention to solving problems.

b). Archaeological techniques and approaches:

1´). Estimates based upon measurements of sites, counts of houses, and their size. One approach to estimates of population has been to determine the number of houses and rooms at a site within a period and from them try to estimate the population. The approach has potential for wide application but also as yet unsolved problems. If the scholar knows the type of occupation and use of buildings, he is nevertheless confronted, especially in tropical areas, with determining the possible settlement at the same time in houses that have disappeared because they were of more perishable material than stone, the extent to which all houses were in use at the same time, and the nature of settlement beyond the area excavated. A study of patterns of occupation may give clues on nature of settlement (19), but there remain thoroughly opposed ideas which will sway judgment in the matter. One of the most important is the dispute whether there were urban centers in America, or whether the admittedly impressive sites that have been excavated should be considered merely ceremonial centers without the concentration of population and facilities and the quickening of human intercourse involved in an urban center (20). The dispute has more reality for students of Meso-America than for those of the Andean area, where large urban settlements are preserved in mud and stone. The question of extent of simultaneous occupation of houses may also be settled by the techniques of microdating of pottery styles now being worked out for Peru. These, when perfected, should permit dating within twenty or thirty year periods, but they have not yet been applied in Meso-America (21). Other problems relate to judgment as to density of occupation even within the boundaries worked out for an urban area. Thus Rene Millon has mapped the urban area of Teothihuacán at its peak as a maximum of 9.5 square miles (22), but he and William Saunders estimate the population at only 50,000-100,000, and find their figure subject to dispute (23). Nevertheless, study of archaeological sites in terms of size of site and numbers and size of houses does give indications that are likely to become the basis for better estimates as evidence on density is uncovered. The evidence at this time is especially good for examining direction of change in occupation and in human numbers.

2´). Estimates from labor needed to erect monuments or to provide surplus. Another approach is involved in a series of studies which have attempted to measure the number of people and periods of time needed to provide the materials and labor that have built monuments (24). Similarly, a long series of studies of cultivation and yields of crops under native systems and with native tools have aimed at finding out what are yields per acre or hectare, the amount of labor needed for cultivation, the amount of labor that a peasant family would be able to provide for other functions such as service and building in the year after feeding itself, and the extent to which a peasant population could provide a surplus for feeding a priesthood, nobility, and artisan and merchant classes (25). The results are still contradictory, and more studies are needed.

3´). Studies based upon stratigraphic analysis. An especially sophisticated approach is to study the strata of human occupation, and to trace the history of erosion in the area by relating deposition in the valleys due to cultivation of the soil, to the parent strata on the hillsides. The approach is especially good for studying changes in human occupation, but also yields estimates of numbers (26). Two especially notable studies are S. F. Cook's, The Historical Demography and Ecology of the Teotlalpan (already cited), and his Soil Erosion and Population in Central Mexico (27), a study of the antiquity of agriculture in central Mexico through analysis of strata.

4´). Determination of density and nature of human occupation through chemical analysis. A new technique now being developed attempts to determine the presence or absence of human population, and its relative density at various periods, through chemical analysis of soil cores taken at various points within the site and beyond it. The determination is based upon the building up of the content in phosphorus and organic matter in soils because of the concentration of phosphorus compounds and certain other elements in large mammals and the impregnation of the soil through their excreta. The technique is especially useful for suspected sites where there are no surviving artifacts (28), and for one area of Jalisco indicates a far denser prehistoric population than had been supposed.

5´). Determinations of technology and diet. A wide variety of kinds of examination used by archaeologists adds up to determination of the prevailing technology and perhaps kind of society. Of such nature are studies of storage areas and middens, the analysis of human feces if they are preserved in dry and protected places, the examination of tools, and even analysis of pollen. What is sought is evidence of the degree to which the prehistoric group derived its food from hunting and gathering or from agriculture. Pollen analysis gives direct evidence of the extent to which cultivated plants were present in the flora (29). From determination of proportion of reliance upon agriculture for food, the scholar can move to an estimate of relative density of population. Just what densities to postulate for each proportion is still under study, but the excavations of Professor MacNeish have gone far to perfect this approach. His studies of the population of the Valley of Tehuacán at various periods during a span of twelve millennia illustrate the methods and conceptions.

c). Estimates by geographers based upon studies of resources and technology. Although all of the categories that have been sketched impinge upon each other, are not mutually exclusive, and

involve studies of resources and technology, geographers in
particular give special emphasis to the study of food resources
available within a given area with its special land forms, soils,
and climate, due attention being given to the prevailing technology
and probable levels of consumption. An estimate of population may
be made through these considerations in one of two terms, either
1) at a density that is found to exist by studying what are
presumed to be similar populations at the present day or at a time
when records give us reasonably firm statements of numbers, or 2)
on the theory that human population will tend over time to build up
to and even pass the available food supply. Perhaps the most
illustrative series of estimates by a geographer, basically at
densities for similar populations at the present day, is by Karl
Sapper for the population of the New World just before the beginning of European disturbance (30).
        A special application of the technique may be seen in the
paper by Professor Denevan in this volume, in which probable size
of population in tropical America on the eve of European disturbance
is calculated in terms of food resources, diet, and patterns of
consumption. Two elements are especially important in his calculations, supply of protein from fish and utilization of a special
technique of mound building for agriculture in the seasonally
flooded regions of tropical South America. Nordenskiold had
noticed such mounds in the Mojos region of eastern Bolivia, but
Professor Denevan has now not merely discovered the far greater
extent of such mounds in the Mojos but also he and James J. Parsons
have found them over wide areas of the Guayas estuary, the coast of
Colombia, and in the Guianas (31). Their work gives new insight
into aboriginal technology and a basis for postulating wider use of
agriculture and far denser human occupation.
2.   Protohistoric Population
        Protohistoric populations in America may be defined as those
Indian groups which underwent change through European influences
that reached them through other Indian tribes or through perhaps
unrecorded, perhaps fairly infrequent European landings, incursions,
and explorations. The concept of a protohistoric period postulates
the possibility and even probability that massive alteration of
population took place once Europeans appeared in America even if
only as traders or casual explorers and that epidemics, territorial
pressures and reshufflings, and changes in technology set loose by
the Europeans travelled far in advance of their actual presence (32).
Only in a few areas of America did the Europeans appear in relative
force on their first landing and begin recording, so that the
population history can be said to have become possible at that point
in time. Hispaniola, central and southern Mexico, much of Central
America and Panama may be said to have moved directly from prehistory
into history; elsewhere the kind of disturbance postulated by the
concept of a protohistoric era must be taken into account. The
meaning of the concept is not that scholars can estimate population
for a protohistoric population, or that there are special techniques
appropriate to such a period, but rather that the first recorded
European statements on Indian populations must be looked at in
terms of this concept, for the statements may refer to a population
that had already undergone massive change in advance of the coming
of European records. At issue is the validity of many statements,

admittedly the earliest on number, as the basis for estimates of number and decisions on the nature of society and technology for Indians in many regions of America as undisturbed prehistoric or pre-Columbian populations, climax populations if one may use the phrase, even though the Indians demonstrably were subject to much protohistoric European influence. Thus our earliest evidence on Indian number for the Mojos region is of 1680 (33) although European expeditions had penetrated the region and there had been a good deal of intercourse with Europeans during the century previous (34). Even for the Inca empire our surviving reports of the last Inca counts of population do not give us an undisturbed people since the counts were made after a massive epidemic of European origin had devastated the empire (35). The concept of protohistoric period places in issue most of the attempts to estimate the pre-Columbian population of temperate North America, especially by Mooney and Kroeber (36), and those for large parts of Latin America.

3.   Period of Initial European Contact

The first years in which Europeans met Indian populations previously isolated from Old World influences form a topic imbued with romance and violent controversy. The exact years varied, of course, from region to region throughout America. That the contact, whether in the form of conquest, warfare, or merely exploration and trade, set up rapid and far-reaching changes in Indian societies is, on the whole, agreed. On the other hand, whether those far-reaching changes were reflected in equally far-reaching changes in Indian numbers, initially at least in massive decline, is hotly debated. The evidence and the methods of analysis are subject to much dispute as to credibility and validity. Kinds of evidence, methods of analysis, and the disputes must be considered at some length. The basic questions are: what was the size of the Indian populations of America (for the debate covers temperate North America as well) in the years before there was disturbance due to European influence or direct contact, and to what extent was there sharp and even disastrous decline thereafter?

The kinds of evidence that become available with the beginning of European contact vary greatly with region and with time. The major addition, of course, is written material, historical evidence in the classical sense of the term. Written materials are far more abundant, in general, for the regions of dense, sedentary Indian occupation, especially wherever in succeeding centuries enough Indian population was present to support a substantial European upper class. The following description of kinds of evidence pertains best to the regions of higher native culture in Spanish America. The categories overlap considerably.

a). Historical Materials.

1´). Descriptions and estimates by Europeans. The first explorers, conquerors, missionaries, and settlers attempted to form an idea of the new region and its inhabitants, and usually gave reports on numbers. These might range all the way from attempts to estimate men engaged in battle to numbers of houses, families, or persons in various categories. The newcomers might attempt to count population on their own or, if there was a native administrative system that could give such information, they might ask the natives. In the latter instance, the Europeans served merely to record native testimony. Of such nature probably were Cortés's early statements on numbers of inhabitants for cities and provinces of Mexico (37).

2´). Native statements of number. Upon questioning by the Europeans, the natives reported such kinds of counts as they might have made for their own purposes. These might be in terms of numbers of warriors in the native population, numbers of families or tributaries or households, or statements in categories that the natives regarded as socially or economically significant in terms of their own system.

3´). Fiscal materials. If the Europeans subjugated the natives in a region, they instituted levies of materials, specie, and service, and kept records. At the outset, such levies were likely to represent a rough adaptation of the native system of taxation to European needs and contained very substantial survivals of native forms. The records kept by the Europeans of such levies are therefore very important for a great variety of studies, including demographic history. For central Mexico, such early tribute records usually give statements of items and frequency of delivery, but do not state the number of the population that was to deliver tribute although there must have been a fairly precise idea of its size and capacity to pay. For Peru, the royal Spanish inquiries into capacity to pay tribute record detailed statements on numbers, categories by social status, sex, maturity, household, and so on.

4´). Missionary and church reports. The earliest Europeans to enter a region either included missionaries or were soon followed by them. If the region was subjugated, the missionaries were able to embark upon general conversion. We owe to missionaries reports on numbers of people converted, baptized, and brought to communion or confession. Wherever a general church organization was established rapidly, there were reports on numbers of faithful in various categories as part of normal parish administration.

5´). Later recording of native tradition; memories of first European explorers, conquerors, and missionaries; and searching of native resources. At some time after the entrance of the Europeans, there was likely to be a series of attempts, some at the direction of the European government, others the normal desire of people to write their memoirs, that give much information on the first years of contact. The famous Relaciones Geográficas, prepared at the command of Philip II, as a set questionnaire on each town or subordinate political unit in America, answered by interrogation of natives and long-resident Spaniards, preserve for us a vast mass of native tradition and much information on pre-Conquest numbers. Native legends and chronicles, originally handed down orally or in native writing, were recorded in the Latin alphabet either in native or European tongues. Later memoirs of Europeans give much information, as do systematic inquiries by Europeans and European-trained natives into what was native society and culture before the coming of the Europeans. The variety and mass of such material is enormous, and has given rise to a special branch of study, half history, half anthropology, called ethnohistory (38).

b). Archaeological, biogeographical, and geographical evidence. The coming of Europeans did not end the usefulness of the materials and techniques of prehistory but merely supplemented them with historical evidence. For many regions, where European recording came late in European contact, or where historical materials are sparse, the techniques of prehistory remain our primary providers of information. The usefulness of each group varies from region to region. Whatever the difficulties of application and interpretation, the techniques of prehistory are far less subject to controversy than are studies based on historical materials.

The mere existence of historical materials seems to increase rather than solve controversy. In general, the testimony of European firstcomers, fiscal evidence, missionary and church reporting, and native testimony and tradition indicate very high figures for the population at the time of the coming of the Europeans, figures which are very much higher than the population in later years. The tendency of many scholars has been to reject contemporary evidence. The famous anthropologist, A. L. Kroeber, has summarized the matter very well:

> "Whoever uses Spanish figures seems almost always to reach
> higher populations than modern ethnologists. The kernel
> of the problem lies here. Shall we pin more faith on
> contemporary Spanish opinions, or on those of professional
> ethnologists who often have not seen an Indian of the
> tribes they deal with?. . . !"(39)

Kroeber, it should be added, rejected most Spanish figures outright himself and upheld the judgment of the ethnologist. Of a piece with the attitude of many scholars are two more rules of thumb of considerable currency today, namely, 1) that all European explorers upon coming into contact with other peoples over-estimate their numbers, usually by substantial margins (40), and 2) that since sixteenth and seventeenth century Europeans were characterized by a relative lack of statistical sophistication, they could not count large numbers or handle fairly complex governmental administration and finance with reasonable accuracy (41).

The challenges to the validity of all historical material on early native numbers do not go unanswered. Other scholars point out that the idea of universal exaggeration postulates a theory of conspiracy among conquerors, missionaries, local officials, administrators sent out from Spain, chroniclers, recorders of Indian tradition, and Indian elders, and that despite their rivalries, quarrels, prolonged litigation, and steady tattling on each other. It demands such unanimity cutting across all animosity and partisan affiliation and across generations and regions that credence in their reporting requires less faith than does disbelief. Furthermore, whatever their lack of sophistication in our kinds of statistics, Europeans of the sixteenth and seventeenth centuries were able to conduct business and government, to trade, to issue bills of exchange and collect on them, to assess and levy taxes, and to keep records of their transactions so that they can hardly be accused with any justice of not being able to count (42). The fiscal records of Philip II's government in Castile have turned out, upon careful inspection, to have been very well kept and give us relatively precise ideas of income, expenditure, and deficit (43).

It is absurd to think that a tribute assessment at the time it was
made meant merely a hyperbolic desire for delivery and that the
justice setting amounts and times and the official or encomendero
supposed to receive payment did not expect delivery of the items in
the quantities and at the times specified.

The differences in approach to the materials on Indian
numbers at the close of the fifteenth century, say on the eve of
the coming of the Europeans, show up very quickly in the range of
estimates for America as a whole. The highest has been 300
millions (44); the lowest, 8.4 millions (45). In our century, when
one might expect that more careful study might moderate the
divergence, it has been brought down at its upper limit to perhaps
100 millions but remains the same at the lower limit. A brief
review of the more seriously made estimates in this century will
give some idea of the differences of opinion. Spinden, who knew
the Mayan area well, postulated 40-50 millions for all of America
for 1492 and a peak at 50-75 millions around the year 1200 A.D.
Rivet in 1924 arrived at a similar figure of 40-50 millions for
1492, but after very considerable criticism of his estimate,
reduced it in 1952 to 15.5 millions (46). Two of the most
impressive and careful statements were by the famous German scholar,
Karl Sapper. In 1924, on the basis of technology, resources, and
comparative examination of extent and densities of human occupation, he estimated 40-60 millions for 1492, of whom 12-15 millions
were in Mexico, an equal number in the Andean area, and 5-6
millions in Central America (47). In 1935, under the impact of
Kroeber's and Mooney's calculations for temperate North America,
Sapper dropped all estimates for temperate North and South America,
on the admission that he knew little about either, and carefully
reexamined his calculations for tropical America. He shaved down
his estimates for most regions and drastically reduced his figure
for the West Indies, but nevertheless, arrived at a calculation of
31 millions (48). The lowest estimates came in the 1930's.
Kroeber, who knew temperate North America well, revised calculations
for temperate North America by James Mooney and added rough
calculations of density of settlement to arrive at a total of 8.4
millions, with Meso-America and the Incan empire each assigned
3.0 millions. In a thoughtful discussion, Kroeber pointed out that
there was little evidence for any decision, that accordingly he
deliberately had chosen low estimates, and invited careful regional
study that might provide better answers (49). At approximately the
same time Angel Rosenblat prepared his study. His estimate for all
of America in 1492 is 13.385 millions (50). More recently, as
detailed regional study has tended to support higher estimates, new
estimates for America as a whole have exceeded the higher figures
postulated early in this century. In 1962, in an admittedly hasty
and general estimate extending proportions based on central Mexico
to the rest of America, I suggested that we might well find in the
end that the population in 1492 was upwards of 100 millions (51).
The anthropologist, Henry Dobyns, applying an average proportion of
decline for populations that did survive, has recently come to an
estimate of 90-112 millions (52).

As one examines the long series of differing opinions and
estimates that have been advanced since at least the middle of the
eighteenth century, it becomes clear that there has been substantial

polarization into two positions which one may dub the Robertson-Bandelier and the Clavijero-Prescott. Although a substantial number of scholars hold to intermediate positions between the two camps, views, attitudes, and arguments have had a remarkable continuity over two centuries. It also becomes clear that involved in the differences over method and interpretation and often underlying them as potent but barely visible forces are a series of conceptual and ideological disagreements that deeply influence judgments on the validity of evidence and techniques of analysis. I shall try to summarize the conceptual and ideological disagreements and then return to the discussion on differences over evidence and techniques of analysis:

a). The nature of pre-Columbian Indian society. The disagreements involve views on the complexity of social structure, extent of social stratification, division of labor, and the extent and manner of production of a surplus from primary production. The range of opinion runs from those who could see merely more elaborate chiefdoms in Meso-America and the Andes to those who see highly complex social structures. Robertson (53) in the eighteenth century and Bandelier (54) in the nineteenth would lie at one extreme; Kroeber and Steward (55) are in an intermediate position that would accept elaborate social structures and, therefore, substantial surplus of primary production for the areas of advanced culture. Cook, Simpson, and I (56) would agree with Prescott (57) in the existence of highly complex societies having at their disposal a huge surplus from the small surpluses created individually by a horde of peasant families. For Mexico and Peru, the picture would be not too dissimilar to pharaonic Egypt. Another form of question, for Meso-America at least, is whether or not the Indians had true urban centers, except admittedly for a few such as Tenochtitlán, or whether the towns were mere ceremonial centers of such low concentration of civic and intellectual interchange that they could not fulfill the same functions as the urban centers of the ancient eastern Mediterranean. The extremes would be Ronald Spores (58) and Michael Coe (59), who deny the extensive existence of urban centers, and Alfonso Caso (60), who finds urban centers widespread and points to the existence of large-scale territorial units of some worthy of the name of empires even for the much earlier periods of Teotihuacán and the culture of La Venta. The discussion on all of these questions comes to sharp focus on density of human occupation and extent of surplus production.

b). Interpretations of the general course of history. We deal here with disagreements over interpretations of the world, past and present.

1'). The idea of progress. For many scholars the idea that the present is superior to the past has an interesting corollary that earlier periods of time must have had smaller populations than later ones; if an earlier population postulated would be nearly equal to or larger than the present-day one in the same area, the estimate must be wrong (61). The opposing view is likely to emphasize fluctuations and even cycles.

2'). The European conscience. The decades in which we live have been the period of the relinquishment of much of direct European political control over other parts of the globe and the reassertion of old native sovereignties or the emergence of new ones searching for ties to traditions antedating the European dominance. Liberation, a consciousness of past exploitation for the profit of the imperial country, and the need for achieving a viable European- ized and economically developed structure lead to a series of views that strongly influence interpretations. In Europe and the United States scholars are strongly influenced by their general views on former colonial areas and current economic and political relations with them (62). The general category may be broken into a number of elements which overlap considerably:

a´). Reparation for historical wrongs to native peoples. The destruction of a large native population and highly organized native political and social structure is held to mean greater European guilt because of conquest and domination; conversely, the existence of a smaller native population which underwent less loss or none at all and the existence of more primitive social and political structures are held to diminish European guilt (63). In Marxist terms the matter may be stated as determination of the extent of capitalist damage to innocent native peoples (64). Marxist statement is especially useful for countries such as the Soviet Union since the fires of revolution have purged the guilt incurred through similar treatment of native peoples (although not American ones) by preceding regimes.

b´). Indigenismo and the search for a non- European basis of national origin and identification. For those countries which have a substantial or predominant proportion of Indian genetic stock in their present populations, the political state attempts to create a sense of nationality through finding values and tradition separate from European culture, with its memories of imperial control. Mexico has had perhaps the most pronounced such movement, but the impulse has shown up in all Latin American countries which were the seats of advanced native cultures and have substantial proportions of native genetic stock in the present population. Attitudes function as in the preceding category.

c´). Exaltation of the European. The counter- current is emphasis upon the European contribution in former possessions and depreciation or lesser emphasis upon previous native society and its contributions to the new national state (65). For Spain, the discussion rapidly touches upon the Leyenda Negra and the opposed Leyenda Blanca or Rosada. An especially interesting and intricate series of attitudes is manifest in the devotees of Las Casas, who tend to emphasize the Spanish conscience and humanitarian impulses, with Las Casas as a principal figure, but are usually not prepared to accept the large aboriginal populations and their brutal destruction as reported by Las Casas himself (66). In general also, scholars of conservative political orientation tend to emphasize the European elements in the national culture since the more radical political elements tend to be anti-European and nativist.

Lest these formulations be considered mere abstractions, let me point out that it is possible for Peru to name a naval vessel Huascar (67) but not Pizarro, that Pizarro may be commemorated in Peru as the founder of Lima but not the present country of Peru, that Cortés goes unhonored in Mexico although much honor is rendered Cuauhtémoc, the last Aztec emperor, and that even now high estimates of pre-Conquest native populations can be denounced as another form of the Leyenda Negra (68).

What one may call ideological perturbations deeply affect the choice and acceptance of method. I have already mentioned in my discussion of historical materials that there is dispute over the reliability of the testimony and over what is then proposed by some as preferable, namely, that the scholar simply apply estimates representing what he is prepared to accept whether or not they have much relation to the data in the historical materials. There are, in addition, other conceptions and kinds of methods which ought to be mentioned, either because they give rise to considerable objection or because they offer new techniques of analysis that in the end will furnish sounder means of arriving at estimates:

a). Estimates derived by application of data on density of occupation for one region to estimates for another. This is simply a form of the technique of estimate already described in the section on prehistory, but used by anthropologists and historians for contact populations. If technology, resources, and kind of occupation are similar in the two regions, the method would seem valid. The major use of the method to date, however, has been to apply conceptions and data derived from study of temperate North America to Latin America. Such application has been objected to as on a par with attempting to estimate the population of Europe or the Mediterranean Basin on the basis of data derived from study of the tribes of northern Siberia (69). The objection would seem just. Another application of the method is a kind of good neighbor policy in historical demography which automatically accords approximately equal postulated populations for the sedentary Indians of either Meso-America or Mexico and those of the Inca empire. Such application would seem to require further study.

b). Examination of data with attention to the ideas of protohistory and a European-induced pandemic. The idea that in many areas there may have occurred disturbances of ultimate European origin in advance of European presence or reporting requires that data be examined carefully to determine the extent to which an undisturbed or altered population is involved. Much of the early reporting on numbers for interior regions of South America, in terms of this conception, must be regarded as applicable to the specific years when it was made but not applicable to a prehistoric population. The formulation of the idea of protohistory is closely related to a more far-reaching conception, namely that during the long centuries and millennia of isolation from contact with the Old World, the Indians of the New World enjoyed relative freedom from epidemics and especially from the major destructive ones of the Old World. When the Europeans in the same centuries began to navigate to most parts of the globe and opened communication on a far larger scale and intensity in the Old World as well as communication with the New, they brought to America not only the diseases which had slowly spread along the paths of trade of Eurasia during millennia, often in destructive epidemics but with opportunity for the populations to recover, but they also brought to America tropical diseases which found fertile territory. There was an American contribution to global diseases but hardly of equal proportions. The European unification of the globe meant that the diseases of the Old World came so quickly into populations hitherto unexposed

that epidemics were unusually destructive and the entrance of new
diseases came in a steady series of blows from which during the
first decades or centuries the native populations seldom or never
had respite in which to recover. Once European-brought diseases
began to have effect, American populations cannot have remained
static (70).

c). The treatment of numerical statements which seem
accurate but are not complete. For areas such as Meso-America,
where European occupation occurred simultaneously with first
European contact, there are available fairly early counts of a
fiscal nature that are usually conceded to be of reasonable
accuracy. Such, for example, is the Suma de Visitas, a count of
perhaps a half of central Mexico carried out between 1547 and 1550.
The problem with finding total population on the basis of such a
document lies in the varied categories used to enumerate the
population (tributaries, heads of families, total persons, persons
over three or four years of age), the exclusion of classes exempt
from tribute, and the failure to achieve complete territorial
coverage. The necessary adjustments to arrive at an estimate of
total population for all of central Mexico are complicated and
give rise to substantial objection at virtually all points (71).
Nevertheless, if the documents are carefully tested and the
adjustments are based upon a reasonable range of evidence, the
method is sound. The problems here are closely parallel to those
of European demographic history.

d). Use of the bi-chronic method. Since so much of the
documentary evidence is fragmentary, arriving at an estimate for
the entire area under study requires use of proportion, that is,
applying the proportion that the area for which evidence is
available bore to the remainder of the region at the nearest time
or times for which there is fuller coverage. For central Mexico,
for which extensive tribute counts in the 1560's cover almost all
of the territory, studies of sixteenth century population usually
take a fix on the 1560's for estimates for other points in time in
the century (72). The method would seem sound provided that nothing
had happened to change the general distribution of populations.

e). Projection and interpolation. This category has
within it the ironic fact that projection is used both by advocates
of high and low estimates but very differently. Rosenblat's low
estimates of population for 1492 are based mostly upon a compilation
of the population of Spanish America formed in the early 1570's by
the Spanish royal cosmographer-general, Juan López de Velasco.
Rosenblat has accepted these figures as applicable to 1570, and
has then projected them backward with slight adjustment to 1492 (73).
However, examination of the sources of López de Velasco, which
became possible with further archival research into tribute counts
and other reports, has demonstrated that the cosmographer-general's
compilation brings together counts carried out at various times over
nearly a quarter of a century, and that use of those counts for
1570 automatically applies a conception of a population that underwent little or no change from 1548 to 1573. Projection backward to
1492 applies fundamentally the same conception. Another and quite
different use of calculation from later counts has been made in
recent years by finding pairs of counts of town populations, one
count being earlier and the other later. The scholar can compute

the ratio and rate of change from one count to the other for each
town and arrive at an average for the region. If the data available
constitute a reasonable and unbiased sample as to number of towns,
territorial coverage, and temporal coverage, the calculation in the
form either of a ratio or a rate is applicable to the entire region.
It is applicable, moreover, to the time span in which evidence
indicates that the same trend obtained, and may be used for calculation of total population at any point in the period of that trend
from a single good fix on total number such as the central Mexican
tribute counts of the 1560's. The method has great usefulness in
settling questions over interpretation of social systems, extent
of exemptions, and so forth when what is at issue is a change in
the fiscal system, for rates of change can be calculated by
examining separately each term of years in which the fiscal system
used a uniform system. (One can calculate on change in quantity of
tribute assessed as well as counts of people.) For central Mexico,
where decrease held relatively steady at an average of 4.5 per
cent a year from 1532 to 1548 and from 1560 to 1590, one is
justified in concluding that increases in the number of tributaries
on the rolls were indeed due to abolition of exemptions, that the
trend from 1548 to 1560 must have been the same, and further that
the initiation of the trend must be referable to the Conquest (74).
The method is statistically sound, but since it resolves all
significant questions of interpretation in favor of the advocates
of high estimates, it is likely to increase an already substantial
dislike of statistical analysis among some scholars.

From what I have said already, it may have become apparent
that in the past decades there has been a steady uncovering of
new historical material and the development not only of techniques
for treating the data but also of growing awareness of the factors
that must be taken into account in interpreting results and in
formulating ideas of what happened to populations in America after
the advent of the Europeans. There exists resistance to such
development and preference on the part of some of the people
writing at present on contact populations for a pleasantly literary
approach to the topic, but in the end more arduous and demanding
methods are certain to prevail. In the past thirty-five years
careful regional studies have begun to supply the detailed
examination of evidence called for by Kroeber. One might mention
for the northwest of Mexico and for California, the studies of
Sauer (75), Cook (76), and Aschmann (77); for central Mexico, the
studies of Sauer (78), Cook, Simpson, and Borah (79); for Yucatan,
a number including the recent paper by J. Eric Thompson (80); for
Colombia, the work of Juan Friede (81); and for the Amazon basin,
the studies of William Denevan (82). For Peru, the publication of
much new material, especially on the provinces of Chucuito (83) and
Huánuco (84), is making available by far the most detailed and
inclusive reporting, which can be the basis for historical-
demographic study going far beyond mere determination of total
number of persons. Clearly most of the work using substantial
masses of historical evidence, careful application of historical
methods of verification, and statistical analysis has been done thus
far on central and northwest Mexico.

4.   The Period of Protostatistical Recording
       Initial European contact, if it meant rapid European

conquest, was followed by early implantation of European systems of
civil and religious administration; if conquest came later, such
implantation was delayed. For central Mexico, for example, one can
talk of a divide in the years 1558-1562 marking the shift from
administration still predominantly using native definitions and
classifications to a far more uniform and Europeanized system; for
a mission frontier such as Lower California, the implantation of
the European system came only at the end of the seventeenth century
and in the early decades of the eighteenth century. The beginning
of the period of protostatistical recording, then, in some regions
was as early as the middle of the sixteenth century. Its end came
after the middle of the nineteenth century with the adoption of an
organized system of civil registration of vital statistics and
census taking in the new fashion of Europe. Within the three
centuries of this period at its longest, one may distinguish three
sub-periods: a). From the middle of the sixteenth century to
perhaps 1770, the implantation of European systems of church
records and reporting and the recording and reporting of the civil
government through fiscal counts, military counts, and occasional
attempts to determine numbers in the population although without a
carefully organized census in our terms; b). The last decades of
the colonial regime, from 1770 to 1810, a sub-period characterized
by massive overhaul of the administration, the institution of much
more careful administration of existing systems of recording, the
beginning of census taking, and development of a reporting system to
a central authority in each colony and in the empire that provided
remarkably good statistics; c). The first decades of independent
regimes in Latin America, a sub-period characterized by sporadic and
largely ineffectual attempts to continue older forms of reporting,
to harness them for the needs of the new states, and the eventual
realization that entirely new forms and organizations would be
needed. The three centuries were not static but rather were marked
by much experimentation, and increasing desire for demographic
information and attempts to gather it, and the steady development of
understanding of the kind of agencies needed for reporting.
     Once the protostatistical European systems of civil and
religious reporting were implanted, they began to yield a wide
variety of data which can be used for demographic study. The
existence of such substantial masses of data tends to change the
nature of examination and discussion. Disputes diminish in scope
and intensity in the presence of relatively abundant data. Although
establishing the size of populations remains important, study
spreads out to such questions as family number, age specific
composition of the population, racial groupings, the sources and
role of migration both from abroad and within the region, direction
and rate of change, causes and rates of morbidity and mortality.
The materials available resemble, although with substantial
regional variations, those found for western European countries at
the same time. As is also true for the western European materials,
examination is just beginning to probe the kinds of treatment
possible and the extent to which the materials will yield answers.
What has already emerged from the studies for Latin America is an
understanding, as the paper by Rolando Mellafe in this volume
shows, that the history of population in the three centuries was
complex and varied widely from region to region. Flight from

oppressive burdens, the opening of frontier areas, and colonization of sparsely settled lands gave population change a dynamic quality.

The kinds of materials of interest for demographic history in this period may be outlined as follows:

   a).   Church reporting.

      1′).   Parish records.   In the middle and last third of the sixteenth century, church dioceses implemented the requirements of the Council of Trent for the maintenance within each parish of registers of baptisms, marriages, and burials _inter alia_.   In much of Latin America the registers were kept in two sets, one for Indians, and the other for non-Indians; in some regions, there were three sets, a third being kept to segregate the Negroes and people of mixed color from both Indians and Europeans.   Few registers of the sixteenth century survive, but for many parishes relatively good series have survived with a start in the seventeenth or early eighteenth century.   As in Europe, the registers vary widely in the care with which they were kept, but many are excellent.   The baptisms are probably the most complete; the marriage registers, although recording all marriages, suffer from the absence of large numbers of unions never solemnized with church rite.   The death registers are usually the least complete, but do give evidence on cause of death and age at death.   The use of parish registers that has been made in France--family reconstruction--is undoubtedly possible for periods and areas of Latin America, but is difficult for the Indians of central Mexico because they tended to use only a few surnames (85).   The excellent records kept in the missions are an unusually promising source of demographic data.   Those for parts of northern Mexico and California have been put to intensive use (86).

      2′).   Church counts.   The clergy of Latin America reported on numbers at irregular intervals.   Bishops during their incumbency were charged with the pastoral visit of their dioceses, and the best executed of such inspections have left us careful discussions of the state of the churches and the parishioners, including records of counts of the population made for the bishop's information and records of the numbers of people confirmed or listed as of age of confession (87).   Under stimulus from the royal government, the dioceses ordered counts of the population, especially in the last decades of the colonial regime, the parish priests carrying out the actual enumeration and reporting.   The paper by Trent M. Brady and John V. Lombardi in this volume is an advance report on a project for computer study of the population of the archdiocese of Caracas using the excellent diocesan counts of the last half century of the colonial period.

      3′).   Church fiscal records.   Although they are not ordinarily thought of as having demographic information, many church fiscal records do.   Those on tithe collection, for example, contain much information on people, their race, activities, and density of settlement as well as economic activity (88).   As far as I am aware, little or no use has been made of such fiscal records for historical demographical study.

   b).   Civil Reporting.

      1′).   Fiscal   counts.   The royal governments in Spanish and Portuguese America made counts for collection of taxes or for assessment of quotas.   Perhaps the most useful subcategory of fiscal

count is the tribute count of Spanish America, a count of the
Indians of age to pay royal tribute, carried out in various
districts and in later years checked against the parish registers to
insure accuracy. The addition to some counts of próximos a tributar
and other groups in the population makes the counts usable for study
of size of family and household, and even a crude form of age
specific analysis (89). The head tax of the period of independence
supplied an equivalent form of listing that covered all of the
adult males.

2´). Counts for other administrative purposes. The
royal governments also carried out counts for purposes other than
directly fiscal ones, such as enrollment of males for militia duty,
listing of whites and non-Indians for verification of right to
residence and for other administrative and economic information (90).
After independence, militia duty became a major reason for registration of population.

3´). Censuses. A special category of count, the census,
which yielded information on number, sex, age, race, and occupation,
and as much else as the central authority wished to inquire into
appeared in the middle decades of the eighteenth century. A series
of experiments carried out with use of civil and religious authorities and testing kinds of information wanted for administrative
purposes slowly perfected the technique in more than a half century.
In 1776-1777 the royal Spanish and Portuguese governments ordered
general censuses in their American possessions, those in Spanish
America being carried out through the bishops, with the parish
priests the reporting agents. Perhaps because of church discipline,
the results, where they survive, include some of the best counts
taken (91). In Mexico, another series of good counts, one of
general population and another of non-Indians (technically for
military information but an excellent report on all ages and sexes
of non-Indians) was carried out in 1790-1794 by the famous Viceroy
Revillagigedo II (92). With the coming of independence, the census
became a necessary instrument for determining apportionment of
representation in the new national and regional legislatures, but
governments trying to develop staff and administrative technique
were able to carry out only local or incomplete ones (93). The
attempt to harness church reporting for the purpose did not work
well, and in any event fell apart in the battle over the role of
the church within the new countries (94).

In general, one may say that the best records of the three
centuries under discussion are those prepared in the last decades of
the colonial regimes, that the most fragmented and variable are
those of the decades after independence. Nevertheless, under
careful study and analysis the records of the three centuries can
yield much information. On the whole, the materials have not been
put to use. The papers by Rolando Mellafe and by S. F. Cook
illustrate uses of the information cutting across types of reporting
and sub-periods. The research group in Buenos Aires and Rosario,
working under guidance of Nicolás Sánchez-Albornoz, has been the
most productive in terms of numbers of papers to date (95).

5. The Age of Systematic Gathering of Statistics

We come now to the present, but systematic gathering of
statistics is really a statement of ideal rather than of omnipresent
practice. Perhaps the Age of the New Reporting would be more

accurate. The attempt to provide national demographic reporting in accordance with the new ideas and systems evolved in Europe embraces essentially the institution of country-wide civil registration of vital statistics and the holding of censuses in accordance with the new conception of a systematic, country-wide count made on a uniform basis and within a period of days, or at most weeks. In the second half of the nineteenth century virtually every country of Latin America adopted both systems. Implementation, however, and completeness and accuracy of coverage vary widely from country to country and even vary by period within each country (96).

The institution of country-wide civil registry meant in each country the abandonment of attempts to use church recording for gathering vital statistics. As in England, the abandonment came about in part because of failure to secure through the parish priests accurate and full coverage; as in France, it was linked usually with a conflict between church and state and between liberals and conservatives over the role of the church. The political and religious conflict has meant that acceptance of civil registry has been very slow and far from complete in many countries. The usual requirement of a civil marriage ceremony as the only one having legal standing for state purposes has led to substantial refusal to repeat a religious ceremony before the civil authorities or simply to resort to free union--a "plague on both houses" reaction (97). For most of Latin America, the civil marriage registers are therefore but a partial and often biased guide to the habits of the people in forming sexual and family unions. Registers of deaths and births are more reliable, those of births most so, but even in a country like Mexico, where after a century of attempts to implant the civil registration of births and steady conciliatory cooperation in recent years between church and state, registration of births is thought now to be almost complete, from 7% to 9% of births are registered at some time after the person involved has begun the second year of life (98).

Similarly the country-wide census has come to Latin America slowly and the results continue to be less accurate than those for western Europe or the United States. A long series of experiments in each country usually led to the creation of a national bureau of statistics supervising the civil register and in charge of the holding of national censuses. Some countries have taken censuses at regular intervals for relatively long periods; others have been unable to do so because of poverty or internal turmoil; others have found it politically expedient not to do so. However, in general, there are useful series for most countries. This is not to say that they are free from substantial difficulties. A simple test, comparing the count of children in the first year of life with those in the second, third, fourth, and fifth years, or tracing the number of children in the first year of life in an earlier census with that of the same cohort in a later one is apt to instill a very real sense of caution in the scholar. A number of difficulties that have appeared seem to be especially Latin American: bad coverage in rural areas of rugged topography because of the low return to poorly-paid census takers; less than good coverage for cities with apartment buildings without elevators; a special mistake in Argentina of making the day of the taking of the census a holiday, whereupon the people joyously went on vacation instead of waiting dutifully to be counted; the difficulty of administering increasingly complex schedules of questions in populations with low proportions of literacy and even lower proportions of acquaintance with the ideas in the schedules; the even greater difficulty of administering such schedules through Spanish-speaking employees in areas of predominantly or almost exclusively Indian speech. Finally, as in most countries today, the introduction of more sophisticated methods of treatment, such as carding the information and computer analysis, introduces the additional errors of the operatives and machines.

I list the problems in recent and current demographic reporting from Latin America not to depreciate the steadily increasing and improving fund of information that is becoming available, but merely to warn that the special alertness of the historical demographer in testing evidence remains necessary in its use. A wide variety of studies makes use of these materials for all countries. Most belong in the category of current demographic study and demographic projection of the immediate future. But the existence of materials covering a period of nearly a century, with magnificent possibilities for analysis of kinds often not easily possible for earlier periods, increasingly lures historical demographers. The paper in this volume by Nicolás Sánchez-Albornoz on "Población y Despoblación Rural en la Provincia de Buenos Aires, 1869-1960" is an example of one kind of historical study that is possible.

(REFERENCES)

1) See the estimates of W. F. Willcox and A. M. Carr-Saunders, in A. M. Carr-Saunders, World Population. Past Growth and Present Trends (Oxford, 1936), pp. 29-45, esp. figures 7 and 8 on pp. 30 and 42. The estimates for Latin America for 1800 are based on the reporting of Alexander von Humboldt, whose reporting in turn derives from the counts carried out by the royal Spanish and Portuguese governments in the last decades of the eighteenth century.

2) Angel Rosenblat, La población indígena y el mestizaje en América (3d ed., 2 vols., Buenos Aires, 1954). For a statement of the previous editions, see pp. 9-10 therein. His estimates are summarized in a series of tables between pp. 20-21, 36-37, and on pp. 58, 88, and 102. The first edition made estimates for 1930.

3) Rosenblat, La población indígena, passim. See also Angel Rosenblat, La población de América en 1492. Viejos y nuevos cálculos (Mexico City, 1967), essentially an expansion and revision of a paper delivered at the International Congress of Americanists, XXXVII, Mar del Plata, September, 1966, and Woodrow Borah, "The Historical Demography of Aboriginal and Colonial Latin America: An Attempt at Perspective," a paper read at the same session and to be published in the proceedings.

4) Rodolfo Barón Castro, La población de El Salvador. Estudio acerca de su desenvolvimiento desde la época prehispánica hasta nuestros días. (Madrid, 1942). For the colonial period the volume is really useful for the study of all of Central America save Panama.

5) Nicolás Besio Moreno, Buenos Aires, puerto del rio de la Plata, capital de la Argentina; estudio critico de su población 1536-1936. (Buenos Aires, 1939).

6) Nicolás Sánchez-Albornoz and Susana Torrado, "Perfil y proyecciones de la demografía histórica en la Argentina," in Universidad Nacional del Litoral, Rosario (Argentina), Facultad de Filosofía, Letras y Ciencias del Hombre, Anuario del Instituto de Investigaciones Históricas, VIII, 31-56 (1965).

7) See the latest article proposing a longer antiquity for man in South America, Edward P. Lanning and Thomas C. Patterson, "Early Man in South America," in Scientific American, vol. 217, no. 5, pp. 44-50 (November, 1967).

8) Inter alia, Richard S. MacNeish, El origen de la civilización mesoamericana visto desde Tehuacán (Instituto Nacional de Antropología e Historia, Departamento de Prehistoria, Mexico City, 1964); Restos precerámicos de la Cueva de Coxcatlán en el sur de Puebla (Instituto Nacional de Antropología e Historia, Dirección de Prehistoria, Mexico City, 1961); "The Origins of New World Civilization," in Scientific American, vol. 211, no. 5, pp. 29-37 (November, 1964). See also the very interesting discussion in José L. Lorenzo, La revolución neolítica en Mesoamérica (Instituto Nacional de Antropología e Historia, Departamento de Prehistoria, Mexico City, 1961).

9)   J. Eric S. Thompson, The Rise and Fall of Maya Civilization
        (Norman, Oklahoma, 1954), pp. 165-170. See also the very
        full discussion in J. Eric S. Thompson, Maya Hieroglyphic
        Writing. An Introduction (2d rev. ed., Norman, Oklahoma,
        1960).

10)   We owe most to Alfonso Caso for decipherment of the Mixtec
        codices. The references are too numerous to cite in full.
        Two of Alfonso Caso's papers are especially informative:
        "El mapa de Teozacoalco," in Cuadernos americanos, año 8,
        vol. 47, núm. 5, pp. 3-40 (1949), which reports on one of
        the key readings; and "Valor histórico de los códices
        mixtecos," in Cuadernos americanos, año 19, vol. 109,
        núm. 2, pp. 139-147 (1960), which gives a general account.
        See also Philip Dark, A Method of Analysis of the Codical
        Art (Oxford, 1958) and Charles E. Dibble, "El antiguo sistema
        de escritura en México," in Revista mexicana de estudios
        antropológicos, vol. 4, núm's. 1-2, pp. 105-128 (1940). The
        forthcoming volumes on ethnohistory in the Handbook of Middle
        American Indians will publish a series of papers in English
        on Meso-American codices, their decipherment to date, and a
        remarkably comprehensive bibliography by John B. Glass.

11)   The forthcoming volumes on ethnohistory in the Handbook of
        Middle American Indians will cover these topics at length.

12)   Julian H. Steward and Louis C. Faron, Native Peoples of South
        America (New York, 1959), pp. 51-54.

13)   See Alfred L. Kroeber, Cultural and Natural Areas of Native
        North America (University of California Publications in
        American Archaeology and Ethnology: 27, Berkeley, 1939),
        pp. 131-181.

14)   Sherburne F. Cook, The Historical Demography and Ecology of
        the Teotlalpan (Ibero-Americana: 33, Berkeley and Los
        Angeles, 1949). See especially pp. 51-59.

15)   For the method, see P. W. Richards, The Tropical Rain Forest.
        An Ecological Study (Cambridge, 1952); P. H. Nye and
        D. J. Greenland, The Soil Under Shifting Cultivation
        (Commonwealth Bureau of Soils, Harpenden, Technical Communi-
        cation, 51, 1960); Special Symposium on Climate, Vegetation,
        and Rational Land Utilization in the Humid Tropics (Bangkok,
        1958).

16)   Ibero-Americana: 46, Berkeley and Los Angeles, 1963.

17)   Ibero-Americana: 36, Berkeley and Los Angeles, 1952.

18)   William L. Thomas, Jr., ed., Man's Role in Changing the Face
        of the Earth (Chicago, 1956); Carl O. Sauer, "Grassland
        Climax, Fire, and Man," Journal of Range Management, III,
        16-21 (1950); The Tall Timbers Fire Ecology Conference,
        Tallahassee, Florida, Proceedings, I-VI (1960-1967, a
        continuing annual series); Heinrich Walter, "Das Pampaproblem
        in Vergleichung ökologischer Betrachtung und seiner Lösung,"
        in Erdkunde, XXI, 181-203 (August, 1967, with an excellent
        bibliography). I am indebted to Professor James J. Parsons
        for assistance on this section of my paper.

19)   Much of the literature on application of archaeological
        method is summarized in two volumes of essays reviewing
        America, region by region: Gordon R. Willey, ed.,
        Prehistoric Settlement Patterns in the New World (Viking Fund

Publications in Anthropology, 23, New York, 1956) and Jesse
D. Jennings and Edward Norbeck, eds., Prehistoric Man in the
New World (Chicago, 1964). The first volume has a general
bibliography; the second one, much larger ones at the end
of each essay. Additional and important material for the
New World will be found in Robert F. Heizer and Sherburne F.
Cook, eds., The Application of Quantitative Methods in
Archaeology (Viking Fund Publications in Anthropology, 28,
Chicago and London, 1960). See further Gordon R. Willey and
Philip Phillips, Method and Theory in American Archaeology
(Chicago, 1958) and S. F. Cook and Robert F. Heizer, The
Quantitative Approach to the Relation between Population and
Settlement Size (Reports of the University of California
Archaeological Survey, No. 64, Berkeley, March, 1965).

20) See the discussion later in this paper.

21) The application is developed in a series of articles by John
Howland Rowe, "Archaeological Dating and Cultural Process,"
in Southwestern Journal of Anthropology, XV, 317-324 (1959);
"Stratigraphy and Seriation," in American Antiquity, XXVI,
324-330 (January, 1961); "Stages and Periods in Archaeological Interpretation," in Southwestern Journal of
Anthropology, XVIII, 40-54 (1962); "Worsaae's Law and the
Use of Grave Lots for Archaeological Dating," in American
Antiquity, XXVIII, 129-137 (October, 1962). The methods are
further discussed in John Howland Rowe and Dorothy Menzel,
eds., Peruvian Archaeology; Selected Readings (Palo Alto,
California, 1967), pp. 146-164 and 177-209. I am indebted
to Professor Rowe for help on this portion of the paper.

22) Rene Millon, "The Teotihuacan Mapping Project," in American
Antiquity, XXIX, 345-352 (1964).

23) Rene Millon, "Décimaprimera mesa redonda de antropología,"
in Mexico. Instituto Nacional de Antropología e Historia,
Boletín, núm. 25, pp. 34-35 (September, 1966).

24) Robert F. Heizer, "Agriculture and the Theocratic State in
Lowland Southeastern Mexico," in American Antiquity, XXVI,
215-222 (1960), is an excellent example, and gives a
bibliography.

25) Ibid.; W. W. Howells, "Estimating Population Numbers through
Archaeological and Skeletal Remains," in Heizer and Cook,
The Application of Quantitative Methods in Archaeology,
pp. 160-162, summarizes work on land use and food consumption
in Yucatán, especially for estimates of population density
prior to the European era. The most concentrated and
extended study on this topic has been done in Yucatán under
the aegis of the Carnegie Foundation.

26) S. F. Cook, Erosion Morphology and Occupation History in
Western Mexico (Anthropological Records, vol. 17, no. 3,
Berkeley and Los Angeles, 1963).

27) Ibero-Americana: 34, Berkeley and Los Angeles, 1949.

28) S. F. Cook and R. F. Heizer, Studies on the Chemical Analysis
of Archaeological Sites (University of California Publications in Anthropology, volume 2, Berkeley and Los Angeles,
1965), with bibliography.

29) See José L. Lorenzo, La revolución neolítica en Mesoamérica, already cited, with bibliography, and Monika G. Bopp

Oeste, La paleobotánica: sus métodos y aplicaciones
(Instituto Nacional de Antropología e Historia, Dirección de
Prehistoria, Mexico City, 1958), also with bibliography.
The Dirección de Prehistoria in the Mexican Instituto
Nacional de Antropología e Historia, under the guidance of
Dr. José L. Lorenzo, has been very active in developing,
applying, and teaching such methods.

30) Karl Sapper, "Die Zahl und Die Volksdichte der indianischen
Bevölkerung in Amerika vor der Conquista und in der
Gegenwart," in International Congress of Americanists, XXI,
The Hague, 1924, Proceeding, pp. 95-104.

31) William M. Denevan, The Aboriginal Cultural Geography of the
Llanos de Mojos of Bolivia (Ibero-Americana: 48, Berkeley
and Los Angeles, 1966), passim but especially pp. 19-28,
58-73, and 112-145; James J. Parsons and William A. Bowen,
"Ancient Ridged Fields of the San Jorge River Floodplain,
Colombia," in The Geographical Review, LVI, 317-343 (1966);
William M. Denevan, "A Cultural-Ecological View of the
Former Aboriginal Settlement in the Amazon Basin," in
The Professional Geographer, XVIII, 346-351 (1966); and
Parsons and Denevan, "Pre-Columbian Ridged Fields," in
Scientific American, vol. 217, no. 1, pp. 92-100 (July, 1967).

32) I am indebted for the concept to Dr. Robert Heizer. See the
discussion on disturbance through disease in Henry F. Dobyns,
"Estimating American Population. I. An Appraisal of
Techniques with a New Hemispheric Estimate," in Current
Anthropology, VII, 395-460 (October, 1966). The reorganization of Indian life in the tribes of the Great Plains through
introduction of firearms and horses secured by interchange
among the Indians themselves for part of the area is one
example of truly massive change. Frank Raymond Secoy,
Changing Military Patterns on the Great Plains (17th Century
through Early 19th Century) (American Ethnological Society,
Monographs, XXI, New York, 1953). The thorough reorganization of Araucanian life in southern Chile may be cited as
another example.

33) Julian Steward, in Handbook of South American Indians (7
vols., Washington, D.C., 1946-1959), V. 662.

34) See the discussion in Denevan, The Aboriginal Cultural
Geography of the Llanos de Mojos of Bolivia, pp. 28-33.

35) Henry F. Dobyns, "An Outline of Andean Epidemic History to
1720," in Bulletin of the History of Medicine, XXXVII,
493-515 (1963); Burr Cartwright Brundage, Lords of Cuzco.
A History and Description of the Inca People in Their Final
Days (Norman, Oklahoma, 1967), pp. 67-70 and 372-373.

36) See the discussion in Dobyns, "Estimating Aboriginal American
Population."

37) An exception would be Cortés's statement on the population of
the native states of Tlaxcala and Huejotzingo: "Hay en esta
provincia, por visitación que yo en ella mandé hacer,
quinientos mil vecinos, que con otra provincia pequeña junto
con ésta, que se dice Guazincango, que viven a la manera
destos, sin señor natural. . ." Carta segunda de relación,
Segura de la Frontera, October 30, 1520, in Hernán Cortés,
Cartas de relación (new ed., 2 vols., Madrid, 1942, I, 56-57).

38)   The volumes on ethnohistory of the Handbook of Middle
      American Indians, now in preparation, will provide for the
      first time a remarkably inclusive survey, bibliographies,
      and general critical introduction to such materials.

39)   Kroeber, Cultural and Natural Areas of Native North America,
      pp. 179-180. See also the discussion in the two studies of
      Rosenblat, passim, and in Dobyns, "Estimating Aboriginal
      American Population."

40)   William Petersen, Population (New York, 1961), pp. 333-341,
      especially 337-338.

41)   See Frédéric Mauro, "Marchands et marchands-banquiers
      portugais au XVIIeme siècle," in Revista portuguesa de
      história, IX, 8 (1961).

42)   See the discussion in Sherburne F. Cook and Woodrow Borah,
      "On the Credibility of Contemporary Testimony on the
      Population of Mexico in the Sixteenth Century," in Summa
      anthropologica en homenaje a Roberto J. Weitlaner (Instituto
      Nacional de Antropología e Historia, Mexico City, 1966),
      pp. 229-239.

43)   See Modesto Ulloa, La hacienda real de Castilla en el reinado
      de Felipe II (Rome, 1963).

44)   Father Riccioli, cited by Francisco Javier Clavijero,
      Historia antigua de Mexico (ed. by Mariano Cuevas, Mexico
      City, 1964), sétima disertación, parte 2, or p. 561.

45)   Alfred L. Kroeber, Cultural and Natural Areas of Native North
      America, pp. 131-181, especially 166.

46)   Rosenblat, La población indígena, I, 13.

47)   Karl Sapper, "Die Zahl und die Volksdichte der indianischen
      Bevölkerung in Amerika vor der Conquista und in der
      Gegenwart," already cited.

48)   Karl Sapper, "Beiträge zur Frage der Volkszahl und Volks-
      dichte der vorkolumbischen Indianerbevoelkerung," in
      International Congress of Americanists, XXVI, Sevilla, 1935,
      Trabajos científicos, I, 456-478. Publication was delayed
      until 1948.

49)   Alfred L. Kroeber, Cultural and Natural Areas of Native North
      America, pp. 131-181. See especially pp. 166 and 177-181.

50)   Rosenblat, La población indígena, already cited. See
      especially I, 102.

51)   Woodrow Borah, "America as Model: The Demographic Impact
      of European Expansion upon the Non-European World," in
      International Congress of Americanists, XXXV, Mexico City,
      1962, Actas y memorias, III, 379-387, especially 381. The
      paper has been published in Spanish in Cuadernos americanos,
      noviembre-diciembre de 1962, pp. 176-185.

52)   Henry F. Dobyns, "Estimating Aboriginal American Population"
      Dobyns's paper gives a careful and very thoughtful review of
      past work, the techniques of estimate employed, and the
      problem of the state of each Indian population at the date of
      earliest report.

53)   William Robertson, The History of America (2 vols., London,
      1777), especially II, 293-302, 409-461, 483-486.

54)   Adolph F. Bandelier, "On the Social Organization and Mode of
      Government of the Ancient Mexicans," in Harvard University,
      Peabody Museum, Annual Report, XII, 557-699 (1879).

55) Alfred L. Kroeber, as already cited; Julian H. Steward, in
Handbook of South American Indians, passim, and in Julian H.
Steward and Louis C. Faron, Native Peoples of South
America.
56) Vide infra.
57) William H. Prescott, History of the Conquest of Mexico and
History of the Conquest of Peru, in many editions.
58) Ronald Spores, The Mixtec Kings and Their People (Norman,
Oklahoma, 1967), pp. 8 and 101 ff.
59) Michael D. Coe, "Social Typology and the Tropical Forest
Civilizations," in Comparative Studies in Society and History,
IV, 63-85 (1961).
60) Alfonso Caso, "Existió un imperio olmeca?" in Mexico, El
Colegio Nacional, Memoria, V, No. 3, pp. 5-52 (1964).
61) The view shows up repeatedly in private and semi-public
discussion, and tends to be associated with relative lack of
concern with present uses of land. The opposing group tends
to be concerned with problems of destructive use of resources
and excessive population. Simpson has been chided by Howard
Cline for his neo-Malthusian views. (Mexico. Revolution to
Evolution, 1940-1960, Oxford University Press, 1962),
pp. 263-264.
62) See the discussion by Richard Konetzke, Entdecker und
Eroberer Amerikas (Fischer Bücherei, Frankfurt am Main,
1963), pp. 7-11.
63) In this connection see Oscar Lewis and Ernest E. Maes,
"Base para una nueva definición práctica del indio," in
América indígena, V, 107-118, especially 115-118 (1945),
and Manuel Gamio, "Consideraciones sobre el problema
indígena en América," in ibid., II, No. 2, pp. 16-23 (1942).
64) F. D. Markuzon, "Naselenie mira ot nachal nashei ery do
serediny XX veka," in V. S. Nemchinov, ed., Vorprosy
ekonomiki, planirovaniia i statistiki (Moscow, 1957),
pp. 388-404; M. L. Al'perovich, Voyna za nezavisimost'
Meksiki (1810-1824) (Moscow, 1964), pp. 54-58, 60-61, 71-72.
65) Mariano Cuevas, Historia de la iglesia en México (5th ed.,
5 vols., Mexico City, 1946-1947), I, passim.
66) Much of the recent literature is reviewed in Lewis Hanke,
"More Heat and Some Light on the Spanish Struggle for Justice
in the Conquest of America," in Hispanic American Historical
Review, XLIV, 298-340 (1964); see further the two classic
works on the Black Legend: Julián Juderías y Loyot, La
leyenda negra; estudios acerca del concepto de España en el
extranjero (2nd ed., Barcelona, 1917), and Rómulo D. Carbia,
Historia de la leyenda negra hispano-americana (Buenos Aires,
1943).
67) The famous Peruvian ironclad, the loss of which turned out to
be decisive in the War of the Pacific.
68) A dinner conversation among teachers of history in Mexico
City, reported to me in November, 1967. The same charge was
raised in a discussion of this paper in Madison in May, 1968.
69) Oral comment by Paul Kirchhoff.
70) See the discussion in Dobyns, "Estimating Aboriginal American
Population;" Alfred W. Crosby, "Conquistador y Pestilencia:
The First New World Pandemic and the Fall of the Great Indian

Empires," in <u>Hispanic American Historical Review</u>, XLVII,
321-337 (August, 1967); the following works by S. F. Cook,
"Demographic Consequences of European Contact with Primitive
Peoples," in <u>The Annals of the American Academy of Political
and Social Science</u>, January, 1945, pp. 107-111; "The
Incidence and Significance of Disease among the Aztecs and
Related Tribes," in <u>Hispanic American Historical Review</u>, XXVI,
320-335 (1946); <u>The Epidemic of 1830-1833 in California and
Oregon</u>, in <u>University of California Publications in American
Archaeology and Ethnology</u>, XLIII, No. 3, pp. 303-326 (1955);
and Saul Jarcho, "The Fielding H. Garrison Lecture: Some
Observations on Disease in Prehistoric North America," in
<u>Bulletin of the History of Medicine</u>, XXXVIII, No. 1, pp.1-19
(January-February, 1964).

71) The <u>Suma</u> has been used as the basis for an estimate of the
population of central Mexico in 1548. Woodrow Borah and
Sherburne F. Cook, <u>The Population of Central Mexico in 1548</u>:
<u>An Analysis of the Suma de visitas de pueblos</u> (Ibero-
Americana: 43, Berkeley and Los Angeles, 1960). The
readings, interpretations, and adjustments have been objected
to at length by Angel Rosenblat, <u>La población de América en
1492</u>.

72) See the discussion in Dobyns, "Estimating Aboriginal American
Population."

73) Rosenblat, <u>La población indígena</u>, I, 83.

74) Development and use of the method may be seen in the following
studies by S. F. Cook and Woodrow Borah: "The Rate of
Population Change in Central Mexico, 1550-1570," in <u>Hispanic
American Historical Review</u>, XXXVII, 463-470 (1957); "Quelle
fut la stratification sociale du centre du Mexique durant la
première moitié du XVIe siècle?" in <u>Annales. économies,
sociétès, civilisations</u>, XVIII, 226-258 (1963); "On the
Credibility of Contemporary Testimony on the Population of
Mexico in the Sixteenth Century," already cited; and <u>The
Population of the Mixteca Alta, 1520-1960</u> (Ibero-Americana:
50, Berkeley and Los Angeles, 1968), chapters 2-3.

75) Carl O. Sauer, <u>The Aboriginal Population of Northwestern
Mexico</u> (Ibero-Americana: 10, Berkeley, 1935).

76) S. F. Cook, <u>Population Trends among the California Mission
Indians</u> (Ibero-Americana: 17, Berkeley and Los Angeles,
1940); <u>The Conflict between the California Indians and White
Civilization</u> (Ibero-Americana: 21-24, Berkeley and Los
Angeles, 1943); "The Aboriginal Population of Upper
California," in International Congress of Americanists,
XXXV, Mexico City, 1962, <u>Actas y Memorias</u>, III, 397-403.

77) Homer Aschmann, <u>The Central Desert of Baja California:
Demography and Ecology</u> (Ibero-Americana: 42, Berkeley and
Los Angeles, 1959).

78) Carl O. Sauer, <u>Colima of New Spain in the Sixteenth Century</u>
(Ibero-Americana: 29, Berkeley and Los Angeles, 1948).

79) Sherburne F. Cook and Lesley Byrd Simpson, <u>The Population of
Central Mexico in the Sixteenth Century</u> (Ibero-Americana:
31, Berkeley and Los Angeles, 1948); Woodrow Borah and S. F.
Cook, <u>The Population of Central Mexico in 1548</u> already cited;

Sherburne F. Cook and Woodrow Borah, <u>The Indian Population of Central Mexico, 1531-1610</u> (Ibero-Americana: 44, Berkeley and Los Angeles, 1960); Woodrow Borah and Sherburne F. Cook, <u>The Aboriginal Population of Central Mexico on the Eve of the Spanish Conquest</u> (Ibero-Americana: 45, Berkeley and Los Angeles, 1963). See also the studies cited in note 71.

80) J. Eric S. Thompson, "The Maya Central Area at the Spanish Conquest and Later: A Problem in Demography," in Royal Anthropological Institute of Great Britain and Ireland, <u>Proceedings. . .for 1966</u>, pp. 23-37, with bibliography.

81) For example, <u>Los quimbayas bajo la dominación española</u> (Bogotá, 1963), with its impressive documentation; "Algunas consideraciones sobre la evolución demográfica en el Nuevo Reino de Granada," a paper delivered at the International Congress of Americanists, XXXVII, Mar del Plata, 1966, and to be published in the proceedings. Also see below.

82) See above, and the paper in this volume.

83) <u>Visita hecha a la provincia de Chucuito por Garci Diez de San Miguel en el año de 1567</u> (Documentos regionales para la etnología y etnohistoria andinas, Tomo I, Ediciones de la Casa de la Cultura del Peru, Lima, 1964).

84) <u>Visita de la provincia de León de Huánuco en 1562, Iñigo Ortíz de Zúñiga, visitador</u> (Documentos para la historia y etnología de Huánuco y la selva central, Tomo I, Universidad Nacional Hermilio Valdizán, Huánuco, 1967).

85) See Nicolás Sánchez-Albornoz, "Les registres paroissiaux en Amérique Latine," in <u>Revue suisse d'histoire</u>, XVII, 60-71 (1967), a revision of a paper presented at the International Congress of Americanists, XXXVII, Mar del Plata, 1966, with a series of general observations; for comments on parish registers as a source for the demographic history of Argentina, see Sánchez-Albornoz and Torrado, "Perfil y proyecciones de la demografía histórica en la Argentina," as cited in note (6), pp. 31-40. Provisional and partial guides to parish registers have been prepared for Argentina and Chile--Aurelio Tanodi, "Los archivos y la investigación en historia social y económica," in Universidad Nacional de Córdoba, Facultad de Ciencias Económicas, <u>Primera reunión argentina de historia social y económica, Córdoba, Argentina, 12 al 13 de julio de 1963</u> (mimeographed report, Córdoba, 1963), pp. 35-37, and Raul Díaz Vial, "Situación de los libros parroquiales," in <u>Revista de estudios históricos</u>, Santiago de Chile, No. 10, pp. 109-122 (1962) (note in <u>Historia</u>, Santiago de Chile, II, 231-232 (1962-1963).) The listing by Tanodi covers some of Argentina; that by Díaz Vial, many parishes in Chile and a few in Argentina. For indications on the history of parish registers in the Archdiocese of Mexico and its suffragan dioceses, Woodrow Borah and Sherburne F. Cook, "Marriage and Legitimacy in Mexican Culture: Mexico and California," in <u>California Law Review</u>, LIV, No. 2, pp. 954-957 <u>et passim</u>. Richard Konetzke, "Documentos para la historia y crítica de los registros parroquiales en las Indias," in <u>Revista de Indias</u>, VII, 581-586 (1946), adds interesting information on the meaning of the racial classifications at the beginning of the

nineteenth century. For examples of use of parish registers for demographic study, see Besio Moreno, as in note (5), pp. 16-90 and Leonardo Manrique Castañeda, "Notas sobre la población de Santa María Chigmecatitlán," in Mexico. Instituto Nacional de Antropología e Historia, Anales, XVI, 199-225 (1963); "Bautizos indígenas según los libros del sagrario de Santiago correspondientes a los años 1581-1596," in Historia, Santiago, IV, 229-235 (1965). For a plan to use similar material for one district in Argentina, see Nicolás Sánchez-Albornoz, "Estudio sobre la demografía histórica del Valle de Santa María," in Universidad, Santa Fe, Argentina, No. 62, pp. 93-104 (1964).

86) See the citations to work on the Californias and northwest Mexico above.

87) Much of the reporting of such pastoral inspections remains in manuscript in Spain or in episcopal archives. Of those published for Mexico, some of the best for demographic study are the inspection of Alonso de la Mota y Escobar as Bishop of Nueva Vizcaya, Descripción geográfica de los reinos de Nueva Galicia, Nueva Vizcaya y Nuevo León (2nd ed., with introduction by Joaquín Ramírez Cabañas, Mexico City, 1940, and various other editions) and the later one, also for Nueva Vizcaya of Bishop Pedro Tamarón y Romeral, Demostración del vastísimo obispado de la Nueva Vizcaya--1765. Durango, Sinaloa, Sonora, Arizona, Nuevo México, Chihuahua y porciones de Texas, Coahuila y Zacatecas (ed. by Vito Alessio Robles, Mexico City, 1937). For a description and analysis of the pastoral inspection of 1768-1770 by Archbishop Pedro Cortés y Larraz of Guatemala, see Barón Castro, pp. 213-223, who consulted a copy of the archbishop's report in the Archivo General de Indias, Seville, the Descripción Geográfico-Moral de la Diócesis de Goathemala, Audiencia de Guatemala, legajo 948.

88) The literature on tithe collection and its records is especially sparse. For evidence on potential, see the articles by Woodrow Borah, "The Collection of Tithes in the Bishopric of Oaxaca during the Sixteenth Century," "The Cathedral Archive of Oaxaca," "Tithe Collection in the Bishopric of Oaxaca, 1601-1867," in Hispanic American Review, XXI, 386-409 (1941), XXVIII, 640-645 (1948), and XXIX, 498-517 (1949) respectively; and those by Michael P. Costeloe, "Guide to the Chapter Archives of the Archbishopric of Mexico," in Hispanic American Historical Review, XLV, 53-63 (1965) and "The Administration, Collection and Distribution of Tithes in the Archbishopric of Mexico, 1800-1860," in The Americas, XXIII, 3-27 (1966). See also Fabián de Fonseca and Carlos de Urrutia, Historia general de real hacienda (6 vols., Mexico City, 1845-1853), prepared in the 1790's, which has much information in its section on Diezmos, novenos, vacantes mayores y menores y escusados, in III, 136-261.

89) On tribute records, see the citations above to the work of Cook, Simpson, and Borah for central Mexico, and the citations for published records for the provinces of Chucuito and Huánuco in Peru. Cook and Borah, The Population of

the Mixteca Alta, 1520-1960, carries the study of tribute
records to the end of the colonial period for the one region
and has a provisional analysis of much seventeenth and
eighteenth century material for all of central Mexico. The
studies of Juan Friede rely upon tribute counts and other
kinds of counts. For a very thoughtful use of such material,
see his study, "Demographic Changes in the Mining Community
of Muzo after the Plague of 1629," in Hispanic American
Historical Review, XLVII, 338-343 (1967), as well as studies
cited previously.

90) See Besio Moreno, pp. 305-351; Barón Castro, pp. 241-259;
Juan Alejandro Apolant, "Padrones olvidados de Montevideo
del siglo XVIII," in Boletín histórico del estado mayor del
ejército, Montevideo, num's. 104-105 and 106-107, published
also as a separatum, Montevideo, 1966 (note from Hispanic
American Historical Review, XLVII, 457 (1967), review by
Karen W. Spaulding). See also the study of the Nueva
Vizcaya padrón of 1604 by Francisco de Urdiñola in Woodrow
Borah, "Francisco de Urdiñola's Census of the Spanish
Settlements in Nueva Vizcaya, 1604," in Hispanic American
Historical Review, XXXV, 398-402 (1955). The two volumes
devoted to demographic studies by the Instituto de Investi-
gaciones Históricas of the Universidad del Litoral, Rosario,
Argentina, under the direction of Nicolás Sánchez-Albornoz
make wide use of administrative counts and records for
historico-demographic purposes. Anuario, vols. VI and VIII
(1963 and 1965). Two studies that illustrate the possibilities of use of varied kinds of materials over broad stretches
of time are: Nicolás Sánchez-Albornoz and Susana Torrado,
"Perfil y proyecciones de la demografía histórica en la
Argentina," and Elda R. González and Roland Mellafe, "La
función de la familia en la historia social hispano-
americana colonial," in Anuario as cited above, VIII, 31-56
and 57-71 (1965). The first article is especially good for
indicating the possibilities of continuing series right
through the changes in recording of the middle of the nineteenth century.

91) Among studies using the census reports for 1777-1779 are
Dauril Alden, "The Population of Brazil in the Late Eighteenth
Century: A Preliminary Survey," in Hispanic American
Historical Review, XLIII, 173-205 (1963), with an excellent
bibliography on Brazilian historical demography and a brief
sketch of efforts at censuses in both Portuguese and Spanish
America in the closing decades of the colonial regimes;
Barón Castro, pp. 224-240, which gives a history for Central
America and analyzes the results for Honduras, the only ones
found so far; Beatriz Rosini, "Estructura demográfica de
Jujuy: S. XVIII," José Luis Moreno, "La estructura social y
demográfica de la ciudad de Buenos Aires en el año 1778,"
and Maria del Pilar Chao, "La poblacion de Potosí en 1779,"
all in Anuario del Instituto de Investigaciones Históricas,
Universidad del Litoral, Rosario, Argentina, VIII, 119-150,
151-170 and 171-180, respectively; and Marcello Carmagnani
and Herbert S. Klein, "Demografía histórica: la población
del obispado de Santiago 1777-1778," in Boletín de la

Academia Chilena de la Historia, año XXXII, primer semestre
de 1965, núm. 72, pp. 57-74. See also Luis Lira Montt,
"Padrones del Reino de Chile existentes en el Archivo de
Indias," in *Revista de estudios históricos*, Santiago de Chile,
núm. 13, pp. 85-88 (1965) (review in *Historia*, Santiago de
Chile, V, 253 (1966)).

92)   The records are preserved in Mexico. Archivo General de la
Nación, in the ramos of *Padrones* and *Historia*. For a
provisional analysis of the materials, see S. F. Cook "The
Population of Mexico in 1793," in *Human Biology*, XIV,
499-515 (1942).

93)   To use again the instance of Mexico, see Felipe Tena Ramírez,
ed., *Leyes fundamentales de México, 1808-1964* (2nd ed., rev.,
Mexico City, 1964), p. 33, giving the text of article 7 of
the Constitution of Apatzingan, 22 October 1814; p. 64,
articles 28-31 of the Constitution of 1812; p. 148, article
2 of the Plan for the Political Constitution of the Mexican
Nation, 16 May 1823; p. 169, articles 10-15 of the Constitution of 1824; p. 212, article 2 of the Bases Constitucionales
de 1836; p. 258, article 24 of the proposed reform of 1839;
p. 313, articles 28 and 34 of the proposed constitution of
1842; pp. 377-381, articles 16-19 and 35 of the second
constitutional project of 1842; p. 410, articles 26 and 27 of
the Bases Orgánicas of 1843; p. 473, article 7 of the reforms
of 1847; and p. 615, article 53 of the Constitution of 1857.
See also the discussion in Mexico. Secretaría de Fomento,
Colonización, Industria y Comercio, *Memoria, 1853-1857*
(Mexico City, 1857), pp. 114-117 and the appendix on
statistics by Orozco y Berra (section IX), pp. 3-31. See
further the excellent account for El Salvador in Barón
Castro, pp. 441-468, and for Argentina in Besio Moreno,
pp. 344-351.

94)   As was done in Mexico in the 1830's and 1840's, and in many
other Latin American countries.

95)   See note 90.

96)   For a survey of Latin American censuses and vital statistics,
with an attempt to estimate probable accuracy and coverage,
see O. Andrew Collver, *Birth Rates in Latin America: New
Estimates of Historical Trend and Fluctuations* (University of
California, Institute of International Studies, Berkeley,
1965). An older bibliography that is especially good for
historical demography is Inter-American Statistical Institute,
Washington, D.C., *Bibliography of Selected Statistical Sources
of the American Nations* (Washington, D.C., 1947). The Inter-
American Statistical Institute publishes continuing reports
on statistical activities and publications. A newer
bibliography is *International Population Census Bibliography,
Latin America and the Caribbean*, issued by Population
Research Center, Bureau of Business Research, University of
Texas (Austin, 1965).

97)   Borah and Cook, "Marriage and Legitimacy in Mexican Culture:
Mexico and California," pp. 969-972.

98)   Mexico. Dirección General de Estadística, *Anuario estadístico de los Estados Unidos Mexicanos, 1960-1961*, table

3.7; Raúl Benítez Zenteno, Análisis demográfico de México (Mexico City, 1961), pp. 26-28, especially table 3 on p. 26.

Additional Note: Two studies, not in these notes, should be mentioned: Günter Vollmer, Bevölkerungspolitik und Bevölkungsstruktur im Vizekönigreich Peru zu Ende der Kolonialzeit 1741-1821 (Beiträge zur Soziologie und Sozialkunde Lateinamerikas, COSAL, 2, Bad Homburg vor der Höhe, 1967), which has a fine discussion of tribute counts and efforts at general counts in Peru in the last eight decades of the Spanish regime, and Enrique Florescano, Precios del maíz y crisis agrícolas en México (1708-1810). Ensayo sobre el movimiento de los precios y sus consecuencias económicas y sociales. (El Colegio de México, Centro de Estudios Históricos, Nueva Serie 4, Mexico City, 1969), which relates movements of prices to weather and periods of plenty and scarcity.

14

HUMAN ECOLOGY AND POPULATION

CARL O. SAUER

UNIVERSITY OF CALIFORNIA, BERKELEY

The human lineage as distinct from other Primates we now know goes back millions of years, hominids living in interior East Africa two million years ago. This indefinitely long period of primitive learning and geographic dispersal, named the Lower Paleolithic by the technic and forms of its artifacts of stone, carried on to a hundred and fifty thousand years ago, by which time man was established over far parts of Africa and Eurasia.

The successful divergent of Primate evolution shows by his anatomy and physiology evidence of his ancestral habitat, the ecologic niche of his origins. He lived on the ground, erect of carriage, walked flat footed, his arms free and not used in locomotion. He lacked pelt, powerful jaws, strong incisors, great strength. He is omnivorous with a widely competent digestive system except for the ingestion of raw starch in quantity. The human infant is born in complete dependence on maternal care, remains so longest, and takes longest to grow to maturity. Sir Alister Hardy has called attention to the superior adaptation of the human body to swimming, absent in other Primates.

It would seem apparent that the usual attribution of human origins to African savannas is improper. These have strong contrast of rainy and dry seasons, wide movement of the herds of game with the availability of forage and water, a balance between fleet game, their predators and scavengers, all drifting across the land. The place thus assigned to man is that of scavenger and predator about the margins of herds, living on crippled, infirm, and young animals, in taking which he competed with carnivores and vultures. The humans are thought of as bands under the control of a strong and aggressive male. The construct is as socially unattractive as it is ecologically incompetent, a poorly equipped Primate, handicapped by dependent and defenseless offspring, venturing into competition

with the functionally specialized predators of the savannas, to
which humans were convenient prey.

A different, proper, and convenient niche was available for
human origins and increase, the forming of its society and the
development of skills, the African shores of the Indian Ocean.
Here there was no lack of food or water at any time, no necessity
to be on the move, so disadvantageous to women and children. The
tides gave a daily change of collecting range on beach and rock.
Sea turtles laid their eggs on beaches. Fish and marine mammals
were stranded occasionally. Estuaries offered a rich harvest as
learning grew. Drinking water of stream, spring, or seep was at
hand at all seasons. There were shells of many sizes and shapes,
bones and carapaces, salt seasoned drift wood, jetsam of many kinds
to be picked up on the beaches. Waves detached rocks from head-
lands and ground them into rounded cobbles, tough and hard, ready
to suit the hand. Abundant and diverse food was at hand and the
materials and forms of stone, shell, wood, and fiber invited use
and fashioning. The coasts were not preempted by other Primates
nor hunted over by the great cats. There was security here as well
as opportunity. Adopting the Hardy thesis of the design of the
human body for swimming, the origin of our kind took form in
aquatic as well as terrestrial habitat.

By the alternate and better option human society was formed
by the women. The Primates in general are rather notorious for
the inattention of the males to the young. The human female had
the responsibility of caring for the young and doing so for so long
that the succession of progeny remained linked to mother and each
other. The human family is unique in its continuity and is based
on the maternal bond. Not band but family is the basis of human
society. The most primitive peoples have the most elaborate
systems of kinship. The simple maternal family readily became an
extended family group by succession of generations that remained
in the same locality, the primordial community. That paternity
was acknowledged and accepted is not basic to the origin of the
family.

Seaside living gave opportunity for permanent habitation,
an innate maternal desire. The man might roam, the woman sought
a place where she could have shelter for her brood and adequate
provision of food, water, and materials. The selection of a proper
site resulted in permanent occupation, the household and home, the
nascent sessile community.

Being amply supplied with food and other necessities the
primordial seaside community continued to increase in numbers.
New sites of similar advantage were occupied and spread about the
Indian Ocean to South Africa and to Java. Some are recorded in
human remains as in Java, more by sites of worked stone preserved
on high coasts. Primitive and early artifacts have been found and
named as to type on sea margins of Morocco and Portugal. Rather
widely distributed early Lower Paleolithic types are known as pre-
Chellean, Abbevillean, and Clactonian from type localities on tidal
sea coast or lower river course in France and England.

By the Second Interglacial, perhaps a half million years
ago, man had colonized far beyond tropical lands and well inland,
as shown by the habitation of Peking Man. This has the oldest
record of his use of fire, preserved there by the rock shelter under

which the people lived. Lacking fire ancestral man was limited by cold and also in his ability to make plant substances palatable and storable. The narrow range of the fireless human was changed into a wide world open to his successful entry when he began his promethean course by taking fire under his control. This I consider was the great achievement of most ancient man, the act by which he began to be the ecologic dominant, freed of climatic restriction. Again I should attribute this to the woman, keeper of the hearth where she learned the varied ways of cooking and at which her family was warmed. At the hearth she found that starchy roots became good food by heat, that bitterness was thus removed from root, stem, and seed, that poisonous plants were made edible, that meat and plants could be preserved. The presence of man beyond tropical climates implies, I think, his use of fire, for warming his living space, and for preparing and storing his food. Thus I should refer nearly all archeologic sites in Europe to the employment of fire, at a time beginning far earlier than that of Peking Man.

Middle Paleolithic time, again by definition and calendar made in France, covers the span from about a hundred and fifty thousand years ago to less than forty thousand (by current Pleistocene reckoning). The innovation was a new breed, Neanderthal Man, and a new culture, Mousterian, the two linked. Both were thought to have evolved in Europe and there was an idea that they were unable to survive the rigor of the last great ice advance. Instead it now appears that they did so and that their range was from western Europe into Mongolia, the Zagros Mountains, and other parts. It was an inland culture, making stone points to use on spears or javelins, perhaps the first to be somewhat specialized for hunting, but also inclined to cave dwelling or rather living under rock shelters. They are the earliest people known to have buried their dead and done so reverently. The range of this culture was from lowland tundra through mixed woodlands to the edge of the desert. Its ecology thus was likely to differ with the habitat with a bent to taking game. I know of no interest in aquatic resources and infer a widely spread population of small groups ranging over small areas and taking advantage of natural shelters.

During Middle Paleolithic time sea level fell by three hundred feet as glaciation increased and rivers discharging into the sea lowered their floors correspondingly. The places and manners of living of waterside peoples of coast and lowland valleys have since been buried under sea and alluvium and are lost to our knowledge. This record is almost a blank though it concerned the largest number of people and the largest concentrations.

The New World was entered by man during Middle Paleolithic time and it may have been entered repeatedly. Under the prevalent doctrine that the New World was not peopled until 'after the end of the Ice Age' good evidence to the contrary continued to be rejected. Radiocarbon dating now is competent to determine age to about forty thousand years. There are sites too old to have radioactive carbon and others are pending. Pleistocene geomorphology thus is having new and more serious attention on the California coast, the Mohave Desert, and high terraces of Texas rivers.

Whether men began to settle the New World during or prior to the
last glaciation has not been determined. At any rate there now is
ample time to fill the New World to its diverse environmental capacities and cultural divergences.

The Upper Paleolithic peoples again were first determined
in western Europe, and the first held to be entitled to the name
Homo sapiens. By current reckoning their time reached from thirty-
five to nine thousand years ago, in rounded terms. These were
hunters of big game, organized for grande chasse, as the Solutreans
for hunting forest horse, Gravettians for mammoth, and Magdalenians
for reindeer. They made fine blades and points of stone by the
technique of pressure flaking and had new precision arms in the
dart thrower and bow and arrow. They engaged in mass drives, most
effective by setting fires in plains, their preferred habitat. In
North America a very similar way of life appeared and at about the
same time, first the Llano/Clovis mammoth hunters, then the Folsom
hunters of an extinct giant bison, and last the Plainview hunters
of the same bisons. The blades and projectile points were as
finely made by pressure flaking as those of the Old World. The
dart thrower was used but not the bow and arrow. These New World
hunters of late Paleolithic time and type occupied mainly the high
plains east of the Rocky Mountains but also lower plains to the
east. In the European and North American plains the hunters and
their major game animals disappeared at about the same time, the
mammoths, horses and bison becoming extinct, the reindeer and
perhaps their hunters withdrawing to more northern tundras.

An ecologic alteration of large extent is implied. The
great game animals were woodland forms and as such unlikely to
mass in large herds. The rapid recession of continental glaciation that set in about eleven thousand years ago was part of a
major climatic change by which arid and semi-arid lands increased
in extent with replacement of mesophytic by more xerophytic vegetation. Humid plains became semi-arid in parts and the forage of
their woodland browsers was diminished. The interpretation that
continuing hunting pressure with increased climatic disadvantage
brought faunal extinction is hardly competent. The major grasslands are plains. This is the quality they have in common, not
any quality of climate. Where there is a break in the plain, as
by the erosion of a valley, the grassy vegetation changes, often
abruptly, to brush or woodland, whatever the climate. Steppe,
savanna, or prairie, the grassland is maintained by burning. If
burning is stopped woody growth enters. The grasslands were formed
by fire spreading across plains during dry weather and, doing so
year after year, suppressed the reproduction of woody perennials.
Man is the agent competent to do this and he has done so since the
time of the Upper Paleolithic hunters. Their pursuit of large
game, such as elephants, giant bison, forest horse, added the use
of fire drives by which the quarry was herded to a place convenient for the killing. Fleeing from the advancing fire they could
be driven over a cliff or become bogged down in wet ground. Such
mass kills are known from Texas to France. The woodland plains
became grasslands, the earlier game and hunters were replaced by
grassland fauna and other hunting people who continued to practice
burning. In its heyday the Upper Paleolithic hunting economy
supported, I should say, more than a minimal population over a

large area. It faded away with the animals on which it had depended.
The plains appear to have been slowly repeopled. In time the plains
bison, pronghorn antelope, and other herbivores restocked North
American plains with as great, perhaps greater supply of game.

At a time when Magdalenian hunters flourished in Europe and
the Plainview hunters in Texas agriculture was being practiced in
Anatolia and in southern Mexico. The oldest places in the Levant
date back ten thousand years, perhaps more, those in Mexico a
thousand years less. The big game hunters lingered in the north,
but a very different way of life was under way to the south in both
hemispheres. In the Levant some of the oldest sites known, such
as Jericho and Chatal Huyuk, were towns of surprising size and construction. These people were unrelated to the hunters of the north
and appear with developed cultures, as to cult as well as to production. They were growers of seeds that had been selected for
cultivation, still for a good while of low yield, but sown, cultivated, and stored. Both in Old and New World these earliest known
parts where tillage was carried on were in interiors of the land,
the Levant having winter rains, Mexico the rainy season in summer,
both in scant amount. Were such the areas and such the plants of
agricultural origins?

The time was the onset of the last melting of the ice caps
and probably that of the modern pattern of climates. Since the
last maximum of glaciation sea level had risen two hundred feet or
more and would rise almost a hundred feet more to its modern level,
reached about four thousand years ago or less. The valley floors
opening to the sea were built up accordingly by alluvium. The
lowlands once inhabited were submerged by water or buried by allu-
viation as the ice melted. As I have thought that these lowlands
were from the beginning the particular domain of man, in which he
learned and increased most, so I look to them as the hearth of
agriculture.

Moving from salt water side through estuaries to rivers and
lakes gave new direction to the manner of living. The tidal zone
of the sea coast has a counterpart in fresh water, in shallows,
swamps, and flood plain, a greatly diverse, accessible, and useful
massing of plants and animals. Here fish spawned, water fowl fed
and nested, amphibious mammals pastured and bred, and edible roots
and shoots could be taken. Canes, rushes, reeds, and lianas provided material for structures and textiles. Man could live in
permanent communities and continue to increase.

The evidence for ancient invention is found in primitive
peoples that have survived or did so into historic time. Those who
lived by suitable waters made water craft of competent and characteristic design, both as to boat and paddle. The dugout canoe was
in widest use in low and middle latitudes of both hemispheres. The
boat-shaped reed bundle float, often miscalled balsa, was used in
widely separated parts of the world, and in part in almost identical design by most primitive peoples, such as the Tasmanians and
the Uru of Lake Titicaca. Having boats fishing in open water as
well as water transport was available. A widespread practice was
taking fish by barbasco, the discovery that certain plants spread
over the water would paralyze or kill fish without impairing their
edibility. This was done by macerating root or other part of a

plant known to have this effect and by scattering from dugouts.
The procedure required specific plant identification and manner of
application and was common to peoples of primitive and high culture,
especially in lower latitudes. The active substances being unstable
and soon dissipated in running water the use of barbasco did not
deplete the fishing waters. In some cases it was under ceremonial
control. Primitive fishing folk also used nets and spears, as in
spearing fish at night by torch light. They dug edible roots in
shallow water and on land.

In situations of superior attraction provision from water
was not limited. Animal protein and fat was in good supply, largely
by fishing. Starch, sugar, and whatever else was needed for a
balanced diet were secured from roots, shoots, and fruits, perennials of lowlands. The transition from collecting to cultivation
was by vegetative reproduction and probably began accidentally.
Digging is the beginning of tillage. Parts that are missed reproduce as separate plants, the more a plot is dug for tubers the
greater its likely stocking. The midden or garbage heap gave a
place for discarded roots and stems to grow. The step to planting
was easy and was done by selecting individual plants. Knowing that
the piece of the plant would be the same as the one from which it
was taken attention was directed to the desirable individual.
Vegetative reproduction became the way to plant breeding by selecting preferred individuals. As such became domesticated forms some
became dependent on man with loss of the ability to reproduce by
seed.

In the Old World the great hearth of fishing and vegetative
farming was in Southeast Asia of abundant monsoon rains and many
rivers, formerly discharging across lowlands now covered by the
South China and Java seas and the Bay of Bengal. Densely populated today on a rice and fish diet, it had the means of feeding a
large population before rice was introduced. The cultivated yams
(Dioscroea) mostly belong here as do the aroids such as taro, all
the plantains and bananas, sugar canes, barbascos, plants needed
for ceremonies, many kinds of plants that have been grown by
cuttings from time unknown.

In the New World a parallel fishing-farming culture occupied
the Caribbean lands, south far into South America and west across
Central America. Manioc, probably the most heavily yielding of all
starch producers, is grown from stem cuttings, as is the sweet
potato. The list of vegetatively grown providers of starch is
large and includes an excellent aroid Xanthosoma (yautia and other
local names), at least one native Dioscorea yam, and arrowroot.
Fish poisons and narcotics were taken into cultivation. Agriculture was carried into the high Andes by the planting of tubers
especially of Solanums that were bred into the great diversity of
potatoes. A tropical terrestrial Bromeliad was made into the pine-
apple, rich in sugar and used to make alcoholic drink.

Both tropical regions of the two hemispheres were directed
to the production of starch and sugar, continuing to rely on their
waters for animal protein and fat. A great diversity of plants was
taken into cultivation by vegetative reproduction and thus bred
into cultigens of high yield. Ample, varied, and constant supply
of food promoted the growth of human populations in sedentary
communities and did so, it is proposed, before this was the case

elsewhere.

The origins of seed cultivation are indicated as geographically marginal to the fishing-farming areas. In the New World the ancestors of the major seed crops, maize, beans, and squash, are thought to be native to central and southern Mexico and northern Central America, mainly in interiors of rainfall limited to summer. The recently extended archeologic record establishes the early cultivation of beans and squash with the absence of maize. When maize appeared it remained for a long time most unimpressive as to yield and quality. The squashes, grown for their seeds, seem to have been more rewarding than the primitive cultivated beans. These oldest Mexican records of seed growing give scant promise of the great and much later development of the maize-beans-squash complex. The inference is that this was an alternative direction northward and inland entered on where the physical conditions were ill suited to the older cultivation. Seed farming, known as milpa agriculture in Mexico, had a long task in making the crop plants we know out of the wild ones. This was done by the same practices used in vegetative planting: 1) Individual selection, the particular squash, ear of maize, or bean desired being kept for seed. 2) Heaping the planting ground into mounds or, less commonly, into ridges. 3) Thrusting a determined number of seeds into the heaped earth at desired depth. This still was planting. Selection for size and color of seed, for size and form of ear, pepo, and pod, and for yield and growth resulted in time in the superior lot of plant forms that supported the large Indian populations of Mesoamerica.

A similar development is suggested for the Old World. Beyond the well watered monsoon lands of Southeast Asia and especially to the west seed bearing grasses and pulses came under cultivation. The process of domestication was not speeded by individual plant selection and planting in mounded earth as in the New World, the seed apparently being broadcast. The amelioration came by mass selection, plants of better yield and ripening at the same time providing more and more of the seed stock. Grasses became the small grains of cultivation, millets, wheat, and barley. Pulses remained small seeded lentils, peas, and Phaseolus beans. In contrast to the New World these beans are small seeded and not diversified as to color. Cucurbits had little attention and least so for their seeds. Flax and hemp were grown for oil and fiber. The attainments of the seed farmers of the Old World are less impressive than those of the New World except for rice, which developed into a great staple in the fishing and vegetative planting complex of the southeast. Animals were not domesticated for the purpose of producing food nor were they significant to human increase until historic time except in the regions of dairying.

Having fire man went to the ends of the earth. Having fire he disturbed the associated biota to his advantage. He helped to increase secondary vegetation of shrubs and herbs, heliophil and precocious, at the expense of forest denseness and shade and thereby increased mammals that browsed and grazed and seed eating birds. I think that during most of his existence he had continuing success in making the world increasingly habitable to himself, by increase of fauna and flora useful to his needs. Very late in his history he domesticated plants and animals. By extending his occupation over the land surfaces and increasing his ecologic dominance man-

kind was able to grow greatly in numbers, perhaps to an equilibrium
with the sustenance available to the skills he possessed. The rise
of sea level in late and post glacial time, which continued to within
four thousand years and submerged lowlands and flooded valleys, took
place at the time when man learned how to grow crops and keep domestic animals, the connection if any being unresolved.

Ecologic equilibrium seems a more attractive thesis than
Malthusian rate of population growth. War and pestilence have
little relevance to simple societies. It is not proved that any
human population breeds until it is arrested by famine. Fecundity
is not fertility nor do we know much about either in 'underdeveloped' or 'primitive' conditions, such as the reduction of conception by ceremonial practices or abstentions.

15

SOCIAL IMPLICATIONS OF CHANGES IN POPULATION
AND SETTLEMENT PATTERN OF THE 12,000 YEARS OF
PREHISTORY IN THE TEHUACAN VALLEY OF MEXICO

RICHARD S. MACNEISH

ROBERT S. PEABODY FOUNDATION FOR ARCHAEOLOGY

ANDOVER, MASSACHUSETTS

This brief paper represents a summary and an
interpretation of some of the information on population
and settlement patterns uncovered by the Tehuacan
Archaeological-Botanical Expedition of the R. S. Peabody
Foundation for Archaeology of Andover, Massachusetts
during their five years (1960-1964) interdisciplinary
investigations in the Tehuacan Valley in northeast
Oaxaca and southeast Puebla, Mexico. In these investigations 456 sites were found in archaeological recon-
naissance and 12 stratified sites with 156 stratified
occupations were excavated. Studies of the 700,000
artifacts and 200,000 botanical and zoological remains
from those archaeological endeavors revealed a long
sequence of culture that has been divided into a series
of dated (by 120 radiocarbon determinations) archaeological phases. Each of these phases was represented by
a series of occupations and components and briefly are
the following (1): the Ajuereado phase that existed from
about 10,000 B.C. to 7000 B.C. is represented by 11
components; El Riego from 7000 to 5000 B.C. has 31
components; Coxcatlan from 5000 to 3400 B.C. has 16
components; Abejas from 3400 to 2300 B.C. has 23 components; Purron from 2300 to 1500 B.C. has only 2 components; Ajalpan from 1500 to 850 B.C. is represented by
13 components; Santa Maria from 180 to 150 B.C. by 40
components; Palo Blanco from 150 B.C. to A.D. 700 by 170
components; and the final phase, Venta Salada, that
starts about A.D. 700 and lasts up until the time of the
Spanish Conquest, has the most components, about 183 to
190. In total, we had a large sample of artifacts and

ecofacts from about 491 occupations for a 12,000 year
period that not only allowed us to reconstruct the culture and environmental change that had taken place in
the Tehuacan Valley, but also could be brought to bear
upon the problems of changing settlement patterns and
population in this region. On the basis of these population and settlement pattern trends plus knowledge of
the subsistence, technology, burial data and other
archaeological data, we have speculated about the evolution of types of social integration and social organization throughout this long sequence.

In these studies our primary problem was to establish a sequence of settlement pattern types. These
settlement pattern types we felt should be the correla-
tions of four sets of information:

1. the ecological and geographical (topographic)
location of our sites
2. the types of settlements
3. the kinds of habitations and;or structures in
the sites
4. the arrangements of the habitations or structures in our sites

First, let us consider the natural zones or micro-
environments of Tehuacan. (see Fig. 1) Tehuacan itself
is situated in southeastern Puebla and northeastern
Oaxaca in Mexico. The floor of the valley varies in
elevation from about 5600 to 3000 feet above sea level
and is flanked to the east by the Sierra Madre Oriental,
or a portion of it named the Sierra de Zongolica, and to
the west by the Sierra de Mixteca, or a part of it
called the Sierra Zapotitlan (2). These two ranges
coalesce to close this portion of the Puebla-Oaxaca
trough in the southern part of the zone (3), while to
the north low hills and areas of higher rainfall seem to
delimit the area about fifty miles north of Tehuacan.
Due to its flanking by high sierras, the valley is in a
rain shadow; between 900 and 400 mm. of rain a year
falls from June through September (4). This results in
the concomitant xerophytic vegetation (5) and a desert
fauna (6). However, more important from the standpoint
of cultural development than its general highland desert
ecology are the micro-environments of the valley. These
have been studied by our cooperating scientists with the
expedition and the results published (7). In summary
they are as follows:

1. The Valley Center Steppe. This area is located
in the center of the valley flanking the Rio Salado and
the broad travertine terraces between it and the Rio
Zapotitlan. To the north it runs at least as far as
Tlacotepec, while to the south it disappears at Ignacio
Mejia just west of Teotitlan del Camino. Although the
vegetation has been considerable altered by man's
activities, it seems to be primarily a mesquite grassland with a more dense vegetation occurring literally
in the bed or banks of the Rio Salado itself. The

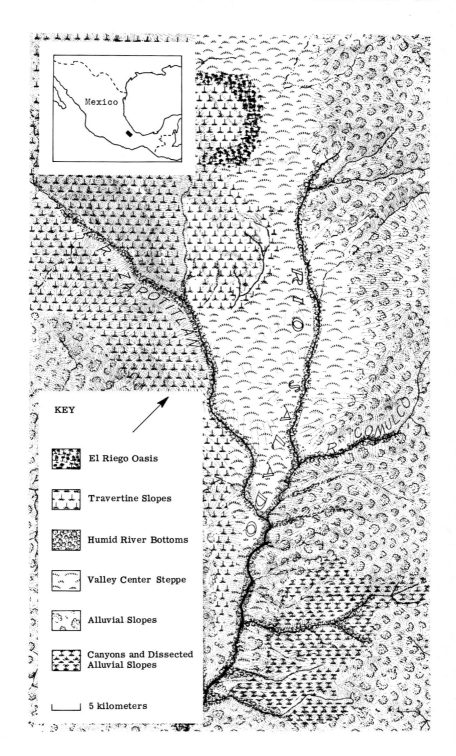

KEY

El Riego Oasis

Travertine Slopes

Humid River Bottoms

Valley Center Steppe

Alluvial Slopes

Canyons and Dissected
Alluvial Slopes

5 kilometers

grassland area includes acacia, reeds, cane, and
various fruit trees(5), and abounds in rabbits, gophers,
kangaroo rats, mice, and birds. Prehistorically this
area probably had coyote, gray fox, skunk, bobcat, and
whitetailed deer, with turtle, iguana, peccary, and
raccoon living at the water's edge (6).

As a whole, it is not an inviting area, but under
certain conditions it or parts of it can be exploited
relatively successfully. One subdivision of it termed
the western travertine slopes and terraces have some
alluvial soils that during the rainy season or with
irrigation can be used for agriculture and during the
rainy season do have some game. Further, in these
slopes and terraces there are deposits of chert and
other materials with a concoidal fracture that can be
quarried. A second subdivision along the waterways can
of course be used for agriculture and plant collecting
at any time of the year, and contains abundant water
fowl and game during the winter dry seasons. The short
grass-steppe region just west of Rio Salado, a third
subdivision, does have some game and edible seeds in the
wet season and, of course, can be turned to agriculture
if canal irrigation is introduced. The other two subdivisions of this zone are mainly differentiated on the
basis of topographical features and are the hills and
hill flanks within this western zone. During the rainy
season, these areas do have some game and can be dry
farmed, but more importantly they can be a good lookout
for game, are defensible in a military sense, and can be
the home bases for farming some of the surrounding subdivision. Finally, it must be mentioned that in all the
subdivisions there are seeps of saline deposits that can
be worked to obtain salt.

2. The Western Travertine Slopes. The area of the
lowest rainfall (under 500 mm.) and most barren soils is
the northwest corner of the valley roughly from just
west of the town of Tehuacan to roughly the northern
edge of the Rio Calapilla and from the flats in the
center of the valley into the Zapotitlan area to the
west of the Tehuacan Valley. The vegetation is predominantly barrel cactus, yucca, lechugilla, garanbullo and
cordon cactus, with mesquite, agave, and grasses occurring in the so-called "wetter" canyon bottoms within the
zones which in turn are also covered with thin alluvial
soils (5). Animal life in the zone is not abundant but
rock squirrel, wood rat, skunk, peccary, gray fox,
rabbit, and occasionally deer do occur in the canyons
(6). One subdivision, the travertine slopes, is a poor
region under any conditions, but it does have salt and
some game and edible plants do occur in some profusion
during the rainy seasons. Much the same may be said of
the canyon eroded into the travertine slopes, but here
at least there are deeper alluvial soils. The other
divisions, the hills and/or hill flanks, are equally bad
for human exploitation but they do have occasional

deposits of onyx, salt, flint, and blocks of stone for
construction as well as offer strategic military positions.

3. The El Riego Oasis. Within the travertine beds
of the western slopes is the Cerro de las Mesas just
north of the town of Tehuacan from whence flows the
famous Tehuacan waters. Because of these springs at the
base of the cliff the adjacent alluvial soils are
covered with lush vegetation including mesquite, guaje,
tule ciruela and other fruit trees, as well as prickly
pear cactus, agave, organ cactus and dense patches of
weeds and grasses (5). As might be expected, a wide
variety of animal life occurs in this oasis area including deer, peccary, skunk, raccoon, gray fox, coyote,
gopher, rabbit, opossum, lizards, rats, mice, and many
birds (6). The micro-environment covers a very small
area, so under primitive conditions would only accomo-
date a small population.

4. The Eastern and Southern Alluvial Slopes. This
is the largest zone extending from the grasslands in the
valley bottoms to well up the eastern and southern
flanks of the hills until the oak-pine forest zone
begins. Exactly where this zone ends to the north was
never well determined in our studies. However, in the
southeast portion of the valley, although broken by the
dissected alluvial slopes and canyons zone, it covers
much of the southern portion of the valley and even
extends up the west side of the valley to the Rio Calapilla and the southern edge of the travertine slopes
zone. This zone is often called the thorn forest zone;
tall legume trees, mesquite and pochote trees cover
much of it. Besides these there are fruit trees such as
chupandilla, cosahuico, and perhaps ciruela, and count-
less thorny scrubs, agave, and a number of different
kinds of cactus (5). Within the zone with its wide
variety of plants was a correspondingly rich fauna
assemblage. Deer, gray fox, peccary, coyote, opossum,
raccoon, skunk, ring-tailed cat, rabbit, iguana, lizard,
rats, mice, and many birds occur in it at one time of
the year or another (6). The statistical data on rainfall is deceiving for it shows that most of the region
has a limited rainfall (under 800 mm.) like the rest of
the valley, occurring only in the rainy season. However
rainfall is much greater in the mountains, occurring
over a longer period of time; some of this flows down
into the arroyos of this eastern zone. In fact, we can
remember one dry, dusty, hot day when we scrambled out
of an arroyo from a torrent of water that had its ultimate source from a thunder storm in the mountains which
we had never even seen or heard. The hilltop and/or
flanks make up the other subdivisions and it must be
added that, besides being defensible, they often over-
look arroyos and valleys that could be conveniently
worked from habitations situated on them. Generally
speaking, this is a liveable subarea for all but the

direst parts of the dry seasons.

5. The Southeast Dissected Alluvial Slopes and Canyons. This area exists in the southeastern portion of the valley, really within the alluvial slopes zone, and could well be considered part of it. The area is characterized by a series of low hills and mesas that have been dissected to form a series of canyons with narrow arroyos or alluvial fans at their bottoms. The sides and tops of the canyons are characterized by scatterings of lechugilla, mala mujer, tall tetecho, prickly pear, and organ cactus. The arroyo bottoms and alluvial fans or terraces also have this type of vegetation but with some mesquite trees, pochote trees, and other legumes, as well as grasses (5). A fairly wide variety of animals occur but none of them appear in very large amounts; most of them only occur seasonally (i.e. spring and summer). The fauna include deer, lynx, rabbit, skunk, fox, rats, mice, gophers, lizards, and iguana (6).

Having briefly summarized the ecological subareas of Tehuacan and their potential (for further details see Byers 1967), let us consider from the limited archaeological evidence when and what zones man did occupy, as well as his possible exploitations of these various ecological niches at various periods (see Table I).

Ajuereado is represented by only eleven occupations six of which came from excavated components in two caves Tc 50 and Tc 35w. Six of these occupations occurred in the alluvial eastern slope--subarea 4, subdivision 1. Furthermore, there was some evidence that four of those occupations were during the Pleistocene when the area was grassland rather than a thorn forest, with herds of antelope, horse, and jack rabbits, instead of whitetail deer and cottontail rabbits. Nevertheless, it would seem probable that the subdivision was occupied by food gatherers during the spring, summer rainy season, and fall. Our subsistence studies seem to indicate that these seasonally nomadic peoples probably collected seeds (in the spring) and leaves and fruits (in the summer), as well as hunted herd animals by lance ambushing or later stalked deer with darts and obtained rabbit meat by drives or trapping. Two other occupations were in the El Riego oasis subdivision and could have been occupied by similar small groups for limited periods during any season, obtaining their subsistence in a similar manner. The one occupation along the Rio Zapotitlan may have been occupied during the dry season when the animals were forced into this zone and man followed them there to hunt and trap them. The other two small occupations were in the canyons and slopes of the western travertine environs of Tehuacan. Unless the environment was far different than it is today, man would have moved into it to hunt or collect plants only during the wet season. Thus, our limited ecological

Table I

Ecological and Geographical (Topographic) Locations by Phase

Areas and subareas	El Ajuereado	Riego	Coxcatlan	Abejas	Purron	Ajalpan	Santa Maria	Palo Blanco	Venta Salada
4. E. Alluvial Slopes (1) valley flanks	6(54%)	10(32%)	3(19%)	5(22%)			1 (2%)	8 (5%)	35(19%)
3. El Riego Oasis	2(18%)	2 (6%)	1 (6%)	?			1 (2%)	9 (5%)	8 (4%)
2. W. Travertine Slopes (2) steep canyons	1 (9%)	2 (6%)	3(19%)	1 (4%)	1 (8%)		1 (2%)	7 (4%)	2 (1%)
1. Valley Center Steppe (2) edges of waterways	1 (9%)	5(16%)	2(13%)	3(13%)	10(77%)	18(45%)		14 (8%)	12 (7%)
2. W. Travertine Slopes (3) hilltops (4) flanks	1 (9%)	0						5 (3%)	5 (3%)
1. Valley Center Steppe (1) travertine terraces		3(10%)	1 (6%)	3(13%)				19(11%)	21(11%)
5. Southeast Canyons (2) canyon flanks		9(29%)	4(25%)	11(48%)	2	1 (8%)	6(15%)	7 (4%)	2 (1%)
1. Valley Center Steppe (6) hill flanks			2(13%)					2 (1%)	9 (5%)

Table I continued.

Areas and subareas	El Ajuereado	Riego	Coxcatlan	Abejas	Purron	Ajalpan	Santa Maria	Palo Blanco	Venta Salada
1. Valley Center Steppe (3)grass steppes						1 (8%)	8(20%)	18(11%)	25(14%)
5. Southeast Canyons (1)canyon floors							4(10%)	1	x 0
4. E. Alluvial Slopes (2)hilltops(3)flanks							1 (2%)	62(37%)	35(19%)
1. Valley Center Steppe (4)hilltops(5)flanks								8 (5%)	18(10%)
2. W. Travertine Slopes (1)valley flanks								5 (3%)	7 (4%)
4. E. Alluvial Slopes (4)hill flanks								5 (3%)	4 (2%)
2. W. Travertine Slopes (5)hill flanks								1	x
Total	11	31	16	23	2	13	40	170	184

subsistence and settlement pattern for Ajuereado would seem to indicate that these early food collectors exploited rather poorly a number (4) of different ecological zones at different times of the year when food resources became available in these different zones--in other words they were seasonally nomadic.

El Riego with thirty-one components shows a similar picture with the majority of the occupations being in the eastern alluvial slopes or canyons therein, probably during the spring to fall seasons. Our subsistence information would seem to indicate that plant collecting had become more important and that because of the changed environment their meat was gained by the more arduous technique of dart stalking and trapping. The El Riego oasis and the valley center was still occasionally occupied during the dry season when they were forced to hunt and trap. A few groups camped in the travertine terraces or steep canyons during the wet season presumably to collect plants and hunt.

Coxcatlan saw a slight shift in their settlement pattern with the majority of their occupations being in the flanks of the east or west canyons, possibly during the wet seasons. Our study of the subsistence remains perhaps gives an explanation of this change. Is it not possible that they moved into these areas so they could better undertake barrancas and hydro-horticulture during the wet season? Valley and hill flanks still were occupied during the spring to fall seasons with food being derived from hunting, collecting, and incipient agriculture. The travertine terrace may have been occupied during the wet season and the river banks during the dry season, and El Riego could have been used briefly during any part of the year.

Abejas peoples seemed to have had a similar settlement pattern and exploited slightly fewer subdivisions. Perhaps in this period barranca horticulture and agriculture occurred not only in the canyon flanks and valley terraces but also along the waterways, and some occupations may have lasted throughout the year. Of course, hunting and collecting continued in all zones but the travertine areas to the west and the valley flanks to the east seemed to have been used less, perhaps because they produced less food in terms of the limited Abejas agricultural techniques.

This trend for occupying the land best suited for barranca agriculture seems to continue into Ajalpan times. During this period, ten of the thirteen sites occurred along waterways and two others in the canyons were occupied during the wet season when the inhabitants were heavily involved in agriculture. The final occupation at Tr 4 in the short grass steppes is more difficult to explain. Its semi-lunar configuration suggests that it too was along a waterway that has since completely disappeared. Even though our sample of Ajalpan sites is very small, this does seem to be the

period when the least number of environments were
occupied and exploited. In the previous periods, man's
subsistence techniques were so unproductive that he had
to live in and exploit a number of different environs,
but with Ajalpan the peoples had one successful kind of
food production during one season--barranca agriculture
--and thus they confined their habitation and their
regions of production to one zone--the barrancas. After
Ajalpan times the environment no longer seems to limit
man's occupations or activities for his new means and
modes of food production with water-control techniques
(plus the amount of food produced) allowed him to exploit more and more successfully an ever wider variety
of ecological niches.

     Santa Maria begins this new trend toward the ex-
ploitation of an increasing amount of new environment
and certainly one of the new techniques of more successful food production that allowed such to happen was
irrigation. Most of the occupations still, however,
were predominantly along the central waterways and
southeast canyon flanks where they could have used
barranca agriculture. It might, however, be added that
even these locations are decreasing from early to late
Santa Maria times. Increasing throughout Santa Maria
times are sites in the canyon floors and in the short
grass steppes and valley bottoms of the Rio Salado.
The preference for those areas would seem to indicate
that as these peoples developed irrigation techniques
for watering these zones they gradually shifted their
residence into these ecological niches. Three occupations still occurred in the valley flanks, at the El
Riego oasis, and in the steep canyon cut into the travertine western slope, but they represent but a very
small proportion of the total population and could have
well been short termed. The only completely new and
different type of area occupied occurred during late
Santa Maria. This was a village located on a hilltop
on the alluvial eastern flanks of the Tehuacan Valley.
As we shall see this area became one of the preferred
zones for occupations during Palo Blanco times. One
cannot help but wonder if this hilltop village was not
the religious and administrative center for both
peasants of that village as well as surrounding hamlets
who farmed the irrigated fields or barrancas in the
region surrounding the hilltop center.

     Palo Blanco sees the apogee of this pattern of
hilltop occupation with valley or slope use of farming
land. The older patterns of living along waterways or
in the irrigated steppes decreased in popularity. It
might also be added that the hilltops not only were used
for residence but also the hills that rise out of
western travertine zones as well as parts of the steppe
zone became the sites of small hamlets or works involved
in the salt industry. Canyon occupations still occur
but now it is by groups using irrigation agriculture.

One other zone of occupation begins to make its appearance and that is hillside occupation. I believe that these reflect the beginning of slash-and-burn dry farming, perhaps assisted by hillside terracing with or without irrigation. The re-emphasis of occupation on eastern valley flanks as well as the new use of western travertine valley flanks for occupation might, also, be part of the same sort of ecological or subsistence adaptation. In fact, one might speculate that use of slopes relatively unproductive under any subsistence system reflect a sudden increase in population that forced some unfortunates to move into a rather marginal area to eke out an existence with poorer subsistence techniques.

Venta Salada sees the use of ecological niches similar to those of Palo Blanco with only slight shifts in the popularity of the zones utilized. Judging by the ecology alone one might conclude that the settlement pattern and land use was much the same as that of Palo Blanco. However, a study of these settlements in terms of subsistence, the published ethnohistorical documents, and certain construction features such as fortifications and saltworks reveal that Venta Salada people were exploiting their ecological niches and settling in them in an entirely different manner, with great heterogeneity of cultural resources.

While the increase in occupations of valley and hill flanks still in part may reflect increasing amounts of slash-and-burn dry farming, there is considerable evidence that the major reasons for the preference for these ecological zones is economic and military. The locations of the three cities as well as the seven major towns in these flank positions may well be due to the fact that in these positions they could control the water resources as well as the military and trade routes into the valley. Some of the hilltop locations are also fortified indicating a military use and a new function of this ecological niche. However, the preferences and reasons for the Palo Blanco peoples occupations of these hills probably still pertained for the Venta Salada peoples. There also was a shift back to the valley steppes and travertine terraces and slopes west of the Rio Salado. This seems due not to changes in subsistence pattern, but to the use of the zones in the salt industry. Needless to say, this final archaeological period sees the occupations in the widest variety of ecological zones which, of course, reflect the widest variety of subsistence activities and the greatest number of economic and social techniques for exploiting the meager resources of Tehuacan. A detailed study of the ethnohistory of many of the towns of the Tehuacan Valley would probably give us more complete data about how and why the various zones were occupied, as well as the kinds of occupations that occurred in them. Even without this information, however, it is apparent that during each of our phases, different ecological niches

Table II

Types of Settlements by Phase

	El Ajuereado	El Riego	Coxcatlan	Abejas	Purron	Ajalpan	Santa Maria	Palo Blanco	Venta Salada
Microband camps	11	21(68%)	8(50%)	10(43%)	2		1 (3%)	22(14%)	7 (4%)
Macroband camps		10(32%)	8(50%)	11(48%)		1 (8%)	4(10%)	16(11%)	15 (9%)
Hamlets				2 (9%)		1 (8%)	18(45%)	34(25%)	49(30%)
Villages						11(85%)	17(42%)	48(30%)	31(19%)
Towns								30(19%)	20(13%)
Salt hamlets								2 (1%)	23(14%)
Fortified hamlets or villages									6 (4%)
Fortified towns									4 (3%)
Cities									3 (2%)
Fortified cities									2 (1%)
Total	11	31	16	23	2	13	40	152	160
Irrigation features							2	4	7
Salt industrial sites								14	19
Shrine									1
Grand total	11	31	16	23	2	13	42	170	187

were exploited in different manners. Moreover, as
distinctive of the phases as the zones they occupied
are the kinds of settlements that occur in each phase
(see Table II).

The simplest kind of settlements occurred in the
Ajuereado phase; at this time all eleven occupations we
uncovered were of seasonal microbands. A microband camp
was composed of one or more individuals, perhaps on a
food gathering, planting, or hunting trip, or of one
to three families who lived together for part of the
year. Archaeologically, such camps usually had less
than two or three hearth areas in them and covered less
than about 100 square meters.

El Riego saw many more occupations. Besides the
twenty-one microband camps, ten seasonal macroband
occupations or camps also occurred. Archaeologically,
these seasonal macroband sites covered an area from 100
to 1000 square meters and had more than three hearth
areas which were used at the same time. They seem to be
occupations of two or more microbands who had banded together for certain periods of the year. These sites
were of course difficult to distinguish from a series of
different occupations of microbands that had lived in
juxtaposition. Lack of overlapping artifact distributions and similar seasonal indicators throughout the
whole site, and the lack of superimposed hearths or
lenses in hearths were archaeological features for distinguishing a macroband camp from multiple juxtaposed
microband camps.

Coxcatlan was little different in terms of kinds of
occupation, but the relative proportions of the two
types of settlement had shifted. There were now as many
seasonal macroband camps (8) as there were seasonal
microband camps. Probably during this period both kinds
of camps were occupied during longer periods or seasons
of the year. This life style of seasonal camps being
occupied for longer and longer periods continued into
Abejas times with the same proportion of macroband
camps (11) to microband camps (10). Abejas, however,
did see the addition of two examples of an entirely new
type of habitation--permanent small hamlets. The hamlets are usually about the same size as the macroband
camps, from 100 to 1000 square meters. However, some
if not all of the people lived in this single area
throughout all the seasons of a year, usually for a
number of consecutive years. Archaeologically, they
were distinguishable from macroband camps in having
some evidence of permanent habitations, even if it was
only wattle and daub.

Eleven of the settlements of Ajalpan were of the
hamlet variety, but a single seasonal microband and
one macroband camp were uncovered. Santa Maria saw the
rise of the first villages (17). Villages are distinguishable from hamlets mainly in having at least one
structure (mound) or plaza area that may be considered

an administrative, economic or ceremonial center. This
area is usually surrounded by evidence of permanent
habitations. These were just slightly less popular than
the hamlets (18). Only a few macroband (4) and microband (1) camps occurred. Two sites with irrigation
features also occurred for the first time. Villages
and hamlets continue to occur in about the same proportions in Palo Blanco times, (48 and 34 respectively)
but additionally there are thirty towns and two salt
hamlets. Towns were distinguished from villages in that
not only did they cover a larger area (over 40,000
square meters) but also they had two or more plazas,
central administrative or ceremonial areas, that were
surrounded by a variety of other structures that showed
some evidence of many full-time specialists. Salt
hamlets were house structures associated with various
salt working features. Microband and macroband camps
continued to occur (22 and 16 respectively) as do irrigation feature sites. Fourteen salt working sites were
another addition in Palo Blanco times. Salt working or
salt industrial sites were distinguishable by features
such as drying bins, salt canals, ovens, and so forth,
connected with the production of salt, but there is no
evidence of habitations. These increase in number
during Venta Salada times as do salt hamlets, but the
rise of cities is the most significant addition during
this final phase.

Cities were distinguishable not only by having two
or more plaza areas, but also the plaza areas themselves
varied in a hierarchical order as to complexity and
associated features. These sites were usually over
150,000 square meters in size and within them had
definite sections or barrios with evidence of work of
a wide variety of full-time specialists. Two of these
five cities were fortified, as were four towns and six
villages or hamlets. The older types of settlements
continued to occur with twenty towns, thirty-one
villages, forty-nine hamlets, fifteen macroband camps,
and seven microband camps.

Although our studies of almost all the settlements
was most superficial there are indications that the
type of constructions or the complex of types of constructions were distinctive for our later phases (see
Table III). The earliest construction uncovered would
be the two pit houses from the Abejas phase. Whether
or not this type of construction continued into Ajalpan
times we do not know, but we do have the remains of at
least seventeen wattle-and-daub walled houses which
appear to be small (2 by 3 meters) and rectangular in
floor plan. Unfortunately, we never carefully excavated
any of these so our knowledge of the details of their
construction is very limited.

Santa Maria saw the continued use of this type of
house and probably this type of construction lasted
right up until historic times--in fact it still occurs.

Table III

Kinds of Habitations and/or Structures by Phase

	Abejas	Ajalpan	Santa Maria	Palo Blanco	Venta Salada
Pit houses	2	17			
Rectangular wattle-and-daub houses		?	51	x	x
Rectangular single-room houses with stone foundations					5
Earth truncated pyramids			13	3,100	1,437
Dry masonry truncated pyramids			19	14	?
Rectangular multi-room houses with stone foundations			7	525	780
Talus-talud type truncated pyramids					2,885
I-shaped ball courts				32	1
II-shaped ball courts				33	3
Structures with cylindrical columns				18	11
Small platforms in middle of plazas					6
Platforms or terraces with monumental staircases					3
Total	2	17	90	3,722	5,131

Grand total: 8,962

However, during Santa Maria times there occurred for the first time a new type of rectangular single-room house, often with a paved floor and dry slab masonry walls. Also at this time are the first truncated pyramids, that is buildings used collectively by the group, probably for group purposes rather than for family usages. The majority of these at this time were earth finished but at least seven had sloping walls of dry-laid slab masonry. There is considerable variation in size and we suspect excavation would reveal a number of different types with various kinds of features such as stairways, types of construction material used, and so forth.

Palo Blanco sees a great profusion of constructions and future excavation would undoubtedly reveal many more types than we will mention here. While wattle-and-daub houses still occur on many sites of various types, i.e. hamlets, villages and towns, a noticeable feature of the period is single-room houses with masonry walls. The building blocks of these walls seem better cut than in the previous period. Furthermore, some of these houses had plastered walls as well as floors or slab paving of the floors. There were also at this time a few rectangular multi-room houses, but they occur mainly during late Palo Blanco times. These may indicate human aggregates larger than the nuclear family but differentiated from the total social group had emerged. Truncated pyramids with an earth covering still occurred but they are far outnumbered by a type with stone covering. Thirty-three of these were immediately recognizable as being of the stepped pyramid variety with vertical walls and talud panelling. Some of the other 525 stone pyramids in poorer states of preservation could well have been of similar construction; a few of them show evidence of a talud and talus construction while others have sloping walls of simple truncated pyramids. Some also abut against other pyramids and a few of them are not rectangular in outline but are L-shaped, U-shaped, and also rectangular-- features that all become popular in Venta Salada times. Palo Blanco is also the period when the first ball courts appear. These are a good sign that an elaborate religious apparatus with complex formal rituals is already present in this area of Mesoamerica by this period. Religion is now a differentiated group activity probably with specialized religious roles (e.g. at least ball players!). Except for the fact that vertical rings appear with the ball courts, much of the architecture of Palo Blanco is very similar to that found in Monte Alban III in the Oaxaca valley to the south.

Venta Salada sees a number of new types of construction and architectural features. Fragments of wattle-and-daub still occur; these were mainly noted at hamlets or villages and resurvey looking for specifically this kind of remains yields none at any of the city sites and at only four of the twenty town sites.

House foundations with masonry walls still occurred, but some of the wall construction had rubble between the interior and exterior masonry. Furthermore, the majority of them revealed plaster covering. However, perhaps of more significance was the fact that there were more than twice as many multi-room houses as there were single-room houses--a situation very different from Palo Blanco. Besides the rectangular multi-room houses, there were many L-shaped, U-shaped, cruxiform, and some had two parallel lines of rooms. Also, some of the rooms were of different sizes--perhaps the small ones with rectangular cists in the floors were kitchens while other small rooms were for storage or were domestic quarters or areas for specialized activities (such as kitchens). Large structures also occurred with cylindrical columns. The pyramids are also different and only one example of the talus-talud type of construction was noted. Most seem to be truncated with sloping walls leading to either horizontal steps or to summits. As mentioned previously, many are not rectangular but rather are L- or U-shaped and sometimes are square or rectangular platforms surrounding a plaza area. A number of the larger ones also appear to have apronlike extensions or low wide platforms attached to one or more sides. Staircases, also, seem wide and are often flanked. In a number of cases wide monumental staircases were noted leading from one plaza area to the next. Again, pyramids more often have stucco or plaster (often painted) associated with them. Also, occasionally a small platform is found in the center of plaza areas. Finally, the ball courts are different from those of Palo Blanco in that they are not I-shaped but often are between two parallel mounds or in rectangular enclosures. All in all, each of our ceramic phases seem to have distinctive types of construction and architectural features.

The arrangements of structures within the various settlements also seem to be diagnostic of our ceramic phases (see Table IV). Unfortunately, however, we dug no sites completely enough to really see the arrangement of structures at a single time period, nor were we able to accurately map the locations of structures within very many settlements. In spite of this, the few sites we did map do give hints of the arrangements of structures as does the general shape of the sites or the shape of the area covered by occupational debris. Both Abejas and Ajalpan had houses arranged in a linear fashion along waterways. Santa Maria sees the dominance of this arrangement, but some linear house arrangements are now clustered or nucleated around a plaza or mound. In a few cases, the plaza associated with this linear house arrangement is U-shaped. Completely new and different was the concentric arrangements of houses around most commonly a U-shaped plaza, but on a few occasions only around a plaza or ill-

Table IV
Arrangements of Habitations or Structures by Phase

Arrangement	Abejas	Ajalpan	Santa Maria	Palo Blanco	Venta Salada
Linear house arrangement	2(100%)	11(100%)	16(49%)	4 (3%)	15(11%)
Linear, with central mound or plaza			7(21%)	7 (6%)	2 (2%)
Circular, around U-shaped plaza			7(21%)	2 (2%)	2 (2%)
Linear, around U-shaped plaza			2 (6%)	2 (2%)	8 (6%)
Concentric, around mound or plaza area			1 (3%)	12(10%)	5 (4%)
Circular, around rectangular plaza				20(17%)	33(24%)
Concentric house arrangement				30(26%)	6 (5%)
Concentric, around clustered rectangular plazas with or without ball courts				22(19%)	32(23%)
House arrangement along contour intervals, with widely distributed mounds or plazas				7 (6%)	10 (7%)
Along contour intervals, with two or more widely distributed rectangular plazas				7 (6%)	13 (9%)
House arrangement around two or more widely separated rectangular plazas				1 (1%)	12 (8%)
Total	2	11	33	115	138

defined plaza. All the older techniques of arrangements of settlements carry on into Palo Blanco times and
all but the concentric arrangements of houses around a
plaza decrease in popularity. The settlement arrangements that become most popular during Palo Blanco are
those in which the houses are arranged in a concentric
pattern. A type without a central mound was the most
popular while houses around a central rectangular plaza
was common and only slightly less popular than the ones
grouped around a cluster of two or more plazas often
associated with I-shaped ball courts. Four other
arrangements occurred. These began in Palo Blanco time
but became popular in Venta Salada times. One of these
(that became one of the most popular in Venta Salada)
sees a series of houses (often multi-roomed) strung out
following roughly the contours of the flanks of hills
or valley slopes. Two other arrangements are similar
but one of those had some sort of plaza area or mound
in among the the houses while the other had two or more
plaza areas situated among the households strung along
the contour lines. It might be added that some of the
larger towns and cities during late Venta Salada have
this sort of household and structure arrangement while
only one example of it occurred during Palo Blanco
times. There is also one more type of arrangement. Of
it we have only one example in Palo Blanco but twelve
in Venta Salada. This type is very similar to the
popular arrangement of Palo Blanco, in having concentric
arrangement of houses or households (usually multi-
roomed) around plaza areas. The difference, however, is
that this later type has its plaza areas widely separated within household clusters or barrios of houses of
specialists rather than having the plazas neatly
arranged together as in Palo Blanco. It might be added
that in Venta Salada times the groups of plaza and
households are often surrounded by a fortification wall,
which appears to indicate that warfare was a threat and
defensive strategic building was a regular standardized
response to it. For some locations fortifications
appear clearly as a defensive need. In others, (as on
fortified hilltop cities and towns) fortified walls are
a stylistic marker of "militaristic-oriented social
activities" rather than a topographical requirement.
　　These four factors, ecological preferences for
habitation, class of settlements, type of structure and
constructions, and arrangements of structures within the
settlements all have temporal significance. By combina-
tion we have attempted to establish types of settlements
that distinguish each phase (see Table V). The
Ajuereado phase is characterized by microbands mainly
on the valley flanks, however some do occur in the
canyons at the El Riego oasis and on the travertine
slopes. In the El Riego phase there were mainly microbands in the same sort of areas, but about one third of
the settlements are macroband camps on the valley flanks

Table V
Settlement Pattern Types by Phase

	El Ajuereado	Riego	Coxcatlan	Abejas	Purron	Ajalpan	Santa Maria	Palo Blanco	Venta Salada
Microband	11(100%)	21(68%)	8(50%)						
Macroband		10(32%)	8(50%)	2					
Hamlet on terraces				10(44%)	1 (8%)	1 (3%)	22(14%)	7 (4%)	
Hamlet on water sources				11(48%)	1 (8%)	4(10%)	16(11%)	15 (9%)	
Village in canyons				1 (4%)	1 (8%)	1	2 (1%)	3 (2%)	
Hamlet in canyons				1 (4%)	10(77%)	1	x	5 (3%)	
Village in east canyons						x	1	x	
Village on steppes and waterways						3 (7%)	2 (1%)		
Hamlet on steppes and slopes						13(32%)	9 (6%)	2 (1%)	
Village on slopes and terraces						4 (3%)	x		
Hilltop hamlet						8 (5%)	5 (3%)		
Hilltop village						23(15%)	17(11%)		
Hilltop town nucleated						1 (3%)	27(18%)	14 (8%)	
Town in valley center						21(14%)	5 (3%)		
Salt hilltop hamlet steppes?						8 (5%)	3 (2%)		
Village on valley flanks						2 (1%)	5 (3%)		
Hamlet on hill flanks						4 (3%)	7 (4%)		
Hilltop town dispersed						3 (2%)	12 (7%)		
Village on hill flanks						1	x	5 (3%)	
Hamlet on valley flanks						1	x	10 (6%)	
Town on valley flanks								7 (6%)	

Table V continued.

	El Ajuereado	Riego	Coxcatlan	Abejas	Purron	Ajalpan	Santa Maria	Palo Blanco	Venta Salada
Salt hamlet or village in valley center									18(11%)
Fortified hilltop hamlet or garrison									2 (1%)
Fortified hilltop hamlet or garrison									4 (3%)
Fortified hilltop village or garrison									4 (3%)
Fortified hilltop town									1 x
Fortified hilltop city									1 x
Fortified steppe city									1 x
Fortified flank city									2 (1%)
Valley flank city									
Total	11	31	16	23	2	13	40	152	160

Grand total: 448

and on the travertine terraces or along the waterways.
Coxcatlan has an equal number of microbands and macrobands. One slight difference is that some of the macrobands are located in the canyons. Abejas also has about
the same number of microbands and macrobands but now one
hamlet along the waterway and one terrace hamlet types ʰ
of settlements occur. Ajalpan has the same types of
settlements occurring, however in very different proportions, as there are one microband camp, one macroband
camp, one terrace hamlet, and ten waterway hamlets.
Those hamlets had wattle-and-daub houses arranged in a
linear fashion. Santa Maria still has four macroband
camps and a single microband camp but waterway hamlets
are the dominant settlement type. Almost unique to
Santa Maria are two new types of settlements--hamlets
in canyons and canyon villages. Also, almost as popular
as waterway hamlets are waterway villages with mounds
around a U-shaped plaza. One example of a new type was
found. This is to become more popular in Palo Blanco--
the hilltop village. Thus, suddenly the number of types
of settlements of Abejas and Ajalpan have doubled from
four to eight by Santa Maria times. Then, the number of
types of settlements in Palo Blanco is double the number
of Santa Maria. Hilltop villages, hilltop hamlets, and
nucleated hilltop towns become dominant. All the types
have a concentric arrangement of structures with single-
room stone foundations on the outer peripheries.
Villages have mounds of talus-talud construction sometimes around rectangular plazas and with or without an
I-shaped ball court. The nucleated hilltop town type
have these features plus a cluster of plazas, mounds,
and ball courts. Other new types that first appear in
Palo Blanco and diminish in Venta Salada are steppe-
slope hamlets, travertine slope villages, and valley
center towns. These have similar structural features
and constructions. Minority types that begin in Palo
Blanco but become more popular in Venta Salada are salt
hilltop hamlets, valley flank villages, hill flank
hamlets, and dispersed hilltop towns. In these types as
well as the eleven new settlement types and all the
older ones, houses more often are multi-room rather than
single-room structures.

One of the most distinctive settlements of Venta
Salada are its cities. These we have divided into four
types, but they might well be considered one type characterized by fortifications and differing internally by
size. These four city types are valley flank cities,
fortified flank cities, fortified steppe cities, and
fortified hilltop cities. Another very distinctive
aspect of Venta Salada is that many other type sites are
fortified and the new types include fortified hilltop
towns, fortified hilltop villages, and fortified hilltop
hamlets. Again, these might well be classified as a
single "fortified" type except for their obvious size
difference as well as the difference in structures.

Valley center salt hamlets are also a very distinctive
settlement type. Three other types have in common the
feature that they are on valley or hill flanks and the
structures are strung along the contour intervals.
Again, however, their size and structure differ. These
have been classified into three new types: hill flank
villages, valley flank hamlets, and valley flank towns.
Thus, our twenty-eight settlement types give us an
additional basis for separating different phases from
each other. The types also show the long development
from microband settlements to the rise of cities.

In the previous paragraphs we have discussed the
ever increasing number of settlement pattern types that
are ever increasing in size and complexity. Can this
data be brought to bear upon the problem of social
changes, size, and population density? Quite frankly,
our information in this line is at best relative and
any attempts to quantify it is at best speculative (see
Table VI). However, we do have some ethnohistoric
source material on the population of Tehuacan and comparison with the archaeological data from our site
survey does give us some basis for estimating earlier
prehistoric populations in that region. Borah and Cook
and others using early Spanish documents about the size
of towns or municipios in the area of our survey give
population estimates that range from 60,000 to about
140,000 people, with a mean figure of about 100,000
people for our Tehuacan ecological zone surveyed (7).
This estimate is in fact an estimate of the population
of the final part of the Venta Salada archaeological
phase. Because of the imprecision and lack of excavation of a sample of a number of habitation areas,
perhaps the only figure from our survey that has any
bearing on the population size of the settlements is the
figure concerned with the size of the area that the site
covered, expressed in square meters. All told, late
Venta Salada sites occupied about 29,847,250 square
meters, but a quick glance at our survey chart reveals
that all are sites that lasted up into historic times
and are included in the Spanish Relaciones such as
Coxcatlan (Tr 62), Tehuacan (Tr 1), Ajalpan (Tr 367,
Tr 368), Teotitlan (Tr 115A), Los Cues (Tr 294), all in
existence in the final quarter of the late Venta Salada
sites and only cover an area of 4,888,584 square meters.
Thus, the site area to population ratio is about one
person to 48.88 square meters of the site area (which we
shall round off to one person per 50 square meters) for
the last century of occupation in the Tehuacan Valley,
roughly A.D. 1450 to 1550.

Although I am well aware the land-to-people ratio
was not constant throughout the periods in the Tehuacan
area, let us now look at the other phases in light of
their figures. For all the Ajuereado occupation we have
only 12,342 square meters of occupied area for a season
or the year and if we consider these occupations as

Table VI

Hypothetical Changes in Prehistoric Population in the Tehuacan Valley

Possible components	Ajuereado 10,000-7000 B.C.	El Riego 7000-5000 B.C.	Coxcatlan 5000-3400 B.C.	Abejas 3400-2300 B.C.	Late Ajalpan 1200-900 B.C.
Possible components	11	31	16	23	13
Total sq. meters covered by sites per century	12,342 617 or 309	108,437 2,760	251,961 7,874	142,333 16,466	155,002 51,162
Proportion of area at historic occupation	1/7800 or 1/15,000	1/1070	1/490	1/290	1/90
Population in 2400 sq. km. or 1500 sq. miles of survey	12 or 6	54	155	329	1,023
Population density per sq. mile per 100 sq. km.	.008 or .004 .5 or .25	.03 2.25	.10 6.25	.22 13.70	.68 42.62
Percentage of diet from agricultural produce	1%	5%	14%	21%	43%

Purron – Early Ajalpan, 2300-1200 B.C.

Table VI continued.

Possible components	Santa Maria 900–100 B.C.	Palo Blanco 100 – A.D. B.C. 700	Venta Salada A.D. 700–1500	Historic sites A.D. 1500–1550
Total sq. meters covered by sites per century	1,511,898 201,453	10,658,755 1,332,344	34,935,500 4,366,938	4,888,584 4,888,584
Proportion of area at historic occupation	1/25	1/4	43/48	1
Population in 2400 sq. km. or 1500 sq. miles of survey	4,029	26,646	87,338	100,000
Population density per sq. mile per 100 sq. km.	2.68 165	16.42 1,110	58.22 3,639	66.57 4,166
Percentage of diet from agricultural produce	58%	65%	75%	

covering ten centuries it is only about 617 square meters
or if the phase is twenty centuries then it is only about
309 square meters. Thus, Ajuereado sites occupied between 1/7800 and 1/15,000 of the area occupied at historic time and may have that small proportion of the
final population of the valley. Using our 50 meters to
one person ratio (that is probably not applicable to this
early time period) this would mean there were six and
twelve people in the valley or two to four nuclear
familites in the valley at the same time. In terms of
population density, since we survey about 2400 square
kilometers or 1500 square miles, this would mean between
.008 or .004 people per square mile or .5 or .25 people
per 100 square kilometers. The El Riego seasonal or
half year occupation covered about 108,437 square meters
and lasted about twenty centuries giving 2,759.9 square
meters per century. This would represent about 1/1070
of the area and perhaps population of historic times.
In terms of land-man ratio this would be about fifty-
four people in the valley and a population density of
.03 people per square mile or 2.25 people per hundred
square kilometers. As may be seen this is from more
than four to eight times increased in population over
that of Ajuereado and has been in part caused by the
shift from a basically hunting and trapping subsistence
to one which also received a large amount of this subsistence from seed collection, leaf cutting, fruit and
pod picking, and incipient agriculture. Coxcatlan
seasonal or half year sites covered about 251,961 square
meters and the phase lasted sixteen centuries or about
7,874 square meters per century. This is about 1/490
of the final area covered and might mean about 155
people in the valley. The general increase in barranca
horticulture and hydro-horticulture over that of El
Riego might account for this threefold increase in population. The population density would have been .10
people per square mile or 6.25 people per one hundred
square kilometers. Abejas in total would see only
142,333 square meters occupied, but since three of the
largest sites were possibly occupied all year round and
since the phase only existed for eleven centuries, the
total square meters per century would be 16,466. This
is about 1/290 of the final prehistoric figure. This
would give a population of about 329 for the valley with
a population density of .22 people per square mile or
13.70 people per one hudred square kilometers.
    Purron and early Ajalpan sites were so rare in the
findings of our survey that even we dare not talk about
population during these time periods. However, from
late Ajalpan, a small period of about three centuries,
we do have some data. In our thirteen components an
area of about 155,002 square meters was occupied or
about 51,162 square meters per century. This would be
about 1/90 of the area covered at the time of Spanish
Conquest. In terms of people, we estimate that perhaps

1,023 were resident in the valley, a population density
of .68 people per square mile or 42.62 people per one
hundred square kilometers. This is about three times
the population of that of Abejas and the general increase in the efficiency of the barranca agriculture
may have been a key factor in this increase.

Our Santa Maria survey information is much more
adequate and even within its brief eight-century span
there are noticeable increases in population as well as
cultural changes. The forty sites of this phase cover
about 1,511,898 square meters or 201,453 square meters
per century, about 1/25 of the final area covered by
the occupations at historic times. In terms of land-
man ratio, this might mean a population of about 4,029
people in the Tehuacan Valley. This would mean a population density of about 2.68 people per square mile or
165 people per one hundred square kilometers. As may be
noted, this is about a fourfold increase over the population of Ajalpan and we would think that a key factor
in this increase would be food production based upon
irrigation. This, also, may be a major factor in the
even larger proportional population increase from Santa
Maria through Palo Blanco times.

Palo Blanco sites show an amazing 10,658,755 square
meters of occupation or 1,332,344 square meters per century, only a little more than 1/4 the area occupied at
historic times. In terms of number of people in the
valley, it might mean as many as 26,646 and the population density would have been 16.42 per square mile or
1,110 persons per one hundred square kilometers. This
is over six times the population of that of Santa Maria.

The population increase from Palo Blanco to Venta
Salada is not so great but is still considerable and
may merely reflect a steady increase in food production
by irrigation techniques as well as importation of food-
stuffs for the exportation of industrial produce (salt,
textiles, and the like). The Venta Salada sites
covered only 34,935,500 square meters, existing for
about eight centuries or 4,366,938 square meters per
century. This is an area only slightly less than that
occupied at historic times, and the population may have
been as high as 87,338 people with the population density of the valley being about 58.22 per square mile or
3,639 people per one hundred square kilometers.

All in all, our attempts at quantifying our population data are not very successful and the results most
speculative. Certainly we hope our crude pioneering
effort will stimulate or provoke others to test our
tentative conclusions or start programs that will yield
better results. Yet, throughout this brief analysis,
there are some interesting and perhaps encouraging
results. For instance, jumps and spurts in population
trends, regardless of the limitations of our data and
methods, must have some meaning in reality. That is,
they seem to tap some isomorphous changes in real

history even though the population figures themselves
may be in error. Comparisons of these trends with
trends in food production seem to have some sort of
causal connection. Does not the population increase
between Lerma and El Riego relate to the jump in the
subsistence trends for the same time period? Does not
the doubling of agricultural produce, the second major
food production spurt between Abejas and Ajalpan, have
some sort of relationship to the population increase
from Ajalpan to Santa Maria? Is not the introduction of
irrigation agriculture in Santa Maria the basic cause in
the great population jump in Palo Blanco times? Do not
these comparisons give us the basis for generalizing
that a major change in food production will result in an
even greater proportioned change in population?

On the basis of our settlement pattern information
we have speculated about population change, so can we
not also speculate about the implications of this data
about the change in social organization that took place
during this long archaeological sequence in Tehuacan?
There is little we can say about the social organization
of the Ajuereado peoples. Our archaeological evidence
would seem to indicate that their subsistence activities
were extremely limited, mainly big game hunting from
ambush, hunting by dart stalking, collecting seeds,
picking fruits, rabbit drive or trapping and perhaps
rarely the collecting of leaves or stalks. It would
appear from our limited knowledge that these activities
were attempted in all seasons in all ecological zones
and that there was little neat scheduling of certain
subsistence activities in certain zones during certain
seasons. We would guess they traveled in small groups
(microbands or nuclear families) only occasionally
gathering together into macrobands for rabbit drives.
Site distributions suggest they were "free wandering",
exploring the land without having evolved territorial
domains. One also might speculate that females married
into the bands and that they were patrilocal bands.
Unfortunately, we do not have many, if any, ethnographic examples of groups with either such a limited
population (.25 or .5 people per 100 sq. km.), nomadic
settlement pattern, or subsistence pattern that are
directly analogous to our Ajuereado phase.

Ethnographic analogies to El Riego and Coxcatlan
in terms of ecology (xerophytic), population density
(from 2 to 7 people per 100 sq. km.), seasonal micro-
band-macroband settlement pattern, and a subsistence
system with a number of kinds of hunting, plant collecting, and incipient agriculture activities that are
neatly geared to exploiting certain environmental niches
in certain seasons are, however, numerous. Intensive
studies of such tribes of bands by J. Steward (8) and
later by Service (9) have found that the above-mentioned
features are usually functionally interrelated and
correlated with band territoriality, band exogamy, and

patrilocality. Also, they found that minimum centralized command control exists only for hunting, ritual,
and a few other communal activitie-. Consequently the
leader has temporary and slight authority based on
personal qualifications rather than ascription. The
religious specialists, however, may control some collective or communal activities such as burial rites and
other rituals (8). Besides this generalization about
patrilocal bands as evidence that El Riego and Coxcatlan
had these social features, there is some other archaeological evidence to bolster this cultural correlation.
I believe that the fact that Coxcatlan and El Riego
components appear in from four to six clusters may be
considered as evidence that groups of microbands and
macrobands are centered in definite regions and that
this is evidence of band territories. The dominance of
males in group burials and the fact that male burials
had most of the grave goods in El Riego and Coxcatlan
certainly indicates a male social dominance, or at
least a dominance as far as ritual life, and it perhaps
may be cited as evidence for patrilocality. The evidence of female and children human sacrifices as well as
other evidence of complex burial rites may be cited as
evidence for at least part-time religious specialists
who controlled at least one collective activity--burial
ceremonies and collective funerary rituals. Studies of
the spatial distribution of artifact types on Coxcatlan
and El Riego floors as well as burials show concentrations of complexes of artifacts indicating specialized
activities by the different sexes--in other words,
division of labor was probably based on sex. On the
basis of the above facts we have classified the El Riego
and Coxcatlan societies as having a cross-cultural type
called "Patrilocal bands."

        Reconstructing the social organization of the
following Abejas and Purron phases is much more difficult. This is not only because of our limited archaeological survey data and lack of excavation of Abejas
and Purron settlements, but also because comparable
ethnological examples have been seldom studies--that is
societies with a settlement pattern of macrobands and
hamlets as well as subsistence systems that is transitional from food collecting to food production. Only
more and better archaeological investigations will yield
data for determining the social organization of this
probably extinct transitional type of society.

        Fortunately, we do have information about the end
result of this period of transition both in the Ajalpan
phase as well as the ethnological record. Ajalpan sees
the rise of a stable subsistence agriculture based upon
flood-plain farming or barranca agriculture. At this
time they were able to grow in the barranca area during
the rainy season sufficient food to last them all year.
Thus they existed in hamlets in or near the barranca

with only occasional trips into other micro-environs
in the non-agricultural drier seasons. Their settlements or hamlets are relatively isolated from each other
and composed of a few households usually arranged in a
linear fashion along waterways. No ceremonial structures are apparent and population density is about
forty-two people per one hundred square kilometers with
there being perhaps from fifty to two hundred people
living in each settlement or hamlet. Chang (10), on the
basis of a study of the cross-cultural human relation
files concluded that societies with this type of subsistence with this sort of linear segmented hamlets or
villages have communities composed of multiple kinship
aggregates. Sahlin and Service (11) would go even
further and suggest that societies with the Ajalpan type
of subsistence and settlement pattern not only have
multi-kinship aggregate villages, but also multi-matri-
lineal clan villages as well as matrilocal residence,
matri-owned territory, leadership in the hands of a male
who represents the kinship group, and a number of other
characteristics. Some of the archaeological data from
Ajalpan components in Zones J through K3 at Ts 368e
tends to suggest a similar hypothesis. The high correlation of certain figurine types with certain house
floors on each of these occupation levels strongly
suggests that the figurines at this time were familial
symbols or descent group symbols, i.e. ritual objects
belonging to household groups which may have been
descent defined. Therefore, their occupations or
hamlets were probably composed of different kinship
aggregates (descent groups?) localized in separate
household clusters. Furthermore, the fact that all
figurines are female suggest that group rituals centered
on female symbols were dominant, perhaps because of an
emphasis on female descent lines or fertility symbolism.
Whether the clusters (3) of Ajalpan sites means descent
group territories or not is difficult to determine, and
there is little evidence to show if there was either
matrilocality, uxorilocality, or virilocality, female
or male inheritance of property or leadership based upon
a male representative of a matrilineal or ambilateral
descent group. Archaeological evidence is rarely
amenable to solving these types of questions.

   Excavations of the Ajalpan household areas gave
little evidence of class or status differences, but one
burial (Ts 204e) does suggest one individual, a male,
who did have special funerary treatment. Furthermore,
the occurrence of a Hollow Red Dwarf figurine in that
burial suggests that this individual was acknowledged
as having high special status, perhaps associated with
religious roles. Is it not possible that there were
full-time ritual specialists in Ajalpan society? Some
of the lapidary artifacts do suggest craftsmen, but
whether they were religious specialists or attached to
secular communities or merely descent group members who

were part-time specialists is difficult to determine.
Also, whether leadership of this type of society was in
the hands of an incipient theocracy or directed by a
group of descent group elders or was an achieved rather
than an inherited role, or some combinations of all of
these is not possible to decide on the basis of our
present evidence.

In spite of these limitations Ajalpan does seem to
represent a cross-cultural type. I prefer to call it a
kin-aggregate type of society.

Santa Maria has many characteristics in common with
Ajalpan but there are some differences and these seem to
have important social implications that indicate that we
are dealing with yet another level of cross-cultural
social development. Santa Maria subsistence is still
agriculture and much of it was still barranca agriculture. However, two important new activities have been
added--irrigation agriculture and orchard culture. The
success of these new means of food production may be
seen in the increased population--perhaps 4,029 in the
Tehuacan Valley and a density of 165 people per one
hundred square kilometers. Hamlets along waterways
with a linear household is still the most popular type
of settlement; there were three hamlets in canyons but
at this time the hamlets seem to be oriented to nuclear
villages with a ceremonial structure or area in it.
The continuation of the Ajalpan type linear hamlets and
the local female figurines suggest that the descent-
household localized system of Ajalpan continued into
Santa Maria times. However, there are many new figurine types (some obviously foreign imports) and many of
these figurine types appear at many households. Moreover, the occurrence of ceremonial structures in the
nuclear village suggests that collective ceremonial
organizations or cults have been introduced in this
society. Thus a new dimension had been introduced into
Santa Maria society and affiliations were not only to
small kinship-linked groups but also to pan-group
(tribal) ritual and burial activities, i.e. the society
as a whole now dominates aspects of life which were
previously domestic in scope. The difference between
burials, the occurrence of tombs, the ceremonial structures, and the orientations of hamlets to ceremonial
nucleated villages suggests that political power was
centralized and localized and there was an (incipient?)
elite to which the rest of the population was subservi-
ent. Furthermore, the settlement pattern as well as the
burials, the public structure (irrigation features,
temples, etc.), and the large importation of foreign
pottery suggests that besides the dominant political
elite (perhaps of religious specialists) and farmers
(peasants?), there was the beginning of a "true"
division of labor in the Durkheim sense, true speciali-
zations--i.e. a class of people who besides or instead
of farming were heavily involved in a series of other

duties or activities (such as trade, public work construction, irrigations, etc.). Thus I believe Santa
Maria represents another level of cross-cultural social
development. Since it occupies a position transitional
to an even more complex type of society this level has
been designated <u>Formative</u>.

This type of society eventually developed in Palo
Blanco times into a type I have called a <u>Priestdom</u>.
Food production was now based mainly upon <u>irrigation</u>
agriculture (which could give three crops a year) rather
than barranca or slash-and-burn agriculture (with its
single rainy season crop). Population jumped both in
terms of actual number of people (perhaps 26,000) as
well as population density and there may now have been
over 1,000 people per one hundred square kilometers.
This population in the main was now concentrated in
hilltop hamlets which were oriented to hilltop villages
or secondary ceremonial centers which in turn clustered
around one or two large hilltop towns. Furthermore,
site distribution studies indicate that there were a
number of clusters of this hamlet-village-town complex
in a number of different regions (often stream drain-
ages) in the Tehuacan Valley. Perhaps these were tribal
territorial units controlled by temple elites (priests).
Figurines appear now as well as the incense burners
depictings gods; they are male and female suggesting
that descent groups were not unilineal (matrilineal or
patrilineal) but perhaps bilateral (ambilateral?). In
terms of marriage, class may have been more important
than descent. There is considerable evidence for a
class structure of this society. The burials in vil--
lages or caves with limited grave goods, the wattle-and-
daub houses in the hamlets or at the peripheries of the
villages and towns certainly may be taken as evidence
of a lower class of peasants. The occurrence of cave
niche burials or rectangular tomb burials as well as
the single-room stone house foundations concentrated
around the central larger structures in the village and
towns, suggest an upper class. There is also a number
of hints in the archaeological record of a whole series
of full-time or part-time specialists. Large numbers
of trade pots suggest merchants, salt hamlets with
rectangular house foundations suggest salt worker
specialists, large constructions in towns suggest
construction works, irrigation works suggest construction men as well as engineers, bureaucrats, and administrators, while temples suggest priests, etc. The
occurrence of house foundations often associated with
the centers of villages as well as with salt hamlets
and irrigation features suggest that the upper classes
were, in the main, composed of various kinds of full-
or part-time specialists. At the top of this system
would be the ruling priestly elite and the elaborate
tombs and their contents, the central ceremonial structure, etc. could be cited as evidence for this conclu-

sion. This society was not only held together by a
series of reciprocal relations both inter and intra the
class, but was further backed by elaborate sacred belief
and political power. It is in this period that we first
can recognize in the figurines, incense burners, and
xantiles some of the gods and goddesses of a pantheon,
part of which lasted to historic times. These, of
course, had at historic times definite duties and functions in running the universe, both physicall and
morally. It might be added that some of these are new
to the Tehuacan Valley, but others such as Tlaloc, the
rain god, Xipe Totec, and Xochiquetzal may have developed from some of the cult deities in the Formative.
     During late Palo Blanco, this type of society seems
at times to gradually break down as we see sites spaced
over a wide area and not in territorial village-town
clusters; multi-dispersed plaza areas in towns and in
the villages lose this neat concentric arrangement of
ascendingly important structures. However, in early
Venta Salada time we see the gradual emergence of our
final type of society which we are calling Despotic
Primitive States in full sway in late Venta Salada
times and at the time of the Spanish Conquest. As
indicated previously, over seventy-five percent of the
sustinence of the Venta Salada came from agriculture
and most of it was obtained by irrigation. However,
the historic documents (12) indicate that Tehuacan was
a major trade center. Archaeology indicates a salt and
weaving industry, also paper, which undoubtedly were
used for export from Teotitlan. These products as well
as others may have been exported in exchange for food
produce imports or manufactured goods. Tribute also
may have brought food produce and craft specialties into
the Tehuacan Valley. Concomitant with the rise in food
production was an increase in population. Documentary
source indicates a population for this valley of between
60,000 and 140,000 at the time of the Conquest, with
perhaps an average of about 85,000 for the Venta Salada
phase. This would mean 3,639 people per one hundred
square kilometers. Much of this population occurred in
about five major cities and in about an equal number of
fortified towns. Clustered around their centers, which
were probably state capitals, would be a whole series
of secondary towns, villages, and hamlets. Early
documents give the names of some of these capitals as
Teotitlan, Los Cues, Coxcatlan, Calipan, Zapotitlan,
Chilac, Tehuacan, and perhaps three or four others.
Furthermore, ceramic and site distributions would seem
to indicate that these Venta Salada sites and these
state capitals were within the historic "empire" called
the Señorío de Teotitlan, an independent ally of the
Aztecs.
     The historic documents give us more information
about the political structure and the intimately
connected class structure. Furthermore, some of the

archaeological evidence from Venta Salada seems to be in
agreement with the documentary sources. In the early
historic documents we have mention of two main estates,
classes, or castes, the principales and macehuales.
These might be called a hereditary noble elite and the
commoners. The large pyramids and structures with
columns on or around them and the more elaborate multi-
room houses in our towns and cities as well as the
cruxiform tombs may well have been those of the princi-
ples or nobles while the single-room house foundations
as well as the wattle-and-daub structures and less
elaborate burials may have been of the commoners. The
documents also indicate that the nobility was divided
into at least two classes, the lordly rulers who were
considered living gods and the minor nobility who
carried out bureaucratic tasks of the rulers' domain.
It might be added that the rulers and nobility who were
members of linked descent lines at least in Coxcatlan,
Teotitlan, and Tehuacan, were nahuatl speakers, while
many of the peasants were mazatec and popoloca speakers.
Furthermore, study of Tehuacan documents and its later
period archaeology could tell us much more concerning
this elite group. The lower group also seems to have
been divided into at least three levels: the full-time
specialists, the peasants, and the slaves. The archaeological records of salt hamlets and weaving in El Riego
Cave and fortifications as well as guard houses indicate
that there were salt workers, weaving specialists, and
soldiers, while artifact distributions within the Venta
Salada site itself indicate localized "barrios" of flint
(blade) knappers, textile workers, salt workers, and
priests. Trade types certainly indicate merchants.
Documentary sources and the illustrations in the Borgia
Codex give evidence of a host of other kinds of specialists. Documents (12) also suggest that there were
novices, assistants, and leaders within each of these
specialized groups and that there was some sort of
educational system. The multi-room houses at salt sites
as well as in the barrios of Venta Salada hint that the
multi-room houses perhaps belonged to the full-time
specialists. Furthermore, the orientation of the Venta
Salada barrios to plaza areas hint that some of these
specialists were under the direction of and payed tribute or taxes to some of the members of the nobility
caste. Below this hierarchal class within our lower
caste would have been the peasants, those who occupied
the wattle-and-daub or single-room stone houses in our
villages and hamlets. At the bottom of the system
according to the documents (12), there would be the
slaves and those destined to be sacrificed. Perhaps
some of the chopped-up burials in El Riego Cave were of
this segment of the society.
     The archaeology of Venta Salada gives us few hints
of the family organization as we have few burials or
figurines or excavated households. On the basis of

similar evidence from nearby groups they were ambilateral. Furthermore, there are hints that marriage was
endogamous within the social classes and that among the
rulers there were even incestuous marriages or marriage
among close kinsmen. Little is known about the rules of
inheritance other than that among the nobility the wives
or eldest offspring inherited the patrimonial domain
rights on land as well as social privileges.

The religion at this time period was an extremely
complex affair (e.g. the Relaciones de Teotitlan has
a complete calendar, a schedule of the year rituals,
etc.). The documents as well as the figurines and
xantiles give evidence of a large pantheon. Many of the
deities are those of the previous phase, but a few have
been added and there are hints that some of these
deities were actual individuals or rulers who became
deified. Documents indicate that there were hierarchical groups of priests for each deity who looked after
the appropriate rituals and ceremonies on the correct
calendrical days. For what little we can tell from the
documents, the priest groups were within the lower
caste and their exact relation to the nobility is
difficult to determine (12).

In the previous pages on the basis of the settlement pattern data plus some additional information, we
have attempted to reconstruct the developments in
social organization in our long Tehuacan sequence.
Much of our reconstruction is speculative and hypothetical. We hope our endeavors will stimulate others to
do the necessary archaeological and ethnohistorical
endeavors that can supplement and test the hypothetical
reconstructions.

(REFERENCES)

1) MacNeish, R.S.
   1964 "Ancient Mesoamerican Civilization."
         Science 143: 531-537.

2) Brunet, J.
   1967 "Geologic Studies." The Prehistory of the
         Tehuacan Valley, Vol. 1. Austin: Univ. of
         Texas Press.

3) Byers, D.S.
   1967 "The Region and Its People." The Prehistory
         of the Tehuacan Valley, Vol. 1. Austin:
         Univ. of Texas Press.

4) Byers, D.S.
   1967 "Climate and Hydrology." The Prehistory of
         the Tehuacan Valley, Vol. 1. Austin: Univ.
         of Texas Press.

5) Smith, C.E., Jr.
   1967 "Plant Remains." The Prehistory of the
         Tehuacan Valley, Vol. 1. Austin: Univ. of
         Texas Press.

6) Flannery, K.V.
   1967 "The Vertebrate Fauna and Hunting Patterns."
         The Prehistory of the Tehuacan Valley, Vol.
         1. Austin: Univ. of Texas Press.

7) Byers, D.S. (Ed.)
   1967 The Prehistory of the Tehuacan Valley, Vol.
         1. Austin: Univ. of Texas Press.

8) Steward, J.H.
   1955 Theory of Cultural Change. Urbana: Univ. of
         Illinois Press.

9) Service, E.R.
   1962 Primitive Social Organization: An Evolu-
         tionary Perspective. New York: Random House.

10) Chang, K.C.
    1967 Rethinking Archaeology. New York: Random
          House.

11) Sahlins, M.D. and E.R. Service
    1960 Evolution and Culture. Ann Arbor: Univ. of
          Michigan Press.

12) Spores, R.
    1965 "The Zapotec and Mixtec at Spanish Contact."
          Handbook of Middle American Indians, Vol. 3.
          Austin: Univ. of Texas Press.

16

THE ABORIGINAL POPULATION OF TROPICAL AMERICA:

PROBLEMS AND METHODS OF ESTIMATION

WILLIAM M. DENEVAN

DEPARTMENT OF GEOGRAPHY

UNIVERSITY OF WISCONSIN

The size of Pre-Columbian native populations in the New World has long been a subject of vigorous discussion. In contrast to the sixteenth-century chroniclers who reported tens of millions of Indians, most modern scholars have been very conservative. Kroeber, for example, estimated only 8,400,000 for the entire hemisphere in 1500 (1). However, the latest estimates have been much higher: Woodrow Borah has suggested 100 million and Henry Dobyns 90 to 112 million (2). The implications of such high numbers for interpretations of the social, economic, and demographic history of both the pre-Columbian and colonial New World are, of course, vast.

Attention thus far has been mainly focused on the highland civilizations of Mexico and Peru where the densest native populations were located. The purpose of this paper, instead, is to examine the lesser known aboriginal situation in the humid tropical lowlands, particularly at the time of initial European contact. For the New World as a whole, good reviews of the literature on estimating native populations and critical discussions of the problems and methodology have been recently provided by Dobyns and Borah (3), and as little as possible of this material will be repeated here.

The areas of concern are those with humid tropical climates below about 5,000 feet elevation (4). The greater part of these lowlands is generally considered to have been sparsely settled, as evidenced by (a) relatively simple socio-economic levels, (b) general lack of documentary evidence of large populations, (c) present low population densities, and (d) low levels of food production by surviving tribes. Nevertheless, a review of a variety of forms of evidence does reveal that locally there were

relatively dense populations, in some areas greater than at the
present time, and that even allowing for a sparse population
density, the areas involved are so immense that very low
densities still project into millions of people.

RATE OF DEPOPULATION

At the outset, it should be emphasized that there are
very few counts, estimates, or even partial enumerations of the
various tropical tribes for the early sixteenth century. The
first such figures generally do not appear until many years or
even centuries later. Even today, the size of many surviving
Amazonian tribes can only be guessed. For example, estimates for
the Campa, the largest tribe in eastern Peru, range from 10,000
to 35,000. The critical problem is then, how much did a given
group decline in numbers from the time of initial contact until
the time a reasonable estimate or count became available? Only
occasionally are there statements from contemporary observers
that the native population had declined by perhaps 50 or 90
per cent of what it was when the Europeans arrived, and these
were only rough approximations.

A major cause of aboriginal population decline was
epidemics of introduced Old World diseases to which the New
World natives had no immunity (5). The rate of decline was
rapid - an estimated 90-95 per cent in many areas within the
first 100 years after initial contact in the opinion of Borah (6).
Dobyns has estimated an average depopulation ratio from first
contact to nadir (date of start of population recovery - usually
100-150 years after contact) of 20 to 1 or 95 per cent. He
proposes a much higher rate of decline for the tropical lowlands,
including complete extinction for many tribes (7). I have
suggested an average for tropical America of roughly 35 to 1
from contact to nadir (8); the decline was much less, of course,
for the more isolated tribes. The higher tropical rate was
partly due to the introduction of malaria and yellow fever (9);
but, in addition, the main highland killers of smallpox and
measles may have been even more virulent in the lowlands.
Different dietary patterns may have been a factor; also viruses
tend to survive better in warmer climates.

However, in the interior tropical lowlands, especially
Amazonia, European contacts for the first 100 years or more were
sporadic and epidemics absent or infrequent. Phelan points out
that in the Jesuit province of Mainas in eastern Ecuador, no
major epidemics were reported from the time Spanish settlers
arrived in 1618 until 1660 (10), although smallpox was at least
present in Borja on the Marañon in the 1640's (11). After 1660,
epidemics were frequent with reductions of mission populations
by 44 per cent in 1660, 25 per cent in 1669, 66 per cent in 1680,
and 72 per cent between 1749 and 1762 (12). Whether epidemics
occurred before 1618 is not known. In contrast, in the Jesuit
Province of Mojos in eastern Bolivia, numerous and severe
epidemics broke out even before the first mission was established
in 1682. On the basis of the probable depopulation in Mojos I
would estimate a crude ratio of decline of between 2 to 1 and
5 to 1 during the first 100 years after initial contact for those
tropical areas where contact was infrequent (13). Steward admits

to a probable reduction in tropical South America by "half or more" during the first 50 to 200 years after initial white contact (14).

Where contact was more intense or frequent, as along most tropical coasts and major rivers, a much higher rate of depopulation occurred. For example, the calculations by Borah and Cook indicate a depopulation ratio of 48 to 1 on the tropical Mexican coasts during only the first 50 years of contact (15). Edwards has determined a decline equal to 28 to 1 for the Island of Cozumel (Mexico) between 1518 and 1587 (16). Even these ratios are low compared to those of other areas where there was near extinction within a few years. For Hispaniola, population estimates for 1492 range up to 5 or 6 million, but even if the very conservative calculation of only 100,000 by Rosenblat is used, the depopulation rate was still tremendous (200 to 1 in 56 years) since only about 500 Indians were left by 1548 (17). The large native population of Jamaica was gone by this time and that of other islands nearly so.

DOCUMENTARY EVIDENCE

The main forms of evidence for estimating aboriginal populations at the time of initial European contact are documentary, archaeological, and ecological. The documentary material, which has received the greatest attention, consists of (a) general estimates by eye witness participants in the early conquests, (b) reasonably reliable but usually late dated estimates and counts, and (c) early but partial enumerations such as numbers of baptisms, tribute records, and mission figures.

The early sixteenth-century chroniclers spoke of populations numbering in the millions on the tropical coasts of Mexico, in western Central America, in Panama, and in the Caribbean Islands. Sauer, for example, is able to cite six Spaniards who gave figures for the island of Hispaniola, or part of it, of "over a million" or 1,100,000, possibly on the basis of a partial census of adults for tribute purposes ordered by Columbus in 1496. And there had already been severe depopulation in 1494-1495. Las Casas, who arrived on the scene in 1502, said the original population in 1492 had been 3 million (18).

How much credence can be given to such estimates? Were they gross falsifications as claimed by many scholars? The figures of Las Casas, Oviedo, and others are invariably said to be much too high as a result of ulterior motives, or because these authors magnified their own deeds by exaggerating the number of natives (19). However, an *a priori* assumption of intentional exaggeration for any reason or because of ignorance is not justified in many instances. Certainly the high early estimates for central Mexico have been at least partly supported by the work of Cook, Borah, and Simpson (20). In treating the initial Spanish activities in the Caribbean (1492-1519), Sauer argues convincingly that the chroniclers had no reason to distort their population estimates, and that they were well qualified to make estimates. "There was neither reason of vanity nor of practical ends to inflate the native numbers" (21). True, most of the early totals were only general estimates, but they should be neither accepted <u>nor</u> rejected without good cause.

Modern historians and anthropologists such as Rosenblat, Kroeber, and Steward obtained their population totals by examination of what they thought to be the first reliable counts for different tribes or areas. For the tropics in particular, these figures are usually for dates long after first contact, and the initial massive depopulation was not fully taken into consideration.

One tribe by tribe calculation is the total of 2,987,060 Indians for tropical South America derived by Steward (22). He pointed out the difficulties in making estimates and the lateness and unreliability of the documentary figures. His "earliest data that appear to be reliable" for given groups are extended to other groups of similar culture and habitat. In some instances the documentary figures are enlarged to take into account some population reduction since initial contact, but in other instances they are reduced because they are believed by Steward to be an exaggeration. Usually the earliest figure itself is used, even though most date one hundred years or more after first contact, by which time tribal numbers had been reduced by amounts ranging up to full extinction. While Steward acknowledges a possible reduction by 50 per cent during the early years, he fails to apply this to his own calculations, although he does say his estimates are probably too low. If doubled, his total becomes 5,974,120, which is comparable to the rough figure of 6,000,000 for tropical South America given by Dobyns, but still considered to be conservative by Sternberg (23).

That many of Steward's tribal figures are far too low is now quite evident. He gives only 6,000 for Mojos in 1680, whereas Jesuit accounts indicate many times that amount in the 1690's (24). He gives figures which can be grouped to total about 125,000 for the Jesuit Province of Mainas in the seventeenth century, whereas Sweet, also using historical sources, arrived at a total of between 187,000 and 258,000 (25). Other examples could be cited.

The densest populations in the American tropics were probably in southern Mexico (Chiapas, Gulf Coast, Maya lowlands of Yucatán), and for some of this area there are partial enumerations for the conquest period. The statistical extrapolation of this data is the most recent and most precise use of documentary evidence. Borah and Cook obtained a population of 1.9 million for the central Gulf Coast north of Tehauntepec, mainly present day Vera Cruz (26). This is part of their total of 25.2 million for central Mexico based on three early colonial records of tribute payments to the pre-conquest Indian rulers. Several arbitrary decisions had to be made in converting the tribute data into population figures, and this has led to considerable discussion of the figures, both for and against (27). But even allowing for a 50 per cent error on the high side, the population would still have been quite substantial.

ARCHAEOLOGICAL EVIDENCE

Except for the Gulf Coast of Mexico, documentary evidence is mostly scanty, late, and of limited value for the humid tropics in view of the unknown but generally drastic early declines. Still, there is need for much more archival research if only to provide secure points of reference along incomplete depopulation curves. However, there are other types of evidence which, although imprecise, can provide some idea of relative population density. One is archaeology. The number and size of village or temple sites give some indication of the number of people required to build them or occupy them. In the Classic Maya area of Yucatán, house sites have been carefully enumerated for dispersed village areas around temples. For a 0.3 square mile area around the Uaxactún temple, Ricketson found 78 house mounds, and then multiplied by 5, which is the average number of persons per house in the area today (28). The problem, of course, is estimating how many house sites were occupied at any one time. Ricketson assumed only 1/4, giving a density of 270.8 per square mile, but Brainard reduced this to only 1/8 for a density of 136 per square mile or only 68 per square mile if each family had two dwellings (29). But the latter is still a sizeable population density for the tropics.

For Amazonia, where the settlement pattern was one of compact villages rather than dispersed settlement as in Yucatán, it is more difficult to identify individual house sites, but village size can be determined from refuse distribution and converted to rough village population size (30). In interior Amazonia the potential of archaeology is greatly lessened by the fact that former habitation sites, having been predominantly located in the river floodplains or on adjacent bluffs, have usually been destroyed by the characteristic meandering of the rivers. Lathrap has calculated that most habitation sites in a given riverine area will be destroyed during a meander cycle of about 500 years. He concludes, therefore, that only a small portion of pre-Columbian sites have survived, and that the failure to find many sites is by no means indicative of a sparse pre-Columbian population (31).

SUBSISTENCE AND ECOLOGY

Another indirect method of estimating aboriginal population is that of determining potential human carrying capacities in relation to the resource base and the subsistence technology and then estimating to what extent the ecological maximum was reached. Such models can be developed with some success for areas with fairly uniform resources and subsistence patterns, although even then it is hazardous to project uniform densities.

There is considerable variation in the distribution of agricultural and wild life resources in the tropics. But for the most part lowland soils are infertile, and once the protective forest is removed cropping is only possible for a few years before yields drop drastically or crop growth is inhibited by weeds. Fertilization was and remains rare, and the common agricultural system both past and present has been shifting cultivation. However, more permanent and intensive forms of shifting cultivation are possible on certain superior soils, such

as the alluvial soils of floodplains, the limestone soils of
Yucatán, and the volcanic soils of western Central America.
Furthermore, the period of necessary forest fallow after a field
is abandoned varies from only a few years to several decades,
depending on soil conditions, temperature, and on the quantity
and seasonal distribution of rainfall. For example, shorter
fallow periods are possible (a) in the foothills where fresh
mineral soil is exposed by erosion and where organic
decomposition is slowed down by lower temperatures than in the
low plains, and (b) in areas of marked dry seasons where leaching
by rainfall is reduced. In general, the more permanent the
agriculture, or the shorter the period of fallow, the more land
there is available at a given time for agriculture, and hence
the greater is the population that can be supported, as long as
there is sufficient fallow time for renewal of fertility.

Population density is not correlated just with agricultural
productivity in the American tropics. For much of the area,
especially in South America and the Caribbean, the staple crops
were starchy tubers, mainly manioc, which are very low in protein
content. Since these tubers dominated the plant food diet, with
only small amounts of the more protein-rich plant foods, the
Indians had a strong dependency on animal protein. Domesticated
animals were of little importance and game was generally sparse,
but fish and other aquatic life were abundant in and along the
large rivers, poorly drained savannas, and coastal waters. Thus,
population tended to be greatest adjacent to water bodies. A
model of an ecological zonation of population density and
cultural level along these lines has been suggested (32). However,
it is only applicable to the root-crop oriented cultures. In
Meso-America the staple crop was maize with a strong emphasis
also on beans. Both are much higher in protein content than is
manioc, and so the maize cultures, such as the Maya, were not as
dependent on animal protein, and an extreme aquatic orientation
of settlement did not develop. There are other reasons for
riverine orientation, such as ease of movement and superior
soils; nevertheless there is archaeological evidence in support
of the protein argument in Reichel-Dolmatoff's observation that
there was a substantial growth of population in the foothills
away from rivers in western Colombia after maize replaced manioc
as the staple crop about 100 B. C. (33).

On the basis of settlement stability, three broad economic
categories of aboriginal culture can be distinguished for the
American tropics: nomadic, semi-nomadic, and village farmers.
The few nomadic tribes were mostly in the interior of South
America, in the interflueve forests and scrub savannas where
they were dependent on hunting and gathering. Population
densities were very low, often less than 0.5 per square mile.
The semi-nomadic tribes were found in similar ecological
situations but practiced some agriculture as well as intensive
hunting. Villages and fields were moved frequently, probably not
so much because of soil decline and social factors as for the
pursuit of dispersed game. Densities ranged up to possibly 2 or
3 persons per square mile, depending on the local resource
situation and village stability. While the densities of both

nomadic and semi-nomadic tribes were quite low, they occupied such vast territories that they may well have totaled over a million people in Amazonia at the time of European contact (34).

In contrast, the village farmers were tribes with relatively stable villages and often fairly dense populations, ranging up to 100 or more per square mile. In South America and the Caribbean the root crop farmers were great fishermen with much less stress on hunting than the nomadic and semi-nomadic tribes. In the Meso-American tropics, where the maize farmers were not as dependent on animal protein, agriculture was generally much more important than either fishing or hunting, and nomadic and semi-nomadic cultures were rare. For all farming cultures, shifting cultivation was the usual farming system. There were instances of relatively stable and intensive agriculture, but unfortunately not too much is known about them.

FIELD REMNANTS: NEW EVIDENCE FOR FORMER DENSE POPULATIONS

In the drier lands of Peru and Mexico, where the high civilizations were found, the agricultural past is still clearly revealed by well preserved remnants of terraces and irrigation systems. However, most traces of Indian fields in the tropical lowlands were rapidly obliterated by heavy rains or covered by forest soon after abandonment. Secondary vegetation can identify a former field site long after abandonment but generally not for as long as 400 years. We do know that some tropical savannas were probably created by Indian agricultural activities in pre-European times.

Our concepts about aboriginal tropical agriculture have been most radically altered by recent discoveries of extensive systems of pre-Columbian fields in lowland South America in open savannas and areas recently cleared of forest (35). The fields consist of earth ridges or platforms alternating with ditches which were dug out as the ridges were built up. They are all found on level terrain subject to seasonal flooding and undoubtedly served to provide dry ground for cultivation. The ridges number in the hundreds of thousands and range in size up to 80 feet in width, over a mile in length, and up to six feet in height. They have been found in the Llanos de Mojos of eastern Bolivia, the San Jorge floodplains of northern Colombia, the Guayaquil area of Ecuador, in coastal Surinam, and in the Orinoco Llanos along the Caño Guanaparo in southern Barinas, Venezuela.

The existence of the ridged fields is alone indicative of dense former populations. Their construction and cultivation required much more effort than shifting cultivation in the forests on well-drained ground. They must have been built because the population had become too dense to be supported on the available high ground and the people had to turn to the less suitable seasonally flooded ground. And, of course, the great extent of the fields is indicative of relatively dense populations. In Mojos there are at least 50,000 acres of ridge and ditch surface. In northern Colombia the total is about 80,000 acres, and there are at least 10,000 acres in Surinam and 4,000 in Ecuador. Since many fields have been destroyed by sedimentation and erosion while others have not yet been

mapped, it is likely that they once covered a total of several
hundred thousand acres.

As with house and village sites, it is difficult to know
or to estimate what portion of the ridges were under cultivation
at any given time. For the San Jorge fields, assuming a conservative two acres of land and water surface per person, Parsons
obtained a total population of 80,000 and a density of 320 per
square mile (36). However, the ridges were undoubtedly fallowed,
and if only cultivated one year out of five, the density would
still have been a substantial 64 per square mile. For the
Llanos de Mojos, there is documentary evidence in the form of
Jesuit counts and estimates for about 112,000 people in the 1690's
over 100 years after initial contact and after at least 20 years
of epidemics. There must have been several hundred thousand
Indians at the time of initial contact in 1580, in contrast to
only about 120,000 people in the entire region in 1961. Using a
contact figure of 350,000 would give a density of 5.0 persons
per square mile, but much of the region is uninhabitable marsh.
Densities must have been considerably higher in the areas of
ridged fields (37).

Undoubtedly, more complete air photo coverage and
refinement of photographic techniques, such as infrared photo-
graphy, will reveal additional traces of ancient field patterns
in the tropics. We do know that many tribes raised mounds
(montones) for their crops, and there should be some remnants
of them. The Spaniards on Hispaniola reported that the Arawak
villages had fields each containing tens of thousands of large
montones, averaging some 9 to 12 feet in circumference and about
3 feet in height (38). This would indicate a tremendous amount
of food production and helps support claims for a large
population on the island in 1492. Unfortunately, little effort
has yet been made to find remains of these montones and determine
their quantity.

Techniques may yet be developed for dating the field traces
and for determining the probable population supported by them.
In any event, the known ridged fields, almost all found where
there is no cultivation today, do indicate a considerable
underestimation of the possibilities for sizeable aboriginal
populations in less than optimum tropical habitats.

POPULATION DENSITY UNDER SHIFTING CULTIVATION

How dense a population can shifting cultivation support
on an aboriginal subsistence level on a permanent basis without
soil and vegetation deterioration? Obviously, this will vary
with the length of fallow time needed for soil fertility to be
replenished; with the amount of unusable land; with the crop
acreage required per person, which varies with technology, soils,
and type of crops; and, where plant food protein is low, with
the availability of animal protein (39). Actual and potential
densities range from only a few persons to over 100 per square
mile. For the present day Kuikuru Indians of the upper Xingu
in Brazil, Carneiro's calculations indicate a potential of 97
persons per square mile, allowing for a 25 year fallow period
(40). Whether the game and fish resources are adequate for such

a density is doubtful, however. Carneiro also calculated an average for the general tropical forest environment of Amazonia, allowing for much more conservative variables including only 1/3 of the land suitable for cultivation, and arrived at 16 persons per square mile. For the southern Maya lowlands of Petén, Cowgill studied contemporary shifting cultivation with a maize staple and a fallow period of 4 to 8 years and arrived at a potential permanent population of 100 to 200 per square mile (41). For northern Yucatán, where a longer fallow period is necessary, the population limit was estimated by Hester at only 59 or less per square mile (42). For La Venta Island (Tabasco) Heizer calculated a potential maximum density of 20 per square mile, and for southern Vera Cruz, Sanders gave the same figure (43). Theoretically, only densities greater than those just cited would result in permanent vegetation and soil damage and, eventually, reduced population carrying capacity, as has happened in much of the modern tropical world. This is one explanation for the population shift away from temple sites by the Classic Maya of Yucatán (44). On the other hand, cultural preferences and prejudices toward the environment and spatial relations between social units can effectively reduce a carrying capacity determined only by technology and resources, as in all the above examples.

Actual aboriginal population densities, both past and present, are mostly well below the postulated potentials. Cowgill estimated that a density as low as 30 per square mile could have accounted for all the ceremonial centers in the southern Maya lowlands (45). The Tupinamba density on the island of Maranhão in 1612 was between 24 and 28 per square mile, but must have been even higher prior to European contact (46). Five islands in the Amazon occupied by the Omagua in 1651 have been calculated to have had an average density of 21 per square mile (47). The present Kuikuru density is only 7 persons per square mile (48). For semi-nomadic tribes, the Yaruro density (Orinoco Llanos) is 2 persons per square mile (49), and the Campa density (east-central Peru) is about 3 per square mile (50). The modern Bayano Cuna density in eastern Panama is 4 persons per square mile (51).

As previously indicated, the densest populations in the Caribbean and Amazon Basin were along the coasts and large rivers where fish were plentiful. A conservative average contact density for riverine Amazonia would be about 15 per square mile, with possibly double that on the broader floodplains and half or less among small streams (52). For the Caribbean islands of Hispaniola, Puerto Rico, and the lesser Antilles, Steward and Rosenblat give contact densities of 13 to 14 per square mile, but other scholars would increase this considerably (53). Thus there is some justification for speaking of moderate population densities for village farmers (5 to 30 per square mile) in much of the Caribbean and South American tropics, with even higher densities (30 or more per square mile) in the Maya lowlands and locally elsewhere, and with low densities under 5 per square mile where tribes were nomadic or semi-nomadic.

For greater Amazonia (tropical interior of South America), I have estimated a total aboriginal population of 5,750,000, with

an average density of 1.5 persons per square mile (54). The
method used was that of determining conservative population
densities, ranging from 0.3 to 30 per square mile, for different
ecological situations, based on known densities for representative
tribes. The method has limitations, of course, because of the
impossibility of knowing whether a density used is truly
representative of a larger but ecologically comparable area. But
I believe that the average densities arrived at are more likely
too low than too high (55), and they are clearly well below
potential carrying capacities. Certainly, the overall average
of 1.5 per square mile is very low compared to known aboriginal
densities in difficult habitats elsewhere in the world.

CONCLUSIONS

In reviewing the wide range of population estimates for
tropical America and the arguments and methods supporting them,
my own conclusion is that the early eye-witness figures were
probably substantially correct, and that the total tropical
population was at least 15 million and probably much more than
that. This is greater than the totals for the entire New World by
some scholars but is well in line with the recent much larger
Hemispheric estimates of Borah and Dobyns. In comparison, the
present day (1960) Indian population for the same area is roughly
between 1,000,000 and 1,500,000, and the overall population
is about 65 million (56).

The arguments for high populations rest on several,
admittedly imprecise, forms of evidence rather than only the
much criticized estimates of the chroniclers: archaeology,
aboriginal carrying capacity, field remnants, tribute and
baptismal records, and known massive depopulation. But neither
do the arguments against large populations stand up well. They
are based on assumptions of low carrying capacity, exaggeration,
unreliability of various forms of evidence, and very low cultural
levels outside the Maya area. The alternative is to rely on the
first reliable counts available, and hence the problem of
determining the preceding degree of depopulation since initial
contact. Too often in the past initial depopulation was not
considered at all, but recently rough depopulation ratios or
curves have been suggested. However, evidence also has been
presented to show that depopulation rates varied greatly, and
more thorough documentary studies of the early post-contact
history of individual tribes is needed to clarify this.

There has been considerable concern over the probable size
of the aboriginal population of the New World. A major reason
is that much of our thinking about New World native peoples will
have to be revised if populations were as large and as dense as
some now claim. Several of the more significant issues are
briefly reviewed below.

First, if a New World population numbering tens of
millions was reduced by 90 per cent or more within a century or
two, a massive depopulation with few precedents in world history,
then we need to do a much better job of analyzing the factors
responsible. In the past the greater blame was placed on
Spanish mistreatment (the "Black Legend"), while more recently
epidemic disease has been considered the overriding factor.

But now the universality of epidemic disease is being questioned. The first reported epidemic on Hispaniola was not until 1518, by which time the native population was already greatly reduced. Sauer believes that the depopulation of Hispaniola was largely associated with a breakdown in the native economy resulting in malnutrition, mainly because of suppression of fishing and hunting which provided essential protein for otherwise starchy diets (57). Consequently, the Indians were much more susceptible to death from brutality, overwork, and sickness. Friede reaches similar conclusions for the province of Muzo in Colombia – that "it was the hard mining life not the plague" that was the chief cause of Indian extinction, and that "when there were epidemics in Spanish America, these were neither general nor of identical consequence (58)." Reproduction declined markedly in many regions, and Sauer associates this with social and family disruption (late marriage, non-marriage, separation of the sexes and parents from children), often leading to a lack of desire to live and reproduce. In addition, Harvey has found that for some Indian tribes, the decline of reproduction can be explained by population displacements that destroyed traditional marriage pools (59). Thus the impact of different depopulation factors clearly varied in time and space, with culture, habitat, and European administration, and much more research is needed to demonstrate and explain these variations.

Second, assuming with Kroeber and Carneiro that a rich culture with a complex social organization is usually an index of a high density of population and vice versa, large tropical populations would suggest greater cultural achievements than many assumed existed outside of Mexico (60). For Amazonia, the typical tropical forest farming community, on the basis of the historical record and present survivals, is usually seen as small in size, temporary in location, and lacking class structure and craft specialization. However, recent archaeological evidence indicates that along the large rivers and in the low savannas this pattern was not representative of the situation prior to European contact (61). There is also considerable evidence for well developed tropical societies ("chiefdoms") in the Caribbean, Central America, eastern Bolivia, and the north coast of South America (62). Hence, arguments for large tropical populations, at least locally, would not necessarily be in conflict with the cultural evidence.

Third is the question of whether aboriginal subsistence technology or intensity was able to support fairly dense populations in the humid tropics. As indicated, the answer is clearly yes, providing there was a balanced diet. Where starchy tubers are the staple, however, limits to population density may be determined more by the availability of animal protein than by agricultural productivity. Otherwise, population density would have an ultimate maximum determined largely by the agricultural system. The maximum may be reduced, however, if there is land deterioration because of an excessively short period of forest fallow or conversion of forest to grassland by burning. The maximum may be increased by changes in ecological or dietary patterns; for example, the introduction of maize as a major food, the reclamation of marginal lands such as by

ridging, or by more intensive forms of agriculture, such as the
use of fertilizers or mulches, which reduce or eliminate the
need of long periods of forest fallow. But even in terms of the
historically known aboriginal carrying capacities, the population
of tropical America could have been considerably larger than the
15 million previously suggested.

On the other hand, it has been argued that for the
pre-industrial societies an increasing population density results
from factors other than increased food production; agricultural
intensification is more likely to be the result of population
growth than the cause (63). It is true that high rural
population densities (over 1,000 per square mile in parts of
tropical Africa and Asia) do reflect a change from long-fallow
forms of shifting cultivation, which require a large amount of
land per capita, to much more intensified forms of agriculture.
For the tropics this usually means a greater frequency of use
of any given plot of land, with a shift from using a plot once
every 25 years or more (long fallow) as in most of Amazonia today,
to a short fallow of only 6-8 years as with the present Maya,
to no fallow period or even several crops a year as in some paddy
rice and horticultural areas of Asia. Since more intensive forms
of tropical cultivation usually require a greater labor input,
at least initially, with lower yields per man hour, than does
long-fallow shifting cultivation, it is unusual for intensive
agriculture to be practiced as long as there is adequate land for
long-fallow cultivation (64). In fact, in central Africa
intensive agriculturalists have been known to revert to simple
shifting cultivation when they move from an area of very dense
population to one of sparse population and available land (65).
The same may well have been true in the New World in the past.
Once intensive agriculturalists came in contact with Europeans
and suffered drastic population reductions, more extensive forms
of agriculture could be turned to. This seems to be the best
explanation for the termination of the construction and use
of ridged fields in the poorly drained savanna lands. The question that needs to be asked, then, is whether pre-Columbian
native agriculture was at times more intensive than what is
known historically (66). And where such can be demonstrated,
as in Mojos, populations denser than those recorded should be
suspected.

Fourth, what were the aboriginal population trends prior
to European contact, and what have they been subsequently?
Presumably there was a steady accelerating increase in
population in the New World up to European contact. There were
undoubtedly local reversals at times, but little is known
about them. The Classic Maya period may have been followed
by a reduction in population. In Amazonia, social deterioration,
as suggested by ceramic sequences, might have been associated
with population reduction (67). Locally, then, the maximum
native populations may well have preceded the European arrival.

The population trends in six areas of the New World during
the first 100 years after contact are shown by Lipschultz (68).
For each there was a sharp reduction during the first 25-35
years and then a more gradual decline. Dobyns found that most
nadirs in native populations were reached between 1570 and 1650,

after which there was usually slow recovery, in part associated
with acquisition of disease immunity (69). In many of the
tropical lands, however, there was no recovery; dozens of tribes
became extinct by 1650. On the other hand, some isolated tribes
suffered little loss until the nineteenth or twentieth centuries
when they were abruptly wiped out and others nearly so. The
remnants of such tribes still have little disease immunity, and
many will not survive. Since World War II, however, many
isolated tribes have received resident missionaries with access
to modern medicines and the means (airplanes) to deliver them to
remote villages faced with epidemics. The result has been a
great population surge among many jungle tribes. A good example
is the Shipibo (eastern Peru), which now has one of the highest
rates of population increase of any group in Latin America. But
where contact was early and constant and native populations were
large, population recovery was early and significant. The lowland
Mayas are the prime example, as they now number over half a
million. Elsewhere in the tropics where there has been long
contact there has been a tendency towards absorption of the
Indian survivors into the mestizo class, both culturally and
physically. It would seem, then, that for many tropical areas
the post-conquest aboriginal population curves are more extreme
and irregular than in temperate lands.

Finally, what is the relevance of aboriginal population
patterns in the American tropics to economic development of these
areas today? Particularly striking is the fact that some areas
were even more densely settled in pre-Columbian times than they
are now (i.e., Mojos, Darién, Quintana Roo, San Jorge). The
underdeveloped nations of Central and South America are making
great efforts to open up empty tropical regions, and frequently
the new settlers find evidence that they were preceded by
substantial numbers of Indians centuries ago. Archaeology and
air photo studies of former settlement and field locations could
show the way to the better lands for modern settlers and to a
reappraisal of some lands now considered unsuitable for
cultivation. Also, much of the present day farming technology
is derived from native shifting cultivation practices. However,
the details of native crop assemblages and systematic fallowing
have often been lost, and now there is pressure to convert
forest to pasture, the result often being serious soil-vegetation
break down. Furthermore, changes in diet have led to severe
malnutrition in some of the new colonies. A knowledge of the
native subsistence ecologies which made possible substantial
and stable agricultural settlement in the American tropics is of
potentially great value today.

In summary, the native demography of tropical America has
scarcely been touched by scholars for either the contact period
or thereafter. Much more is known about the highlands of Mexico
and Peru, which is understandable in view of the much greater
documentary material existing. The native population patterns
and trends in the tropics do seem to have been somewhat different
from those in the highlands, and every effort should be made to
gain a better understanding of them utilizing the variety of
forms of evidence available. In this paper I have focused on the
size of the tropical native population at the time of initial

contact. Contrary to general belief, while much of the tropical lowlands were very sparsely occupied, it is quite clear that many areas did contain substantial numbers of Indians. Unfortunately, the size of these populations has been masked by their very rapid destruction during the early years of European conquest and settlement.

(REFERENCES)

1) A. L. Kroeber, <u>Cultural and Natural Areas of Native North America</u>, University of California Publications in American Archaeology and Ethnology 38 (Berkeley, 1939), p. 166.

2) W. Borah, "America as Model: The Demographic Impact of European Expansion Upon the Non-European World," <u>Actas y Memorias, XXXV Congreso Internacional de Americanistas</u> (Mexico, 1964), Vol. 3, pp. 379-387, esp. p. 381; H. F. Dobyns, "Estimating Aboriginal American Population: An Appraisal of Techniques with a New Hemispheric Estimate," <u>Current Anthropology</u>, Vol. 7, 1966, pp. 395-416, esp. p. 415.

3) Dobyns, see footnote 2; W. Borah, "The Historical Demography of Aboriginal and Colonial Latin America: An Attempt at Perspective," <u>Actas del XXXVII Congreso Internacional de Americanistas</u> (Argentina, 1966), in press; W. Borah, "The Historical Demography of Latin America: Sources, Techniques, Controversies, Yields," See this collection.

4) The Caribbean Islands, most of Central America, Mexico east and and south of the Isthmus of Tehauntepec plus the central Gulf Coast, Amazonia, the Orinoco-Guiana region, the Central Plateau of Brazil, the northern Chaco, and coastal Ecuador-Colombia-Venezuela.

5) For a recent discussion of the impact of epidemic disease in aboriginal America, see A. W. Crosby, "Conquistador y Pestilencia: The First New World Pandemic and the Fall of the Great Indian Empires," <u>Hispanic American Historical Review</u>, Vol. 47, 1967, pp. 321-337.

6) Borah, see footnote 2, p. 382.

7) Dobyns, see footnote 2, pp. 409-410, 413-415. For example, there is documentation of the decline of the Sabané group of the Nambikwara in Mato Grosso from about 1,000 in 1926 shortly after first contact to only 21 in 1938 12 years later. The Cayapo of the Araguaya River declined from between 6,000 and 8,000 in the early 1900's to only 27 by 1929.

8) W. M. Denevan, Comment on "Estimating Aboriginal American Population," <u>Current Anthropology</u>, Vol. 7, 1966, p. 429.

9) Malaria seems to have been a major cause of native deaths in Yucatán; see J. E. Thompson, "The Maya Central Area at the Spanish Conquest and Later: A Problem in Demography," <u>Proceedings of the Royal Anthropological Institute of Great Britain and Ireland for 1966</u> (1967), pp. 23-37.

10) J. L. Phelan, <u>The Kingdom of Quito in the Seventeenth Century</u>, (Madison, 1967), p. 47.

11) D. G. Sweet, <u>The Population of the Upper Amazon Valley, 17th and 18th Centuries</u>, Unpublished Master's Thesis. (Univ. of Wisconsin, Madison, 1969), p. 126.

12) Juan de Velasco, <u>Historia del reino de Quito in la América meridional</u> [1841-1844] (Quito, 1960), Vol. 3, pp. 820-826.

13) W. M. Denevan, <u>The Aboriginal Cultural Geography of the Llanos de Mojos of Bolivia</u>, Ibero Americana 48 (Berkeley, 1966), pp. 118-120.

14) J. H. Steward, "The Native Population of South America," <u>Handbook of South American Indians, Vol. 5, Comparative Ethnology</u>, J. H. Steward, ed., Bulletin of the Bureau of

American Ethnology 143 (Washington, 1949), pp. 655–668, esp. p. 657.

15) S. F. Cook and W. Borah, "On the Credibility of Contemporary Testimony on the Population of Mexico in the Sixteenth Century," Suma antropológica en homenaje a Roberto J. Weitlaner (Mexico City, 1966), pp. 229–239, esp. p. 236.

16) C. R. Edwards, Quintana Roo: Mexico's Empty Quarter, Report of Field Work Carried Out under ONR Contract 222 (11) NR 388 067, Dept. of Geography, University of California (Berkeley, 1957), pp. 128, 132.

17) A. Rosenblat, La población indígena y el mestizaje en América (Buenos Aires, 1954), Vol. 1, pp. 102, 298.

18) C. O. Sauer, The Early Spanish Main (Berkeley, 1966), pp. 65–69.

19) For example, J. H. Steward and L. C. Faron, Native Peoples of South America (New York, 1959), pp. 51, 55; Rosenblat, see footnote 17, Vol. 1, p. 101.

20) W. Borah and S. F. Cook, The Aboriginal Population of Central Mexico on the Eve of the Spanish Conquest, Ibero Americana 45 (Berkeley, 1963), pp. 81–82; also see other studies cited therein.

21) Sauer, see footnote 18, p. 65. Also, see Cook and Borah, footnote 15.

22) Steward, see footnote 14. Data is based on Rosenblat and on the Handbook of South American Indians.

23) Dobyns, see footnote 2, p. 415; H. O'R. Sternberg, "Man and Environmental Change in South America," Biogeography and Ecology in South America, E. J. Fittkau, et. al., eds. (The Hague, 1969), pp. 413–445, especially p. 418.

24) Denevan, see footnote 13, p. 116.

25) Sweet, see footnote 11, pp. 153–156.

26) Borah and Cook, see footnote 20, pp. 81–82.

27) Critics include A. Rosenblat, La población de América en 1492: Viejos y nuevos cálculos (Mexico, 1967); and W. T. Sanders, Review, American Anthropologist, Vol. 68, 1966, pp. 1298–1299. On the other hand, Dobyns (see footnote 2, p. 415) has suggested an even larger figure of 30,000,000.

28) O. G. and E. B. Ricketson, Uaxactún, Guatemala, Group E, 1926–1931, Carnegie Inst. Wash. Publ. 477 (Washington, 1937), .p. 16

29) S. G. Morley and C. W. Brainerd, The Ancient Maya (Stanford, 1956), p. 262. .

30) B. Meggers and C. Evans, "The Reconstruction of Settlement in the South American Tropical Forest," Prehistoric Settlement Patterns in the New World, G. R. Willey, ed., Viking Fund Publications in Anthropology 23 (New York, 1956), pp. 156–164.

31) D. W. Lathrap, "Aboriginal Occupation and Changes in River Channel on the Central Ucayali, Peru," American Antiquity, Vol. 33, 1968, pp. 62–79.

32) D. W. Lathrap, Yarinacocha: Stratigraphic Excavations in the Peruvian Montaña, unpublished Ph.D. dissertation (Harvard, 1962), Vol. 1, p. 549; W. M. Denevan, "A Cultural-Ecological View of Former Aboriginal Settlement in the Amazon Basin," The Professional Geographer, Vol. 18, 1966, pp. 346–351;

R. L. Carneiro, "The Transition from Hunting to Horticulture in the Amazon Basin," presented at the International Congress of Anthropological and Ethnological Sciences, Tokyo, 1968; W. T. Sanders and B. J. Price, Mesoamerica: The Evolution of a Civilization," (N.Y., 1968), pp. 89-94.

33) G. Reichel-Dolmatoff, Colombia (New York, 1965), pp. 73-75, 80-81.

34) W. M. Denevan, "The Aboriginal Population of Western Amazonia in Relation to Habitat and Subsistence," Actas del XXXVII Congreso Internacional de Americanistas (Argentina, 1966), in press.

35) J. J. Parsons and W. M. Denevan, "Pre-Columbian Ridged Fields," Scientific American, Vol. 217, 1967, pp. 92-100. For the most recent published report, see J. J. Parsons, "Ridged Fields in the Río Guayas Valley, Ecuador," American Antiquity, Vol. 34, 1969, pp. 76-80.

36) J. J. Parsons and W. A. Bowen, "Ancient Ridged Fields of the San Jorge Floodplain, Colombia," The Geographical Review, Vol. 56, 1966, pp. 317-343, esp. pp. 342-343.

37) Denevan, see footnote 13, pp. 112-120.

38) W. C. Sturtevant, "Taino Agriculture," The Evolution of Horticultural Systems in Native South America: Causes and Consequences, J. Wilbert, ed. (Caracas, 1961), pp. 69-82. esp. pp. 72-73.

39) The concept of critical population density for shifting cultivation systems has been well developed for tropical Africa by W. Allen, The African Husbandman (New York, 1965). For a critique of the concept, see J. M. Street, "An Evaluation of the Concept of Carrying Capacity," The Professional Geographer, Vol. 21, 1969, pp. 104-107.

40) R. L. Carneiro, "Slash-and-Burn Agriculture: A Closer Look and its Implications for Settlement Patterns," Selected Papers of the Fifth International Congress of Anthropological and Ethnological Sciences (Philadelphia, 1960), pp. 229-234.

41) A. M. Cowgill, "An Agricultural Study of the Southern Maya Lowlands," American Anthropologist, Vol. 64, 1962, pp. 273-286, esp. p. 109.

42) J. A. Hester, Jr., Natural and Cultural Bases of Ancient Maya Subsistence Economy, Unpublished Ph.D. dissertation (U.C.L.A., 1954), p. 109.

43) R. F. Heizer, "Agriculture and the Theocratic State in Lowland Southeastern Mexico," American Antiquity, Vol. 26, 1960, pp. 215-222; W. T. Sanders, "The Anthropo-Geography of Central Vera Cruz," Revista Mexicana de Estudios Antropológicos, Vol. 13, Nos. 2-3, 1953, pp. 27-78, esp. p. 51.

44) The latest statement of this sort is by W. A. Haviland, who believes that skeletal studies in the Tikal area suggest that a "marked reduction in stature in Late Classic times may be indicative of a situation of nutritional stress" from land failure, and that this "may have had something to do with the collapse of classic Maya civilization" in about 900 A.D.; see "Stature at Tikal, Guatemala: Implications for Ancient Maya Demography and Social Organization," American Antiquity, Vol. 32, 1967, pp. 316-

325, esp. p. 316.

45) Cowgill, see footnote 41, p. 110.

46) There were 10,000 to 12,000 Indians in 1612 in an area of 422 square miles; see Claude D. Abbeville, História da missão dos padres Capuchinos no Ilha do Maranhão, (São Paulo, 1945), pp. 139-145.

47) Sweet, see footnote 11, pp. 41-43.

48) Carneiro, see footnote 40, p. 231.

49) A. Leeds, "Yaruro Incipient Tropical Forest Horticulture: Possibilities and Limits," The Evolution of Horticultural Systems in Native South America: Causes and Consequences, J. Wilbert, ed. (Caracas, 1961), pp. 13-46, esp. p. 21.

50) Denevan, see footnote 34.

51) C. F. Bennett, Jr., "The Bayano Cuna Indians, Panama: An Ecological Study of Livelihood and Diet," Annals Association of American Geographers, Vol. 52, 1962, pp. 32-50, esp. p. 35.

52) Denevan, see footnote 34.

53) Steward, see footnote 14, p. 664.

54) Denevan, see footnote 34. These figures are corrections of the originally calculated total of 7,600,000 Indians with a density of 2.0 per square mile.

55) Using historical documents, Sweet obtained figures for Maynas that were 15 to 60 per cent higher than mine; see footnote 11, p. 157.

56) The total present Indian population of tropical America is mainly based on Boletín Indigenista, Special Issue, "Guide to the Indian Population of America," Vol. 21, 1961, pp. 169-266; however, it must be kept in mind that there is little consistency in the definition of an Indian. The total human population is based on a large number of recent census sources.

57) Sauer, see footnote 18, pp. 203-204.

58) J. Friede, "Demographic Changes in the Mining Community of Muzo after the Plague of 1629," Hispanic American Historical Review, Vol. 47. 1967, pp. 338-343.

59) H. Harvey, "Population of the Cahuila Indians: Decline and its Causes," Eugenics Quarterly, Vol. 14, 1967, pp. 185-198. Also see, C. Wagley, "Cultural Influences on Population: A Comparison of Two Tupi Tribes," Revista do Museu Paulista, Vol. 5, 1951, pp. 95-104.

60) Kroeber, see footnote 1, p. 180; R. L. Carneiro. "On the Relationship Between Size of Population and Complexity of Social Organization," Southwestern Journal of Anthropology, Vol. 23, 1967, pp. 234-243.

61) Lathrap, see footnote 32, Vol. 1, pp. 498-575.

62) Steward and Faron, see footnote 19, pp. 174-251.

63) E. Boserup, The Conditions of Agricultural Growth: The Economics of Agrarian Change Under Population Pressure (Chicago, 1966).

64) P. Gourou, The Tropical World (New York, 1966), Chapter 9. This is a major reason why it is difficult to establish stable colonies of new settlement with permanent agriculture on the fringes of Amazonia.

65) Gourou, see footnote 64, p. 104.
66) Eric Wolf in <u>Sons of the Shaking Earth</u> (Chicago, 1959), p. 78, suggests that the Maya must have had intensive systems of agriculture, even though we have no evidence of it, "which allowed them to maintain stable centers of control." On the other hand, it has recently been suggested that relatively dense populations in the lowland Maya area, the Caribbean Coast of Panama and Colombia, and elsewhere were supported by an agricultural system even more extensive than shifting cultivation but more permanent and productive, which involved the reduction of large forest areas to "orchard-garden thickets" dominated by useful wild and cultivated plants; see B. L. Gordon, <u>Anthropogeography and Rainforest Ecology in Bocas del Toro Province, Panama</u>, Report on Field Work Carried Out Under ONR Contract 3656 (03) NR 388 067, Department of Geography, University of California (Berkeley, 1969), pp. 69-75.
67) Lathrap, see footnote 32, Vol. 1, pp. 561-572.
68) A. Lipschultz, "La despoblación de las Indias después de la conquista," <u>América Indígena</u>, Vol. 26, 1966, pp. 229-247, esp. pp. 234, 239, 242.
69) Dobyns, see footnote 2, pp. 415.

17

THE APPLICATION OF COMPUTERS TO THE ANALYSIS OF CENSUS DATA: THE BISHOPRIC OF CARACAS, 1780-1820

A CASE STUDY

TRENT M. BRADY   UNIVERSITY OF TORONTO

JOHN V. LOMBARDI   UNIVERSITY OF INDIANA

The programs and policies of the Spanish Bourbon reformers have been the subject of numerous studies ranging in topic from imperial reorganization to improvements in mining, agriculture, and public health. One aspect of Spain's Century of Enlightenment, however, has been neglected: the institution, in both Spain and Spanish America, of comprehensive and systematic population counts. In fact, in the field of census taking Spain was a pioneer. Of the enumerations conducted in the eighteenth century, only those in New France (1665), Ireland (1703), Sweden (1749), and several of the Italian States preceded the various censuses taken in the Spanish Empire from 1750 on.(1) The abundant census data now available to scholars testifies to the magnitude of the reformers' achievement.

The Caracas Padrones

The Venezuelan census records constitute one of the largest available collections, comprising roughly 8,000 individual censuses covering a period of more than half a century from 1760 to 1820. In addition, the records include the books of Bishop Mariano Marti whose visit to the province of Venezuela from 1771 to 1784 represented the first attempt at a complete population count for the region.(2) The censuses, to be sure, contain a number of defects having to do with accuracy of reporting, completeness of enumeration, and consistency in the representation of data. Yet in spite of these deficiencies the Venezuelan censuses remain indispensable for the study of that nation's economic, political, and social development during the period of transition from colony to independence.(3)

The population counts had several basic objectives. The most important and obvious of these was to determine the total number

of inhabitants in each parish in each succeeding year. Distinctions
based on sex and marital status provided information on the number
of persons of both sexes who were married, unmarried, or widowed.
Continual refinement in the taking of annual inventories of population eventually led to reporting by age and to the division of
the census population into a series of general age categories,
such as one to seven years, seven to sixteen years, and so on.

The earliest censuses presented a marked contrast to later
developments in population accounting. The scattered censuses
for the period 1760-1771 were mere lists of names of Spanish heads
of households, their families, servants, and slaves, and for this
reason are not included in the present case study. Ultimately
the census data was expressed in a purely quantitative form with
the numerical entry for each census category inserted in the
appropriate blank in a set of ruled columns.(4) The development
of systematic population counts reflected the padrones' increasingly secular character, even though parish priests were used as
reporting agents in all instances. During the period 1785-1800,
for example, the censuses were based in part on a three category
system of classification which served as a record of compliance
with the sacramental obligations of the Church. The specific
purpose of the categories was to distinguish persons admitted to
the sacraments of Communion and Confession from those eligible
for Confession only and from infants and minor children.(5) After
1800 the ecclesiastical categories were discarded and replaced
by a system based, again in part, on distinctions of age and
marital status.

By far the most important system of classification, however,
was that which attempted to divide the census population into a
hierarchy of "social races."(6) Here too the authorities strove
for constant refinement in their attempt to differentiate on the
basis of physical traits (the somatic norm images associated with
particular racial groups) and social status. Among the general
determinants of classification were type of occupation, extent of
Hispanization, period of time elapsed since manumission, and type
of racial and ethnic mixture. This last was clearly the most
important. In the five category system used in the Marti _visita_
from 1776 on and throughout the Bishopric after 1800, (7) three
categories--whites, Amerindians, and free Negroes--were explicitly
racial in designation. The two remaining categories--slaves and
pardos--comprised both Africans and peoples of mixed European-
African-indigenous origin.

The social character of the categories is partly evidenced by
the length of time necessary for the authorities to develop a
uniform set of classifications and to apply these throughout the
parishes of the Bishopric. The earliest padrones in the Marti
visita employed very rudimentary categories. From 1771 to 1776
the census counts distinguished between parishioners living within
the bounds of the parish and within the _pueblo_ or town, and those
living outside the town but still within the parish; in other
cases the censuses distinguished between Amerindians and all other
groups taken together.(8) During the remaining period of the
visita (1776-1784) the Bishop was directed to apply the five
category system to his jurisdiction by a Royal Order of 17 November
1776. Not until 1800 were all priests in the Bishopric directed

to apply the Marti census of 1776 to their separate annual enumerations.

While the Marti visita provided an impetus to the taking of censuses, the period of 1776 to 1800 was marked by the use of a variety of socio-racial distinctions, since the Royal Order initially applied only to the visita. The following examples included the major variations. The _indio_ group was divided into tribute-paying and free Indians, that is those exempted from tribute. Both pardos and slaves were divided into subcategories on the basis of racial or ethnic descent which included those individuals of predominantly Negroid characteristics, as well as the European-African mixtures (called _mulatos_) and the African-Amerindian mixtures (called _zambos_). The reporting agents did not, however, apply the foregoing categories uniformly in all of the more than two hundred parishes in the Bishopric. In addition, changes in classification sometimes occurred within single parishes in succeeding years.

From 1800 to 1820, the censuses, with one exception, followed the Marti form. The exception, the 1813 padron, is particularly noteworthy for its distribution of the population by age and used a somewhat different set of socio-racial categories. _Mestizos_, who were expressly included with _blancos_ in the directives of 1776 and 1800, were again placed in a separate category. Surprisingly, the 1813 census did not distinguish slaves as a separate group; a single catchall category--_de las demas castas_-- brought all afro-mestizos together as one group irrespective of legal status or racial descent. In this context the term _castas_ applied to lower status groups of mixed racial origin, not to all socio-racial categories.

Changes in category designation should not obscure the authorities' genuine and consistent interest in distinguishing the European, indigenous, slave, and mixed blood populations,(9) for all but the earliest of the padrones attempted to maintain such distinctions. The institution of the five category system after 1800 brought final uniformity to census classifications. There is as a consequence a sizeable body of comparable data on which to plot changes in the racial and ethnic composition of the Venezuelan population.

Given the variety, quality, and bulk of information contained in the collection of padrones described above, the only feasible way to organize and analyze it is through the application of computer technology. The project of preparing this material for computer analysis is being carried out in four stages. The first is the organization and reproduction of the padrones. The second is the coding and key-punch operations. The third is the computer analysis, and the fourth is the publication.

Organization and Reproduction

Before the information contained in the padrones of the Caracas Archdiocesan Archive can be manipulated in any way, it is necessary to bring all of the useable padrones together in an easily consultable form. We chose to microfilm the entire collection of statistics as the only practical method of preserving the material for future consultation. Moreover, by using microfilm we would be assured of having various copies of the padrones available for our use, thereby reducing the difficulties inherent in a joint operation of this type. A further advantage of microfilm is that it lends itself to xerography by which process we were able to get copy-flo reproductions that could be easily read and easily annotated.

Once the microfilming phase was completed and the entire collection had been reproduced on Xerox paper the next phase of this effort could begin.

Coding

Before the information available on the padrones can be used by computers it must be transferred to punch cards. Given the proper instructions it is quite possible for a key-punch operator to transfer the numerical data on the padrones directly to an IBM card. However, we chose to add another step to this process in the interests of increased accuracy.

Because these padrones were compiled in a period of great change in Spanish America, and because they represent an innovation in clerical bookkeeping, the consistency of notation used by individual priests varied widely. The existence of this somewhat idiosyncratic notation in addition to the physical deterioration of a number of padrones convinced us that we should make ourselves responsible for translating the data into readable form in order to reduce the possibility of error in the key-punch operation.

To put the data in punchable form, it is necessary to transfer it to coding sheets specially designed for this purpose. In addition to the numerical data, code numbers had to be devised to cover a variety of nonstandard situations. For example, there are occasions when priests included widows and widowers with the single persons rather than with the married persons. It is also necessary to include pertinent, nonnumerical information with each padrón. For example, some padrones are for only half a parish, some are for the rural area only, others are for a parish whose boundaries had been changed since the previous census, and so on. Because these padrones cover the period of the Venezuelan wars for independence, there are instances when a parish priest will note that his flock is smaller than at the last census because of heavy enlistments or heavy casualties. It is also possible that a significant population change may be noted by the census taker as having been caused by a natural disaster such as earthquakes or pestilence. All of these items must be assigned a number code and entered in the appropriate column on the coding sheet so that when the cards representing a particular padrón are punched, they will contain every bit of relevent material that can be extracted from the document.

Another informational category that must be included on the coding sheet is a legibility index. Needless to say, all the padrones are not of equal legibility. Sometimes only part of a document can be read. We have, therefore, worked out a method of accounting for such variations that allows us to distinguish between blank entries and illegible entries.

Computer Analysis

Once the coding and the key-punch operations have been completed, the analytical stage of this project will begin. Since all the information contained in the padrones will be transferred to punch cards, there are practically no limitations on the kinds of questions that can be asked. One of the first series of inquiries we plan to put to the machine will concern the completeness and reliability of the information contained on the cards. From this question we will discover the chronological periods or subperiods where the information appears to be the most reliable and complete. Then, using these as base years, it will be possible to project population trends for those periods or areas where coverage is not complete.

With the information derived from this first series of calculations we can begin to ask more detailed questions. For example, one series of queries might be directed at establishing the boundaries of ethnic regions and subregions within the bishopric of Caracas. Another intriguing possibility lies in the opportunity for the calculation of vital rates of population change. The excellent geographic and chronological coverage of the padrones combined with the inclusion of an age category--that of the parvulos--will allow a reliable computation of rates of population change. Moreover, it will also be possible to establish the differing rates of change within each ethnic group. In any case, these are only a few of the possibilities for demographic analysis afforded by the Caracas padrones.

But demographic analysis is not the only use for this data. The statistics obtained through computer analysis will, for example, help settle the long standing controversy over the destructiveness of the Venezuelan wars for independence. Was the demographic loss due to the war heavy or moderate? Economic historians can use the data from the padrones in the analysis of the early economic development of Venezuela. Populations shifts resulting from the introduction of new crops could be verified through these statistics. And of course, the padrones are indispensable for any analysis of the immensely important social phenomena of mestizaje in Venezuela.

Publication

What sort of publication is possible from the data collected and processed under the project? By and large, our intention is to collect the basic statistical data for the Venezuelan population in this core period. In addition to standard charts of population by parish at perhaps five year intervals showing ethnic classifications, we would also include some of the answers to the question series mentioned above. Moreover, it should be possible to make some rather accurate population projections into the nineteenth century and to compare these projections with the census information available from the republican governments. The choice of exactly which tables we will use and in what form we will present them must, of course, await the results of computer analysis. Nonetheless, our goal is to provide a manual of reliable population statistics that will give students of the period a secure statistical base for their interpretations.

One of the values of computer technology in this type of project is that the scholarly community is not required to rely exclusively on our selection criteria. Anyone interested in asking different questions of our data aimed at some special demographic problem can easily obtain copies of the IBM cards when the entire collection of padrones has been recorded.(10)

REFERENCES

1. A,M.Carr-Saunders, World Population (London, 1964),p. 6-7. The Italian states were: Sardinia (1773, 1795), Parma (1770), and Tuscany (1766).

2. The visita is published in Caracciolo Parra León, ed., Relación de la visita general, 3 vols., (Caracas, 1928).

3. The records in the Archivo Arquidiocesano supersede all previous estimates of the Venezuelan population based on the following sources:

a. "Estado grāl en extracto de la población y producciones de la Provincia de Venezuela formado por D. Josef de Castro y Araoz..." 1781. MS in Biblioteca del Palacio, Madrid. Miscelánea de Ayala XXIX, f. 303.

b. Alexander Von Humboldt, Personal Narrative of Travels to the Equinoctial Regions of the New Continent, 3rd ed., 6 vols. (London, 1822-1826).

c. Francois Depons, Voyage a la partie orientale de la Terre-Ferme..., 2 vols. (Paris, 1806).

d. Angel de Altolaguirre y Duvale, Relaciones geográficas de la governación de Venezuela, 1767-1768 (Caracas, 1954).

e. Joseph Luis de Cisneros, Descripción exacta de la Provincia de Benezuela (Caracas, 1950).

4. All padrones were hand ruled. Only in rare instances were printed forms used.

5. The age range for parvulos was 0-7 years, i.e., to the age of reason according to the precepts of the Catholic Church. The more explicit term ninos was sometimes used. Interestingly, a person was considered single from the age of seven on. Letter from Woodrow Borah to Trent Brady, 30 June, 1967.

6. Charles Wagley, "On the Concept of Social Race in the Americas," in Dwight Heath and Richard N.Adams, eds., Contemporary Cultures and Societies of Latin America (New York, 1965), p. 531-545.

7. Real Orden, 25 July 1800, cited in the padrones from the Archivo Arquidiocesano.

8. See the Marti visita in Parra León, Relación, I and II, passim.

9. That Spanish-American creoles were generally concerned with the problem of maintaining racial balance in America is clearly seen in the interest they had in censuses of population based on racial distinctions. In the Representación to the Cortes of Cadiz dated 20 July 1811, the representatives of the Ayuntamiento, Consulado, and Sociedad Patriótica in Havana expressed their interest in a population count that would tell them the various percentages of whites, free Negroes, and slaves in the islands and that would show the relative rates of increase of these three groups. Doc. No. 9 appended to the Representación del Ayuntamiento, Consulado y Sociedad Patriótica, La Habana, 20 July 1811. Archivo General de Indias, Indiferente General, Leg. 2827.

10. We want to take this opportunity to thank the organizations and individuals that have helped make this project possible. In Caracas, Venezuela we are deeply indebted to the kind co-operation

of Padre Gómez Parente and the Director of the Archivo Arquidiocesano de Caracas, Padre Cesáreo Armellada, for their assistance in
the consultation and microfilming of the collection of padrones.
Moreover, we also are grateful to Don Manuel Pérez Villa and the
directors of the Fundacion John Boulton, Caracas, for their
generous assistance in the microfilming phase of this project.

The authors wish to express their thanks to the Research
Committee of the Graduate School of the University of Wisconsin,
Madison, for assistance in making the reproduction and key-punch-
ing phases of this project possible. We should also extend our
gratitude to Mr. Eduard Glaaser, Assistant Director of the Social
Systems Research Institute, Madison, for the preparation of the
coding format. Encouragement and support have been graciously
extended by Professors John L. Phelan and Karl E. Taeuber of
the University of Wisconsin.

18

MIGRATION AS A FACTOR IN THE HISTORY OF MEXICAN POPULATION:

SAMPLE DATA FROM WEST CENTRAL MEXICO, 1793-1950

SHERBURNE F. COOK

DEPARTMENT OF PHYSIOLOGY

UNIVERSITY OF CALIFORNIA

BERKELEY

Rates of change as well as the character of the population are well known to be conditioned not only by fertility and mortality but also by migration, the movement of people from one habitat to another. Frequently there is a large scale, or even sensational mass transfer from one area to another, as in the predominant immigration to the United States throughout its history or in emigration from Ireland in the middle nineteenth century.

In Mexico the influx of foreigners subsequent to the sixteenth century consisted of a very moderate, steady immigration from Europe, chiefly Spain. This immigration almost entirely ceased with the War of Independence, 1810-1820. Not until approximately 1920 was there a resumption in sufficient volume to influence perceptibly the national racial or ethnic composition. Hence any demographic study of a Mexican region, apart from the capital itself, which involves only the period 1820-1920, can substantially ignore this demographic component.

On the other hand, during the same century the population itself was by no means completely static. Several slow but profound internal readjustments were occurring, in particular the gradual aggregation to form cities, and the steady pressure of settlement into the northern or interior provinces. We present here data for selected regions of the West Central area, that is the five states of Michoacán, Colima, Jalisco, Nayarit, and Aguascalientes, as an exploration of the potential of studies of internal migration for Mexico. The time covered is from the end of the eighteenth century to 1950.

For our study all direct information relative to the shift of persons is lacking. That is to say, no systematic registration has ever been made of change of residence at the time it occurred, such as is frequently done by the police of many European countries. We must resort, therefore, to two types of document, each of which

states both the present domicile and the place of origin for every
individual recorded. One of these is the census, and the other is
the Civil Register. Both of these possess the common feature that
there is no fixed interval between the moment of origin (i.e. birth)
of the person and the moment at which the present residence is
specified. In other words, persons of a wide range of age are
included in a single group and, as a result of this limitation, no
more than a very diffuse temporal relationship with respect to
migration can be secured. Furthermore, neither the biological age
nor the calendar year can be established at which the actual transfer for any person took place.

A census, of course, states the place of origin of each
living person, irrespective of age, at a given secular point, e.g.
a year. The Civil Register, on the other hand, is a continuous
record of a certain event: birth, marriage, or death. Hence for
comparison with census data, the civil registrations must be
tabulated for as short a time period as is feasible, in order to
coincide with the census, and this means that the number of cases
must be reasonably large. Moreover, all classes of registration
are not equally useful. Births obviously tell nothing about
spatial movement. Deaths can be employed with the Mexican Registro
Civil, because not only is the place of origin of the decedent
given but also that of his parents or other close survivors. On
the other hand, with deaths, the time span is greatly lengthened.
Marriages, where the place of origin of the participants is given,
are the most valuable for the age span is restricted in essence to
the period 18-35 years.

The mass of source material for the study of internal
migration is potentially great. The censuses of 1777 and 1793
stated place of origin at least for heads of families, and we
possess many volumes of padrones from these dates. The same
considerations hold for many subsequent censuses. Those instituted
by the National Government since 1895 have systematically tabulated
the inhabitants of each state according to state (but not town) or
origin. Finally, the Registro Civil has been preserved in most
state capitals and contains the place of origin of many millions of
persons who married or died from 1860 to the present.

To exploit fully such an array of material would be a task
of impossible magnitude. Consequently we shall limit our exploration to a few major sources as illustrating the type of analysis
which is possible, and suggest a few conclusions which may be drawn.
I.   The census of 1793

The famous count taken by order of Viceroy Revillagigedo II
gives personal information on each adult, including place of origin,
for a number of provinces, partidos, and other territorial divisions
of what are now the west central states. From these we have
selected three moderately small units as representative: the
partidos of Colima, Ahuacatlán, and Motines. For each, Table 1A
shows the segregation into broad categories. These are arranged,
as well as can be done, according to distance of origin and hence
distance of migration. The first major group is local born, and
the term is taken to mean birth in any town within the circumscribed
area. Thus for the partido of Ahuacatlán a man originating in
either Ahuacatlán, Jala, or Ixtlán is considered as local regardless
of which of the three towns was his residence at the time of the

census. A similar procedure is used with the other two regions.

The second major group includes all those adults born outside the partido. This group is further divided in three parts.

A. From contiguous provinces or territories. This gets us
one step away from home. It is recognized, of course, that contiguous areas may vary enormously in size, common boundaries, and
other characteristics. Nevertheles, we have to conform to the
areas in existence and mentioned by name in the Padrones. For
Colima these are Jalisco (including much of Nayarit) and Michoacán.
For Ahuacatlán they are the remainder of Nayarit and Jalisco. For
the Motines they are Colima, Jalisco, and the remainder of
Michoacán.

B. The residue of Mexico. Here no distinction is made
between geographical regions within Mexico, for the number of
persons involved is very small and there is wide scattering.

C. Europe. This category includes almost entirely
Spaniards, who were migrating to Mexico in still appreciable
numbers. This immigration was abruptly terminated by the War of
Independence.

In Table lA are shown the actual numbers of adults, together
with the percentage distributions as based upon (1) total population, which includes of course the local born, and (2) immigrants
only. In Table lB are given more detailed data on the number and
percentage of the immigrants, excluding the Europeans. For this
purpose state lines are used and Jalisco is divided roughly through
Guadalajara into a northeastern and a southwestern portion.

The results are clear. The general pattern in Colima and
Ahuacatlán demonstrates the great majority of adults to have been
local born. Among the newcomers those from nearby regions, i.e.,
adjacent provinces, predominate heavily, followed in order by those
from other Mexican districts and from Europe. In a very crude,
but still genuine manner, the place of origin of the people varies
inversely as some undetermined power of the distance from the
census locality, thus in appearance simulating the law of gravity,
the intensity of illumination from a point source, and other
physical processes. In other words, the distribution of the place
of origin around the population focus expresses a tendency for
migrants to travel only short distances. There are relatively few
instances of long jumps. Here the pattern deviates sharply from
that seen throughout the history of the United States where, after
the initial settlement of the Atlantic seaboard, pioneering migrants
uniformly travelled great distances from their original homes to
their final resting place, these distances commonly stretching over
hundreds or thousands of miles. In contemporary times pure
distance has almost ceased to be a factor in interstate migration.

The Motines, in 1793, shows a picture quite different from
that played by Colima and Ahuacatlán, with only 28 percent of the
adults local born. The reason lies in the fact that whereas
Colima and the partido of Ahuacatlán were long established,
continuously well-populated communities, the Motines was empty land.
The original inhabitants had been wiped out in the sixteenth
century, and except for a few tiny villages and mining camps this
great area had lain relatively deserted for nearly two centuries.
In the late eighteenth century it was beginning to fill up again,
and the majority of the inhabitants were immigrants from nearby

areas who were moving in to fill the vacuum. The Motines thus
demonstrates a phenomenon typical of central and southern Mexico
since perhaps 1600 A.D., the resettlement of vacated land,
primarily along the coasts.

A few further comments may be made concerning the three
areas shown in Tables 1A and 1B. The distribution of Europeans was
relatively consistent: 2.7%, 4.6%, 1.2% of the immigrants to
Colima, Ahuacatlán, and the Motines respectively. Similarly the
migrants from other Mexican provinces were respectively 10.1%,
11.9%, and 5.1% of the total. Thus the slow flow of migration
from the outer world was spread quite evenly over these remote
territories.

Another feature of interest is the apparent tendency for
people to migrate from very restricted areas. For instance, of
those moving to Colima from contiguous provinces, 714 in all (see
Table 1A), 111 came from the town Zapotlán, Jalisco, 91 from Sayula,
Jalisco, 57 from Tepalcatepec, Michoacán, and 58 from Cotija,
Michoacán. Of 237 from contiguous provinces going into the Motines,
80 came from Colima, 25 from Zapotlán, Jalisco, and 16 from Autlán,
Jalisco. It looks very much as if emigration was governed to a
considerable extent by local report and customs.

The conditions just described, let it be again pointed out,
apply specifically to 1793 and generally to the period 1750-1810.
It is interesting and significant that we shall find the patterns
established during this epoch persisting into the twentieth century.

II.   The census of 1822 in Guadalajara

It was the intent of the government to record the place of
origin of all inhabitants of the city, but various circumstances
render incomplete the data actually in our hands. Of the 24
cuarteles, or wards, the census sheets for only 18 are preserved
in the Archivo General Municipal of Guadalajara. Of these 18, only
7 are usable. With the other 11 the place of origin either was
omitted entirely or was given so carelessly as to be valueless for
numerical purposes. Of the 7 mentioned, cuarteles nos. 11, 12,
and 23 are meticulously reported and in full; No. 1 is complete
for only five blocks, but these can be included here. Number 20 is
complete except for the last four or five census sheets. Number
6 gives place of origin for heads of families only but these can be
used. In Number 17 the place of origin is recorded for whole
families but probably omits many scattered individuals.

Despite the gaps, about one-third of the city is represented,
and in distribution within the town the sample is adequate and as
far as can be determined is without bias. The latter point is
assured by the fact that the relative number of migrants to the
city lies between 25 and 40 percent of the population in every
cuartel, the average being 35 percent. This variation is entirely
within expected limits. The total number of persons involved is
over 8,000.

The distribution of place of origin is shown in Table 2.
Since we are dealing with a point concentration of population rather
than an intensive area, the first category of origin is within the
point, or city, itself. The second embraces the closely surrounding
territory, which for present purposes can be defined no more exactly
than within the modern state of Jalisco, Guadalajara lying very
close to the center thereof. (If time and space permitted, a

detailed town-by-town analysis could be made with the data at hand, and the influence of the nearer suburbs could be evaluated.) The third order of distance includes the contiguous states of Zacatecas, Aguascalientes, San Luis Potosí, Guanajuato, Michoacán, Colima, and Nayarit (although Nayarit at that time was a canton of Jalisco). The fourth order is Mexico at large which in turn may be divided for convenience into three portions: 1) northern and western states, 2) southern and eastern states, and 3) the Federal District. The fifth and final category includes all persons born outside of Mexico, at this period mostly from Europe.

From Table 2 it is clear that the inverse distance principle noted with the 1793 census holds here also. Thus two-thirds of the recorded population were born in Guadalajara, one-third having moved there from other places of origin. Of the latter group about 50% came from the state of Jalisco, 40% from adjacent states, and 10% from all other regions. If the towns of origin were analyzed in detail, it could be shown that fully one-third of those migrating from within the state of Jalisco were born in villages not more than one day's horseback or walking journey from the city itself.

One further matter deserves attention. From Table 2 it will be noted that of those migrating from contiguous states approximately three-quarters originated in the plateau states of Zacatecas, Aguascalientes, San Luis Potosí and Guanajuato, whereas less than a tenth moved out of the coastal states of Colima and Nayarit, the remainder being derived from Michoacán, which is both plateau and coastal. It is quite true that the population reservoir to the north and east of Guadalajara was much greater than to the south and west. Nevertheless, there is a differential in favor of the interior. The most logical explanation is that the coast as a whole was an area of immigration and resettlement, whereas the plateau was relatively saturated demographically and was exporting rather than importing people.

III.   Marriage data, Guadalajara, 1875-1955

Table 3 shows in terms of percentage the distribution of origin of 34,299 persons who registered for marriage licenses at the civil registry in Guadalajara from 1875 to 1955. Although these figures cannot be compared directly with those derived from the 1822 census, nevertheless in themselves they cover a period of 80 years, and in principle demonstrate the same type of pattern as is seen in the earlier tabulations.

The books of the Registro Civil for the municipality of Guadalajara have been preserved since approximately the year 1860, and of course are still being written. The civil certificates of marriage state the age and place of birth of each conjugal partici- pant. For purposes of this study, one or two year samples were taken at ten year intervals, all marriages in a given year being included. Since the annual or biennial total of names reaches several thousand, the sampling is quite adequate, and little would be gained by extending the number over the intervening years in each decade. The initial date is 1875, and the terminal date 1955.

There have been established several categories of locality of birth or origin which vary somewhat from those used for the 1822 census, but which conform to the principle of distance. The first consists, as would be expected, of the native born children of Guadalajara. The second covers the state of Jalisco.

With Jalisco a difficulty is encountered in that many, indeed perhaps one-third of those indicating their origin as the state of Jalisco, do not specify the town or village. Such persons, therefore, can be allocated only to the state in general, not to any special portion thereof. In order to get some notion of the contributions furnished by political or ecological regions within the state we may use only those individuals the exact place of whose origin is known. Since, however, such cases are in the majority, and since there is no known bias affecting the origin of those Jalisco natives whose town or village of birth is not stated, it is proper to utilize that fraction for whom we do know the exact place of birth.

Very broadly, as was suggested in connection with the census of 1793 (see also Table 1B), Jalisco may be split into two primary divisions, one consisting of plateau country, the other of the rather broken escarpment and coast. In detail obviously no hard and fast line can be drawn, but a general segregation is possible. The northeastern portion of the state (NE in Table 3) is considered to lie north and east of an imaginary boundary which extends from the great barranca of the Río Santiago southeastward and runs just west of Guadalajara to the western end of Lake Chapala. It includes San Cristóbal and Zapopan, Guadalajara itself, and the southern villages of Santa Anita, Tlajomulco, and Jocotepec. Indeed it runs along National Highway No. 15 from Guadalajara to Lake Chapala.

On the other side the southwestern portion includes Hostotipaquillo, Magdalena, Tequila, Tala, and Santa Ana Acatlán. It also embraces all of Jalisco south and southeast of Lake Chapala. One notes that the city itself and the immediate suburbs are in the northeast sector, since to split the city would not be feasible, and furthermore, the basin of the Rio Atoyac is definitely on the plateau. As a result, even excluding the urban area, the weight of total population favors the northeast sector, a factor which must be considered in evaluating the relative number of migrants from the two sectors to Guadalajara. This relationship is designated "ratio NE/SW" and is shown in Table 3.

Beyond Jalisco, we reach the ring of contiguous states described in connection with the census of 1822. These varied widely in the number of persons who migrated to Guadalajara. Fine distinctions, however, cannot be drawn because of the additional variation among these states with respect to other factors such as total population, length of boundary common with Jalisco, distance from Guadalajara as compared with that from Mexico City and other metropolitan units, etc.

The fourth category is Mexico beyond the adjacent states. Here, as previously, we consider three subordinate divisions of the country: 1) north and west, from Sinaloa eastward to include Tamaulipas; 2) south and east, from Querétaro and Mexico east to include Veracruz; 3) the Federal District. The fifth category includes those born outside of Mexico, with no attempt to segregate by race or national affiliation.

In Table 3 all these categories are shown for each sample year in terms of percent of total individuals applying for marriage licenses in Guadalajara. In addition each of the four non-native categories is expressed as a percentage of the total immigration (rather than total persons married).

The tabulation demonstrates both a spatial and a secular
pattern. The spatial pattern is that previously encountered and
embodies what we have called the inverse distance principle. Thus
the predominant element is consistently the native born inhabitants
of Guadalajara. Next in order are those born in non-metropolitan
Jalisco, those from contiguous states, those originating elsewhere
in Mexico, and finally the foreign born. This order of relative
number has been preserved even to the present day, although the
quantitative internal relationships appear to have been undergoing
transition.

The secular pattern is a function of the spatial pattern.
From 1875 to 1955 there is a steady increase in the number of
immigrants to the city, resulting in a decrease in relative number
of native born from about 75% to 35% of those marrying. There
undoubtedly was no reduction in absolute number of native born, but
this component suffered relatively due to the extremely rapid
increase in number of outsiders.

Immigration, particularly during the early phases of the
period, has been predominantly from the neighboring parts of
Jalisco. But the number arriving from contiguous states increased
faster than those from nearby Jalisco. (The percent of immigration
from Jalisco fell from 83 to 55 while that from contiguous states
rose from 14 to 21.) At the same time the immigration from the
remainder of Mexico increased still faster (from 2 to 19% of the
immigration).

Looking at the entire picture, we see an expanding sphere of
influence. The distance through which migration to Guadalajara
takes place has consistently increased until it seems to reach out
to all parts of Mexico. The ultimate equilibrium may well resemble
the pattern of the United States where distance as such becomes
clearly subordinate to other factors in determining the extent and
character of migrants to a great metropolitan area.

A point of special interest concerns the source of migrants
from inside the state of Jalisco. As shown by the line in Table 3,
designated "ratio NE/SW," in 1875 more than three times as many
persons marrying in Guadalajara came from the northeastern half of
the state than from the southwestern half. Part of this preponder-
ance, as suggested previously, may have been referable to the
greater total population in the northeast. Yet in subsequent years
the ratio progressively fell until in 1955 more persons came from
the southwest than from the northeast. Such an unequivocal shift
during 80 years is clear indication that whereas in the late nineteenth century the plateau was an area of emigration, and the
lower, warmer region one of immigration, during the past several
decades conditions have reversed themselves. The southwestern
sector of Jalisco has substantially filled up, or the northeastern
sector is under reduced emigration pressure, or both processes
have been under way. Regardless of the interpretation, the facts of
the matter have definite bearing on the composition and characteristics of the contemporary plateau, as compared with the coastal
population.

IV.   Interchange between states as shown in the national censuses,
1910-1950
For the modern period we may examine internal migration as

measured by the crossing of state lines. Selecting as representative the censuses of 1910, 1930, and 1950, we find that each of
these (see notes to Tables 4 and 5) provides a set of figures for
each Mexican state showing the state of origin, i.e., birth, for
every recorded inhabitant. This makes possible the construction of
tables for the five west central states, jointly and severally,
setting forth the source of immigrants and the destination of
emigrants. Table 4 deals with immigration, parts A, B, C, and D
setting forth the three censuses and the five-state totals
respectively. Similarly Table 5, A, B, C, and D, concerns
emigration.

     For the indicated censuses and areas, Table 4, A, B, C, and
D gives the total population, the number and percent of persons
born in the state or area, those born in contiguous states, those
born elsewhere in Mexico, and the foreign born. Then are shown the
total number born in the state or area who are now living in other
states (i.e., emigrants), the total number born elsewhere now living
in other states (i.e., immigrants), and finally the net exchange
expressed as number of persons, and as percent of the total population. Table 5, A, B, C, and D, is constructed in an analogous
manner, but deals only with the present distribution of emigrants
from each state or area.

     Inspection of these tables brings to light many features of
interest, some of which may be summarized briefly.

     A. Immigration has been consistently greater into Nayarit,
Colima, and Aguascalientes than into Jalisco and Guanajuato.

     B. In all three censuses Guanajuato and Jalisco show a net
loss of persons, that is emigration exceeds immigration. Nayarit
and Colima have always shown a net gain. Aguascalientes passed
from a gain in 1910 to a loss in 1950. The five-state total records
a consistent loss, due largely to the population weight of
Guanajuato and Jalisco.

     C. The magnitude of net loss, 1910 to 1950, in Jalisco and
Guanajuato has increased. (Consider also the change from gain to
loss in Aguascalientes.) Meanwhile the magnitude of the gain in
Colima and Nayarit has decreased.

     D. These facts demonstrate a slowing down in 40 or 50 years
of the movement to the middle west coast. There has been a transition from immigration to emigration, resulting in an increased
migration deficit which has affected all five states.

     E. The fact should not be overlooked that the shift in
migration pattern has been masked in recent decades by the simultaneous enormous increase in gross population of all five states due
to the widening differential between birth and death rates. Even
in Guanajuato, which according to the census of 1950 had lost a
quarter of a million native born citizens by emigration, the
population rose by approximately 30 percent between 1930 and 1950.

     F. The retardation of the movement into the west central
states, and particularly coastal Jalisco, Colima, and Nayarit, was
evidently in progress by 1910. Such a view is supported by the
progressive reduction of the ratio of migrants to Guadalajara
from the northeast with respect to those from the southwest which is
observed in the marriage records. The time span here is 1875 to
1955. The corresponding ratio as derived for the migrants to
Guadalajara shown in the 1822 census was roughly 2.4. This figure

coincides with the values found from the marriage data for the period prior to 1905 and suggests that the slowing down of the southwestward movement actually began during the last two decades of the nineteenth century.

G. The broad scheme of immigration in the modern censuses is consistently present. The great majority of inhabitants of each state (over 90 percent) are native born. A small number have come from contiguous states and a still smaller number from elsewhere in Mexico. The principle of distance, therefore, applies in this century to interstate migration. At the same time there has apparently been some outward progression of the source of origin. Between 1910 and 1950 there has occurred a decrease from approximately 96% to 93% native born in the five state total, together with a parallel increase in the number of those born in contiguous states or beyond.

H. Concerning emigration, the localities to which individuals went are predominantly local (i.e., to adjacent states--for we have no information in the national censuses on intrastate movements). Nevertheless, it is worth pointing out that there has been a very heavy increase in movement to the Federal District, a definite increase in movement to the north and northwest, but a decline in movement to contiguous states and to the south and east. An unequivocal, but slow increase in the radius of emigration thus seems to be in progress.

We may now formulate three final conclusions brought out by the evidence presented in the preceding discussion.

1. There has been for fully two centuries a clearly demonstrable movement of population from the plateau to the central west coast, a movement which may now be in its terminal phases.

2. Migration from one interior point to another has followed and still follows a pattern determined by distance from the source: the number of people moving is an inverse function of the distance through which they move.

3. The mean distance traversed appears to have been slowly increasing for several decades and may increase more rapidly in the future.

Table 1A

Place of Origin of Adults, 1793 Census

Area	Local Born	Contiguous Provinces	Other Parts of Mexico	Europe	Total Immigrants	Total Persons
				Immigrants		
Colima (1)						
Number Persons	2857	714	83	22	819	3676
Percent of Persons	77.7	19.4	2.3	0.6	22.3	100.0
Percent of Immigrants	--	87.2	10.1	2.7	100.0	--
Ahuacatlán						
Number Persons	921	51	11	3	65	986
Percent of Persons	93.4	5.2	1.1	0.3	6.6	100.0
Percent of Immigrants	--	78.5	11.9	4.6	100.0	--
Motines						
Number Persons	103	237	13	3	253	356
Percent of Persons	28.9	66.6	3.6	0.9	71.1	100.0
Percent of Immigrants	--	93.7	5.1	1.2	100.0	--

Table 1B

Place of Origin of Adults, 1793.
Extended Detail of Place of Origin of Migrants.
Europeans Omitted.

Living in Colima

From:

	Jalisco: coast and escarpment	Jalisco: Lake Chapala, north and east	Michoacán Valladolid and west	Nayarit: (Tepic)	Aguascalientes	Guanajuato: south and west	Zacatecas	Central Mexico	Total
Number	371	151	182	1	2	39	38	13	797
Percent	46.6	19.0	22.8	0.1	0.2	4.9	4.8	1.6	100.0

Living in Ahuacatlán

From:

	Nayarit (Tepic)	Jalisco: coast and escarpment	Jalisco: Lake Chapala, north and east	Michoacán	Aguascalientes	Guanajuato	Zacatecas	Central Mexico	Total
Number	10	31	10	3	2	0	4	2	62
Percent	16.1	50.0	16.1	4.8	3.2	0.0	6.5	3.2	100.0

Living in Motines

From:

	Colima	Michoacán: west	Jalisco: coast and escarpment	Jalisco: Lake Chapala, north and east	Aguascalientes, Guanajuato, Zacatecas	Central Mexico	Total
Number	80	56	92	13	6	6	253
Percent	31.7	22.1	36.5	5.1	2.3	2.3	100.0

References to Tables 1A and 1B

1)   Mexico, Archivo General de la Nación, ramo de Padrones,
vol. 11, passim. The adjacent or contiguous provinces are
Jalisco (including Tepic) and Michoacán. Other Mexican
provinces include principally Guanajuato and Zacatecas.
The local born are from the Villa of Colima and closely
surrounding towns, all within the northeastern half of the
present state of Colima.

2)   Padrones, vol. 14, passim. This tabulation is based upon
adult Españoles and mestizos, the negroes and mulattos not
appearing in the census. Since the partido of Ahuacatlán
forms the eastern corner of Nayarit the contiguous provinces
will be Jalisco and the remainder of Nayarit itself. Other
Mexican areas include all else.

3)   Padrones, vol. 21, passim. Tabulation based upon adult
Españoles and mestizos. The contiguous provinces are
Michoacán, Colima and Jalisco.

Table 2

Origin of Adults in 7 Cuarteles of Guadalajara,
According to the 1822 Census.   (1)

Place of Origin	Number of Persons	Percent of Total	Percent of Immigrants
Guadalajara	5552	66.2	
Jalisco	1454	17.3	51.1
Zacatecas	388	4.6	13.6
Aguascalientes	148	1.8	5.2
San Luis Potosí	25	0.3	0.9
Guanajuato	294	3.5	10.3
Michoacán	175	2.1	6.2
Colima	33	0.4	1.2
Nayarit (Tepic)	65	0.8	2.3
Total Adjacent States	1128	13.5	39.7
Federal District	69	0.8	2.4
Northern States (2)	24	0.3	0.8
Central and Southern States (3)	62	0.7	2.2
Total Balance of Mexico	155	1.8	5.4
Latin America	18	0.2	0.6
Europe	70	0.8	2.5
Undetermined (4)	19	0.2	0.7
All others	107	1.2	3.8
Total immigrants	2844	33.8	100.0
Total persons	8396	100.0	

References to Table 2

1)   See the text for discussion.

2)   In this table and in Table 3 the north and west of Mexico is
        considered to consist of the following states, when any of
        such states is not the home of the population tabulated, nor
        is adjacent, or contiguous to that state: Colima, Nayarit,
        Jalisco, Aguascalientes, Guanajuato, Sinaloa, Zacatecas,
        San Luis Potosí, Durango, Tamaulipas, Nuevo León, Coahuila,
        Chihuahua, Sonora, Baja California.

3)   The south and east in an analogous manner consists of the
        following states (excluding the Federal District):
        Michoacán, Queretaro, Hidalgo, Mexico, Morelos, Guerrero,
        Tlaxcala, Puebla, Veracruz, Oaxaca, Chiapas, Tabasco,
        Campeche, Yucatán, Quintana Roo.

4)   A few names on the census sheets are illegible, or unrecog-
        nizable. They are probably minor localities in Jalisco.

Table 3

Percent of Persons Married in Guadalajara
Who Were Born in Areas Designated

Area	1875-1876	1885-1886	1895-1896	1905	1915	1925	1935	1945	1955
Total Persons	5048	4212	4881	3072	5004	3312	3130	3672	1968
Guadalajara	66.29	75.44	73.49	74.48	61.27	54.44	43.02	33.84	36.50
Jalisco	28.22	19.96	21.08	20.05	27.84	32.94	41.32	43.49	34.95
Ratio NE/SW	3.17	2.49	2.86	1.87	1.43	1.53	1.44	1.16	0.89
1) Zacatecas	1.64	0.43	0.88	0.65	1.68	1.93	2.14	2.61	2.79
2) San Luis Potosí	0.14	0.14	0.00	0.23	0.16	0.21	0.35	0.46	0.56
3) Aguas-calientes	0.91	0.74	0.39	0.07	0.22	0.54	0.38	0.60	0.97
4) Guanajuato	0.81	0.59	0.84	0.49	1.14	1.00	1.34	1.44	1.88
5) Michoacán	0.57	0.62	0.68	0.89	2.03	3.13	3.58	4.55	4.32
6) Colima	0.06	0.17	0.18	0.36	0.86	0.33	0.61	1.31	1.27
7) Nayarit	0.58	0.40	0.33	0.42	0.86	1.03	1.79	1.91	1.52
Total Contiguous states	4.71	3.08	3.30	3.20	6.95	8.17	10.19	12.88	13.31
Ratio 1,2,3,4/5,6,7	2.90	1.60	1.78	0.82	0.85	0.82	0.71	0.66	0.87
NW Mexican States	0.28	0.40	0.59	0.81	1.58	1.57	1.69	2.53	4.01
SE Mexican States	0.10	0.38	0.43	0.29	0.74	1.06	1.09	2.39	3.41
Federal District	0.22	0.24	0.33	0.49	0.74	0.94	1.92	2.61	4.37
Total	0.60	1.02	1.35	1.59	3.06	3.57	4.70	7.53	11.79
Foreign Countries	0.18	0.50	0.78	0.68	0.88	0.88	0.77	2.26	3.45
Percent immig. from Jalisco	83.74	81.26	79.52	78.57	71.89	72.28	72.52	65.72	55.02
Percent immig. from Contiguous States	13.95	12.55	12.45	12.54	17.94	17.95	17.88	19.48	20.98
Percent immig. from Mexico	1.78	4.15	5.09	6.23	7.90	7.84	8.25	11.38	18.57
Percent immig. from Foreign Countries	0.53	2.04	2.94	2.66	2.27	1.93	1.35	3.42	5.43

Table 4

Regions From Which Immigration Occurred, 1910 (1)

	Guanajuato	Aguas-calientes	Jalisco	Nayarit	Colima
Total Population	1,081,651	120,511	1,208,855	171,173	77,704
Born in State					
Number	1,058,165	101,349	1,185,265	138,396	64,714
Percent	97.83	84.10	98.05	80.85	83.28
Born in Adjacent States					
Number	19,371	15,282	9,836	22,943	11,801
Percent	1.79	12.68	0.81	13.40	15.19
Born in Other Mexican States					
Number	2,625	3,309	12,250	9,140	979
Percent	0.24	2.75	1.01	5.34	1.26
Foreign Born					
Number	1,480	571	1,504	694	210
Percent	0.14	0.47	0.12	0.41	0.27
Living in Other States but Born in This State	102,696	16,579	97,386	6.158	3,963
Total Born Elsewhere but Living Here	23,486	19,162	23,590	32,777	12,990
Net Exchange:					
Number	-79,210	+2,583	-73,886	+26,619	+9,027
Percent	-7.32	+2.14	-6.11	+15.55	+11.62

Table 4B

Regions From Which Immigration Occurred, 1930 (2)

	Guanajuato	Aguas-calientes	Jalisco	Nayarit	Colima
Total Population	987,025	132,890	1,255,340	167,694	61,914
Born in State					
Number	947,931	100,560	1,199,578	141,552	49,957
Percent	96.03	75.68	95.56	84.41	80.68
Born in Adjacent States					
Number	28,272	26,116	41,153	18,628	10,260
Percent	2.87	19.65	3.28	11.11	16.58
Born in Other Mexican States					
Number	8,855	5,602	11,913	7,062	1,555
Percent	0.90	4.21	0.95	4.21	2.51
Foreign Born					
Number	1,967	612	2,696	452	142
Percent	0.20	0.46	0.21	0.27	0.23
Living in Other States but Born in This State	154,436	26,471	154,720	18,336	9,004
Total Born Elsewhere but Living Here	39,094	32,330	55,762	26,142	11,957
Net Exchange:					
Number	-115,342	+5,859	-98,958	+7,806	+2,953
Percent	-11.67	+4.40	-7.88	+4.65	+4.77

Table 4C

Regions From Which Immigration Occurred, 1950 (3)

	Guanajuato	Aguas-calientes	Jalisco	Nayarit	Colima
Total Population	1,333,655	188,055	1,737,764	290,111	112,312
Born in State					
Number	1,269,889	150,051	1,649,858	243,685	84,904
Percent	95.22	79.81	94.95	84.00	75.58
Born in Adjacent States					
Number	37,936	29,985	45,673	35,379	23,400
Percent	2.84	15.93	2.84	12.13	20.85
Born in Other Mexican States					
Number	22,883	7,135	37,365	10,700	3,829
Percent	1.72	3.79	1.72	3.75	3.41
Foreign Born					
Number	2,947	884	4,868	347	179
Percent	0.22	0.47	0.27	0.12	0.16
Living in Other States but Born in This State	322,735	49,411	326,635	27,803	16,437
Total Born Elsewhere but Living Here	63,767	38,004	87,906	46,426	27,408
Net Exchange:					
Number	-258,968	-11,407	-238,729	+18,623	+10,971
Percent	-19.40	-6.06	-13.73	+6.41	+9.76

Table 4D

Regions From Which Immigration Occurred - 5 State Totals

	1910	1930	1950
Total Population	2,659,894	2,604,863	3,661,897
Born in State			
Number	2,547,889	2,439,578	3,398,387
Percent	95.78	93.69	92.81
Born in Adjacent States			
Number	79,233	124,429	172,373
Percent	2.98	4.78	4.70
Born in Other Mexican States			
Number	28,303	33,987	81,912
Percent	1.07	1.30	2.24
Foreign Born			
Number	4,459	5,869	9,225
Percent	0.17	0.23	0.25
Living in Other States but Born in This State	226,892	362,967	743,010
Total Born Elsewhere but Living Here	112,005	165,285	263,510
Net Exchange:			
Number	-114,887	-197,682	-479,500
Percent	-4.32	-7.59	-13.08

Table 5A

Regions to Which Emigrants Moved, 1910 (4)

Now Living In	Guanajuato	Aguas-calientes	Jalisco	Nayarit	Colima
			Born In		
Adjacent States					
Number	29,852	4,683	55,082	4,037	1,441
Percent	29.1	28.2	56.5	65.6	36.4
Federal District					
Number	46,044	2,013	16,307	507	718
Percent	44.8	12.2	16.8	8.2	18.1
North and West Mexican States (5)					
Number	10,637	9,016	19,401	1,331	1,455
Percent	10.4	54.4	19.9	21.6	36.7
Central and South Mexican States (6)					
Number	16,163	867	6,596	283	349
Percent	15.7	5.2	6.8	4.6	8.8
Total Emigrants					
Number	102,696	16,579	97,386	6,158	3,963
Percent	100.0	100.0	100.0	100.0	100.0

Table 5B

Regions to Which Emigrants Moved, 1930

Now Living In	Born In				
	Guanajuato	Aguas-calientes	Jalisco	Nayarit	Colima
Adjacent States					
Number	39,941	8,522	72,166	10,432	3,612
Percent	25.9	32.1	46.6	56.9	40.1
Federal District					
Number	75,365	3,759	40,853	2,761	1,797
Percent	48.8	14.1	26.4	15.1	20.0
North and West Mexican States					
Number	23,347	12,435	29,883	4,286	2,448
Percent	15.1	46.9	19.3	23.4	27.2
Central and South Mexican States					
Number	15,773	1,755	11,818	854	1,147
Percent	10.2	6.9	7.7	4.6	12.7
Total Emigrants					
Number	154,426	26,471	154,720	18,333	9,004
Percent	100.0	100.0	100.0	100.0	100.0

Table 5C

Regions to Which Emigrants Moved, 1950

Now Living In	Guanajuato	Aguas-calientes	Jalisco	Nayarit	Colima
Adjacent States					
Number	47,702	12,755	115,803	13,249	5,447
Percent	14.8	25.8	35.4	47.7	33.2
Federal District					
Number	190,602	12,169	105,229	4,029	4,891
Percent	59.1	24.6	32.2	14.5	29.7
North and West Mexican States					
Number	58,851	21,908	83,191	9,019	4,832
Percent	18.2	44.4	25.5	32.4	29.4
Central and South Mexican States					
Number	25,580	2,579	22,412	1,506	1,267
Percent	7.9	5.2	6.9	5.4	7.7
Total Emigrants					
Number	322,735	49,411	326,635	27,803	16,437
Percent	100.0	100.0	100.0	100.0	100.0

Born In (column group header over Guanajuato, Aguas-calientes, Jalisco, Nayarit, Colima)

Table 5D

Regions to Which Emigrants Moved

Born in 5-State Area

Now Living In	1910	1930	1950
Adjacent States			
Number	95,095	134,673	194,956
Percent	41.9	37.1	26.2
Federal District			
Number	65,589	124,535	316,920
Percent	28.9	34.3	42.7
North and West Mexican States			
Number	41,840	72,399	177,801
Percent	18.5	20.0	23.9
Central and South Mexican States			
Number	24,348	31,347	53,344
Percent	10.7	8.6	7.2
Total Emigrants			
Number	226,872	362,954	743,021
Percent	100.0	100.0	100.0

References to Tables 4 and 5

1) These figures are excerpted from the Boletín de la Dirección General de Estadística, Número 5, Secretaria de Fomento, México, D.F., 1914. The figures for native born Mexicans are on pages 19-31, and for foreign born on pages 32-53.

2) From the individual state volumes of the Quinto Censo de Población, 1930. The immigration is always in cuadro no. 25 of the state volume. Emigration is found in the Resumen General, cuadro no. 41, pages 119 et seq.

3) From the Séptimo Censo de Población, 1950, Resumen General, cuadros nos. 27 and 28, pages 129 et seq.

4) The sources for emigration in this census are the same as for immigration.

5) See note 2, Table 2.
6) See note 3, Table 2.

19

THE IMPORTANCE OF MIGRATION IN THE VICEROYALTY OF PERU

ROLANDO MELLAFE

CENTRO DE INVESTIGACIONES DE HISTORIA AMERICANA,

UNIVERSIDAD DE CHILE

Traditional historiography has accustomed us to a static view of colonial Hispanic American Society. It has given us a picture in which the ancient village communities and the new cities founded by the invaders finally stagnated for two long centruies of inactivity, the roads and inns deserted. Nothing could be farther from the truth than such a picture. A glance at any kind of colonial documents, if the scholar holds firmly in mind the concerns of social history and the ideas of demography, will bring conviction that the opposite was true. We could even affirm that the basic characteristic of colonial Hispanic American people was geographic mobility for there was constant movement of people in all senses of the term. Furthermore, if we study any society as though its members remained fixed in one geographic locale, we fail to notice one of the most important aspects of the process of change; we miss the mechanism that steadily brings society up to date and transforms it. These are considerations that tend to be absent from a historiography too much concerned with descriptive narrative. As a counterweight, we might even advance a global interpretation of colonial Hispanic-American society as one in constant flux because of continuing and widespread movement of people (1). While neither claiming nor wishing to explain all the historical development of Hispanic America during the colonial period on the basis of migrations, we propose to present in the following pages a discussion of the most important points which must be taken into account if, in studying the society, we wish also to be aware of the extent and forms of migration that it underwent and the results that migration impressed upon it. Starting with a very general methodological approach, we consider that the whole phenomenon of migration in colonial Hispanic America should be examined in three different aspects: the causes and characteristics of the migrations, their direction and rythm; and their social results. Let us look at each of these aspects.

Causes of Migration:

If we consider the territory of the Viceroyalty of Peru
and its area of influence, we should distinguish between external
and internal causes of migration. The former have to do with
the expansion of Europe, manifest in the Conquest; the latter
with the processes involved in the seizure of power and subsequent
economic and social adjustments of the invaders, who superimposed
themselves in every way upon the Indian strata.

The first stage of Spanish expansion in the territory
of the Viceroyalty of Peru found institutional form in the organization of the expedition of conquest (la Hueste Indiana) (2).
In terms of migration, the expedition of conquest was a stratified micro-society, composed of varied ethnic elements. It was
a social group that included at one and the same time people
who were to form the earliest and most powerful structure of
power in the viceroyalty, and also such elements as prostitutes,
free servants, and Indian and Negro slaves. (3) It included
the most diverse sub-groups of Europeans, Negroes, and Indians,
the latter from the vast regions of America stretching from
Mexico to Panama (4). In short, it was an uneven, very rich,
and motley cultural mixture which superimposed itself upon the
more homogeneous cultural complex that we call the Inca Empire.
In terms of migration, then, the Conquest meant continuing
waves of immigrants who superimposed themselves in a relation
of mastership upon extensive layers of Indian communities with
their distinctive cultures.

The success of Spanish conquest and expansion in Peru
resulted in large measure from continuing connection with the
outside, that is, from uninterrupted immigration that took on
institutional form and lasted almost three centuries. For
example, in the years 1540-1559 alone, Peru received from the
Old World 3,228 immigrants, who represented 37% of total
immigration to America (5). Other regions politically and
economically linked to the Viceroyalty of Peru, such as the
Kingdom of Chile, also received significant reinforcements of
European immigrants, many of whom because of great mobility
among regions of America eventually settled in Peru. In the years
1540-1567, 2,391 Europeans entered Chile, of whom 306 later left
the realm (6).

After the end of the early and most important period of
Spanish expansion, immigration to the Viceroyalty of Peru occurred
usually in four different ways: entrance of whites, almost
invariably Europeans coming from outside America; entry of Negroes
and Orientals, who came always as slaves from other continents;
creoles, other people of unmixed ethnic stock and mestizos from
other Hispanic colonies in the New World; and finally Indians
of various cultural groups, who came from the periphery of the
viceroyalty. Of special importance among such Indian immigrants
were those from Chile, northwest Argentina, Paraguay, Brazil,
the eastern slope of the Andes, and the Amazon Basin.

Among internal causes of migration, the expedition of
conquest must be considered one of the most important in the

earliest period. The disturbances and disruptions that it
produced as it remained in one location for a while, underwent
reorganization, or moved to new locations among the Indian rural
communities has already been pointed out elsewhere (7). If
the shifts in population caused by the Conquest itself, therefore,
are not discussed in this essay, there remain those caused by
settlement of Europeans, including in the concept the economic
adjustments consequent to such settlement. If we list in
chronological order the most important developments and factors,
they would be the following: the foundation and maintenance
of cities as urban centres of control, the Civil Wars and other
disturbances, changes in the means of communication and transport, including the difficulties of maintaining the network of
facilities of communication, the mita (levy of a percentage of
the adult males for compulsory labour) as the normal means of
supplying workers in varies uses and in seasonal surges of need,
and the appearance of a plantation economy in various zones of
the viceroyalty.

     The developments listed are too well-known for there to
be necessary any description of them. We should like, nevertheless, to comment on some of their features as causes of migration.
The great cities founded by the Europeans usually functioned
as centres of attraction for immigration often within radii of
hundreds of kilometers. However, at times in special circumstances they became centres for the dispersal of migrants. The
most usual of such instances were, for example, the opening
of new zones of economic opportunity, severe epidemics, times
of plentiful harvests in the surrounding rural regions, prolonged
economic crises, the revival of customs or policies forbidding
the intermingling of races, etc. Since the greater part of
the urban population was mestizo, whenever such expulsive factors
began to operate, there was movement during the seventeenth and
eighteenth centuries from the large to the smaller, to the more
recently founded cities, or even to Indian towns. Thus large
numbers of mestizos of all shades of skin colour formed districts
of outsiders within provincial urban centres.

     When we refer to the Civil War and other disturbances,
we do not refer solely to the wars for power that occurred among
the Spanish conquerors, which traditionally have been called
the Civil Wars, but also to struggles that took place within
native Indian society. We need merely mention the wholesale
shifts of population that occurred during the struggles that
kept the Inca Empire in crisis when the Spanish appeared or those
that took place later in the resistance of Illatopa and other
Incas in exile (8).

     Until the use of mules became common in the course of
the seventeenth century, and actually even after mules did come
into common use, the transportation of goods and passengers,
the sending of messages and orders, the maintenance of bridges,
roads, and inns was a steady, continuing reason for migration
of all kinds and at the most varied times (9). The use of
Indians for such needs were blamed from the early sixteenth
century for the evils of what at the time was given the striking

name of the uprooting (el desarraigo). For remedying the evils, the
Spaniards attempted extreme measures that now after careful study
do not seem at all excessive. For example, Lic. Cristobal Vaca de
Castro at Cuzco in 1543 issued his well-known ordinances for inns,
distances from one to another, ways of making Indians carry loads,
and the duties of the appropriate magistrates, which although
considered harshly restrictive, yet allowed each Spanish traveller
to take with him from seven to eleven Indians, either his own
servants or others, recruited from those Indians required under
the mita to serve in inns and transport (10).

One cannot stress enough the importance of the various
kinds of mita as a cause of migration, especially the levy or
workmen for mining, for the raising of coca, and for the so-called
mita de plaza, which furnished labor to the small landholders and
farmers of urban centres and the territories nearby. The mita
for mining had begun to make inroads into existing Indian communities before it was organized systematically by Viceroy Francisco
de Toledo. The inroads became far greater after the Indian males
available for labor were registered in lists and fixed percentages
set for the laborers who must be sent to various and distant
places. As a cause of migration, the mita had a two-fold effect
from the end of the sixteenth century, for it not only meant
the sending of contingents of workmen to chosen places, but it
was also one of the major reasons for flight by Indians and thus
furnished immigrants to the rural areas surrounding the territory
of the communities held to the more onerous forms of levy and
service.

If the cities and mining cnetres, the latter through the
mita, became causes of migration, the same function soon became
characteristic of all areas of intensive need for agricultural
labour. We shall return later to this point and do not wish to
deal here with Indian community lands, but agricultural activity
which could not secure its supply or workmen through the mita,
caused all kinds of movements of population: seasonal, within
zones, between zones, over considerable distances, permanent,
etc. Of all movements that took place, undoubtedly those
involving the largest numbers were to regions of plantation
economy: cotton and sugar plantations, vineyards, and olive
orchards on the coast; coca and sugar plantations in the valleys
at low altitudes in the interior.

The direction and rhythm of migration

The direction and rhythm of migration are easily
determined for the years of Spanish expansion into Peru, a movement that may be considered as lasting until the 1570's.
In this period, we may distinguish three waves of migration of
relatively short duration in which the destinations of the migrants
dictated enormously different spatial differences. For the
earliest migration, say until the 1540's the Europeans and all
other groups who found shelter in the expedition of conquest,
especially the native yanaconas (serfs) and the uprooted of all
classes and cultures, tended to concentrate in what is today the

north coast of Peru, forming what can be called the expansive
axis of Trujillo-Cajamarca. Immediately afterward, settlement
concentrated in the central zone of Peru in a triangular area
formed by the focal points Lima, Cuzco and Arequipa. In the
1540's there developed a second wave of migration of wide geographical dispersion that reached to the south and north of the
areas of the first movement. Instances of the movements of
people in this second wave are the discovery and conquest of
Chile, and the forced migration of yanaconas and other Indians
held to service from the south of Peru and from the region of
Quito to Popayan (11). In many sectors of this expansion and
migration to the south and the north, there really took place
movement in parallel lines which in general corresponded to
the routes of the Coast and the Sierra since part of the movement
relied upon the existing network of Inca roads (12).

The third wave, which we might consider as lasting until
1580, moved to occupy what had been the eastern frontier of the
old Inca Empire. Thus the direction of migration changed sharply
to west-east. The change in our opinion involved two powerful
factors arising because of economic expansion: a) the growth
of Potosí, which meant need for labour in its mines and need
for agriculture to feed the dense population that mining created,
and b) the urge to connect the world of the Andean plateau with
the agricultural regions of the east (Cordoba and Tucuman) and
to obtain an outlet via the Parana River, the Rio de la Plata,
and the Atlantic Ocean. What was at first an urge became
driving economic need in the last years of the sixteenth century.

Aside from the strict supervision and legal requirements
for the passage of Spanish and other Europeans to the Indies, it
is difficult to discover what we might call official policy on
these great movements of migration. Nevertheless, there existed
between 1532 and 1580 at least two completely divergent points
of view on the matter. Until 1548 the administrators of the
viceroyalty, including Lic. De la Gasca, held that Spanish cities
should be founded wherever there was a dense native population
and, therefore, that European immigrants should be urged to
settle in such cities. On the other hand, Viceroy Francisco de
Toledo held that the native labour force should be concentrated
in those regions that because of favourable opportunities for
economic exploitation had already been settled by Europeans; in
other words, Indians should be settled where Spanish entrepreneurs
could use this labour. This is one of the basic meanings of the
so-called _fundaciones toledanas_ (settlements founded by Viceroy
Toledo) (13).

With the end of the initial period of massive movements
in migration that were part of the Conquest and the earliest
settlement in urban areas, the direction and rhythm of migration
became much more complex. The student of the following period
must take into careful account the various economic zones of
the viceroyalty, the periods of high and low demand for labour
in them, and the changes that took place in two centuries.
Unfortunately we know very little about such matters and research
on them is one of the most urgent needs for the study of the

economic history of the Viceroyalty of Peru. Because of our lack
of information, we shall, at this time, have to use the scanty
information that our own study has made available to us and
sketch a statement based almost entirely on theory.

If one looks at the problem in very general terms, it
is obvious that in the sixteenth and seventeenth centuries there
were at the same time areas in which population became concentrated and which attracted immigrants, other areas which lost
population, and yet others which because at one time they
attracted immigrants and at another lost people through emigration,
we may call mixed in nature. The picture becomes even more
complicated if we take into account the additional feature that
some groups in the society of the viceroyalty, essentially ethnic
subdivisions, tended to concentrate by choice in some areas
and not in others. In this already complex picture, we may say
that the migrations show selection by the migrants.

The permanent areas of attraction for immigrants were
five; their characteristics in brief were the following:

Coastal plantations: Until the end of the colonial
period, they attracted workers who were Negro and part-Negro.
Rather than entire families, the immigrants came as individuals
of suitable ages for work and reproduction.

Highland plantations at medium altitudes (1000 to 2000
metres): The immigrants were Indians and came as relatives of
people already established or as complete families. They were
fleeing from encomiendas and long-established communities.

Plantations of highland type but at lower altitudes
(from 0 to 1000 metres; those in the valleys called yungas in
some regions): The immigrants were of a very complex social
status; they included free and fugitive Indians, yanaconas
(Indians held in semi-servile status), free Negroes, fugitive
Negro slaves, and various mixtures of Indian, European, and
Negro. Among them were very few creoles or immigrants from
Europe.

Indian lands and communities at medium altitudes: The
immigrants were especially Indians of all kinds of social status,
mestizos, creoles, and even immigrants from Europe.

Small towns of Indians and mestizos: Such towns might
be at any altitude but most were at medium ones. The immigrants
were of the same kind as in the category just above. For this
category as for the one just above, the process of attraction
of population during the seventeenth and eighteenth centuries
was closely linked to such important phenomena as the pressure
on and seizure of the lands of the Indian communities, the loss
of Indian population in the highlands, the flight of mestizo
population from the larger cities, and the breakdown of some
of the traditional institutions for production and furnishing
labor, especially the encomienda and the mita.

Among those areas that provided emigrants and that
served, therefore, as centers of dispersion, there were at least

three that may be easily distinguished:

Lands and communities at high altitudes, called de punas
(punas being Andean pastures at very great altitudes, over 3000
meters): The loss of population in such lands and villages was
particularly a phenomenon of the seventeenth century and undoubtedly linked with extensive occupation of land for sheep raising
and the appearance of numerous workshops for woollen textiles.

Mining cities and centers: From the second half of
the seventeenth century onward, contraction of output in the
mining industry of the viceroyalty brought about the progressive
abandonment of various of the towns that had sprung up in response
to the development of the industry. In other instances, as
happened in Potosí itself, decrease in yield brought about a
substantial departure of workers, merchants, and others dependent
on the industry. The nature of the urban population in the
period was such that the emigrants were of a great diversity of
ethnic categories and kinds of juridical status.

Zones marginal to the Conquest and the settlements of
the sixteenth century: These were regions, like the country of
the Chiriguano Indians, which lay beyond the frontiers of the
Inca Empire and, further, were not conquered in the first
Spanish advance. But shortly after the Conquest, the Spaniards
began to take Indians from such regions as cheap labour in semi-
servile status, or to expel the inhabitants from the most fertile
lands, especially those suited for tropical crops. All of this
meant successive movements of Indians of a level of culture
inferior to that on the Inca Empire toward the centers of
attraction for immigration within the viceroyalty.

There remain for listing the areas that we have called
mixed, which have that quality because of changes at various times
and varying combinations of factors already enumerated. The
following geographic and human categories may be called mixed:

The majority of the older cities: These were particularly successful in receiving immigration from zones that had
ceased to be attractive as mentioned above.

Mining zones and centers of workshops: Both types of
centers of economic activity opened and closed down at various
times in the course of a century because of exhaustion of ore
deposits, unfavourable market conditions, shortage of labour,
restrictive legislation, etc. Gold and copper mines were especially affected by exhaustion of deposits.

Haciendas bound to the economy of the above zones: A
very large proportion of possible agricultural production for
market was always bound to supply of the needs of the mining
centers and the relatively dense population of those regions
that had workshops with their concomitant condition of monopoly
of the services of their workers. Upon the decay of the mines
that they supplied, some of the haciendas went out of existence
as productive entities or became less able to employ labour.

The effects of migration.

It is evident that the migrations within the Viceroyalty of Peru had direct effects upon society and economy at any level that we may wish to study. Nevertheless, we shall never be able to measure such effects nor to know how and with what intensity they operated if we do not first take account of two types of structures. One is of the structure of the migrations as such; the other, the social structures directly affected by the migrations. Unfortunately, it is precisely these aspects of the social history of Hispanic America that are the least studied as that history is slowly and only recently developed. Once again we must resort to a theoretical sketch that makes use of the few scattered bits of evidence that have been uncovered.

Discussion of the structure of the migrations brings us to three other aspects with which it is in close connection. If for any flow of migration whatever we could manage to determine the number of people in it, their sexes, and ages, we could arrive at the fundamental relation between migration and population. If for the same flow of migration, we could determine whether it was seasonable, permanent, intrazonal, or taking place over long distances, we should be in better wise to study the themes already mentioned of the direction and rhythm of the migrations. This second aspect will always be fundamental for any study of social and economic history. A possible example would be the seasonal and permanent intrazonal migrations brought about by the economic enterprises of encomenderos in some of the moutain regions of the viceroyalty (14). Furthermore, if for one group of migrants in the society of the viceroyalty, we could detect and study the social and ethnic character or the elements that composed it, we should come closer to accurate determination of the over-all social composition of the viceroyalty and we could examine underlying phenomena for which there is no adequate explanation at present. The example of the social group called yanaconas illustrates this point well.

During the three centuries of the colonial period, the word yanacona was used to designate at least fifteen different groups of Indians, the variation in usage being due to place, circumstances and date. Of the usages, three can be defined merely by rapid examination in terms of chronological order of ordinary records. Two of these three usages have their origin in migration. The first yanaconas were those that the Spaniards found under that designation on their coming to Peru, that is, the status of the yanaconas was pre-Conquest and Inca; the majority of those yanaconas became free after a few years through refuge in the cities or the protection of Spanish dominion. Another totally different usage covered Indian common whom the Spaniards reduced to the status of yanaconas in the y the Conquest and immediately thereafter. They were some lled yanaconas of the Conquest. They acquired their statu uprooting and transfer despite the fact that around roy Francisco de Toledo tried to settle them in assigned ith allotments of land and the obligation to pay a speci e. The third usage covers new and extensive groups that o

existence during the seventeenth and eighteenth centuries. They
had highly diverse origins and socio-economic status but certain
common characteristics: they had come to their status of
yanaconas through uprooting, flight, or forced migration; they
performed agricultural labor; they paid little or no tribute;
they had no precise juridical recognition or definition of their
status; and they lived under the special protection and control
of certain sectors of owners of large agricultural holdings who
found in them the only means of obtaining labor at almost no cost.

Unless we steadily keep in mind the continuing process
of migration in the Viceroyalty of Peru, we can explain hardly
any of the major phenomena of change in the family or in the
Indian communities. Any kind of continuing migration -- especially
to so striking an extent as we have just sketched for the viceroyalty -- together with the complications of pervasive conflicts
within the population, must have brought radical changes to the
systems of matrimony and of family structure, which in the end
were deeply affected by continuous changes in the definitions of
residency and the rights attached thereto (15). Changes of a
contradictory nature affected relations based on kinship and
descent, and so brought into play factors of social-psychological
and even biological impact.

Lest anything that has been said appear in exaggeration,
let us merely remember in regard to the biological impact of the
migrations the changes brought about in food and sexual customs,
in the nursing of infants, and in births among the people subject
in substantial numbers to forced temporary migrations, as in the
mita for mining or for coca plantations, in both of which the
people forced to migrate underwent violent changes of altitude
and climate.

The psychological relations of the immigrants, among
themselves, with the members of the new community, and with natives
of the district, showed different patterns that varied according
to the period, the place, and other circumstances. Conflict came
to be normal from the second half of the seventeenth century
onward, for by that time migrations had been occurring steadily so
that within the Indian communities and indeed in the entire
population attitudes toward the newcomers, whether favorable,
indifferent, or hostile, had already been formed. By that time
there had also come into common usage some expressive terms that
have arrich sociological content: indio fugado (fugitive Indian),
indio forastero (Indian stranger), indio intruso (Indian
trespasser).

The importance of migration in the Viceroyalty of Peru
may be seen in the single point that in the second half of the
sixteenth century the viceregal capital of Lima, despite the fact
that it had an Indian population of several thousands, with whole
districts of the city people by Indians, contained so few Indians
born within the territory of the city that they were designated by
the special term indios criollos (creole Indians).

References

1) See, for example, the interesting essays publ
   Louis Hartz, The Founding of the New Societie;   in
   the History of the United States, Latin Ameri
   Africa, Canada and Australia (New York, 1964)

2) Silvio A. Zavala, Las instituciones jurídicas
   conquista de América (Madrid, 1935).

3) Rolando R. Mellafe, La introducción de la esc   ra
   en Chile. Tráfico y rutas (Universidad de Ch   os
   de Historia Económica, N° 2, Santiago, 1959).

4) Instances of the presence of Indians from Mex   ala,
   Panama, etc. may be found in The Harkness Col   the
   Library of Congress. Peru 1531-1651. Calend
   (Washington, D.C., 1932).

5) Peter Boyd-Bowman, "La procedencia de los esp
   América: 1540-1559," in Historia mexicana, XV
   (Mexico City, 1967).

6) Tomás Thayer Ojeda, Reseña histórico-biográfi
   eclesiásticos en el descubrimiento y conquist
   (Santiago, 1921).

7) Rolando R. Mellafe, "Problemas demográficos e
   colonial hispanoamericana," in Temas de histo   a
   hispanoamericana (Colección Nova Americana N°
   1965).

8) Evidence can be found, for example, in Relaci   de
   la conquista del Perú, 1534, or in El anónimo   e
   1534, both in Raúl Porras Barrenechea, Relaci   /as
   de la conquista del Perú (Cuadernos de Histor
   N° 2, Paris, 1937).

9) Rolando R. Mellafe, "La significación históri
   puentes en el virreinato peruano del siglo X\
   Historia y cultura, I, N° 1 (Lima, 1965).

10) Revista histórica. Órgano del Instituto His1
    III, N° 4 (Lima, 1909).

11) Much evidence on the presence of large numbe1
    de la conquista living in special communities
    Popayan at the end of the sixteenth century (
    of the seventeenth may be found in the Archiv
    Cauca in Popayan, sections of Civil-Gobierno
    Tributos.

12) Rolando R. Mellafe, "La significación históri
    puentes," cited above.

13)   See, for example, Roberto Levillier, ed., Gobernantes del
      Perú.   Cartas y papeles.   Siglo XVI, I, p. 107 (Madrid, 1921).

14)   Some examples may be found in Rolando R. Mellafe,
      "Agricultura e historia colonial hispanoamericana," in Temas
      de historia económica hispanoamericana cited above, and in
      "Consideraciones históricas sobre la visita de Iñigo Ortiz de
      Zúñiga," in Visita de la provincia de León de Huánuco en
      1562, I (Huánuco, 1967).

15)   Further discussion of this subject, especially on the
      relation between family and population, may be found in
      Rolando R. Mellafe, "Problemas demográficos e historia
      colonial hispanoamericana," in Temas de historia económica
      hispanoamericana cited above, in "Consideraciones
      históricas sobre la visita de Iñigo Ortiz de Zúñiga," also
      cited above, and in Elda R. González and Rolando R. Mellafe,
      "La función de la familia en la historia social hispano-
      americana colonial," in Anuario del Instituto de
      Investigaciones Históricas, VIII (Universidad del Litoral,
      Rosario, 1965).

20

RURAL POPULATION AND DEPOPULATION IN THE PROVINCE

OF BUENOS AIRES 1869-1960

NICOLAS SANCHEZ-ALBORNOZ

NEW-YORK UNIVERSITY

Between 1869 and 1960, that is between the First and the Fifth National Census of the Republic of Argentina, the Province of Buenos Aires, the leading state in size and population, grew from 307,761 to 6,776,108 inhabitants. This means an increase of almost 22 times at a sustained annual growth rate of 1.9%. The importance of this growth as well as the area concerned -- 307,804 sq. km. -- justify, even in an international perspective, a demographic study of this province. The different circumstances under which this exceptional growth took place give such a study an even greater significance.

1. From the viewpoint of physical geography, the countryside of the Province of Buenos Aires comprises the greatest part of the Pampas prairie, a plain unique in Latin America for its size and its temperate climate.

2. Historically, the Province of Buenos Aires has played a central role in the building up of present day Argentina, one of the leading countries in Latin America. The province has developed in harmony with the objectives proposed by the Federal Capital by virtue of the close association existing between the Capital and the Province in the economic, social and political field.

3. Economically, the Province grew rapidly, impelled by an exceptional foreign demand for its farming and livestock products. This production has given and continues to give the country the greater part of its foreign currencies.

4. At the beginning of the period under examination, the territory considered was only sparsely populated. A large part of it, still under Indian control, remained uninhabited. The growth concerns the total area of the province during the period under consideration as well as the number of inhabitants. It should be noted that while the population density has increased from 1 inhabitant per square kilometre in 1869 to 22 in 1960, it still continues to be very low. Excluding Greater Buenos Aires the density of the Province still reaches only 9.7 inhabitants per square kilometre. (1)

5. Such population increase could not have happened without immigration. Although part of it originated in the other provinces, the main flow came from overseas. The Province of Buenos Aires received the huge flow of immigrants who left Europe while it passed through its phase of demographic revolution. As in the rest of Argentina, most of the immigration in the Province of Buenos Aires took place during the half century from 1880 to 1930.

6. Simultaneously, with a dissemination of the immigrants over the countryside, the Province went through a process of urbanization. This has been most notable in recent years.

These are all well known facts; what is less evident however, is that the Province of Buenos Aires offers an example of an early change in fertility and mortality. The Province first went through a period of population explosion characterized by a high birth rate and a low death rate. This was followed by a period with low birth and death rates. The first change occurred at a time when changes caused by the present demographic revolution were not even foreseeable in any other Latin American country.

It was not long before the province again experienced changes in fertility and mortality. Apart from neighbouring Uruguay, few regions of Latin America have birth and death rates as low as the rates for the province of Buenos Aires. This change, however, has not affected the rest of the country nor had it the necessary dimension to affect and to alter the Latin American trends in fertility and mortality as a whole. In the perspective of the general evolution of Latin America, the Province of Buenos Aires plays the role of a precursor. By examining its evolution the other parts may foresee the future which awaits them.

The decrease of the rural population, characteristic for the socially and economically advanced nations, has, in recent years, also affected the Province of Buenos Aires; this evolution however has been masked by the increase in the total number of inhabitants of the province. In the countryside, the sustained growth has come to an end and has changed into a decrease of the rural population.

The Province of Buenos Aires is a very singular case of a territory that, over a period of some 70 years, has been rapidly colonized by a large mass of peasants who, as soon as they had settled, started to migrate once again. In Latin America there are many examples of rushes of peasant populations for open unsettled land, that for short-term reasons were abandoned. These often were abandoned in an even shorter time and to a greater extent than in the Province of Buenos Aires. The depletion of the fertility of the soil, a world wide decrease in the demand for the crops produced or the attraction of newly discovered more fertile lands may all cause such a phenomenon. However, without dismissing ab initio the incidence of analogous factors of the countryside of Buenos Aires, it is our impression that the rural depopulation is not due to particular circumstances, but rather to something deeper.

What follows is far from a complete study of the topic; it merely attempts to present the problem, to contribute some evidence and to suggest lines of further research. The formulation of more definite conclusions will require more time and more effort.

Scarcity of data concerning certain periods and/or certain aspects on the one hand and the lack of homogeneity in registration and data recording on the other hand were the main obstacles we had to face. Our principal sources of information were, in addition to the provincial censuses of 1881, 1890 and 1938, the five National Censuses of 1869 (I), 1895 (II), 1914 (III), 1947 (IV) and 1960 (V) respectively: in other words, eight censuses irregularly spread over a period of almost one century. (2) During the period of maximum demographic changes, i.e., between 1895 and 1938, the inter-censal periods are far too long (19 and 24 years respectively); therefore a number of important questions cannot be answered. An additional difficulty is that the provincial census of 1938 was never published and that the only information that it contained (on some typewritten sheets kept in the library of the Dirección Nacional de Estadistica y Censos (National Board of Statistics and Censuses)) was the total population by sex and <u>partido</u> (county). For most of the data categories we must indeed compare 1914 with 1947, which in fact increases our inter-censal period of 24 years to a 33 year interval. In addition to this, a number of censuses do not contain certain types of data, such as the breakdown by age at the partido level; the grouping of data may also differ from one census to another.

An additional difficulty is the way "rural population" has been defined for census purposes. When the censuses distinguish between rural and urban population, any population, be it dispersed or grouped in nuclei of 2,000 inhabitants or less, is qualified as rural. It is, however, our opinion that this definition is no longer acceptable: a number of nuclei having a population of 2,000 and more may well be predominantly rural. The mechanisation of the agricultural sector promotes the growth of centers in which a growing number of services geared to the rural sector are concentrated. Meanwhile, the development of communications allows people to live in places which, although strictly statistically speaking are non-agricultural, are more typical of the countryside. The change of dwelling place does not necessarily produce an occupational transfer to non-agricultural activities as shown in the eloquent example of the <u>contratistas</u> who specialize in harvesting and who live, with their machines, in the towns. (3) Thus, many county capitals are considered urban centers in the censuses, although there are no signs of non-agricultural economic activity whatsoever in the whole county. Why should one make a distinction between urban and rural populations in partidos such as Pila with a total population of 2,978 inhabitants, Laprida with 8,721 or Tapalque with 9,443 inhabitants to cite only a few examples? On the other hand, is there any reason to assume that a community of 2,000 inhabitants one century ago was less rural than a present one? Probably not. An additional reason for not respecting the statistical definition of a rural population is that the distribution of the houses in most settlements of the Pampa do not attain the degree of concentration equal to that found in the mediterranean villages for example, and which would partially justify the fact that they be considered urban centers.

For all these reasons we are compelled to propose an alternate definition which is, however, not entirely satisfactory to us and which has to be considered experimental: it will be acceptable when the definition has proved itself to be workable. We shall consider as rural the population of those partidos whose economic structure is predominantly rural. Consequently, this definition excludes the 23 partidos of the Buenos Aires agglomeration as well as the two other large cities of the Province, Mar del Plata (partido of General Pueyrredón) and Bahía Blanca (partidos of Bahía Blanca and Coronel L. Rosales).

According to our definition, the rural population is a residual
that in no way can be identified with the total population of the
countryside. In the first censuses, the area covered by the
present metropolitan area comprised a large number of peasants who
are, according to our definition, excluded from the actual rural
population. On the other hand, the partidos which we considered
to be rural, comprise at present an important segment of the
population that is not only urban in terms of location but that is
employed in the secondary sector, the latter defining more clearly
its non-rural character. This is the case for the districts that
border the banks of the Paraná where we find steelworks, refineries
and metallurgic, paper, textile and food industries. Olavarria
also boasts an important secondary sector. In the analysis which
we will be making, we shall, of course, not draw any examples from
the above mentioned cases.

Despite the apparently arbitrary nature of the definition,
the distinction made will allow us to operate with homogeneous
entities throughout the study. On the one hand we have the
agglomeration of Buenos Aires as well as two large southern
cities; on the other hand, the countryside of the Province. While
small or medium sized cities appear here and there, they do not
distort the specific rural character of the rural part of the
province.

The differences in the average annual rate of inter-censal
growth between the different areas amply justify the perspective
in which they have to be seen.

Table 1

Average Annual Rate of Inter-Censal Growth
(per 100 inhabitants

	1869-1881	1881-1890	1890-1895	1895-1914	1914-1938	1938-1947	1947-1960
Province	4.4	3.9	3.8	4.2	2.1	1.9	3.4
Urban area	4.4	8.4	0.2	5.5	3.4	4.9	4.4
Rural area	4.4	2.6	4.8	3.7	1.2	-1.4	1.3

Between 1869 and 1960, the population in the urban area increased
at an average rate of 2% a year and in the rural area at only 1.6%
a year. The difference can be explained by in that the
importance of the agglomeration of Buenos Aires on the whole had
been increasing steadily. In 1869, and in spite of the absence of
any population in the interior of the Province, the agglomeration
accounted for only 18% of the total population. In 1960, however,
after the colonization of the interior, the same agglomeration
plus the two southern cities amounted to no less than 70% of the

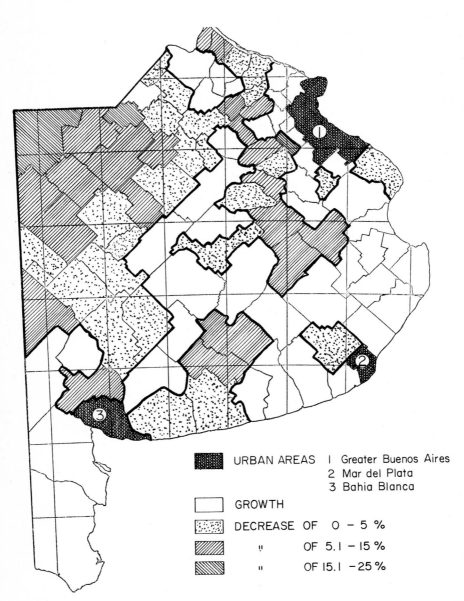

URBAN AREAS   1 Greater Buenos Aires
              2 Mar del Plata
              3 Bahia Blanca

GROWTH

DECREASE OF 0 − 5 %

        "   OF 5.1 − 15 %

        "   OF 15.1 − 25 %

MAP I   PROVINCE OF BUENOS AIRES: INTERCENSAL VARIATION 1938–1947

total population. The Province had obviously become highly
urbanized. A unique growth of the urban area can be observed
between 1881 and 1890. The foundation of La Plata, the new
provincial capital was responsible for the exceptional high growth
rate of 8.4% in the urban area between 1881 and 1890. The old
partido of Ensenada, which had a population of 6,962 inhabitants
in 1881 saw a new city built within its boundaries and had its
name changed; nine years later, in 1890, no less than 65,610
inhabitants were living in the new city. A phenomenon of this
magnitude could not but have a deep impact upon the indices.
     Between 1869 and 1881 the population of the three areas
considered (the rural and urban areas as well as the entire
province) increased at a surprisingly high and uniform rate. The
reason for the growth of the rural population was that in that
period there was a very strong push towards the lands in the
south of the province; between 1881 and 1890, however, the growth
rate of the rural area dropped considerably. Two very distinct
processes took place: a very high population increase in the
South and in the Center of the Province and a low increase in the
region near Buenos Aires that had been settled in earlier times
and that was most highly populated. Between 1890 and 1895 the
difference in trend between the urban and rural areas was quite
noticeable. While the population of the periphery of the city of
Buenos Aires hardly grew, the rural area registered a record
growth of 4.8 percent. It should be remembered that this five-
year period followed the economic crisis of 1890, which hit
Argentina so hard that many immigrants coming from overseas
returned to their country of origin. (4) Similarly, the crisis in
the urban area pushed a large number of people from the coast into
the interior of the Province.
     Between 1895 and 1914, the trend reverted to the previous
patterns: an urban growth that exceeded the rural, with both
areas possessing a high growth rate. It should be noted that in
the following years none of the areas would experience such high
growth rates. Between 1914 and 1938, the growth rate for the
province dropped by 50 percent. The slowing down in growth seems
larger in the countryside than in the urban area, where it
continued to be quite intense. Between 1938 and 1947, a period
influenced by the effects of World War II, urbanization once again
became more distinct without however reaching the rhythm of the
early part of the century. This was the period when the
industrialisation of Greater Buenos Aires took place. In the
meantime, the population of the countryside decreased substantially.
The map of the inter-censal variation between 1938 and 1947 (Map I)
confirms this fact and indicates where the decreases took place.
In 48 partidos, representing more than half of the rural area
partidos, the population decreased in absolute terms: in 24
partidos with less than 5 percent, in 21 between 5.1 and 15% and
in 3 with more than 15.1 but less than 20 percent. The depression
zone covered the entire western part of the province (a region
known for its winter grazings), a large part of the north (a
typical maize district), the center (specialized in cattle
breeding) and the south (with its cereal culture). In other words,
the depression affected those regions where the typical products
of the Province were grown. The only regions spared from the

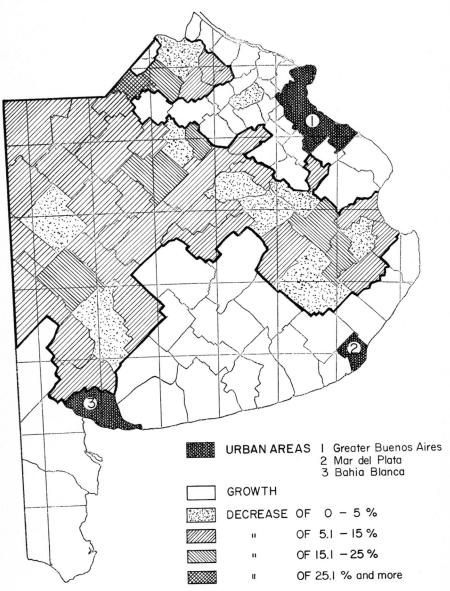

MAP II   PROVINCE OF BUENOS AIRES: INTERCENSAL VARIATION 1947-1960

decline were the lowlands on the banks of the River Salado, the
central coast, the center of the Province around Olavarría, Azul
and Tandil, the two Patagonian departments as well as the region
adjacent to the metropolitan area, noted for its dairy farming
and specialized agriculture.

Between 1947 and 1960, while the urban area continued its
rapid ascent, the rest of the province also resumed a positive
trend of growth. The average yearly increase of 1.3% may,
however, be misleading since half of the rural partidos suffered
population losses. In general terms the same regions which were
affected by a decrease in population between 1938 and 1947,
continued to drop thereafter. In 1960, 45 rural partidos had a
population smaller than in 1947. Of these, 8 lost between 0 and
5% of their inhabitants, 28 partidos (a clear majority) between
5.1 and 15%, 8 others between 15.1 and 25% and only one partido
lost more than 25.1% of its original population. It should be
noted that in the preceding inter-censal period no partido lost
more than 20% of its original population. The number of partidos
affected by the reduction of the rural population was approximately
the same in both inter-censal periods. While in some of them the
population ceased to decrease in the second period, the decrease
started in the other: the latter compensating for the former.
The decline came to an end in the northern and southern coastal
areas, while the following areas joined the zone of depression:
the northern interior, the center and the lowlands of the Salado
on the eastern coast. Between 1938 and 1947 the majority of the
declining partidos lost less than 5% of their population, but
between 1947 and 1960 an even greater majority lost between 5.1
and 15% of their population. This constituted an unequivocal sign
of a general aggravation of the situation.

How can we explain the fact that, between 1947 and 1960
and in spite of a 1.3% yearly increase (as compared to the 1.4%
decrease in the previous period), the countryside continued to
lose inhabitants? (5) Obviously some kind of a process of
urbanization had developed inside this area. The industrialization
of the region along the Paraná, and, on a lesser scale, of some
parts of the Center, had given impetus to small and medium sized
towns whose growth stopped the decline of the region in which they
were located. The partido of San Nicolás, for example, lost
5.4% of its inhabitants between 1938 and 1947, while after the
development of an industrial park, the population increased by no
less than 60.4% between 1947 and 1960. (6)

With the growth of services a number of towns also grew.
These included Chivilcoy, Junín and Nueve de Julio in the western
zone. Thus, the rural area had entered a new phase in its
evolution.

The decline of the peasant population together with the
urbanization of the interior may well be indicators of the process
of modernization. This phenomenon was not just the result of the
attraction of the metropolis, although this attraction really
existed. During more than half a century, the population
concentration around the city of Buenos Aires had been perfectly
compatible with rural development. It was also not a question of
a simple response to a short term agrarian crisis, as it might have
seemed at the beginning of the crisis of 1930. The demographic

and agrarian crisis situations are still existing: they cannot anymore be considered as accidents, since they have now become the "structural situation".

Even in the case where tagnation in the agrarian economy could be mastered by reforming the system of land tenure and exploitation, the mechanisation which necessarily accompanies these changes would not allow the countryside to absorb a greater mass of peasants, unless it moved into a system of extremely intense cultivation which was not always possible nor profitable. According to the productive structure adopted in the past, the economy seems to have reached a ceiling and the population a point of saturation. While industrialisation seems to be the answer to the first problem, urbanization seems to be the answer to the second one.

If there was modernization it must make itself felt in another way; namely through the changes in fertility and mortality. Is there any evidence of changes in fertility and mortality? Are there still districts characterized by the traditional high birth and death rates? When did the drastic fall in the death rate begin? Has the birth rate also fallen and if yes, then when? Simultaneously, with the death rate or later? Has a new equilibrium at a lower level been reached in any area? In other words, how far has the Province of Buenos Aires been affected by changes in fertility and mortality? In order to try to answer these questions we must rely on the vital statistics and on the age structure of the population of selected partidos at specific moments.

In 1960 the crude birth and death rates of the Province were respectively 16.0 and 7.9 per thousand; the natural growth was 8.5. The crude birth rate for the rural area was 15.4 as compared to the 16.9 per thousand for the urban area; the crude death rate was 9.5 per thousand for the rural area and 6.6 for the urban area. The rate of natural increase for the rural area was a low 5.9 and for the urban area a high 10.3. (7)

That, contrary to all predictions, the birth rate of the agglomeration of Buenos Aires was higher than the rate in the rural area may tentatively be explained in two ways. Greater Buenos Aires had been receiving many immigrants in the past years in conditions where there was no marked predominance of one or the other sex. Since migrants tended to be persons in their reproductive age, the reproductive capacity of the area had probably increased. A second reason could be that, the migrants generally come from other provinces or neighbouring Latin American nations, both with more traditional fertility patterns than Buenos Aires, they brought with them the higher fertility characteristics of their province or country of origin; on the other hand, they enjoy a lower death rate thanks to the better health conditions prevailing in Buenos Aires. Both circumstances maintain the process of "demographic revolution" in Greater Buenos Aires through which the interior of the Province, or at least many zones of it, have already passed. Naturally these explanations are only hypotheses which need to be verified. Finally, the lower rural birth rate may well have resulted from an opposite phenomenon: the departure of migrants from the countryside would leave the remaining population with a smaller group belonging to the reproductive ages and subsequently with a decreased capacity of reproduction. It should, however, be noted that the crude death rates in both regions were close to the provincial average. This meant that the health conditions in both parts of the province were equally advanced. The slight difference in favor of the city was probably due to more deficient health conditions in the countryside and to the attachment of the old people to the land.

In observing the spatial distribution of the fertility and mortality patterns of the rural area, we discern several differences. There were three large zones where the birth rates were higher than the average: the entire west, the center east and a strip bordering the north and west of Greater Buenos Aires. There were also three zones with low birth rates or rates close to the average: a zone to the south of Greater Buenos Aires, the northern part of the province (a predominantly maize raising district) and the south. The low death rates can be traced back to areas along the coast, in the interior of the Bay of San Borombón, in the mountain ranges from Tandil to the coast, in a large part of the west as well as in some departments near the agglomeration of Buenos Aires. The high death rates seem concentrated in the agricultural north, the cereal region of the south and in part of the cattle raising center. When combining both types of rates, district differences in natural growth also appear: the north and the south exhibit low birth rates and high death rates resulting in a lower than average natural growth; the west had a high birth rate and a "normal" death rate and consequently a high natural growth; the area to the south of the agglomeration of Buenos Aires had low birth and death rates and hence a slow natural increase; the center-east area where a high birth rate was coupled to a varying death rate, increased rapidly. It could be said that the natural growth in the agricultural regions of the north and the south was lower than in the winter grazing lands of the west and than in the cattle raising lands of the east. In the dairy farming belt surrounding the metropolitan area, the situation differed between the south and the south-east. All of these are broad features requiring a more penetrating analysis. The previous enumeration attempts to link the demographic behavior to the predominant productive activities of each zone as a possible explanation of that behavior. The incidence of these economic factors on fertility and mortality is, however, too complex a problem to be undertaken in this paper.

Over the past century the fertility and mortality patterns have evolved in a very significant manner throughout the province. A hundred years ago high death and birth rates were typical; these rates changed gradually, finally reaching their present level. We will compare, for the years 1869, 1881, 1914 and 1960, some representative partidos. Our comparison, however, will to an extent suffer in that the above dates are unevenly spaced: shorter periods would have been more convenient. A second problem arises from the fact that the western and southern regions were, in 1869 and 1881, sparsely populated and without any administrative organization. In these zones our analysis will be even more limited. In addition, since the Registration was not organized until the end of the last century, the rates calculated for the

first two dates are based on the number of baptisms and burials
for 1869 and 1881 of the parish in question divided by the
recorded population of the partido. In many cases, clear
incongruities appeared due to the fact that the church and civil
jurisdictions were not necessarily identical. Although the samples
chosen are not affected, we wished to draw attention to certain
problems.

Table 2

Evolution of Crude Birth and Death Rates
and of the Rates of Natural Growth in
Selected Partidos

(per 1,000 inhabitants)

Partido	Year	Birth Rate	Death Rate	Natural Growth Rate
1. Rojas	1869	51.8	24.5	27.3
	1881	42.3	24.9	17.4
	1914	36.3	11.3	25.0
	1960	16.1	10.6	5.5
2. Ranchos (later General Paz)	1869	46.4	32.2	16.4
	1881	41.9	20.9	21.0
	1914	37.0	13.2	23.8
	1960	15.2	7.2	8.0
3. Rauch	1869	-	-	-
	1881	44.2	20.0	24.2
	1914	32.5	11.6	20.9
	1960	24.0	8.0	16.4
4. Puán	1869	-	--	-
	1881	-	-	-
	1914	46.9	9.2	37.7
	1960	21.2	6.7	14.5
5. 9 de Julio	1869	-	-	-
	1881	42.5	15.5	27.0
	1914	44.3	12.4	31.9
	1960	19.8	10.3	9.5
6. Navarro	1869	55.4	23.6	31.8
	1881	37.5	19.3	18.2
	1914	31.6	13.4	18.2
	1960	19.2	9.3	9.9
7. Juárez	1869	-	-	-
	1881	45.6	25.1	20.5
	1914	27.9	8.2	19.7
	1960	14.7	8.2	6.5

Graph I̅ POPULATION PYRAMIDS for NAVARRO and RANCHOS (1869, 1947, and 1960)

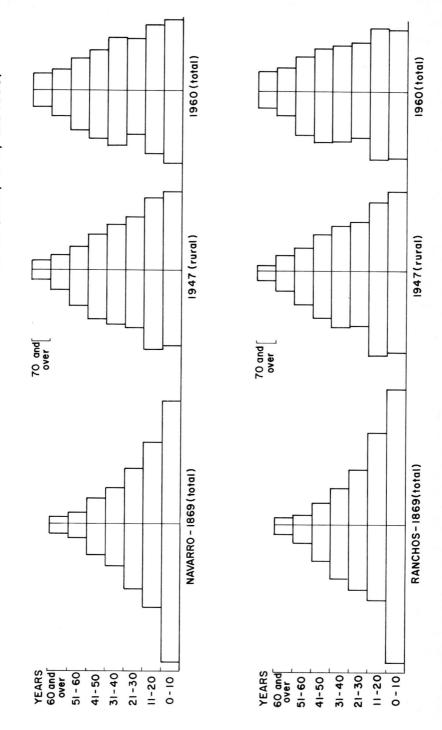

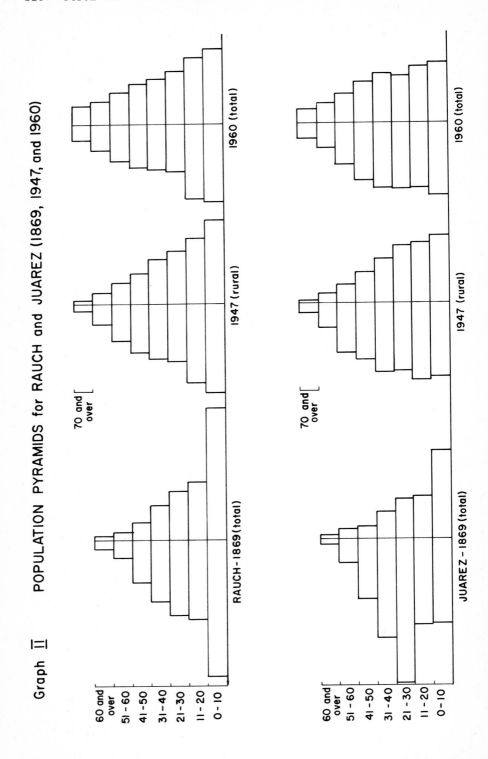

Graph II   POPULATION PYRAMIDS for RAUCH and JUAREZ (1869, 1947, and 1960)

Graph III   POPULATION PYRAMIDS for ROJAS and NUEVE DE JULIO (1869, 1947, and 1960)

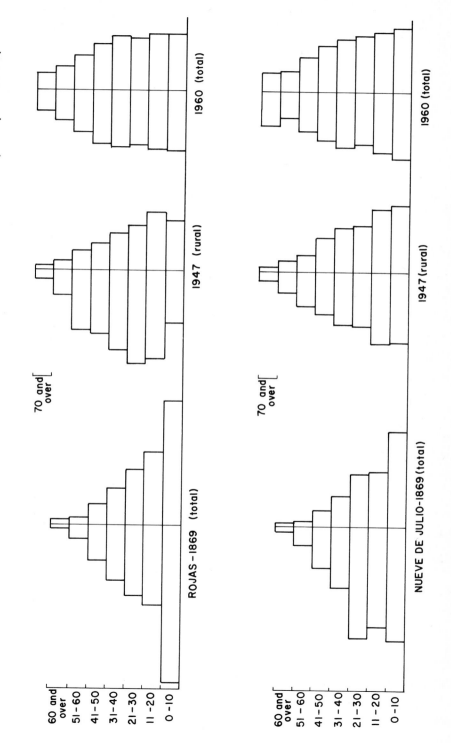

Of the seven partidos selected, the partidos of Rojas, Navarro and Ranchos were originally military posts built on the Indian frontier after the creation of the Viceroyalty of Rio de la Plata in the last quarter of the 18th century: consequently these partidos are territories that were long ago incorporated to the countryside of Buenos Aires. They all have undergone different evolutions: Rojas had developed into an agriculture area, while Navarro and General Paz have conserved their original character as cattle raising areas. The partidos of Nueve de Julio, Rauch and Juárez were founded in 1865, just before the First National Census, on land which had been recently settled. Puán, however, was not won until the military expedition of 1875, ordered by Alsina. The subsequent "conquest of the desert" finally consolidated its precarious incorporation allowing the foundation of the partido in 1886.

Without entering into the details or into a discussion of the possible deficiencies of our figures, we wish to make the following observations:

-- The initial birth and death rates were high, as one would expect;

-- The first rate to drop was the crude death rate which resulted in the rise of the natural growth rate in various places;

-- Afterwards, the birth rate declined rapidly, while the death rates remained almost unchanged;

-- Chronologically the decline of the crude death rates occurred before 1914 while the decrease of the birth rate took place after that date. The period of high birth rates and low death rates occurred shortly after the colonization. Over time, the gap between the two rates narrowed, with the natural growth reaching a stage of maturity characterized by its low level.

When comparing the population pyramids of Rojas, Navarro, Ranchos, Rauch, Nueve de Julio and Juárez for 1869, 1947 and 1960 (8) one can make the following observations:

1. The pyramids of Rojas, Navarro, Ranchos and Rauch for 1869 are -- with their very broad base -- characteristic of a young population: the population between 0 and 20 years accounted for 55 to 60 percent of the total population. There is also a very clear distinction between the different age frequencies. Finally, the older age groups are very small.

2. The shape and the sex structure of the population pyramids of the four districts are identical. The males predominate in the age groups 21 to 60: the reason for this may be that the manpower shortage, affecting farming and cattle raising

areas which were in full expansion, was met by
immigration from overseas.

3. The pyramids of Juárez and Nueve de Julio reveal
    a young female population. The age structure,
    however, is very irregular. There is also a
    large proportion of men 11 years and over especially
    in the age group 21-30 years. These peculiarities
    are probably caused by the fact that both partidos
    are frontier-partidos. The territories had only
    recently been occupied, causing the arrival of
    pioneers, some with their families, although
    most of them were single men between 21 and 50 years
    of age.

4. The rural population of these partidos had aged
    in a noticeable way in 1947. The base of the
    pyramids had become smaller: the population
    between 0 and 19 years accounted for from one-third
    to 44 percent of the total population. The
    distinction between the different age frequencies
    had become considerably less, while the older
    population, and especially the age group 60-69,
    became more important.

5. In each age group men outnumbered women. The sex
    imbalance of 1869 in the frontier partidos had
    been absorbed over the course of the generations.
    The sex imbalance had now become very marked
    for the partidos with mainly agricultural or
    mixed economic activities such as Rojas and
    Juárez. This was especially visible in Rojas
    where there were twice as many men as women
    between the ages of 20 to 39 years: from 39 years
    onward the proportion of men increased. The
    same phenomenon can, to a certain extent, be
    observed for partidos surrounding Rojas.

6. The population pyramids for 1960 show a notable
    ageing of the rural population. The population
    between 0 and 19 years only represent between
    30 and 40 percent of the total population.
    Meanwhile, the percentages of the people aged
    60 years and over increased from 1-2% in 1869
    to 10-14% in 1960, the extreme case being Rojas
    where the frequencies for 50 years and more
    was almost identical to the frequency at
    50 years.

7. The excess number of males was larger in Rojas
    and Juárez than in the other partidos.

The masculinity ratio in the Province was nearly the same
in 1869 and 1947: 105.5 and 105.1. Both ratios are, of course,
much lower than the ones recorded for the years of massive
immigration: 111.9, 115.5 and 110.1 respectively in 1895, 1914
and 1938. In 1960, the numberical differences between the two

sexes had almost disappeared (the masculinity ratio being only 100.6), a sign that the effects of immigration had been wiped out and that the Province was increasingly dependent on its own human resources.

In this final paragraph of our paper we wish to present some conclusions. It is hoped that we have been able to prove them satisfactorily.

The distinction made between urban and rural areas seemed to be useful from an analytical point of view.

The population evolution of the countryside of Buenos Aires had, as it were, completed a full cycle during which a phase of intense growth was followed by another phase of progressive depopulation which as yet, has not been concluded. During the phase of growth, a high natural increase, caused by high birth rates and a sharp decline of the death rates, was coupled with a large influx of immigrants from overseas.

During the second phase, the rural area evolved towards fertility and mortality levels typical for the more developed countries: low birth and death rates, which seem to be lower than the ones for the remaining part of Latin America, a marked ageing of the population and a freeing of peasant manpower from agricultural and cattle raising tasks. The changes occurring in the division of labor caused a rural depopulation, causing in its turn a reversal in the direction of the migratory movements: the positive migration balance changed into a negative one; instead of exercising a pull upon the migrants, the rural area was now responsible for a push phenomenon, causing an increased urbanization.

The first phase apparently culminated in the thirties, the second phase starting shortly thereafter. More detailed research on this problem would definitely be welcomed by all researchers.

References

1. By Greater Buenos Aires we mean the territory made up of the
    partidos surrounding the city of Buenos Aires. Partidos are
    the territorial and administrative units into which the
    Province is divided. At present there are 121 partidos with
    an average area of some 2,500 sq. km. each. These
    dimensions vary considerably from one region to another.
    Those that are most populated are not necessarily the largest
    in area: 20 partidos of Greater Buenos Aires cover only
    3,447 sq. km. in total.

    According to the census of 1960, Greater Buenos Aires (aside
    from the Federal Capital) is comprised of the partidos of
    Almirante Brown, Avellaneda, Esteban Echeverría, Florencio
    Varela, General San Martín, General Sarmiento, Lanús, Lomas
    de Zamora, La Matanza, Merlo, Moreno, Morón, Quilmes, San
    Fernando, San Isidro, Tigre, Tres de Febrero, Vicente
    López and Berazategui which was founded at the end of the
    census year. In a larger sense we should also include
    Escobar, the city of La Plata (capital of the Province)
    and the bordering partidos of Ensenenda and Berisso: 23
    jurisdictional districts in all with a population of
    4,261,400 in 1960. This is done by the Proyecto DISABO
    of the Ministry of Public Health aof the Province (La Plata,
    1965). In this paper Pilar and San Vincente are also
    included within the conglomerate since various of the
    partidos of present day Greater Buenos Aires were
    established through segregation of the original territory.
    Among the inhabitants registered there in the first censuses
    it is now impossible to disaggregate those who lived within
    the limits of the present partido and those who lived in the
    area later set apart. In order to operate with homogeneous
    entities throughout almost a century, it seems advisable
    to include both partidos although they presently lack the
    urban characteristics appropriate for being included in
    the metropolitan area.

    For clarification let us insist at once again on the
    vocabulary: the city of Buenos Aires is the Capital of
    the Republic; Greater Buenos Aires includes the 20
    partidos surrounding the city; the conglomerate of
    Buenos Aires includes these 20 as well as the capital of
    the Province and two of its bordering partidos (for
    historical reasons we have also included Pilar and San
    Vicente); the metropolitan area is comprised of the
    Federal Capital plus the conglomerate.

2. The listing of the sources may be found in Nicolás Sánchez-
    Albornoz and Susana Torrado, "Perfil y proyecciones de la
    demografía histórica en la Argentina", Anuario del Insituto de
    Investigaciones Históricas, 8, Rosario, 1965, pp. 31-56.

References (Continued)

3.   Daniel Slutzky, "Aspectos sociales del desarrollo rural en
     la pampa húmeda argentina", Desarrollo económico, 29,
     Buenos Aires, 1968, pp. 95-135.

     Contratistas are men who operate with their own machinery and
     a team of workers, hired for performing many agricultural
     tasks.

4.   G. Beyhaut et alt., Inmigración y desarrollo económico,
          Departamento de Sociología, Universidad de Buenos Aires,
     1961.

5.   While the population census of 1947 gave a "statistical"
     rural population of 1,223,155 persons for the whole
     Province, that of 1960 claims 882,113.   The decrease of
     341,042 units represents 27.8% less, in other words, a
     yearly drop of 2.4%.   There are places like the partido of
     General Arenales, where a kind of break up took place.
     Of the 20,008 inhabitants classified as rural in 1947, the
     census-takers found only 7,370 thirteen years later.

6.   There are curious cases such as that of Pergamino.   Despite
     the increase of the urban population from 32,382 to 41,612,
     according to the censuses of 1947 and 1960, during a period
     of industrial bonanza (textiles), the drop in rural
     population was so sharp that it overshadowed the urban
     growth.   Consequently, the partido as a whole decreased
     slightly.

7.   The rates have been calculated on the basis of the vital
     statistics data published in the Boletín Estadístico of
     the Province of Buenos Aires, Vol. III, Demográfico 1958-65.

8.   The age groups of the censuses of 1869, on the one hand,
     and 1947 and 1960, on the other, are not the same.   The first
     distinguishes children in the first year of life, those from
     the second to the fifth and those from the sixth to the
     tenth.   We have grouped them together in a category covering
     11 years.   The censuses of 1947 and 1960 group all children
     between 0 and 9 years in one category covering 10 years.

21

QUELQUES TRAITS CARACTERISTIQUES DE L'EVOLUTION

HISTORIQUE DE LA POPULATION DE BRESIL

OLIVER ONODY

BANQUE NATIONALE DU DEVELOPEMENT ECONOMIQUE

MINISTERE DE LA PLANIFICATION,

RIO DE JANEIRO.

I. Les données statistiques.

a) La population totale du brésil.

Les estimations et les résultats des recensements de la population du Brésil, qui suivent n'englobent que les habitants
de la partie du territoire national où la civilisation et la
culture portugaises ainsi que l'administration publique ont
déjà pénétré.

Tableau 1: La population du Brésil

Année	Population		Année	Population	
1550	15.000	(1)	1819	4.222.000	(10)
1560	30.000	(2)	1819	4.396.000	(11)
1568	17.000	(3)	1824	4.000.000	(12)
1583	57.000	(4)	1830	5.340.000	(13)
1588	88.000	(5)	1832	4.471.000	(14)
1600	100.000	(1)	1838	5.300.000	(15)
1660	184.000	(1)	1840	6.218.000	(16)
1690	300.000	(1)	1842	3.116.000	(17)
1700	300.000	(2)	1851	5.000.000	(18)
1766	1.500.000	(6)	1851	7.344.000	(19)
1776	1.900.000	(7)	1854	7.677.000	(20)
1780	2.523.000	(1)	1860	8.418.000	(19)
1798	3.000.000	(6)	1864	10.045.000	(21)
1798	3.250.000	(1)	1872	10.112.000	(22)
1800	3.650.000	(8)	1880	11.748.000	(16)
1808	4.000.000	(9)	1890	14.333.000	(22)
1810	3.618.000	(10)	1900	17.318.000	(22)
1819	3.596.000	(4)	1910	23.414.000	(23)

Année	Population	Année	Population
1920	30.635.000 (22)	1968	89.815.000 (24)
1930	33.568.000 (24)	1970	93.292.000 (prévis.)
1940	41.236.000 (22)	1975	107.182.000 (prévis.)
1950	51.944.000 (22)	1980	123.000.000 (prévis.)
1960	70.967.000 (22)		

Sources: (1) Contreiras Rodrigues:Traços da economia social e politica do Brasil Colonial; (2) R. Simonson, Historia
ecoômica do Brasil; (3) Gândavo, Tratado da terra do
Brasil, 1576; (4) P. Calogeras, Formaçao historica do
Brasil; (5) Coisas notaveis do Brasil (Manuscrit de
Madrid), 1589; (6) T. Ewbank, Life in Brazil, 1856;
(7) Abbé Correa da Silva; (8) Humbolt; (9) Premier recensement officieux (IBGE, Anuario Estatistico, 1936);
(10) A. Balbi, Essai statistique sur le Royaume de Portugal, 1844; (11) Enquête du conseiller Veloso de Oli-
veira; (12) Rugendas, Voyage pittoresque dans le Brésil,
1835; Humbolt, Evaluation numérique de la population du
nouveau continent, 1825; (13) Malte Brun (IBGE, Anuario
Estatistico, 1936); (14) F. Denis, Brésil, 1838; (15) H.
Say, Histoire des relations commerciales entre la France
et le Brésil, 1839; (16) Buescu et Tapajos, Historia do
desenvolvimento econômico do Brasil, 1968; (17) Adalbert
von Preussen, Reise nach Brasilien, 1857; (18) Nathenson;
(19) IBGE, Anuario Estatistico, 1954; (20) Enquête dont
les résultats sont publiés dans le rapport du Ministère
de l'Empire; (21) Wappäus, Handbuch der Geographie und
Statistik des Kaiserreichs Brasilien, 1871; (22) les
différents recensements de la population; (23) Ministerio
da Agricultura, Industria e Comercio, Anuario Estatistico,
1916; (24) Estimations de l'Institut Brésilien de Géographie et de Statistique.

Le pourcentage des brésiliens dans la population mondiale et
de l'Amérique Latine a évolué comme suit:

Tableau 2.

Année	Monde	Amérique Latine
1804	0.5%	18.09%
1845	0.6	20.00
1890	1.0	23.83
1910	1.4	30.00
1930	1.7	30.63

Sources: Mulhall, The dictionary of statistics, 1899; La popu-
lation mondiale, Société des Nations, 1930; Carr-Saunders,
World Population. Past Growth and Present Trends,
Oxford, 1936.

b) La population des deux villes, les plus grandes.

Nous présentons çi-après quelques données statistiques sur la
population des villes qui ont connu l'accroissement de la population le plus spectaculaire.

Tableau 3: La population de Rio de Janeiro, fondée en 1565.

Année	Population	Année	Population
1568	560 (1)	1860	197.000 (6)
1588	4.000 (2)	1872	274.000 (8)
1690	20.000 (3)	1890	522.000 (8)
1725	40.000 (4)	1900	811.000 (8)
1807	50.000 (5)	1912	975.000 (9)
1817	110.000 (5)	1920	1.157.000 (8)
1821	112.000 (6)	1940	1.764.000 (8)
1830	124.000 (6)	1950	2.303.000 (8)
1842	170.000 (7)	1960	3.307.000 (8)
1850	169.000 (6)	1968	4.230.000 (9)

Sources: (1) Gândavo, Tratado da terra do Brasil, 1576; (2) Coisas notaveis do Brasil (Manuscrit de Madrid), 1589; (3) Simonson, Historia econômica do Brasil; (4) Rocha Pitta, Historia da America, 1725; (5) Spix et Martius Reise nach Brasilien, 1823; (6) IBGE, Anuario Estatistico, 1936; (7) Adalbert von Preussen Reise nach Brasilien, 1857; (8) les différents recensements; (9) Estimations de l'IBGE.

Tableau 4: La population de Sao Paulo, fondée en 1554.

Année	Population	Année	Population
1606	190 (1)	1910	346.000 (6)
1765	3.900 (2)	1920	579.000 (5)
1817	30.000 (3)	1940	1.326.000 (5)
1835	21.000 (4)	1950	2.198.000 (5)
1872	31.000 (5)	1960	3.825.000 (5)
1890	64.000 (5)	1968	5.835.000 (7)
1900	239.000 (5)		

Sources: (1) G. Barros, A cidade e o planalto; (2) Enquête ordonnée par le Morgado de Mateus; (3) Spix et Martius, Reise nach Brasilien, 1823; (4) D. P. Müller, Ensaio dum quadro estatistico, 1838; (5) les différents recensements; (6) Ministerio da Agricultura, Industria e Comercio, Anuario Estatistico, 1916; (7) Estimation de l'IBGE.

c) La population indigène.

Les indiens du Brésil (1), appartenaient principalement comme on le sait, à deux grandes catégories, qui au début vivaient séparées: a) les tribus marginaux, l'immense famille des Tupis de la côte; b) les tribus de la forêt tropicale, les Tapuias et les Tupis du "sertao". Les données statistiques qui réfèrent à cette population autochtone sont extrêmement précaires et peu véridiques et ceci pour trois raisons:

1. Il y a encore aujourd'hui de vastes régions où pas un homme blanc n'a pu pénétrer. Il est évident qu'on ne peut pas faire des estimations sérieuses pour une population avec laquelle on n'est pas encore entré en contact. Il faut noter ici que quatre tribus vivant encore dans un état primitif, furent découverts entre 1960 et 1968.

2. Dans les estimations il y a eu très souvent confusion

entre les indiens civilisés (2) et la population indigène se trouvant en dehors du sphère de la culture
portugaise.
3. Pour une partie des historiens anciens, la population
indienne qui avait rejeté le contact avec la civilisation
européenne, n'intervenait simplement pas dans les calculs
démographiques.
Malgré qu'elles sont très contradictoires, nous donnons quelques-
unes des estimations relatives à la population indigène totale
du pays.

Tableau 5: Estimations de la population indigène du Brésil.

Année	Population	Source
1500	100.000.000	Abreu e Lima
1500	10.000.000	Antônio Baêna, Jean de Lery
1500	1.500.000	M. de Albuquerque
1550	1.000.000	Varnhagen
1700	800.000	P. Calogeras
1798	252.000	C. Rodrigues
1798	650.000	Buescu-Tapajos
1800	470.000	Humbolt
1810	259.000	Balbi
1834	300.000	Rugendas
1900	1.250.000	Premier recensement anthro-pologique-culturel, réalisé par l'éthnologue Luis Bueno Horta.
1922	1.000.000	Handbook of South American Indians
1940	500.000	id.
1940	1.500.000	Rondon
1940	1.117.000	Angel Rosenblatt
1941	827.000	Ministério da Agricultura, Aspectos geographicos do Brasil, 1942.
1948	90.000	Procureur chargé de l'enquête criminelle sur les atrocités commises contre les indiens.
1950	45.000	IBGE
1957	68.000	Darcy Ribeiro
1960	50.000	Service de protection des indiens.
1968	75.000	Time, 3 May 1968.
1969	100.000	Fundação Nacional do Indio: Plano de integraçao indigena; population disperée dans 15 états fédérés.

Malgré l'absurdité de quelques estimations, - 100.000.000
d'âmes - on peut conclure que la population indigène à l'époque
de la découverte du Brésil, devrait être sensiblement plus
nombreuse qu'affirme Varnhagen - un million d'âmes -, car presque tous les témoins contemporains ont été profondement im-
pressionés par la densité de la population de cet immense

territoire, faisant dans leur subconscience une comparaison
avec le petit Portugal, qui comptait à l'époque à peine
1.500.000 d'habitants. Orrelana et Acuna (1541) constatèrent
que les indiens dans le bassin de l'Amazone communiquaient d'un
village à l'autre par le son de martel et pierre et que ces
villages s'étendaient sur deux lieus de profondeur dans tout le
territoire de l'Amazonie. L'abbé Durant pour sa part pensait
que les indigènes étaient aussi nombreux que les mouches. Selon
Bertoni, dix millions d'indiens vivaient entre Belem et Gurupa.
Carvajal estima qu'à Grao Para seul, il y avait au 16e siècle,
plus d'un million d'indiens. Simao de Vasconcelos, chroniquer
de la Compagnie de Jésus, affirmait en se basant sur des lettres
conservées jusqu'à nos jours, que les premiers portugais
croyaient que la nation des tapuias à elle seule était plus
nombreuse que la population de toute l'Europe. Le Père Antônio
Vieira (1640) par exemple, compta à l'époque plus de 500 peu-
plades entre Sao Luis et Gurupa, comptant chacune 4.000 à
5.000 guerriers. Finalement, il faut mentionner Piso (1635)
qui croyait que la population du Brésil pouvait être la plus
nombreuse du monde.

d) La population noire.

La plus grande difficulté qui se présente lors de l'estimation
de la population noire du Brésil trouve sa cause dans les
différentes classifications qui figurent dans les documents
historiques. Il est, par exemple, très souvent impossible de
savoir si la classification "esclaves" inclut oui ou non des
indiens (3).
La distinction entre "pardos", pretos crioulos" et "africanos"
(4) ne facilite certes pas les recherches historiques. En
plus, la distinction entre les divers croisements n'est toujours
pas très claire dans les sources disponibles. Ainsi l'ex-
pression "métis" englobe-t-elle tous les métissages (caboclo,
cafuso, mulato, etc.) ou seulement les descendants de nègres
et de blancs (5). Finalement, le manque de précision dans la
définition d'un blanc et d'un mulâtre rend pratiquement impossible toute comparaison entre les statistiques brésiliennes
et les données étrangères (6).

Tableau 6: La population noire du Brésil.

Année	Nombre	% de la pop. totale	Source
1538	14.000	24,56	Père Anchieta
1600	20.000	20,00	Simonsen
1650	33.000	19,41	Père Vieira
1655	40.000	22,22	Varnhagen
1660	50.000	27,17	Gaspar Dias Ferreira
1780	600.000	23,78	Dieudonné Rinchon
1798	1.988.000	61,17	Contreiras Rodrigues
1800	1.600.000	48,49	Abelardo Romero
1805	1.960.000	53,70	Humbolt
1817	2.887.000	76,31	Fr. Tannenbaum
1818	2.515.000	65,88	Balbi
1818	2.128.000	55,75	Arthur Ramos

Année	Nombre	% de la pop. totale	Source
1818	1.930.000	45,71	G. Keith
1819	1.107.000	30,78	Calogeras
1819	1.728.000	42,66	Rinchon
1820	2.000.000	48,19	Buxton
1824	1.987.000	49,68	Rugendas
1835	2.100.000	42,00	F. Denis
1850	3.250.000	54,16	Rinchon
1851	3.100.000	62,00	Nathenson
1870	1.191.000	11,91	Gouvernement brésilien(1)
1870	1.500.000	15,00	Sénateur Otoni
1870	1.750.000	17,50	Sénateur Pompeu
1870	1.800.000	18,00	Sénateur Franco
1884	3.000.000	25,00	H. Johnston
1908	2.718.000	12,39	H. Johnston
1940	6.035.000	14,63	Recensement (2)
1950	5.692.000	11,00	Recensement
1968	5.500.000	6,12	Jornal do Brasil, 12 mai 1968 (3)

Notes:(1) La raison de cette diminution doit être recherchée dans deux circonstances. Premièrement on n'a pas inclus dans les chiffres, mis en avant pendant les débats parlementaires, le nombre des nègres déjà affranchis. Secundo, la prohibition d'importer des noirs, le blocus naval anglais ainsi que la grande mortalité ont eu certaines répercussions sur ces chiffres.

(2) Le nombre de noirs dans les statistiques des trente dernières années a été affecté par la création d'une catégorie séparée groupant les "mulâtres".

(3) On ne publie plus des données sur la couleur de la population, car officiellement la discrimination contre les nègres a cessé d'exister en vertu de la Loi d'Alfonso Arinos (1951). Au fond, une discrimination raciale contre les nègres n'a jamais existé au Brésil. Il existait cependant, une discrimination assez forte de caractère juridique (entre esclaves et affranchis), remplaçée plus tard par une discrimination moins brutale de couleur (rendant très facile le passage à la catégorie des blancs); actuellement, il y a une discrimination assez délicate d'ordre économique, ce qui explique le fait qu'il n'y a que 5% de nègres dans la cadre des officiers, 3% aux Universités et 2% dans le service public.

Dans les diverses parties du pays, les pourcentages des noirs, au siècle dernier étaient:

Tableu 7: Importance numérique des noirs dans certaines parties du Brésil.

Année	Région	% de la population	Source
1808	Minas Gerais	41,58	180.000 nègres:Echwege

Année	Région	% de la population	Source
1814	Rio Negro	4,83	729 nègres:Spix et Martius.
1814	Ceara	65,78	97.800 nègres:Patriota, mai 1814.
1814	Santa Catarina	24,63	8.143 nègres: Patriota, mai 1814.
1814	Rio Grande do Sul	33,90	Mulhall
1815	Sao Paulo	20,73	44.591 nègres:Spix et Martius.
1819	Minas Gerais	26,90	Calogeras
1819	Rio de Janeiro	23,40	id.
1819	Bahia	30,40	id.
1819	Pernambuco	26,30	id.
1819	Maranhao	66,60	id.
1819	Goias	42,50	id.
1819	Rio Grande do Norte	12,86	id.
1829	Mato Grosso	53,20	Mëmoria Estatistica
1829	Minas Gerais	52,24	id.
1829	Maranhao	42,85	id.
1862	Rio Grande do Sul	24,64	Mulhall
1874	Sao Paulo	24,00	M. E. Marquês

e) L'immigration.

L'immigration au Brésil se laisse diviser en deux grouples: les portugais d'une part et les immigrants appartenant à d'autres nationalités de l'autre.

Quant aux lusitaniens, on a connu quatre formes d'immigration:

a) L'immigration forcée: il faut classer ici les bandits et les prostituées. L'arrivée des "cristaos novos" après le massacre de Lisbonne de 1506, doit être considéré comme un exode demi-forcé car il se faisait en vertu de la loi d'expulsion promulguée par le roi Manuel I, le 5 décembre 1496.

b) La venue en mission et de service: cette catégorie inclut entre autres les missionnaires, les soldats, les fonctionnaires publics.

c) L'immigration dirigée: on peut citer ici le cas des jeunes filles orphelines envoyées du "Recolhimento de Nossa Senhora da Encarnaçao" dans les années 1552, 1553 et 1557, ainsi que les couples açoréens destinés au sud du pays(7).

d) Finalement il existe une immigration spontanée, qui a prédominé pendant les dernièrs siècles.

En ce qui concerne les immigrants d'autres nationalités on peut distinguer plusieures périodes dans l'histoire du Brésil:

a) 1500-1580: Au début, et malgré les luttes contre les français, les anglais, etc., il était relativement facile pour les étrangers de s'installer au Brésil et d'y excercer n'importe quelle profession.

b) 1580-1750: Ce fut avec l'unification du Portugal et de l'Espagne que commençaient les restrictions imposées aux étrangers.

c) 1750-1808: Pendant cette période, pratiquement seul des
portugais avaient le droit d'entrer dans le pays.
d) 1808-1818: Pendant cette période transitoire, après
l'arrivée du souverain portugais, le Brésil ouvrait
graduellement ses ports aux étrangers. D. Joao, dans un
document officiel expédié le 28 mars 1808 à l'Intendant
de l'Or, déclare: "Les nations étrangères (ãles étrangers)
qui viennent, contribuent à l'expansion de ce continent
non seulement par leurs populations, mais aussi par leurs
fonds, services et talents dans l'agriculture et l'industrie, ce qui apportera les plus heureuses conséquences
ainsi qu'augmentation de la prospérité du Brésil."

L'immigration des autres nationalités pouvait se faire de deux
façons: soit individuellement soit orientée. Ce fut de cette
dernière façon que commençait la colonisation regulière du
pays (8). Le premier contrat de colonisation fut conclu avec
le représentant du canton de Fribourg (Suisse), S. N. Gachet,
et fut approuvé par le décret du 16 mai 1818. C'est ainsi que
naquît la ville de Nova Friburgo. La colonisation allemande
commença en 1824, avec la fondation de la colonie de Sao Leo-
poldo dans le sud du pays. D'autres villes apparaissaient
telles que Petropolis (fondée par J. Koeler), Brusqui (Baron
von Schneburg), Juiz de Fora (fondée par Halfeld), etc. Entre
1818 et 1849 vingt colonies furent créées. Dans la période
1850-1866 54 autres colonies furent fondées. La colonisation
italienne commença en 1874 et l'immigration japonaise en 1908
avec l'arrivée, le 18 juin, du bateau Kasato Maru, avec 680 immigrants à bord. La dernière immigration organisée, d'une
certaine envergure, était celle des hollandais.
Les immigrations individuelles non-organisées donnèrent
également lieu à la création de colonies, qui, faute d'appui
officiel, ne parvenaient pas à se développer. Il suffit de
mentionner ici les "vilas" Colônia Arpad, Colônia Bocskai,
vila de Rei, Sao Estevao, etc., toutes fondées par des immigrés
hongrois.
L'estimation numérique de l'immigration globale blanche
au Brésil se heurte à une difficulté insurmontable: le manque
de données statistiques.
Pour la période 1500-1777 on ne possède rien de précis
et il faut se fier aux documents historiques qui réfèrent à
l'origine européenne des habitants du Brésil (9). Les Archives
Nationales ont publié en 1963 la liste de 601 étrangers entrés
dans cinq capitaineries du Brésil entre les années 1777 et 1819.
L'énumeration n'est pas complète puisqu'il manque les lettres de
A à D, ainsi que les données relatives aux autres capitaineries.
En vertu d'un ordonnance du Ministre des Affaires de Guerre et
des Affaires Etrangères, on ouvra à la police (le 29 mars 1808)
le premier "livre pour la légitimation des étrangers". A base
de ce livre on peut reconstruire le nombre des étrangers arrivés,
en Brésil à partir de ce moment:

```
1808-1822 : 4.234 personnes (10
1823-1830 : 4.446      "
1831-1839 : 6.968      "
1840-1842 : 3.770      "
```

Malheureusement, en mai 1842, les registrations dans le livre des étrangers furent suspendues pour des raison inconnues (11). Il faut noter que ces chiffres ne comprennent pas l'immigration portugaise, ni la colonisation organisée. Cependant une grande partie de ces étrangers s'est établie d'une façon définitive, acquérant ainsi la nationalité brésilienne. Le nombre des naturalisations a monté à environ 140.000 dans les années 1847-1965 (12). Quant aux portugais arrivés au Brésil, leur nombre monta à 24.000 entre 1808 et 1817 (13).

Selon l'Institut Brésilien de Géographie et de Statistique (IBGE), l'immigration dans la période 1820-1963, présentait l'aspect suivant:

Portugais	:	1.768.974 soit	31,97%
Italiens	:	1.624.981 "	29,37
Espagnols	:	718.750 "	12,98
Allemands	:	256.448 "	4,64
Japonais	:	242.150 "	4,38
Autres	:	922.453 "	16,66%

Il faut remarquer qu'à partir de 1965 l'IBGE ne publie plus les données relatives à l'immigration, probablement à cause de la diminution de celle-ci; la diminution elle-même est la conséquence de la mauvaise situation économique, de l'inflation, de la xenophobie, de l'instabilité sociale et politique du Brésil, du mauvais fonctionnement des organismes d'immigration ainsi que de la prospérité des pays européens. On a estimé le nombre des immigrés à 9.38, 8.175 et 11.000 respectivement pour les années 1965, 1966 et 1967. Le Brésil a également cessé d'être le pays adoptif préféré des Portugais. Les pays de destination des émigrant portugais étaient (en ordre de préférence) en 1966: France (73.419), les Etats-Unis (13.376), l'Allemagne (9.686), le Canada (6.795), l'Afrique du Sud (4.721), le Vénézuela (4.697) et enfin le Brésil (2.607).

II. Les facteurs déterminants de la composition de la population brésilienne.

a) La population peu nombreuse de la mère patrie.

Au temps de la découverte du Brésil, le Portugal n'avait que 1.500.000 à 2.000.000 d'habitants. La population était tellement insuffisante que la plus grande partie du territoire du Royaume au 16e siècle était inculte et se trouvait abandonnée. A part de cela se fut avec cette population que le Portugal devait se battre en Afrique et en Asie, qu'il devait défendre son territoire européen et qu'il devait peupler ses possessions en Amérique du Sud. Par conséquent le Portugal se vit obligé, d'une part de suppléer l'immigration régulière par des solutions de fortune (métissage, importation forcée d'étrangers, etc.), et d'autre part de rendre difficile la sortie du Brésil (14) et de restreindre sévèrement l'émigration (15). Il convient de noter que la croissance démographique au Brésil était très faible au début de l'ère coloniale. L'interdiction de fonder

de nouveaux couvents au Brésil, décrétée le 16 octobre 1609,
ne changeait pas grand'chose à la situation.

b) La vastité du territoire.

Le Brésil avec ses 8.511.965 km2 de superficie, possède une
des plus basse densités démographiques dans le monde: approximativement dix habitants par kilomètre carré. Cette faible
densité a forcé les autorités portugaises, y compris l'église,
d'employer dans le traitement des indigènes des méthodes relativement indulgentes -au lieu des solutions extrêmes ren-
contrées dans d'autres colonies- et d'essayer d'épargner les
indiens (très souvent contre la volonté même des colons) et
d'encourager les mariages mixtes entre soldats portugais et
femmes autochtones, comme ce fut le cas en Amazonie.

c) Différences de fécondité entre les races.

Pour quelques races l'activité sexuel dépassait la moyenne:
ce fut ainsi pour les femmes indiennes (16), pour les mulâtres
des deux sexes (17), les italiens, les japonais (18) ainsi
que pour les sémites et surtout pour les arabes.

d) Bannissement.

Il est vrai qu'une nouvelle ambiance, résultant d'un immigration a un effet régénératif très fort sur l'individu en
question et il est également vrai qu'une grande partie des
raisons se trouvant à la base des bannissement de jadis -et
de caractère sexuel ou religieux- ne constitueraient aujourd'hui même pas une contravention. Le grand nombre de
"degredados" parmi les premiers habitants blancs du Brésil a
eu cependant une très profonde influence sur l'évolution de la
population. Même les deux premiers européens (un s'appelait
Afonso Ribeiro) laissés dans la colonie nouvellement découverte
par Pedro Alvarez Cabral, étaient des bannis. A partir de
1536 le Portugal a généralisé la pratique de déporter les
bannis au Brésil. Plus tard, en 1551 cette colonie devenait
le lieu de destination de tout bannissement du 3e degré. Au
début, les "degredados" furent répartis sur tout le territoire.
Dès 1620, ils étaient surtout envoyés à Maranhao, puis à Santa
Catarina en vertu de la loi du 30 juin 1794 et finalement, à
partir du 20 novembre 1797, au Mato Grosso et en Haute Amazonie.
Quand le premier Gouverneur Général, Tomé de Souza, arriva au
mois de mars 1549 il amena avec lui 400 bannis. Plus tard
presque tous les voyageurs se montraient surpris du grand
nombre de criminels bannis, vivant au Brésil: Pyrard de Laval
(1610), Aldenburgk (1624), Nieuhof (1641) et l'abbé Raynal
(1782). Selon O. Burger, on envoyait en 1797 à Santa Catarina,
les condamnés du bagne de Güstrow (Mecklenburg). Simonsen
dans son Histoire Economique parle de 2.000 forçats napolitains
qui furent transférés au Brésil durant le siècle passé.
Plusieures lettres témoignaient de l'influence désastreuse de
ces éléments sur la nouvelle société: ce fut dans ce sens que
Duarte Coelho écrivit au Roi le 20 décembre 1546; au mois de
septembre 1551 ce fut le Père Nobrega qui protesta et le 31
mars 1560 ce fut le tour au Gouverneur Général, Mem de Sa.

e) Les célibataires et les hommes seuls.
  Tandis que la colonisation des Etats-Unis par exemple était
basée sur la famille et le travail, la civilisation brésilienne
avait comme origines l'individu et l'aventure. Les portugais
qui venaient pendant les premiers siècles étaient soit des
célibataires, soit des mariés, laissant leur famille au Portugal et n'ayant pas l'intention de rester puisqu'ils venaient
seulement pour faire fortune. Le fait est qu'ils sont restés
quand'même, fondant une nouvelle famille avec des indiennes
ou des femmes noires. Ceci est une des raisons de l'énorme
métissage qui s'est effectué au Brésil. Il faut cependant
admettre que le portugais venait au Brésil déjà très métissé,
croisé surtout avec du sang africain. Les hollandais qui oc-
cupaient pendant trente ans le Nord du pays n'étaient guère
plus purs, à cause de l'influence espagnole aux Pays-Bas.

f) L'esclavage indien.
  Europe prit connaissance de l'existence de l'esclavage indien
au Brésil au moment où, en 1504, le premier navire amena
quelques esclaves. En 1511 et sous le commandement de Cristo-
vao Pires, une quarantaine de captifs furent amenés au Portugal.
L'existence de l'esclavage fut également confirmé en 1515 par
la "Nova Gazeta do Brasil". Herrera signale l'existence en
1527 d'une factorerie florissante au Brésil où l'on faisait
la traite des Indiens. Selon l'estimation de P. Merea (19)
il y avait en 1548 déjà 3.000 esclaves autochtones au Brésil
et le Père Anchieta (1553) trouvait à Pernambuco 2.000 captifs
indiens et a Bahia 3.000. D'après Simonsen, l'industrie du
sucre occupait à elle seule au 17e siècle 170.000 forçats
indiens. Il est compréhensible que le colon portugais venant
avec des capitaux privés et avec une certaine tradition et expérience esclavagistes, avait tout de suite besoin de main-
d'oeuvre forcé afin de faire fructifier ses capitaux. Au début
cependant, cet esclavage fut masqué par des cadeaux sans valeur
(miroirs, perles en verre, etc.) que les indiens acceptèrent
comme rétribution de leur travail. Cependant, quand l'intérêt
des indiens pour ces objets insignifiants diminua, la cruauté
des conquérants augmenta et l'esclavage indien se généralisa
à partier de l'année 1530.
  Les souverains portugais pour leur part ont essayé de
défendre les indiens contre les abus de l'esclavage. Le Roi
ordonna en 1565 la protection des indigènes et la lettre royale
du 20 mars 1570 interdisait la traite des indiens sauf en cas
de guerre "juste". La loi du 11 novembre 1594 définit la
notion de la guerre "juste" et la loi du 30 juillet 1609 pro-
clama la liberté formelle de la population autochtone du
Brésil. Le 10 septembre 1611 cependant Philippe II revint un
pas en arrière et permit aux colons d'acheter des prisonniers
de guerre. En 1652 D.Joao IV décreta une nouvelle prohibition
et en 1679 la traite des indiens fut à nouveau condamnée.
Finalement une dernière loi dans ce domaine, promulguée le
6 juin 1755, confirma la liberté des indigènes à Para et
Maranhao. La direction du "Diretorio dos Indios", le 3 mai

1757, assura cette liberté dans tout le territoire national,
soit-il d'une façon théorique.

g) L'esclavage des nègres.

Pour les portugais arrivant au Brésil l'esclavage n'avait rien
de neuf. Déjà en 1443 les premiers envois importants de nègres
arrivèrent au Portugal et vers 1550 10% des habitants de Lisbonne étaient des noirs. Quand le lusitanien émigré au Brésil,
s'est aperçu des difficultés provoquées par l'installation de
l'esclavage indien, il a tout de sute commencé à importer des
noirs d'Afrique, perdant 30 à 50% des "pièces" pendant le
trajet. Au marché de Bahia prédominaient les soudanais et à
ceux de Pernambuco et de Rio de Janeiro les "congos" d'Angola.
L'esclavage noir était un esclavage "parasitique" qui per-
mettait aux propriétaires de vivre aux dépens de leurs captifs
et non pas un esclavage "symbiotique". La raison peut être
trouvé dans le fait que l'esclavage noir était plus un esclavage de plantation qu'un esclavage domestique. L'esclavage
indien de son coté s'approchait davantage du type symbiotique.
La traite des indiens était devenu plus difficile à cause de
la réaction des indiens, leur résistance physique très faible,
leur productivité très basse ainsi que le degré primitif de
leur civilisation. Le découverte des mines a fourni aux blancs
les ressources financières permettant la substitution de l'esclavage indien par l'esclavage noir. Dans quelques régions,
comme à Pernambuco et Bahia, cette substitution s'est effectuée
très rapidement entre 1690 et 1700. Dans les autres parties
du territoire cette substitution était très lente, comme en
Amazonie et à Sao Paulo, et le processus s'y prolongea jusqu'au
19e siècle. La date exacte à laquelle le premier nègre fut
importé au Brésil est incertaine. Elle est située entre 1525
et 1545 (20). En ce qui concerne le nombre de nègres arrivés
au pays on ne possède guère de données exactes, exception faite
pour les importations légales pour quelques années. En outre,
les sources nous ne renseignent pas sur le nombre de nègres,
entrés clandestinement. Say, par exemple, affirme qu'en 1837
seul, 40.000 nègres entraient par contrebande. L'importation
des esclaves noirs présente l'image suivant.

Tableau 8: Importation d'esclaves noirs au Brésil.

Année	Nombre	Source
1576	14.000	Pierre Verger
1575–91	50.000(a)	Rapport présenté à Philippe II par le vicomte Paiva Manso
1580–1836	1.600.000(a)	James Duffy
1612	10.000	Pierre Verger
1620	13.000	id.
16e–17e s.	10.000 par an	Marques de Lavradio: A aboliqao da escravatura.
16e–18e s.	30.000 par an	W. Guthric
1636–45	23.163(b)	Simonsen
1637	4.000(c) par an	Varnhagen
1680–1700	10.000(d)	Obligation de la Compagnie de Monopole.

Année	Nombre	Source
1700	10.000 par an	Duffy
17e s.	40.000 à	
	50.000 par an	Calogeras
1741	25.000 (e) par an	Romero
1759-1803	642.000 (a)	Frank Tannenbaum
1800-1850	40.000 à	
	50.000 par an	Spiegel, The Brazilian Economy
1807-1847	1.801.000	Rinchon
1824-1834	80.000 par an	Rugendas
1831-1841	220.000	Romero
1840-1844	20.000 par an	Calogeras
1840	30.000	Rinchon
1841	16.000	Rinchon
1842	17.435	Ministère des Finances
1843	19.095	id.
1844	22.845	id.
1845	19.453	id.
1846	50.325	id.
1847	56.172	id.
1848	60.000	id.
1849	54.000	id.
1850	23.000	id.
1851	3.278	id.
1852	700	id.
1853-54	512	id.

Notes: (a) d'origine angolaise
(b) à Pernambuco
(c) à la colonie hollandaise du Brésil
(d) à Maranhao
(e) à Bahia.

Le dernier transport d'esclaves noirs arriva à San Matheus à bord du navire nord-américain "Mary Smith".
Il y a également de grandes divergences dans l'estimation de l'importation globale de nègres au Brésil.

Tableau 9: Estimations du nombre de nègres importé au Brésil.

Nombre	Source
9.000.000	W. Guthric
6.000.000	P. Calmon, Historia do Brasil
15.000.000	Calogeras
4.800.000	Carneiro, A nacionalizaçao do negro
8.000.000	Ramos, The Negro in Brazil
4.830.000	Statistiques officielles.
3.000.000	Chaves, Memorias econômico-politicas.
3.000.000	Pereira, Breve historia da America
3.500.000 (a)	Simonsen
6.723.850	Buescu

Notes: (a) l'estimation de Simonsen se laisse répartir comme suit:
17e siècle: 350.000 destinés à l'industrie du sucre
18e-19e siècle: 1.000.000 pour l'industrie du sucre
600.000 destinés aux mines
250.000 pour les plantations de café
1.100.000 pour les autres secteurs de l'économie.

Il est très difficile de présenter des chiffres plus précis; car après l'abolition de l'esclavage le Ministère des Finances ordonnait l'incinération de tous les documents relatifs à l'ancien régime d'esclavage, imaginant naïvement que l'on pourrait réparer de cette façon les injustices multi-séculaires, mais causant en réalité des pertes irréparables aux recherches historiques. Cette incinération fut ordonnée par le décret du 14 décembre 1890 et exécutée par la circulaire du 13 mars 1891.

L'abolition de l'esclavage nègre fut un processus très long et très douloureux aussi pour les esclaves que pour les maîtres (pour qui cela signifiait une perte de capitaux) ainsi que pour l'empereur Pedro II, pour ce processus entrainait la perte de son trône. Les phases de cette libération graduelle étaient les suivantes:

1816 (17 avril)	: Décision royale limitant la traite sur les côtes occidentales de l'Afrique entre le 10e et 25e degré et sur les côtes orientales entre le 5e et le 10e degré.
1818 (27 janvier)	: Loi sur la punit on -avec bannissements- des négriers au nord de l'Equateur.
1831 (7 novembre)	: Loi sur la libération des esclaves entrant les ports du Brésil, suivie le 12 avril 1832 par un décret relatif au même problème.
1850 (4 septembre)	: Loi d'Eusebio de Queiros, interdisant le trafic des esclaves sur le terri-toire brésilien, suivi d'un décret datant du 14 octobre 1850.
1853 (28 décembre) et 1864 (24 septembre):	décrets sur l'émancipation des africains affran-chis, dont le nombre monta à 1.027 entre 1855 et 1864.
1871 (28 septembre)	: "Loi de ventre libre", sur la libé-ration des enfants nés d'une esclave.
1883 (13 mai)	: "Lei aurea", abolition totale du régime d'esclavage.

Malgré toutes ces mesures prises, le nombre d'esclaves restait, au siècle dernier, assez élevé dans certaines régions du pays.

Tableau 10: Nombre d'esclaves au Brésil au 19e siècle.

Année	Capitainerie ou Province	Nombre	Source
1814	Rio Negro	729	Spix et Martius
1814	Ceara	17.208	Patriota, mai 1814

Année	Capitainerie ou Province	Nombre	Source
1821	Pernambuco, Ceara, Paraiba, Rio Grande do Norte	523.000	Balbi
1824	Minas Gerais	290.000	Rugendas
1835	Sao Paulo	326.902	Müller
1858	Rio Grande do Sul	282.547	Rapport du Président de le Province.

h) L'intolérance religieuse en Europe.

L'intolérance religieuse en Europe avait également des répercussions sur l'évolution de la population brésilienne.
L'épisode des "cristaos novos" est la plus significative par
le grand nombre concerné. Un certain Gaspar da Gama apparte-
nait à l'expédition de Cabral tandis qu le premier fermier du
Brésil, Fernando de Lorohnha (1505-1512) était lui aussi un
nouveau chrétien. Les nouveaux chrétiens dominaient surtout
l'industrie du sucre, la première compagnie privilegiée du
Brésil (1647) ainsi que le fermage des impôts. Pyrard de
Laval (1610) et Frézier (1712-1714) étaient impressioné par
leur nombre. Les huguenots à leur tour ont laissé au 16e
siècle de nombreux descendants à Rio de Janeiro. Il y aussi
une correlation entre les progroms russes et la grande vague
l'émigration juive vers le Brésil au siècle passé. Les années
1939-1945 voyaient l'arrivée de plusieurs milliers de commerçants et d'intellectuels. Diverses sectes russes, vivant
en Chine, venaient au Brésil après la Deuxième Guerre Mondiale
et y établirent quelques colonies.

i) L'intolérance politique.

Des nords-américains, réfugiés de la guerre de sécession,
fondirent la ville prospère de Americana, dan l'état de Sao
Paulo. C'est en grande partie aux très nombreux techniciens,
ingénieurs et savants venus de l'Europe Centrale après la
Deuxième Guerre qu'on doit l'énorme stimulant qu'a reçu l'industrialisation dans les années 1950-1960. Le nombre d'hongrois arrivés au pays après 1956 n'était pas aussi grand que
l'on avait espéré, car il existait des conditions économiques
plus favorables dans les autres pays d'immigration.

j) Le surpeuplement dans quelques pays étrangers.

Ce phénomène n'est pas resté sans importance pour le Brésil
surtout en ce qui concerne l'immigration italienne et japonaise. L'immigration italienne atteignait son maximum dans
la décade 1880-1890 avec 690.000 nouveaux-venus tandis que
l'immigration japonaise atteignait son point culminant avec
la venue en 1960 de 7.746 immigrants.

k) L'exode allemand des années 1945-1952.

Cet exode fut provoqué par la crise résultant de la guerre.
Néanmoins la plupart des immigrants a retourné en Allemagne

suite des difficultés économiques du Brésil, de l'ambiance peu acceuillante vis-à-vis des étrangers et surtout à cause du "miracle économique allemand".

1) La politique du Portugal.
La politique particulière du Portugal en ce qui concernait le Brésil et le climat qui en était le résultat ont déterminé le caractère de l'immigration. Contre les tentatives française, anglaise, hollandaise ainsi qu'espagnole d'arracher la colonie à ses découvreurs, le Portugal essayait de se défendre par un isolement total du Brésil: ceci força la Métropole de cacher toutes les ressources naturelles qui existaient dans cette partie de l'Amérique Latine. Le roi Manuel I interdisait en 1504 de faire apparaître le Brésil sur les cartes géographiques portugaises. Le 23 novembre 1708 Woodes Rogers constata personnellement que "les portugais n'aimaient pas dire la vérité sur leur industrie du sucre." Les livres "Cultura e opulência do Brasil" d'Antonil, publié en 1711, et "Histoire de l'Amérique Portugaise" de Pitta Rocha, édité en 1727, furent confisqués parcequ'ils contenaient des déscriptions économiques.

m) Le climat.
C'est le climat qui détermina la préférence pour le Brésil des émigrants quittant l'Europe méridionale, l'Afrique du Nord et le Proche Orient. D'autre part les conditions climatiques ont causé une certaine rédistribution des immigrants à travers le pays. Les allemands, les slaves, les nordiques ainsi que les hongrois se sont établis dans les régions les plus froides, tandis que les italiens, les africains du nord ainsi que les immigrants du Proche Orient se sont établis dans les régions tropicales.

n) Finalement le nationalisme brésilien (jeune et virulent) et le catholicisme (économiquement faible, mais très fort du point de vue politique), contribuent pour des raisons différentes (politique ou dogme) au maintien et à la conservation de taux de natalité très élevés. Ils croyent tous les deux l'objectif principal d'une politique nationale est la densité de la population (c'est-à-dire peupler le pays d'une multitude de gens misérables, malades et analphabètes) et non pas l'élévation du niveau de vie de la population présente.

III. Tendances se manifestant dans la
composition de la population.

a) La disparition des indiens.
La population autochtone du Brésil est en train de disparaître complètement (21) les raisons pour cette dispartion sonts les suivantes.

1) Le contact même avec la civilisation. Dés le début, l'église a forcé les indigènes de couvrir leur "hont" (vergonha) de vêtements, ce qui avait pour conséquence de

répandre la pneumonie fatale. De nombreuses maladies avaient
des conséquences mortelles pour les indiens ne possédant pas
la même immunité des blancs: la grippe, le syphilis, la
gonorrhée, la tuberculose, les maladies vermineuses, etc.   Il
est un fait que les quelques tribus encore non contactées
par la civilisation sont saines et fortes, tandis que les
indiens civilisés sont malades, dégénérés et en train de
disparaître, comme indique le chiffre de la population de
quelques tribus:

	1948	1968
Munducurus	19.000	1.200
Nhambiquaras	10.000	1.000
Carajas	4.000	600
Xocreus	800	200
Xicaos	00	53

Par ailleurs la connaissance des effets pernicieux sur les
indiens du contact entre les deux races forçait les jésuites
d'essayer d'isoler la race rouge dans des missions, réussis-
sant de réunir par exemple à Maranhao le nombre de 50.000
indiens (1686).

2) L'absorption par les races blanche et noire. L'indien n'a-
vait pas de possibilité de croiser avec la femme européenne
et il considérait comme dégradant tout métissage avec une
négresse. L'indienne au contraire, recherchait toujours la
relation avec des européens et très souvent aved des nègres:
le résultat furent de très nombreux croisements. Quand il
s'agissait d'étrangers, qui ne sont pas restés au Brésil,
comme par exemple les normands à partir de 1501, les hollandais ou les anglais plus tards, les enfants nés de ces
métissages continuèrent d'appartenir à la communauté indienne primitive, mais s'ils étaient devenus plus clairs,
comme cela arrivait à 2.000 Acurinis, vivant près du Xingu
en Amazonie. Les enfants nés des relations entre les femmes
indigènes et les portugais, les "mamelucos" (22), étaient
perdus pour la population indie ne car ils se rangèrent du
côté de leurs pères, combattant sauvagement la race de leurs
mères. Etant donné que la majeure partie des indiens brésiliens avait la peau assez claire, sans traits mongoliques
très forts, on pouvait distinguer difficilement cetter première génération métisse des portugais venant de la partie
méridionale de la péninsule. Finalement, les enfants nés
du croisement des indiennes et des nègres les "cafusos"
étaient classés par la société, avec la population noire,
diminuant ainsi, dans les statistiques, le nombre de la
communauté indienne.

3) La guerre. Après un début assez idyllique, où prédominèrent
des relations amicales pleines de curiosité réciproque, les
conquérants voulaient introduire l'esclavage, d'où, à partir
de 1530 environ, de conflits extrêmement sanglants. En 1657
le Père Vieira informa le roi Alfonse IV, que les portugais
avaient tué sur la côte entre San Luiz et Gurupa en quarante
ans plus de deux millions d'indiens.

4) Divers prétextes. Quand les souverains portugais commençaient à défendre la population autochtone contre l'agres-
sivité des colons, ces derniers trouvaient toujours des
moyens pour éluder les prohibitions. Un des moyens le plus
souvent utilisé était celui de placer une croix près d'un
campements indien: après que cette crois eut mystérieusement
disparue dans la nuit, les colons, évocant la "juste guerre"
anéantissaient le camp (voir le compte-rendu d'Acuna, etc.).

5) La contamination bactériologique. Quand la pression des
indiens sur les villages blancs augmenta, les portugais
laissèrent, près des camps indiens, des matériaux de cou-
chage infectés de variole, ce qui décimait les indiens.
Même à présent se sert-on encore de cette pratique. Ce fut
de cette manière qu'on éliminait les Pataxos à Bahia (Jornal
do Brasil, 5 mai 1968). Le pasteur adventiste Wesley
Stevens a dénoncé récemment la contamination des indiens
au Mato Grosso par le virus du typhus.

6) La provocation. Les portugais s'efforcèrent d'evénimer les
luttes tribales afin de pouvaoir obtenir des esclaves de la
tribu victorieuse.

7) La politique d'induire au vice. Par exemple en favorisant
consommation de l'alcool que les indiens ne supportent pas
aussi bien que leur boisson, le cauim.

8) L'emploi de poison. Les "Beiços-de-Pau" au Mato Grosso, ont
été tués par l'insecticide mélangé au sucre (Jornal do
Brasil, 5 mai 1968), les "Cintas Largas" au Para par un
mélange de sucre et de strychnine, ainsi que par des bonbons
contenant de l'arsenic (Fatos e fotos, avril 1968).

9) Distribution des produits anticonceptionels par des mis-
sionaires étrangers tels que la DIU, le serpentine, etc.

10) Le cannibalisme. C'est-à-dire la croyance qu'en mangeant
son ennemi vaincu on pouvait acquérir les qualités du
guerrier tombé.

11) Destruction complète des structures sociales indiennes.
Comme par exemple les liens de parenté tribale, la poly-
gamie, le culte de la nudité, la religion, la langue, le
folklore, la musique et toute de superstructure des mythes.

12) Le génocide par les armes. Le premier à s'en servir fut le
Gouverneur-Général Tomé de Souza qui au 16e siècle fit in-
cendier 70 villages indigènes et assassiner les habitants.
Puis vint la destruction par les paulistes de onze missions
jésuites dans la région de Parana et Paraguay (1628-1630)
suivie en 1638 par la destruction des missions au Mato
Grosso. Le massacre des indigènes continue même à nos jours.
Les indiens "Caraôs" à Goias furent anéantis en 1941 (Jornal
do Brasil, 7 mai 1968). Le numéro d'avril 1968 de la revue
"Fatos e fotos" nous renseigne sur l'emploi de dynamite.
Les Pakaanovas ont été mitraillé par des immigrants grect
(Jornal do Brasil, 24 mars 1968). Les Maxacalis à Minas
Gerais ont été tué par des "pistoleiros" contractés par
les propriétaires terriens (Jornal do Brasil, 5 mai 1968).
Sept mille Tapanhumas furent tués au Mato Grosso. Les
Kaingangs furent tués pendant la construction du chemin de

fer du Noroeste. Le numéro de juin 1968 de la revue En-
ciclopedia parle de la disparition, par la violence, des
Botocudos à Espirito Santo et des Xoklengs à Santa Catarina. Dans une action punitive, 60 Atroiris furent dé-
capités en Amazonie en 1959 (Jornal do Brasil, 20 décembre
1968). Il convient finalement de noter que l'instruction
criminelle ordonnée en 1968 par le Ministre de l'Intérieur
contre le Service de Protection aux Indiens (SPI) créé en
1910, a constaté dans son rapport de vingt volumes les
crimes suivants: massacre, assassinats (parmi lesquels
des pendaisons et des crucifixions par les fonctionnaires
même du Service-Jornal do Brasil, 5 mai 1968), viols,
tortures médievales, etc. (42 crimes). Il faut rappeler
ici qu'une enquête similaire, entreprise en 1964, avait
relevé les mêmes faits. Cependant, le procès n'avait
pas pu être conclu, à cause d'un incendie mystérieux qui
détruisait à Brasilia les archives du SPI. Comme résultat
de ces enquêtes, une Fondation Nationale de l'Indien fut
créée, absorbant l'ancien SPI, le Service du Parc National de Xingu et le Conseil National de Protection à l'Indien. Trente-trois fonctionnaires du SPI dissous furent
évincés. En 1964 l'explorateur Paul Lambert protesta
contre l'extermination des indigènes. Au mois d'avril
1968, 138 ethnologues étrangers -parmi lesquels Claude
Levi-Strauss, auteur des "Tristes Tropiques"- demandaient
dans une lettre envoyée au Président de la République,
une protection adéquate pour les indiens brésiliens.

Les raisons apparentes de ce génocide sont multiples:
  -exploitation des ressources naturelles: le sapin
   (Parana), la cassitérite, la balata, et la seringue
   (Rondonia, Amapa), l'or (Minas Gerais), du bois (Bahia,
   Para, Maranhao), la tantalite, le titane et la "poaia"-
   ipeca (Mato Grosso).
  -l'élévage (Goias).
  -l'occupation de terres nouvelles par des grands propriétaires (23).
  -l'achat de terres par des étrangers (Amazonie)(24).
  -la construction des lignes de chemin de fer.
13) La prostitution. Il suffit de référer ici à l'étude faite
    en 1968 par le directeur de l'Institut de la préhistoire
    de l'Université de Sao Paulo.
14) La divulgation d'une fausse nouvelle concernant la riches-
    se d'un "garimpo" de pierres précieuses, ce qui attire
    des milliers d'aventuriers armés.
b) Les traits dominants des races.
    En général quand deux races se croisent, les traits de la race
    la plus forte prédominent dans la descendance métisse. C'est
    ainsi que dans la règle on retrouve dans le métissage blanc-
    noir la prédominance des qualités physiques du nègre et les
    caractéristiques intellectuelles du blanc. Au Brésil par
    contre on se trouve devant un phénomène contraire: le physique
    perd peu à peu le caractère noir. Il suffit de remarquer

qu'une ville comme Bahia devient visiblement de plus en plus
blanche sans qu'il y a immigration. L'art et la culture primitive des africains ont pris le dessus sur le folklore européen, comme par exemple dans la musique et ont même transformé
complètement la culture portugaise.

c) Taux d'accroissement élevé.

Les taux annuels d'accroissement ont évolué comme suit (25):

$$
\begin{array}{rl}
1872-1890 &: 2,01\% \\
1920-1940 &: 2,05\% \\
1940-1950 &: 2,38\% \\
1950-1960 &: 3,10\% \\
1968 &: 3,60\%
\end{array}
$$

Il faut noter que les dernières prévisions de 1969 du Ministère
de la Planification prévoient une diminution de ce taux qui
baisserait jusqu'à 2,9%. L'accroissement de la population
n'est pas le résultat de l'immigration qui est d'ailleurs in-
signifiante, mais est dû exclusivement à l'accroissement naturel qui est grandement influencé par la stabilité du taux
brut de natalité et la diminution du taux brut de mortalité(26).
Ce qui nous semble inexplicable est l'uniformité de ce taux
d'accroissement pour toutes les classes sociale, y comprise
la classe moyenne, et son augmentation malgré le fait que le
revenu per capita s'est accru soit-il d'une façon modérée.

d) L'importance du groupe d'âge de 0 à 24 ans.

La proportion de la population totale représentée par le groupe
d'âge de 0 à 24 ans est très élevée(27):

1872 : 56,38%		1940 : 62,51%
1890 : 60,36%		1950 : 61,97%
1900 : 63,78%		1960 : 61,65%
1920 : 63,44%		

e) L'espérance de vie à la naissance.

L'espérance de vie à la naissance du brésilien est la plus
basse du monde, exception faite des Indes et de quelques pays
africains et latino-américains(28):

	Hommes	Femmes
1940-1950	41 ans	45 ans
1950-1960	49 ans	54 ans

Les espérances sont les plus basses dans les états fédérés
suivants:

Mato Grosso	: 36,3 ans	Rio de Janeiro	: 38,1 ans
Amazonas	: 37,9 ans	Alagoas	: 38,8 ans
Para	: 38,1 ans		

L'espérance de vie élevée de Rio Grande do Sul (53,0 ans) se
laisse expliquer par le climat et par la manière de vivre de
sa population qui est originaire de l'Europe Centrale et du
Nord de l'Europe.

f) Augmentation de la population active.

Entre 1940 et 1960 la population totale s'est accrue plus fort que la population économiquement active: un taux annuel d'accroissement de 2,7% contre seulement 2,4% pour la population active. Les pronostics prévoient pour les années 1965-1975 une inversion de ce trend avec des taux d'accroissement de 2,8 et 2,9%.

g) Le rôle de l'immigration.

Dans la période 1850-1950 approximativement trois quarts des immigrants se sont définitivement fixés dans le pays et avec leurs descendants ils ont contribué 6.800.000 âmes à l'augmentation de la population, ce qui représente 15% de la croissance démographique. La contribution de ces éléments étrangers à l'accroissement de la population était de 23% entre 1890 et 1900; 10% entre 1900 et 1920 et à peine 1% entre 1940 et 1950; entre 1950 et 1960 cet pourcentage s'est de nouveau accru jusqu'à 4%.

h) Pourcentage élevé d'analphabètes.

Le pourcentage d'analphabètes reste toujours très élevé:

1890 : 67,2%		1950 : 51,6%
1920 : 60,1%		1960 : 39,2%
1940 : 56,4%		

i) Déplacement des centres de gravité.

Il y a eu un déplacement constant des centres de gravité en ce qui concerne l'accroissement de la population. Ceci ressort clairement des données contenues dans le tableau 11.

Sous réserve qu'il s'agit pour chaque phénomène d'un cercle vicieux, on peut dire que les facteurs qui ont influencé les fluctuations régionales de la population étaient les suivants:
-Bahia: transfert de la capitale (1763).
-Rio de Janeiro: siège de la capitale entre 1763 et 1960 ainsi que l'essor du commerce extérieur.
-Sao Paulo: les "bandeirantes", l'immigration et surtout l'industrialisation.
-Pernambuco: industrie de la canne à sucre.
-Espirito Santo: le "Pau Brasil".
-Minas Gerais: la production de l'or, de diamant et plus tard de fer.
-Rio Grande do Sul: l'immigration, l'élevage et la culture de froment.
-Para: économie exploitation végétale.
-Amazonas: caoutchouc et jute.
-Parana: plantations de café (1872:1,28% en 1960:6,03% de la population brésilienne).

j) L'intégration.

L'idée d'intégrer le "hinterland" s'est manifestée durant toute l'histoire du Brésil. Les "bandeirantes" paulistes du 16e au 18e siècle, penchaient involontairement dans cette direction, c'est-à-dire d'inclure dans l'économie nationale l'intérieur du pays, malgré le fait que leur but déclaré était la chasse aux indiens. Plus tard il y avait la création des "territoires" de Ponta Pora, Amapa, Acre, Guaporé et Rio Branco

Tableau 11:   Evolution de la population au Brésil (par état et en pourcentage de la population totale du pays)

Etats	1571 (a)	1725 (b)	1772 (c)	1815 (d)	1872 (e)	1890	1900	1920	1940	1950	1960	1968
Bahia	27,00	19,16	18,52	13,65	13,89	13,39	12,15	10,87	9,50	9,31	8,44	7,82
Rio de Janeiro (f)	2,33	-	13,84	14,57	13,42	13,42	14,61	12,65	13,04	13,58	14,12	14,92
Sao Paulo	8,66	6,66	7,50	6,14	8,43	9,66	13,08	15,00	17,41	17,59	18,28	17,24
Pernambuco	16,66	5,83	15,41	10,61	8,47	7,18	6,77	7,04	6,52	6,54	5,83	5,33
Espirito Santo	3,33	-	-	-	-	0,95	1,20	1,49	1,82	1,66	1,67	1,68
Minas Ger.	-	9,3	20,59	12,46	20,55	22,21	20,61	19,22	16,34	14,86	13,81	13,02
Rio Grande do Sul	-	-	1,33	2,57	4,38	6,26	6,57	7,12	8,05	8,02	7,67	7,42
Amazonas et Para	-	-	4,17	4,00	3,35	3,32	3,99	4,40	3,36	3,16	3,20	3,22
Autres Etats	-	-	-	39,96	32,22	30,91	30,30	29,77	32,52	34,44	36,30	38,65

Notes: (a) Gandavo; (b) Rocha Pitta et Simonsen; (c) Dauril Alden, The population of Brazil in the late eighteenth century; (d) Calogeras et Spix-Martius; (e) les recensements de 1872 à 1960; (f) y compris Guanabara.

qui devenaient des unités administratives indépendantes; il y
avait aussi la fondation de diverses Surintendances (pour le
Nord-est, l'Amazonie, le Centre-ouest), des Conseils Régionaux
du Dévéloppement, ainsi que des banques officielles de caractère régional ainsi que l'élaboration des plans régionaux.
La construction d'une nouvelle capitale sur le "Planalto"
appartient à ce groupe de manifestations séculaires. Le
transfert de la capitale aurait pu être considéré comme l'in-
cident le plus pittoresque de l'histoire moderne du Brésil
(à cause de son caractère pharaonique), s'il n'avait pas eu
de conséquences tellement fâcheuses -conduisant en 1964 presque
à la guerre civile- et causées par l'inflation qu'entrainait
ce transfert par son importance, le rythme et le moment auxquels il s'effectuait. L'idée du transfert d'une capitale
n'est pas nouvelle. Il y a aussi des exemples en dehors du
Brésil. Dans ce pays, les origines de ce problème remontent
peut-être déjà à la décision prise en 1575, de diviser le pays
en deux parties avec deux capitales ayant égalité de droit.
Ce qui changeait cependant était la motivation d'un tel transfert: indépendence politique(29), salubrité(30), sécurité
militaire(31), manque de produits naturels, cherté et luxe
à Rio de Janeiro, colonisation et intégration(32), développement de l'agriculture(33), etc. Le 17 mai 1891 fut créée la
"Commission Exploratrice du Plateau Central" qui avait pour
mission de démarquer la zone réservée au District Fédéral.
Toutes les constitutions contiennent à partir de 1891 une
clause concernant le transfert de la capitale, qui fut finalement décider par la Loi no. 3.273 du 1 octobre 1957 et qui
devait être réalisé en trois ans. Pendant cetter période une
ville moderne devait être construit en plein forêt vierge, au
milieu d'animaux sauvages et d'indiens non-civilisés. Ce cas
d'intégration provoqua la concentration démographique suivante:

Tableau 12: La population de Brasilia

1957 :	12.000	1963 :	231.000
1958 :	28.000	1964 :	263.000
1959 :	64.000	1965 :	314.000
1960 :	142.000	1966 :	360.000
1961 :	168.000	1967 :	405.000
1962 :	200.000	1968 :	451.000

IV. Conclusions: Les effets de l'évolution
     démographique sur le comportement social
     dans le domaine économique.

a) Les effets negatifs.

1) La productivité extrêmement basse. Ceci est sans doute le
problème numéro un de l'économie brésilienne. Le Brésil est
aussi grand que toute l'Europe et ses ressources naturelles
sont peut-être plus abondantes que celles des Etats-Unis.
S'il n'y avait pas le problème de la productivité, le Brésil

devrait avoir aujourd'hui le même degré de développement de
l'Amérique du Nord. Nous allons examiner les raisons du grand
décalage existant entre les deux pays. Il y a sans doute le
facteur climat et peut-être en partie la différence dans la
fertilité du sol, mais cela ne suffit pas pour expliquer la
dimension de l'écart. Nous ne toucherons pas aux causes
chroniques de la basse productivité dans les pays sous-développés, comme le manque de capitaux, de main-d'oeuvre qualifié,
d'automatisation et de magasinage. Nous n'énumerons que les
causes spécifiquement brésiliennes de ce niveau de productivité,
causes qui se rapportent au comportement social qui est déterminé par les considérations d'ordre démographique. Ces
causes sont les suivantes: le manque de sens d'organisation,
d'assiduité(34 et d'hygiène, le fatalisme, l'incompréhension
de la notion de précision et de ponctualité. De même l'anti-
intellectualisme rend extrêmement difficile la formation des
spécialistes. Le Portugal pour sa part a maintenu au Brésil,
pour ne pas le perdre, un climat d'obscurantisme. L'empire
brésilien a hérité cette mentalité. Un rapport du Ministre
des Finances mentionnait encore en 1845 que pour obtenir la
permission d'immigrer au Brésil il fallait "être pauvre et
appartenir à la classe des servants": c'est-à-dire qu'on devait
être analphabète. Il allait de même après la Deuxième Guerre
Mondiale, quand un nombre de savants européens devaient cacher
leur diplômes d'Universités afin de pouvoir entrer au Brésil
comme simples manoeuvres, sans qualification. Il est vrai que
ces restrictions formelles à l'immigration de personnes quali-
fiées n'existent plus: elles ont été substitué par l'intolérance professionnelle et par la xénophobie. Caio Prado Junior
affirme dans son Histoire Economique que le niveau culturel
très bas du Brésil colonial ne trouvait pas non égal en Amé-
rique(35). Il faut mentionner aussi la préférence brésilienne
pour la promiscuité et le bruit. Tandis qu'à l'étranger existe
une tendance très nette de séparer les personnes, surtout dans
les secteurs intellectuels, on préfère au Brésil des grandes
salles avec 10 à 40 personnes, qui passent la majeure partie
du temps en conversant, produisant ainsi un nombre énorme de
décibels, ce qui réduit sensiblement la productivité. Le fait
que la population brésilienne (sauf pour une couche sociale
très mince) vivait toujours dans un état sous-nutrition chro-
nique, peut être expliqué beaucoup plus facilement par la
basse productivité que par l'état colonial ou le régime féodal.
Finalement en considérant l'aspect macro-économique du problème, il ne faut pas oublier que 66,5% des brésiliens (âges
0-19 ans et 60 ans et plus) vivent au frais de la population
active (19-59 ans).

2) Absence d'intérêt pour l'entretien et la conservation des
biens de capital. Mary Graham constatait déjà en 1821 le
manque de propreté dans les rues de Salvador. Aujourd'hui on
pourrait dire la même chose des deux grandes villes du pays:
Rio de Janeiro et Sao Paulo. Les hôtels les plus luxueux,
comme l'hôtel Amazonas à Manaus par exemple, deviennent rapidement inhabitables. Les wagons les plus modernes, achetés en

Europe avec des emprunts étrangers deviennent inutilisables
en quelques années. On s'est abstenu de la construction, dans
les grandes villes, de passages sousterrains, étant donné que
leur saleté empêche toute utilisation après quelques semaines.
La vie des équipments n'est que le quart de ce qu'il est à
l'étranger. Après la première mauvaise récolte on change de
culture ou on fait les semailles ailleurs au lieu d'engraisser
la terre. Finalement, une grande partie du territoire national
a été dévastée sans qu'il y ait eu reboisement ouvrant ainsi
la voie à l'érosion et à la création de déserts. Les raisons
de cette négligence, qui a provoqué un gaspillage énorme, sont
le nomadisme héréditaire des indigènes, l'économie de rapine
des premiers colons, le manque de sens publique et le niveau
culturel bas de la population.

3) L'absence d'épargnes. Le capital privé joue un role très
important dans le dévéloppment économique d'un pays non-soci-
aliste. Or, c'est ce qui manque au Brésil. Les raisons principales de cette défaillance dans les pays sous-développés
sont soit d'ordre structurel (revenu national bas, demande
intensive pour des biens importés, etc.) soit d'ordre social
comme le manque d'épargnes ce qui découle du comportement
social qui est en large mesure dicté par le fait que le future
ne lui est guère favorable. L'inexistence de l'hiver, la
cueillette facile de fruits dans n'importe quelle région humide
du pays et à n'importe quelle époque de l'année, ainsi que le
nomadisme séculaire ont privé le brésilien de tout sens de
prévision. Il dépense promptement tout ce qu'il gagne et ne
pense même pas au proche avenir, car il espère constamment
de trouver un "jeito" (c'est-à-dire une possibilité de vivre
aux frais de quelqu'un) ou, à la rigueur, des fruits d'un
bananier.

4) Le taux très élevé d'accroissement de la population empêche
l'augmentation du revenu national per capita ce qui amplifie
la partie marginalisée de la société.

5) La xénophobie économique. Le dévéloppment économique brésilien dépend actuellement de capital étranger dans une mesure
de 20 pourcent. Bien que sollicité ce capital n'est pas bien
reçu en Brésil et il est entouré immédiatement de toute sorte
de précautions et méfiances, devenant la cible de chaque dé-
monstration de rue. L'élément humain qui accompagne ce capital
est à son tour soumis à d'innombrables restrictions, dont une
partie est sanctionnée dans la constitution même. Les raisons
de cette xénophobie sont bien connues: héritage de la politique
de secret du Portugal et le complexe d'infériorité des brésiliens. Il nous paraît cependant paradoxal d'adopter le
système des classes discriminées de nationaux-cas d'ailleurs
unique dans le monde moderne-dans un pays dont le dévéloppement
dépend en large mesure du capital et du know-how étrangers.
Le résultat inévitable de cet état d'esprit est que plusieurs
secteurs économiques du Brésil n'ont pas été développés.

6) Manque de sens de réalisme économique. L'état émotionnel

dans lequel on attaquait les problèmes économiques ne permet-
tait presque jamais d'élaborer un budget de prévisions réaliste.
C'est la raison pourquoi seulement 23 exercices se sont termi-
nées par un bilan positif durant les 145 années qui sont dé-
coulées depuis l'indépendance du pays. En général les grands
plans économiques ne peuvent pas être exécutés étant donné
qu'ils ne furent pas élaborés sur une base réaliste. Le fait
que presque tous les organismes de l'état ainsi que les socié-
tés semi-publiques, semi-privées travaillent avec un déficit
budgetaire se laisse également expliquer par ce manque de vision réaliste.

7) Finalement l'individualisme extrême n'a pas permis le dévéloppement d'un sentiment de solidarité économique dans la
société brésilienne, ce qui condamne à l'échec toute politique
économique.

b) Les effets positifs.
Parmi les effets positifs il faut mentionner l'extraordinaire
aptitude commerciale du brésilien, so résistance au climat
tropical ainsi que sa vitalité biologique. Sa faculté de perception est plus grande que celle d'un européen et il est plus
intellectuel que l'américan. Sa patience et sa philosophie
pratique dans des situations difficiles ont fait école. Il a
une très grande habilité manuelle et il reste maître de ses
nerfs quand il conduit un moyen de transport ou en dirigeant
n'importe quelle machine.
    Ces qualités -et il y en a d'autres- ont contribué à la
conservation de l'intégrité de son immense territoire, ce qui
contraste singulièrement au fait que la partie espagnole de
l'Amérique Latine s'est désintégrée en plusieurs états indé-
pendants.

Références

(1)   Selon A. Hrdlicka, d'origine asiatique, selon P. Rivet
      maléo-polynésienne et australienne.

(2)   Nombre d'indiens civilisés: en 1538 pour tout le Brésil,
      25.000 (Père Anchieta); en 1583 pour tout le Brésil, 18.000
      (Calogeras); en 1588 pour tout le Brésil, 28.000 (Coisas
      notaveis do Brasil); en 1814, 11.435 dans la Rio Negro et
      50.000 dans Para (Spix et Martius), Rio Grande do Sul,
      61395 (Camargo, Quadros Estatisticos e Geograficos, 1868),
      Ceara, 9.196 (Patriota, mai 1814); en 1821, 4.000 dans Per-
      nambuco, Paraiba et Rio Grande do Norte (Balbi); en 1835
      pour Sao Paulo, 825 (Müller).
      Les dernières "pacifications" étaient celles de Kaingangs
      (Santa Catarina) en 1912, Botocudos (Minas Gerais, Espirito
      Santo) en 1911, Umotinas (Mato Grosso) en 1918, Parintinins
      (Goias) en 1928, Xavantes (Mato Grosso) en 1946 et celle de
      Kaiapo-Kuben-Krau-Kegu (Para) en 1952.
      Selon la "Memoria estatistica do Imperio do Brasil, 1829",
      89% de la population de la Capitainerie de Rio Negro et
      35% de la Province de Para étaient des Indiens. D'après
      Horta Barbosa, en 1942, les 1.244.000 Indiens vivaient
      principalement dans les états suivants: Mato Grosso (40%),
      Acre (24%), Amazonas (16%) et Goias (12%).

(3)   Par exemple en 1588 il y a 43.000 esclaves (Coisas notaveis
      do Brasil).

(4)   D. P. Müller, Ensaio dum quadro estatistico da Provincia de
      Sao Paulo, 1838.

(5)   Mestiço: 1805: 300.000   (Humbolt);
                 1810: 628.000   (Balbi).

(6)   Mulâtres au Brésil:
              en 1798:   221.000 ou 7,36% de la population totale
                         (Contreiras Rodrigues);
              en 1824:   628.000 ou 15,70% (Rugendas);
              en 1908:   5.582.000 ou 25,37% (H. Johnston);
              en 1940:   8.744.000 ou 21,20% (Recensement);
              en 1950:   13.786.000 ou 26,54% (Recensement).

(7)   Le décret du 1 septembre 1808 fit venir pour la Capitainerie
      de Rio Grande do Sul, 1.500 familles originaires des Açores.

(8)   La loi no 601, du 18 septembre 1850, autorisa le gouvernement
      de faire venir, aux frais du trésor public, des colons pour
      l'agriculture, l'administration ainsi que pour la formation
      de colonies. Par les décrets nos 1.584 du 2 avril 1855 et
      2.158 du 1 mai 1858 furent approuvés les Statuts de L'Asso-
      ciation Centrale de Colonisation, fondée pour une période
      de dix ans avec un capital de 1000 contos. Elle avait pour
      but importation d'agriculteurs et d'ouvriers d'industrie
      et elle jouit d'une subvention gouvernementale. Plus tard
      le gouvernement brésilien signait un contrat avec John Beaton,

représentant de la compagnie Brazilian Coffee States, fondée
en 1872 (décret no 5.128 du 30 octobre 1872 et décret no
5.269 du 26 avril 1873), visant l'importation du 5.000 immigrants du Nord de l'Europe, n'ayant pas atteint l'age de
45 ans. 95% de ces immigrants seraient des agriculteurs
pour les plantations de caféiers et de coton et 5% seraient
des artisans. Les subventions reçues par cette compagnie
étaient:
–à Londres: 6 livres par immigrant entre 11 et 45 ans et
    trois livres pour tout immigrant entre 2 et 10 ans.
–au Brésil: 110 milreis par colon entre 11 et 45 ans et
    55 milreis par colon entre 2 et 10 ans.
–une prime, payable après quatre ans de 30.000 milreis.
–transport gratuit au Brésil.
–franchise de douane.
En même temps un autre contrat fut conclu (décret no 5.373
du 6 août 1873) cette fois avec Savino Tripoli pour l'importation de 400 familles originaires de l'Allemagne et de
l'Italie.

(9)   Population blanche du Brésil:
                1549: 4.000   (Castro Barreto)
                1570: 21.000   (Engel Slinter)
                1583: 25.000   (Calogeras)
                1600: 30.000   (Simonsen)
                1616: 44.000   (Razam do Estado do Brazil – 12.385
                            "povoadores", "vezinhos")
                1640: 100.000   (Castro Barreto)
                1700: 200.000   (Simonsen)
                1798: 1.010.000   (Contreiras Rodrigues)
                1819: 2.488.743   (id.)

(10)   35% d'Espagnols, 23% de Français, 14% d'Anglais, 4% d'Alle-
        mands, 4% d'Italiens, 2% de Suisses et 1% de Suédois.

(11)   Etrangers au Brésil: en 1872: 382.041; en 1920: 1.513.635;
        en 1940: 1.283.833 et en 1950: 1.085.287.

(12)   Recensements des naturalisés: en 1920: 52.326; en 1940:
        122.735 et en 1950: 128.897.

(13)   Spix et Martius.

(14)   Pour pouvoir retourner à la Metropole, les portugais avaient
        souvent besoin d'une permission royale.

(15)   Lettres royales du 3 septembre 1667, 28 avril 1674 et du
        21 mars 1694; décrets du 26 novembre 1709, du 19 février
        1711 et du 4 mars 1720.

(16)   Certains auteurs, comme A. Romero par exemple dans son ou-
        vrage "Origem da imoralidade no Brasil" trouve une expli-
        cation pour ce phénomène dans la déficience priapique de
        l'homme indigène.

(17)   Spix et Martius constataient déjà en 1817-1820 que les nègres
        du Brésil avaient beaucoup moins d'enfants que les blancs.

Les statistiques récentes confirment ce fait. Taux de fécondité féminine (pour les femmes de 15 à 45 ans):

	1930-1940	1940-1950
Blanches	176,50	171,02
Mulâtres	188,65	195,87
Négresses	173,43	167,45

(18)   Taux de fécondité féminine des japonaises au Brésil:
       en 1930-1940: 194,25 et en 1940-1950: 200,30.

(19)   Historia da colonizaçao portuguêsa.

(20)   1525 Rinchon, La traite et l'esclavage des congolais par
       les Européens); 1531 (C. Prado Junior, Historia econômica
       do Brasil); 1533 (A. Romero); 1539 (Description faite par
       le Père Anchieta); 1542-46 (Varnhagen).

(21)   Nombre des tribus relevées: en 1900: 230 (Darci Ribeiro);
                                      1950: 140 (id.)
                                      1960: 100 (Première enquête
                                                 du SPI).

(22)   Marcgraf: Qui natus est ex patre Europaeo et matre Brasili-
       ana, nominatur mameluco (1640).

(23)   Selon la constitution brésilienne, les indiens se voient
       garanti le droit à la possession des terres qu'ils habitent
       et à l'usufruit de toutes les ressources naturelles qui s'y
       trouvent.

(24)   Dénonciation du Ministre de Justice.

(25)   Ministério do Planejamento e Coordenaçao Economico: Diagnos-
       tico preliminar da demografia.

(26)

	Taux brut de natalité	Taux brut de mortalité
	pour mille	
1872-1890	46,5	30,2
1920-1940	44,0	25,3
1940-1950	43,5	20,1
1950-1960	41,5	11,5

(27)   Min. do Planejamento e Coordenaçao Economico: Diagnostico
       preliminar da demografia.

(28)   Idem.

(29)   Les "inconfidentes" de Minas Gerais (1789-1792).

(30)   Le climat mentionné par le Prince Régent (Lettres de l'am-
       bassadeur Strangford, 1808).

(31)   Correiso Brasiliense, Londres, 1812.

(32)   Varnhagen: Memorial Orgânico, Madrid 1848-49.

(33)   Premier projet du Sénat sur le transfer, 10 juin 1853.

(34)   Observé en 1843 par Castelnau et en 1856 par Dubot.

(35) C. Prado J.: "Il ne reste aucun doute que l'ignorance du colon portugais a toujours constitué le principal obstacle au développement de ses activités économiques.

Soc
HB
849
P58
1968